DATE DUE			

My Road to Opera

By Boris Goldovsky

Bringing Opera to Life: Operatic Acting & Stage Direction

By Curtis Cate

Antoine de Saint-Exupéry: His Life and Times

George Sand

The Ides of August: The Berlin Wall Crisis — 1961

My Road to Opera

The Recollections of Boris Goldovsky

as told to

Curtis Cate

Illustrated with Photographs

Houghton Mifflin Company Boston 1979

Library of Congress Cataloging in Publication Data
Goldovsky, Boris.
My road to opera.

Includes index.
1. Goldovsky, Boris. 2. Opera — Biography.
I. Cate, Curtis, date II. Title.
ML422.G613A3 782.1'092'4 [B] 78-20846
ISBN 0-395-27760-4

Printed in the United States of America
V 10 9 8 7 6 5 4 3 2 1

These recollections are dedicated to the memory of Fritz Reiner, Ernst Lert, and Serge Koussevitzky.

Preface

I HAVE NEVER KEPT a diary or wished to write an autobiography. As a musician — that is, as someone whose artistic language is the played or sung note rather than the written word — I have long felt that there was a certain impropriety involved in transgressing the tenuous borderline that separates the world of music from the world of prose. Wagner and Berlioz, being compulsive writers as well as exceptionally gifted composers, were unusually qualified to be authors of their own memoirs. Yet even their recollections resemble, at least to some extent, the thirty or more autobiographies of composers, singers, actors, and musicians I have added over the years to the other books in my library. Most of these supposedly "factual" chronicles are in reality highly subjective ego trips into the past, in the course of which the author's talents and triumphs are exaggerated, his weaknesses soft-pedaled or ignored, his occasional setbacks often blamed on others.

Every successful performer knows what a sense of giddy intoxication is induced by public adulation. Composers, conductors, and stage directors can just as easily succumb to vanity and become boastful egomaniacs, in the belief that their particular way of composing music, conducting an orchestra, or producing an opera is the only proper way. Because they have for so many years basked in the limelight, it is only natural that they should not wish to retire from active life without adding a final literary flourish to their memorable achievements. But I must confess that I have never had much taste for such self-serving effusions.

I should add that I find writing both difficult and time-consuming. This may come as a surprise to those who, for so many years, have listened to my intermission broadcasts from the Metropolitan Opera, and who have been led to believe that I can write as glibly as I speak or play the piano. A lecturer I have been on countless occasions, but I make no claim to be a writer. If I have had a vocation in life, it has been that of an educator. I have written very little for the sheer fun of it, and my longer literary efforts have been more like textbooks than anything else. *Bringing Opera to Life, Bringing Soprano Arias to Life* (with my colleague Arthur Schoep as co-author), and *Touring Opera,* a manual for small companies (put together with the help of my nephew Thomas Wolf), were essentially written for the benefit of opera performers and producers and deal for the most part with technical matters.

For years my wife, Margaret, like so many others, kept repeating, "Boris, you *must* write your memoirs!" But having so long frowned on the exhibitionism of some of my colleagues, I felt no burning desire to follow their example. My feelings in this respect might never have changed but for the insistent prodding of Curtis Cate, who had somehow felt — even since our first meeting in the autumn of 1955 (at a time when he was working for the *Atlantic Monthly*) — that I was somebody who had a story to tell. He began by asking me for articles — several of which I wrote — and then ended up by suggesting something more ambitious. But it was only after he had finally volunteered to do the actual writing — by which time he had produced two fine biographies (one of Saint-Exupéry, the other of George Sand, so interesting for me because of the Chopin connection) — that I gave my reluctant consent.

The resultant voyage into the past turned up a number of surprises. Distant events that had been telescoped or otherwise displaced were restored to their proper chronological order. Long forgotten reasons were rediscovered as to why, at such and such a moment, I was involved in this enterprise or that. This was particularly true for the years following the Russian revolution when the pressure of political and personal events forced me to shuttle from city to city: from Moscow to Odessa and back to Moscow; then from Berlin to Paris and back to Berlin; finally, from New York to Budapest to St. Jean de Luz and back to Budapest. Only slightly less difficult to reconstruct was the period of the early 1930s when, first in Philadelphia and then in Cleveland, I was drawn into the musical life of the United States.

If I have a story to tell, it is above all because I began my musical life as a hearty despiser of opera, a prejudice I harbored for more than twenty-six years before finally seeing the light. Since many of my readers may once have felt the same way, it may interest them to discover how a person who hated opera because it was so inferior to the dramatic intensity of Stanislavsky's theatrical productions in Moscow was finally converted to the realization that this most complex of art forms could be even more vibrant and exciting when properly directed and performed. It may also interest them to know how I was influenced by Artur Schnabel, at a time when I still thought myself destined to become a keyboard virtuoso, and how later I succumbed to the spell of Ernö Dohnányi, the most gifted all-round musician I have ever known, who did so much to broaden my musical knowledge and horizon.

For many, and particularly the young, Josef Hofmann too is now little more than a name, though in the late 1920s he was still widely regarded as the greatest pianist alive. It was he who, by vetoing my piano career, forced me into another and doubtless more fruitful direction. As for my transformation into an "opera expert," it was made possible by three extraordinary men — Fritz Reiner, Ernst Lert, and Serge Koussevitzky — to whose memory this book is dedicated.

These reminiscences extend as far as the year 1951, by which time my artistic metamorphosis was complete. Some day, health and time permitting, I may add a kind of coda, to explain in greater detail how the musical and dramatic ideas I had elaborated during my apprentice years were later applied and developed, and how they have affected the staging of opera in the United States.

Brookline, September 1978 BORIS GOLDOVSKY

Contents

My Road to Opera

1

Childhood in Russia

IN JUNE OF 1976 I happened to be lecturing and acting as master of ceremonies on a European "Music Cruise" that was circumnavigating the Scandinavian countries when our liner, the S.S. *Daphne*, put in to the port of Leningrad. My wife, Margaret, decided to go ashore on a guided tour, as did our son, Michael, and our daughter-in-law, Lillian, but I preferred to remain on board. I had been warned by the State Department officials who had issued my passport that they could do nothing to help me if the Soviet authorities chose to detain me because I was Russian-born. Although there was little likelihood of my being arrested while on this guided tour, I was in no mood to expose myself to the good graces of the local police. As I watched the visitors disembarking, under the close scrutiny of armed soldiers and police inspectors who took away the passports of the Americans as they filed past — doubtless to keep the potential malefactor from selling it on the black market to some Soviet citizen, desperately anxious to flee his homeland — my feeling of disgust kept growing. The passengers were treated as though they were about to visit a prison or a penitentiary, full of dangerously antisocial elements who must under no circumstances be allowed to flee from their present place of confinement. The spectacle sickened me and strengthened my resolution not to set foot again in that unfortunate country, which had lived for the past fifty-nine years in the grip of an implacably totalitarian regime.

Instead of sightseeing, I spent my time pacing up and down the deck, haunted by the memory of the day — in September 1921 — when my mother and I had reached this same city, still known as Petrograd, by train in order to board the steamer that was to take us across the Baltic to Stettin. Did we realize that we were saying goodbye forever, that something irrevocable and irremediable was taking place, and that we would never set foot on Russian soil again? Possibly Mother did. But for months, and indeed for years, we — and above all my father, who said that all this couldn't last — had expected the Bolshevik experiment to blow over like a rainstorm or a bad attack of fever, after which the sun would shine again and things would return to normal. But things hadn't returned to normal. Instead, they seemed to have grown worse with each passing month, and that was why it was finally decided that Mother would accept an invitation to go to Germany on a violin concert tour, the understanding being that Father would join us later with other members of the family.

There were many things then I did not realize, for I was only thirteen years old. Simply to have been born in Moscow in the year 1908 was in itself a privilege not granted at the time to many persons of Jewish origin. My mother, Lea Saúlovna Luboshutz, like her parents, had been born and brought up in Odessa, which, with the Black Sea littoral, lay south of the *cherta ossyedlosty* — the "settlement line," as it was known — south of which Jewish families were allowed to live.

The line, of course, was not hermetic, for it had always been possible for "house Jews" — those who were quick-witted — to establish themselves in cities like Saratov or Tula, or even in the two capitals of Tsarist Russia, Moscow and St. Petersburg. Such was the case, for example, with Anton Rubinstein, a virtuoso pianist who was allowed to leave his native town of Kherson, in the Ukraine, and settle in St. Petersburg, where he soon became court pianist before founding and directing the Imperial Conservatory of Music. Another was the virtuoso fiddler, Leopold Auer, who was lured away from his native Hungary when he was still in his twenties to train a new generation of violinists at the St. Petersburg Conservatory. One of his students was a Pole named Emil Mlynarski, who after studying for some years under Auer in St. Petersburg, moved south to Odessa to give violin instruction at the local Music School. Whether this was a deliberate plan on Anton Rubinstein's part, I do not know, but the result was electrifying. The realization that gifted violinists could escape from the "ghetto" by obtaining scholarships to the St. Petersburg Conservatory of Music had a galvanizing effect on many Jewish parents in Odessa, who began waking up their offspring at six o'clock in the morning, and this when they were barely big enough to hold a miniature fiddle in their hands, in the hope that through extra hours of prebreakfast practice, they might develop into another Auer or Mlynarski and thus be allowed to migrate northward beyond imperial Russia's Mason-Dixon line to those distant, beckoning El Dorados — or perhaps one should say Yukons, since they were often snowbound — St. Petersburg and Moscow.

I should add, for those unfamiliar with musical technique, that to play the violin, or for that matter the cello, really well, one must begin very young — as is also true of ballet dancers. An adolescent who begins at the age of twelve or later can almost never develop the digital dexterity needed to play a string instrument with the sureness of touch it takes to become a virtuoso. The extraordinary number of first-class instrumentalists of Jewish origin that burgeoned during the two or three decades preceding the First World War was unquestionably due to the hothouse training they were subjected to as infants in the belief that this was the surest way of having them overcome their geographically restricted or ghettolike status.

Something remarkably similar has recently occurred in Japan, largely as a result of the "Suzuki method," which is based on the simple idea of having parents attend their children's violin lessons so as to be able to guide their practice drill at home. Today, thanks to this remarkable teaching method, Japan has turned out literally hundreds of exceptionally talented violin players nine, ten, or eleven years old. While the credit undoubtedly belongs to Suzuki, I doubt that his inspirational genius alone could have accomplished this had the Japanese, after Pearl Harbor and their defeat in World War II, not felt a special need to seek respectability in more pacific pastimes than those in which the warrior samurais had once excelled. Like the Jews of Eastern Europe, they have responded brilliantly to the stigma or stimulus of humiliations that needed to be overcome.

My mother, born in 1885, was one of the first of this new generation of hothouse fiddlers who were to spring up, with precocious maturity, in various Russian-Jewish centers — a generation that was to include Efrem Zimbalist (born in Rostov-on-the-Don in 1889), Mischa Elman (born in the Ukrainian town of Talnoye in 1891), Toscha Seidel (born in Odessa in 1899), and Jascha Heifetz (born in the Lithuanian city of Vilna in 1901). Some of the credit obviously belongs to my maternal grandfather, Saúl Luboshutz, who was something of a fiddler, though his proficiency probably did not much exceed the occasional demands placed upon it by family reunions, Jewish weddings, and gregarious occasions of that kind. He knew enough about bow work and proper fingering to be able to guide his elder daughter's violin drill during those early morning sessions when he would wake her up and have her practice for an hour or two before going off to school. But most of the credit must be given to Emil Mlynarski, who gave her professional instruction during the five or six years he spent in Odessa before recommending her to Vassili Safonov, a former colleague he had known in St. Petersburg who was named head of the Moscow Conservatory of Music in 1899.

On the strength of his recommendation Safonov made a first visit to Odessa in that same year of 1899 to tap the reservoir of musical talent which this fragrant, sun-blessed city had begun to accumulate. A single audition sufficed to win the fourteen-year-old Lea Luboshutz a scholarship to the Moscow Conservatory — to the understandable delight of my grandparents, overjoyed to see those many hours of digital torture thus handsomely rewarded.

And so it was that my mother moved to Moscow. She was followed a year or two later by her sister, Anna, who was something of a beauty, with striking red hair and a swanlike neck which won her the nickname of *Sheya* ("neck") Saúlovna, sister of Lea Saúlovna, the violinist. Aunt Anna's instrument, however, was not the fiddle but the cello. Why this was I honestly don't know. But my grandparents must have decided to develop their children's talents in different directions almost from the start.

The youngest, Piotr — or Dyadya (Uncle) Petya, as he came to be known — was thus harnessed at a tender age to the piano. He too developed sufficient musical proficiency to impress Safonov during a later visit to Odessa, and he was thus able to follow his two sisters to the Moscow Conservatory. But being a restless adolescent with a marked taste for the fair sex, he spent as much time at the conservatory chasing girls as he did practicing on the keyboard. This proved his "undoing" — if such it can be called — for when put to the test at the end of his conservatory years, he failed to match the superlative standard set by his two elder sisters, both of whom had been awarded the prized Gold Medal. Dyadya Petya had to content himself with a distinctly second-class Silver decoration. But more than this was needed to throw the young pianist off his buoyant stride, and though obviously not destined to become another Anton Rubinstein or Liszt, he was expert enough to become the third member of the celebrated Luboshutz trio.

All of this, of course, I only discovered later, when I was old enough to be taken for walks as far as the Moscow Conservatory, which then (as now) consisted of two buildings set back a bit from the Nikitsky Boulevard in a setting of lawns and trees. The building to the right contained the main concert hall, known as the *Bolshoy Zal,* while the building to the left contained the classrooms and a smaller chamber-music hall known as the *Maly Zal.* And it was here, on a tall, square plaque adorning the right wall of the entrance hall that my boyish chest would almost visibly swell at the sight of Mother's name, followed a little further down by Aunt Anna's, among the honored recipients of the coveted Gold Medal. But — *pozor, pozor!* (shame, shame!) — of Uncle Petya's name there was not a trace on the ground floor, though one could find it by going upstairs to another part of the building, where the plaque listing the Silver Medalists was displayed.

It was always regarded in the family as something of a joke and not to be taken too tragically — this inability of Dyadya Petya to make the topmost grade. Certainly it did nothing to inhibit his zestful joie de vivre, which he exhibited at home as elsewhere in the most disarming way. He was a born clown and entertainer and in this respect quite different from his more serious sisters. Also, being some years younger than they, he was much closer in age to my brother, Yuri, and myself than were our own parents — the difference in years being no more than sixteen.

In our fifth-floor apartment on the Trubnikovsky Pereulok — about a mile and a half to the west of the Kremlin — Dyadya Petya occupied a bedroom at the far end of the central corridor which cut the apartment in two. My brother, Yuri, and I used to call this bedroom "Dyadya Petya's fortress" — a fortress which, like all fairy-tale castles and cloud-wreathed citadels, invited periodic attacks. Simulating a full gallop down the corridor we would hurl ourselves, like two human battering rams, against the fortress's closed and bolted door. The reverberations from these repeated assaults must have been quite trying to the stoic chatelain, who sat or lay behind his closed portcullis pretending to hear nothing. One day, however, he finally lost patience and resorted to a ruse which thoroughly discomfited the two boldly charging knights. The bedroom door, though seemingly closed, was left imperceptibly ajar — with the result that when we raced down the corridor and banged against it at full speed, the door flew open and both of us landed on our faces. We were treated to a severe beating on the spot and told to desist from further assaults of this kind.

Children being what they are, we developed a new game. Instead of galloping down the corridor like Galahads, we took to creeping up to the closed door like Indians, whispering to each other: "Shush . . . softly . . . Dyadya Petya is sleeping" — then turning the doorknob stealthily to see if this was really so. This too soon got us into trouble. One morning, while we were pushing the door open for a peek inside, Dyadya Petya, who was wide awake, leaped out of bed and chased the two impertinent voyeurs down the corridor and into the living room, through the dining room and back, to the startled horror of our Latvian governess, Katya Rigert, who was so overcome by the sight of this naked man wildly racing around chairs and tables that she stood transfixed, protesting in her native German: *"Aber Peter Saúlovich! Aber Peter Saúlovich!"*

This was one of the rare occasions on which we actually saw him barefooted. For each of Dyadya Petya's feet had an extra toe — six instead of the usual five — a deformity which, like the slight curvature of his spine, he always took pains to conceal — from us as from his female conquests, mesmerized by his gaiety and dark liquid eyes.

Whereas Dyadya Petya finally went off to live in a little bachelor's flat of his own, our redheaded governess, Katya Rigert, was a permanent fixture in our Trubnikovsky Pereulok apartment. She had been imported from Riga and lodged in a bedroom next to Dyadya Petya's to teach us German, just as later Yuri and I were taught to speak French by a mademoiselle who came to give us private lessons once or twice a week. In this respect too I realize how exceptionally privileged I was, particularly when I compare my polyglot upbringing to the monolingual childhood of most young Americans. Our father, a lawyer by profession, found it quite natural to speak French or German at table, and so did Mother, who would have had trouble on her concert tours abroad if she had been limited to Russian.

With his graying beard, thinning hair, and piercing dark eyes, my father, Onissim Borissovich Goldovsky, was a most imposing figure. I don't recall ever having seen him dressed in anything except formal suits that looked like morning coats. He was twenty years older than my mother, and indeed the exact age of my maternal grandmother, and this superiority in age — he must have been close to fifty when my brother and I were only seven and six — greatly enhanced his parental prestige, making him something of a guru in our childish eyes. As a *preesiazhny poviérenny* — a "sworn confidant" or attorney — who headed some kind of legal firm or office, he was seconded by a small staff of *pomoshchniki* (assistant barristers), who kept turning up at the apartment with bulging briefcases and thick files. There was something magisterial about Father which may unwittingly have influenced my later life, for he was an erudite person with a well-stocked library who always gave one the impression of having vast funds of knowledge to impart. From him I almost certainly inherited, if only by virtue of example, a love of lecturing and of sharing knowledge which has remained with me to this day.

Yet, oddly enough, there was never any question in those early days of our following in Father's footsteps. It was taken for granted that like Mother, Aunt Anna, and Dyadya Petya — who gathered almost daily in our living room for their trio rehearsals — Yuri and I would be "artists" and thus beings of a higher order.

Like many a younger brother I suffered dreadfully from the privileges Yuri enjoyed simply because he was a year — to be exact, one year, two months, and eighteen days — older than myself. Having to go dutifully to bed at eight-thirty while he was allowed to stay up until nine struck me as the most humiliating injustice —

particularly since it was often during that crucial half-hour that the most exciting surprises and visits would occur. Lying in bed, still awake, I would strain my ears in vain to hear exactly what Dyadya Petya was saying, after walking in all dressed up and on his way to some party; his latest wisecrack or anecdote would send the company assembled in the living room into gales of laughter, on the foaming crest of which I could so poignantly hear my elder brother's silvery soprano peal. I would console myself with the thought that Yuri too, though present and laughing his head off with the rest, was probably just as much in the dark as I. The laughter of grown-ups was such a mysterious thing.

Not until much later did I understand why I would be dispatched with Yuri to the kitchen to fetch Father a glass of "really cold water." For some reason Yuri, if left to his own devices, would never leave the tap open long enough. So I would be delegated to accompany him to the kitchen sink, where I would hold my finger under the stream of water until it began to turn blue. Returning solemnly to the dining room, we would find everyone in stitches, apparently amused by the sight of the water carrier trying not to spill the frigid liquid while his assistant sought to warm his frozen finger. The real source of the merriment was Father, who had sent us to the kitchen so as to be able to tell a bawdy joke and whom we would find on our return, seated at the head of the table with a faint smile on his face and pretending to be puzzled by this outburst of irreverent hilarity.

For the rest I did my utmost to minimize the difference in our respective ages, going as far as to claim that Yuri was only six months older than myself. Curiously enough, I could get no one to believe it, even though this six-month interval struck me as being far closer to the truth in expressing the difference in our relative size and strength than the one year and two months that actually separated our two births. But it was years before I could understand the cause of this adult incredulity and merriment.

Yuri must have been about seven, while I was still six years old, when we were one day summoned to a conference with our parents. We were now old enough to be given music lessons, so the question was: what instrument did each of us wish to play? Yuri, being the elder, spoke up first. He wanted to play the piano. Since this was his choice, the piano it would be. And now what about Boris? . . . I too wanted to play the piano, but since Yuri had already chosen it and I was not going to be a copycat, I had to choose something else. "I want to play the fiddle, like Mama!" I stoutly declared, not realizing what I was letting myself in for.

It was several months before I was finally able to test my childish resolution. Good piano instructors could easily be found in Moscow at this time, but good violin teachers were apparently a rarity. Mother offered to give me my first lessons, but this proposal I vehemently rejected. What could be more babyish than studying with one's own mother? Father agree that this was an outlandish suggestion, quite unworthy of a resolute young man. There was also the problem of locating a suitable fiddle. When I heard that I was to start out with a half-size job, I protested indignantly. What a humiliation! No, I wasn't going to learn to play on a pint-size violin. I was going to learn to play properly, on a full-size instrument, and I was going to show everyone that I was big enough to do it. After all, I imprudently added, I had already tried my hand a bit on Mother's Amati. This rash admission brought the roof down on my head. There was a lot of angry shouting, and I was sternly lectured and warned of the dire punishment that would be meted out to me if ever I dared approach Mother's violin case again.

Finally, after several wasted months, a teacher was found: a kind, elderly gentleman named Rifkind. As a compromise I was offered a three-quarter-size violin. We were now ready to begin. I tried hard and the patient Rifkind tried even harder to make a fiddler out of me, for it was a rare honor to be tutoring Lea Luboshutz's talented little boy. Talented? One could begin to doubt it. My talents, whatever they were, obviously lay elsewhere.

I just couldn't reconcile myself to the contortions through which I was put in assuming the correct violin-playing stance. The twisted position of the left elbow, with the accompanying strain on left shoulder, wrist, and chin, the upside-down manipulation of the left-hand fingers coupled with the horizontal undulations of right elbow and wrist — all this baffled and offended my sense of anatomical proprieties. I experimented with other, less cramping ways of handling bow and fiddle, but without success. We were obviously not made for each other, and as far as the violin was concerned, I was what one of my German teachers was later to term an "antitalent."

Between these excruciating sessions — as painful to the ear as they were to arm and shoulder — I started a clandestine affair with the piano. It was love at first touch. What was so depressingly difficult with the violin — getting a pure, ungrating sound — seemed here to solve itself with no effort at all. I found it easy to pick out simple tunes and sequences and even add a harmony or two.

One day Uncle Petya surprised me while I was fooling around on the keyboard. Sitting down beside me, he showed me a few scale fingerings, then assigned me some simple studies for beginners. I mastered them so quickly that he went to Mother and said: "This is ridiculous! It's a waste of time trying to teach Boris to play the violin. He's no more made for it than I am. But he gets on wonderfully with the piano. He likes the keyboard and it seems to like him."

Father and Mother finally yielded to Dyadya Petya's pleas, and the good Rifkind was informed that his services were no longer needed. I was now entrusted to a musical pedagogue named Gelman — as the German name of Hellmann is pronounced in Russian — who had been giving piano lessons to Yuri. I made such startling progress that in a few months' time I caught up with and even overtook my elder brother, who did not seem to possess my digital dexterity. This marked a turning point in the lives of both of us. Piano playing now became the central focus of my existence, the goal toward which my youthful sights were set, while for my brother it gradually dwindled to a peripheral activity, one he finally abandoned altogether in favor of "more serious" pursuits.

It was also Uncle Petya who later removed me from the pedagogic ministrations of Gelman and personally introduced me to a really first-class teacher, Karl Avgustovich Kipp, who was to remain my piano instructor until I left Russia four years later. Professor Kipp was a small, meticulous German whose friendly pink face was surmounted by an even pinker patch of baldness, fringed by slopes of snow-white hair. He had spent most of his life in Moscow, where he had helped to train several generations of Russian pianists. Though not particularly concerned with subtleties of expression, he was uncompromising in his insistence that his pupils acquire a solid grounding in finger technique.

I was fortunate, I now realize, in being exposed to this digital drill years before I sold my soul to the metaphysicians of Berlin, high priests of musical profundities who could not be bothered with anything as trivial as piano-playing technique. Under Kipp's exacting tutelage one practiced scales and more scales until one was blue in the face. Then came arpeggios and more arpeggios, followed by the technical exercises of Hanon, Czerny, Cramer, and finally Bach. One had to play accurately. Dear God, did one play accurately! Everything had to be precisely right — the notes, the different rhythms, the fingerings, the pedal work, the crescendos, the diminuendos, everything.

Years of teaching had convinced Karl Avgustovich that all of his young pupils were either careless, lazy, or both. In my case he was right. I was lazy. I loved to improvise, to sight-read, to practice Bach, but I detested scales and arpeggios. Above all, I abhorred those deadly dull digital calisthenics, those totally unmusical permutations of the seven white keys known as the Hanon — or as they were called in Russian, the Ganon — exercises. Kipp, however, was a firm believer in the virtue of the Hanon drills, insisting that his pupils practice them daily and also transpose them into all the other keys. The result, I once calculated in a moment of exasperation, was a repertory of musical torture which when extended to all twelve major keys could keep one occupied for one hundred and seventy-eight hours of continuous playing.

But one day I made a startling discovery: I could put my fingers through the Hanon drill while thinking of other things, and even better, while reading a book. This was a revelation. What had hitherto been an irksome chore ceased to be an ordeal. I could now practice for hours without feeling any distress because my brain, instead of being chained to these mind-numbing exercises, was garnering the rich delights of Frances Hodgson Burnett's *The Secret Garden* and *Little Lord Fauntleroy,* the novels of James Fenimore Cooper and Jack London — all immensely popular in Russia — and even something like *David Copperfield,* though this was rather a bulky tome to conceal behind a page of the Hanon score. To this day I cannot think of these stories without rehearing the sound of those tedious tonal sequences.

Karl Avgustovich Kipp, I soon discovered, was an expert psychologist as well as an inflexible disciplinarian. Realizing that a regime of constant reprimand and lecturing is apt to lose its force through repetition, he had developed a special shock treatment to combat the inveterate indolence of his pupils. I was exposed to it about six months after the start of my lessons with him and at a moment when everything seemed to be going very smoothly. I had perfected my ability to read a book while my fingers went through the mechanics of the Hanon exercises — a simple flick of the music page being enough to hide the book from my mother or anyone else who might wander into the living room during my practice hours. Indeed, my eagerness to practice for hours on end had begun to alarm my parents, who were afraid that I was about to undermine my health.

Kipp, though strict as usual, seemed satisfied with the progress I was making. Then one day I received a shock. He criticized my scales and arpeggios and commented acidly on my Hanon exercises — to my amazement, for I had put in eight solid hours of drill work during the preceding three days in order to finish Jack London's *The Call of the Wild.* Finally I was told to play Bach's three-part invention in F-minor, which has remained one of my favorites notwithstanding the shattering experience I am now going to describe. I had barely started playing when Kipp jumped all over me. Everything about it was wrong. In the sixth measure he made several simultaneous corrections. One of the left-hand notes had to be held a little longer while the other notes, also played by the left hand, had to be performed semilegato. He made changes in my right-hand fingering and introduced new, tricky pedaling effects. In trying to correct one detail, I neglected others, until in my confusion the entire passage was a shambles.

Kipp began to lose patience. The angrier he got, the more nervous I became. Finally, I made four or five mistakes at once. Kipp blew up. "You are lazy!" he shouted. "You are inattentive, you are stubborn, you insist on doing things *your* way — which is the *wrong* way!" and so on. He had me start again from the beginning. But by this time I was in such a state that I could not have played a proper C Major scale.

"Why am I wasting my time with a clumsy oaf like you!" exploded Kipp. Seizing the volume of Bach's inventions from the piano rack he flung it furiously to the floor.

"Now get out of here!" he cried, pointing imperiously toward the door. "Leave my house this minute and never let me see you here again. I'm not going to teach you anymore, do you hear? Tell your parents that you are no longer my pupil. You are simply not good enough. They will have to find someone else to try to teach you something. But that's their problem, not mine."

Outside, for it was winter, it was bitterly cold. As I trudged homeward in my thick wool coat and snow boots, I couldn't hold back my tears, which froze on my cheeks until melted by the hot tears that kept flowing. Our Trubnikovsky Pereulok apartment was about a mile and a half from Kipp's place, but I cried the whole way and was quite a sight by the time I reached home.

Mother did her best to console me. Yes, she said, she would take the matter up with Kipp and see if she couldn't persuade him to relent. But Kipp at first was adamant. No, he wasn't going to take me back. I had been indolent, I hadn't been practicing assiduously enough, etc. But after three agonizing days — the darkest of my young life — he finally gave in and agreed to reconsider, provided I practiced diligently and carried out my assignments to the letter.

I was overjoyed and practiced furiously for my next lesson. My reading for the time being was neglected. In an unprecedented burst of zeal I decided to present Kipp with a new, refined rendition of the Hanon exercises, obtained by having the right hand play in a key with sharps while the left hand played the same exercise in another key with flats. This was really expiation for my sins, for it demanded undivided attention and made book-reading impossible. The resultant cacophony, however, was more than the other members of the household could endure, and I was forced to abandon an experiment which, for all I know, might have brought a smile to Karl Avgustovich's rosy face.

Seven or eight months after this first catastrophe Kipp staged a second "expulsion," and a year or so later he kicked me out again. But from talks with other Kipp pupils I gathered that I was not alone in this respect. At one time or another all of them had been shown the door and requested never to darken his threshold again — only to be readmitted later. It was obviously a routine pedagogic device and probably scheduled in advance. For it really did not matter to Kipp whether the pupil had done his homework or not. By making several "corrections" in the same passage, he was certain to throw his young trainee off his stride and to make him feel clumsy and confused. The flustered student would begin to make additional mistakes, giving the instructor ample cause for working himself into a rage.

From all this I learned a lesson probably not intended by my piano professor: how easy it is to make any musical performer look stupid by scattering his (or her) powers of concentration. Much later in life, when I became involved in complex musico-dramatic problems, I understood why opera singers, who have to act, sing, and be musically accurate, all at the same time, are often accused of being stupid. It is too much to expect a singer not to make musical mistakes while he or she is learning details of stagecraft, and even the ablest of virtuoso performers could quickly be made to look like a monkey were Kipp's methods to be applied to him.

I was six years old when the First World War broke out in August of 1914, and of this dramatic happening, which was to transform the life of Europe, and incidentally my parents', I have only a dim recollection. Mother and Father had left for the Côte d'Azur, from which they returned as quickly as they could. Father then insisted that Mother give up her violin recitals "for the duration," and she did not thereafter appear in public, though she continued to participate in chamber-music events whenever Aunt Anna and Uncle Petya would gather in private living rooms for a musical soirée.

The war, which caused so much hardship and suffering at the front, did not particularly affect our daily lives. There were no shortages of food, and for my brother, Yuri, and myself almost half of the daylight hours — three in the morning, three in the afternoon — were now spent at school learning the rudiments of Russian grammar, history, geography, and mathematics.

Toward the end of each May, when the school year was over, we would all pile into a droshky and be driven to the station, where we would board the local train that was to take us out in a northeasterly direction beyond the city's suburbs to the village of Ivankovo, where our parents had a dacha. These migrations, though full of promise and excitement, were at the same time a bit upsetting for me, as they happened to coincide with my birthday which, according to the Julian calendar, fell on May 25 (June 7, by our present Gregorian-calendar reckoning). Whereas Yuri, born in early March, could celebrate his birthday in style with school friends invited over to share in the festivities, my own would pass virtually unnoticed and unobserved in the general confusion of packing as we prepared to leave, or of unpacking once we had reached the country.

The dacha itself was a pleasant summerhouse surrounded by a garden full of bushes, many of them with berries which we enjoyed picking. There were evergreens and the white-trunked *beryozy* — or birches — so dear to the Russian heart, and woods where we went to look for wild strawberries and mushrooms. The trees were full of songbirds which chirped and warbled, and every now and then we would be thrilled by the unmistakable two-note call of the cuckoo — which, as I was later astonished to learn while staging Humperdinck's *Hansel and Gretel,* no North American had ever heard in the woods of his own country. There was also a river nearby, in whose cold water we would go bathing when it was hot and the sun was shining brightly. A tennis court was available for the sportively inclined, a distinct minority, as I recall, compared to those who liked to move sedately from one wicket to the next banging a croquet ball with a wooden mallet. In the summer of 1915 a big brown and white cow made her appearance, adding a bucolic touch to the pastoral environment. Happy to have brought two sons into the world, Mother named her *Dochka* — for the daughter she would have liked to have and was in fact to give birth to the following year.

A quarter of a mile or so away was a far more elegant dacha, more like a country mansion or chateau, which belonged to a textile magnate named Krestovnikov, a good friend of Father's. Madame Krestovnikova was very much a grande dame, with a magnificent assortment of broad-brimmed hats, trailing skirts and sashes, and descending ovals of pearls festooning her ample bosom. Being invited to their palatial residence was always a special treat for Yuri and myself, because we would find the house swarming with other children, eager to play games. During one of these games, I remember, I was sent alone into an adjacent room while the rest of the children chose a certain phrase I would have to guess. The room where I was made to wait must have been a bedroom or a boudoir, for lying on a table there was a beautiful jeweled brooch. It glowed at me like something conjured up by the genie out of Aladdin's magic lamp, just too irresistibly lovely to be ignored. Picking it up, I fingered its gleaming surfaces and then slipped it into my jacket pocket.

The theft was soon discovered and there was a tremendous hue and cry in the neighborhood. Feeling more and more guilty, I finally went back to the Krestovnikovs' house with the jewel, but as I couldn't bear to admit I had stolen it, I explained that I had found it on the ground while playing in the village street that ran between our two houses.

Most children, of course, experience such moments of temptation, culpability, and extreme remorse, and many of them invent childish lies to conceal their guilty actions. But my claim to have "found" something I had in fact pocketed must, I now realize, have been in my childhood linked to a general pattern of behavior concerning original "discoveries." Among the many volumes in Father's library was a pamphlet about human dreams and sleep. This booklet made a great impression on me. After reading it carefully I explained to anyone willing to listen what happens to one who is asleep and dreaming. When asked how I knew all this, I would proudly answer: "Because that is how it is. This is something I have discovered." As I grew older I found less and less pleasure in decking myself out in the borrowed plumes of Aesop's fable. Information derived from books struck me as less impressive than what I could manage to discover through my own efforts. In this sense, though I have read many books and derived a great deal from them, I have never been or sought to be a scholar. I have always had the feeling that it is not really proper to quote, as scholars do, from this book or that, and that footnotes are not real intellectual knowledge, but a form of "borrowed plumage." Years later, after *Bringing Opera to Life* was finished, I noticed that it contained almost no quotations from other sources.

There was of course a piano in the country dacha just as there was one in the living room of our Moscow apartment. I could thus continue practicing during the carefree summer months and even forget the tiresome Hanon exercises as I let my fingers wander over the keyboard. All aspiring pianists, I imagine, dream of becoming a Mozart or a Chopin. For me the great composers occupied the seventh heaven, the uppermost sphere in the firmament of music. Famous divas and gifted virtuosi might win more money and applause while in their prime, but the great composers did not need that sort of glamour since they were immortal. And so, in a deliberate exhibition of self-deceit, I would let my fingers run over the keyboard, improvising sweet-sounding melodies and graceful harmonies. I did this even though I knew perfectly well that it was just a trick, that I was doing no more than rearranging familiar patterns, whereas real composition is something entirely different, depending as it does on one's ability to invent new themes and give them a definite, convincing form.

Then one day, to my surprise, I found myself mysteriously inspired. We had returned to Moscow, as we usually did in early September, when the days were less warm and the nights often chilly. It suddenly came to me while I was lying in bed — a sad, haunting theme. It was a sentimental waltz in D Major, with subtle harmonies and a coherent musical structure. For several successive nights it haunted me until I knew it by heart.

Finally I sat down and reproduced the waltz on the piano, playing it over and over until my fingers were familiar with every note.

"What's that you're playing?" I was asked.

"Oh, just something I heard in a dream," I would answer.

I soon came to believe it. How else could I have hit on anything so entrancing except in some sort of inspired dream? After all, why not? Hadn't Tartini's *Devil's Trill* violin sonata, which

Mother and I often played together, been written as the result of a dream in which the composer had heard it personally played to him by the Devil? So this D Major composition became my own "Dream Waltz," an original creation which nobody in the family — neither mother, nor Uncle Petya, nor even Aunt Anna, who had a fabulous musical memory, had ever heard before.

Ten years were to pass before I was to discover the secret of this oneiric inspiration — which I shall relate in due course. But at the time it helped to enhance my reputation as a budding "child prodigy" who might — who knows? — be destined to follow in the footsteps of Borodin, Rimsky-Korsakoff, or Tchaikovsky. I had devised an easy way of memorizing Russian noun declensions and short-cut methods for multiplying certain arithmetical figures, and with the conceit of youth I fondly imagined that there was not a book in Father's library that I could not understand. By this time I had left the fairy tales of Perrault and of the Comtesse de Ségur, Wilhelm Busch's *Max und Moritz,* and the fables of Krylov and La Fontaine far behind, and I was learning a lot of Pushkin by heart. I had absorbed *The Three Musketeers* with gusto, devoured *The Hunchback of Notre Dame* with relish, and I was about to tackle Tolstoy's *War and Peace.* But before taking on this monumental opus, I one day heard my parents discussing a play by Anton Chekhov entitled *Vishniovy sad* — known to English readers as *The Cherry Orchard.* In Russian the word *sad* means "garden," and in my innocence I imagined that this *Cherry Garden* was going to be something as enchanting as *The Secret Garden,* which had so beguiled me a year or two before. So I plowed through all four acts of Chekhov's play in vain search of a magic that wasn't there, and though I thought I understood every word uttered by the various protagonists, I found myself bored and baffled by those endless monologues and nostalgic effusions and wondering what all the fuss was about since nothing ever seemed to happen.

Fortunately, not all dramatic works affected me in this way. I think it was in Victor Hugo's *Hernani* that I encountered secret passages where people hid and took part in plots and counterplots. The whole thing was tingling with excitement and got me so aroused that I decided to try my hand at writing a play of my own. I sat down and wrote a gripping melodrama, at the end of which there was nothing left but corpses. All the main characters were dead, having been murdered or having committed suicide or having succumbed to horrible accidents of one kind or another. Feeling quite pleased with this little brain child, I took it to Father, who read it through and then congratulated me on it. "You know, you seem to show a considerable gift." At that I began beaming, until he added: "Yes, a considerable gift . . . In fact, I'm seriously thinking of having you apprenticed to a butcher!"

Childhood for most young people is a prolonged exercise in frustration, and mine was no exception. It was bad enough having to sit at table listening to Father telling stories which neither Yuri nor I really understood, though they caused a lot of laughter. But never did my brother and I feel more profoundly humiliated than on those evenings when Feodor Chaliapin came to dinner. The great basso was a good friend of the family, and Mother had once even accompanied him to the United States on a music tour. It was always a thrill to see this fabulous person invade our apartment with his overpowering presence, to hear his extraordinarily resonant voice, and occasionally to feel his regal hand resting on my head. But we youngsters were never granted more than fleeting glimpses of this larger-than-life figure. For no sooner had we finished our supper than Yuri and I were unceremoniously hustled off to bed, leaving the grown-ups to savor the entertainment that followed. And what entertainment that was! Perhaps the greatest Russian raconteur of modern times, Chaliapin had an inexhaustible fund of bawdy stories which were quite unfit for childish ears, particularly when recited with a Rabelaisian verve which left nothing to the imagination.

Already, as a six- or seven-year-old child, I had been taken to see several ballet performances. One of them was Tchaikovsky's *Nutcracker Suite*. Another, which I loved, was Shchedrin's *Konyok Gorbunok,* a children's ballet about a little hunchback horse. Yuri and I even attended a few ballet classes at a school directed by Fokine, though we both gave this up quite soon.

The first opera I ever heard — even before I saw it performed on the stage — was Tchaikovsky's *Eugene Onegin*. Everyone around me knew its melodies and arias, could sing or play them on the piano, and of course recite the lovely verses from Pushkin's most famous poem. The only other opera that enjoyed anywhere near as much popularity in Moscow was Bizet's *Carmen,* but *Eugene Onegin,* being the combined creation of Russia's greatest poet and Russia's greatest composer, had a unique place in our affections. I was too young to appreciate the Byronic irony and social criticism to be found in Pushkin's poem, in which the emptiness and futility of everyday life in aristocratic circles during the reign of Tsar Nicholas I is mercilessly exposed. All I cared about was the romantic love story, with its sad, unfulfilled conclusion. Tatiana, naturally, was my favorite — the beautiful young heroine, so pale, so terribly in love. I shared her agony in writing that passionate letter to Eugene, in which she poured out all that her throbbing heart contained. It was so thrillingly unconventional. Weren't men the ones who were supposed to make avowals of this kind to the young ladies they were wooing?

The music of the Letter Scene, I might add, does full justice to Pushkin's passionate verses. I particularly loved the opening phrase depicting Tatiana's feverish yearning, then the breathless, interrupted gasps building up to an almost intolerable suspense, crowned by Tatiana's romantic declaration (which every soprano in Russia was ready to sing at the slightest provocation): "Even though I should perish, I will first yield to that blinding ray of hope and drink the magic poison of desire!"

When I finally saw this opera performed on the stage, I was profoundly shocked to hear Onegin declare in the last act that he was in love with Tatiana after all, and to do so in almost the identical words and music that she had used when she was penning her passionate letter to him. I could not forgive Tchaikovsky for not having composed another aria for the baritone, since this one should have been left as Tatiana's exclusive property.

I experienced much the same disappointment, though for quite different reasons, when, after months of pestering my parents, I was finally allowed to accompany them to the Bolshoy Theatre to see *Boris Godunov.* I had read Pushkin's drama, which had inspired Mussorgsky's score, and it had a special place in my heart, if only because Tsar Boris and I shared the same first name. Often in fun people would quote the famous line: "Boris, Boris, all trembles before you!" and I would enjoy a moment of exaltation as the imaginary Tsar of All the Russias. I also wanted to see Mussorgsky's opera because Tsar Boris — a complex character who, though originally a murderer and a usurper, is also portrayed as a kind father and a strong, sagacious ruler — was one of Chaliapin's great roles.

In my youthful fancy I expected Chaliapin to appear on stage with the very first notes and to stay there, singing, plotting murder, getting himself elected Tsar, fighting the Pretender Dmitri, and generally dominating the situation. But what I saw was quite different. The first scene of the prologue began with a chorus, after which a man appeared and sang a pretty solo. At first I was sure it was Chaliapin, but I soon realized that this was not the Tsar at all but some kind of nobleman who had come out to tell the people that Boris was unwilling to be crowned. In the next scene there was much ringing of bells and more choral singing, and Chaliapin did finally appear, looking splendid in his tall imperial bonnet and regalia. But after a couple of minutes he disappeared, leaving the stage to the chorus while the bells rang out wildly once again. The prologue was followed by a long intermission, after which we returned to our seats to watch the first act. In its first scene two men sang for what seemed an interminable time, and then after a short intermission, other characters filled the stage and sang, but not one of them was Boris. There was another long intermission, after which I fell asleep, so that all I heard from Chaliapin that evening was the short acceptance speech in the prologue.

Many people, I imagine, come away from their first exposure to opera with some such feeling of acute disappointment. Later I heard Chaliapin sing in *Russalka,* an opera by Dargomizhsky, in which he played the part of an insane old miller. The make-up was extraordinary and so convincing that nobody could have guessed that this was the same man who had earlier impersonated Tsar Boris. Chaliapin was a consummate make-up artist as well as a supreme actor. But his mighty talent was so overpowering that it made everyone else on stage look dwarflike and insignificant. This third operatic experience thus did nothing to reconcile me to lyrical dramatics — *le théâtre lyrique,* as the French call it — which struck me as being a singularly ponderous and stilted art form.

There were other reasons for my aversion to opera. My young years in Moscow happened to coincide with a golden age of Russian drama, dominated by Konstantin Stanislavsky's celebrated Art Theatre. One of the regular visitors to our Trubnikovsky Pereulok apartment was Ivan Moskvin, a short, stubby actor with a nondescript face which he could transform into anything he liked, so that one always had difficulty recognizing him on stage. Moskvin loved music and would often tiptoe into the living room while I was at the keyboard, intrigued by the sounds I was making. If it was something by Bach, he would sink into a chair and listen in rapt silence. Delighted to have an appreciative listener to whom I could play something more inspiring than the insufferable Hanon, I would entertain Moskvin with long extracts from *The Well-tempered Clavier.* In return he offered me tickets for performances at Stanislavsky's theater. I didn't realize it at the time, but these were worth a king's ransom. And thus it was that as a fascinated young boy I saw Moskvin and Stanislavsky and Kachalov play the most varied roles in Griboyedov's *Gorye ot ouma* (*The Woes of Being Too Witty*), Gogol's *Revizor* (*The Inspector General*), Chekhov's *Chaika* (*The Seagull*), and Gorky's *Na dne* (*The Lower Depths*).

No wonder I could not generate enthusiasm for opera. Compared to these marvelously vital and lifelike characterizations, the pompous posturings and artificial gestures of the operatic stage seemed unbearably wooden.

Some of these inspiring evenings at the theater must have taken place after the first Revolution of February 1917, which led to Emperor Nicholas II's abdication, or after the second Revolution of October, which led to the overthrow of the Kerensky government and the triumph of Lenin's Bolsheviks. Though Father was never actually a member of the parliamentary Duma, he was unquestionably a liberal and had long favored the development of democracy in Russia. He thus welcomed the February Revolution, which promised an end to somber palace intrigues and the machinations of half-educated charlatans like Rasputin. The names of Kerensky and Miliukov were forever on Father's lips, and it was evident from the excitement with which he spoke of them that he considered them great men.

I was too young to grasp the intricacies of these political upheavals, though I vividly recall one of their first consequences: the issuance of a new currency which had shrunk physically as well as in purchasing power to postage-stamp size, so that one now needed fifty twenty-ruble "notes" to make up a 1000-ruble sheet in order to be able to buy something.

The summer of 1917 was destined to be the last we were to spend at our dacha in the country. The war, still raging hundreds of miles away to the west, seemed as distant as ever while we roamed the woods looking for wild strawberries or lapped up the deliciously warm, sweet milk abundantly provided by Dochka, the brown and white cow. Dochka, however, was no longer the privileged recipient of undivided attention. For Mother's secret wish had been fulfilled the previous December by the birth of a baby daughter named Irina, who thus came into the world eight and a half years after the younger of her two brothers.

The February Revolution had provoked a lot of verbal excitement in our household, but otherwise our lives had not been much affected. However, with the October Revolution our world was turned upside-down. Suddenly there was firing in the streets, and for a number of days we were more or less forced to stay indoors and were not allowed to sally forth with the red-haired Katya Rigert when she went on errands — like going to buy coffee, for example, which was quite a procedure, since our parents insisted on a special three-variety blend composed of mocha, Medina, and Livanskoe (that is, Lebanese).

The "counterrevolutionaries" having been dispersed with rifle fire or bayonetted into submission, the Bolsheviks lost no time establishing a new social order. As a lawyer, Father was automatically classified as a *bourzhoui* — a derogatory term corresponding to the French *sale bourgeois* or "filthy bourgeois scum." As an exploiter of the downtrodden proletariat, Father lost his right to employ a cook and a maid. Varvara, the cook, who had slept upstairs on a floor reserved for domestics, was thus sent packing, as was Fevronia, the all-purpose maid who had occupied a small bedroom next to the kitchen. We were, however, allowed to retain the services of Katya. The *shveitsar* — which is to say, the janitor — was likewise freed from his menial occupation and disappeared overnight.* Not content with that, the authorities closed off the front entrance of number 15, Trubnikovsky Pereulok, thus condemning the elevator. We were no longer permitted to use the

* *Shveitsar* — literally "the Swiss." Ever since the time of Peter the Great, Swiss guards had been imported into Russia to protect important buildings, and from this the term had spread to cover any doorman or porter.

front stairwell; instead we had to use the back staircase, climb five flights, and enter the apartment through the kitchen door.

This was only the beginning of our tribulations. The apartment, with its three large south- and southwest-facing rooms, four bedrooms, and one maid's room, was declared too spacious for a family of six (two parents, three children, and one governess). We were thus required to take in a family of complete strangers. Fortunately they were simple working folk, who made a minimum of fuss when it came to sharing the kitchen, the water closet, and the bathroom. But to accommodate the newcomers, Mother and Father had to give up their master bedroom next to the vestibule and move to the other end of the central corridor into what had once been the dining room, with its chandeliers, bookcases, handsome wallpaper, and the dark blue porcelain with gold incrustations which was brought out for special occasions. Those special occasions — when Chaliapin, Ivan Moskvin, and others had come to enliven the evenings — were now a thing of the past; and though the Steinway grand piano was allowed to remain in the living room, the elegant Louis XV–style armchairs had to be pushed against the walls to make space for the dining room table, on which we and the newcomers took turns with meals.

The meals too grew steadily more meager as the winter progressed. One of the first consequences of the Bolshevik takeover was the closing down of almost all of Moscow's shops. Normal monetary transactions virtually ceased to exist and were replaced by ration coupons which had to be exchanged once a week for the most basic foodstuffs. For the first time in our lives we learned the meaning of permanent, unremitting hunger.

The new masters of the country, though brutal and often brutish in their ways, did not wish to appear totally "uncultured" — an adjective which to this day is almost a term of abuse in the Soviet Union. And so it came about that one day a representative of some factory club arrived to ask if Mother would consider giving a violin recital for the benefit of the workers there. Mother had not given any concerts since the beginning of the war, but when informed by the club representative that in payment she would receive a dozen eggs, ten pounds of potatoes, and that unheard-of luxury — a box of granulated sugar — she accepted. However, she added, she would need an accompanist. Now what kind of fee could they offer him? The answer: apples and herrings.

A suitable date was agreed upon, several weeks hence, and the factory management said it would take care of the transportation problem by having Mother and her accompanist — her brother, Piotr Luboshutz — picked up and driven out to the suburbs in a factory truck. But an unexpected hitch developed when Uncle Petya informed his sister that he could not free himself from another engagement on that particular day.

I don't recall just who first suggested that I be chosen in Dyadya Petya's place. It was probably intended as a joke. But no sooner was the suggestion in the air than I grabbed at it with both hands. What was so ridiculous about the idea of a nine-year-old boy accompanying his violin-playing mother on the piano? What had age got to do with it, I argued — with a heated eloquence worthy of Father's — if I was competent enough to do the job? And who could doubt my competence, since I had by now mastered Tartini's *Devil's Trill* sonata, Schubert's (not Franz, but a lesser-known C. F. D. Schubert's) *The Bee,* and Kreisler's "Liebeslied Waltz." By practicing day and night I could even double this slender repertory during the next two weeks. It was silly, I added, to let all those tempting apples and herrings go to someone else when the family had a second professional pianist available and willing.

My earnest pleading cut no ice with the grown-ups, who prevailed on a certain Samuelson to act as substitute for Uncle Petya. By way of consolation I was told that I could go on practicing with Mother, in the hope that at some future and presumably distant date I might be good enough to accompany her at concerts. Determined to show these doubting Thomases that I was every bit as good as this Samuelson intruder, I practiced furiously for the next twelve days. And it was a good thing I did so, for shortly before the concert, Samuelson came down with influenza and two days later I found myself being triumphantly driven out with Mother in a truck to the suburban factory.

This was the first of a number of factory concerts at which I accompanied Mother — anything but an easy task, as I quickly discovered. She had not performed in public for some time, and playing by heart made her nervous and taxed her memory. She often suffered "blanks," and as she couldn't stop at such moments, saying: "Sorry, but I've forgotten how it goes from here on," she would simply jump to another section of the composition and I would have to catch up with her as quickly and smoothly as possible. While still very young I thus received a quite unusual training in alert listening and quick musical reactions, which was to be of immense value in the future.

Mother must have performed at half a dozen factories in the outskirts of Moscow, when one day the representative who had extended the first invitation reappeared, asking Mother to come out for another concert. This time the promised fee included several pounds of butter, then virtually unobtainable, as well as ten pounds of potatoes. After which he added: "Oh, and be sure to bring that little boy who came with you the last time. The workers were intrigued with your young accompanist, and this time they would like to hear him play something all by himself. . . . We'll give him some candy and maybe a few extra herrings, as well as apples."

A few days later, after accompanying one of Mother's violin pieces, I was thus called upon to perform a solo. The piece was Mendelssohn's *Rondo capriccioso,* which has remained one of my favorites to this day. I cannot play it without a strong feeling of nostalgia for the Moscow of my youth, mingled with a feeling of relief at the realization that I don't have to play it anymore to obtain a few apples and herrings.

In the late spring of 1918 I was forced to give up these factory concerts when Mother and Father decided to send Yuri and me down to our maternal grandparents in Odessa. The Treaty of Brest-Litovsk had not yet been signed and the Germans still occupied large parts of the Ukraine. This vast agricultural region had always been the breadbasket of Russia, and the food situation in Odessa was apparently far less grim than in northern cities like Moscow and Petrograd.

I recall little of our southbound trip, except for a moment of excitement when we reached the frontier separating the Russian from the German forces. Though hostilities had virtually ceased and even given way to a certain amount of fraternizing between once hostile soldiers, getting across the no man's land between the two lines was a perilous undertaking. My brother and I were bundled into a big covered cart and driven by a local peasant over a rough country road until we were told that we were no longer on Bolshevik territory. At the nearest station we were put on a train and made the rest of the trip by rail.

Our maternal grandparents — which is to say Saúl and Gitel (in Russian, Catherine) Luboshutz — occupied a ground floor apartment in a large stone house on one of Odessa's main streets. The house had probably seen better days, but now it was crowded with refugees like ourselves, and the inner courtyard stank most unpleasantly of unremoved garbage. The house was big enough to accommodate a school so that Yuri and I had only to descend two flights of stairs from our second-story rooms and walk around the corner to the classrooms. On the other hand, I had to walk quite a distance for my piano lessons, which were given to me at her home by a Mrs. Weiss.

Though Grandfather Saúl (with the accent on the *u*) had once played the fiddle well enough to coach Mother and to launch young Anna and Piotr on their musical careers, he was now little more than a supernumerary and seemed to spend most of his time praying and going to the synagogue. This was something of a novelty for Yuri and myself, who had been brought up in a liberal and artistic rather than in a religious atmosphere, though there were certain feast days — like the Day of Atonement — which we had regularly observed in Moscow.

In Odessa the dominant personality was clearly Grandmother, or Babushka, as she was called, who wore the pants and ran the shop. Next to her ground floor apartment was a kind of combination salesroom and workshop, where secondhand pianos were repaired, retuned, and generally spruced up so that they could be sold at several times the price she had paid for them at local auctions or private sales. Grandfather, who was sometimes put to work with soap and sandpaper, cleaning and polishing the ivory keys until they turned from dirty yellow to gleaming white, was always expelled from the shop the moment a customer appeared, lest he undermine Babushka's canny bargaining by innocently agreeing with an outraged client that he was being overcharged for the "miserable piece of junk" he was thinking of purchasing.

Some months after our arrival we were joined in Odessa by Katya Rigert and our almost three-year-old sister, Irina. Mother, who had accompanied them, then returned to Moscow to be with Father. A few months later the Revolution caught up with us again, as Red Army cavalrymen and footsloggers trotted or trudged into Odessa, now abandoned by the "Whites" and the French and Greek detachments that had occupied it until April 1919. Uncle Petya was hurriedly dispatched from Moscow to help Babushka look after and protect us. He used his spare time, of which he had a lot, to woo the local girls — one of whom, named Elena Mikhailovna, he decided there and then to marry. This unexpected addition to our household aroused quite a bit of tension, for Aunt Elena and Babushka took a violent and pointed dislike to each other, filling the air with their shrill comments and complaints.

Of the eighteen months we spent in Odessa I most vividly recall the outings which Yuri and I took part in as Boy Scout "cubs." We were taught how to put up tents, build fires, prepare outdoor meals, and initiated in certain handicrafts, like the making of small brushes. As our camp was located by the shore, we were also taught how to swim and paddle a boat. There was a lot of exercising and footracing and competitive games of one kind or another. Anxious as ever to excel and in my desire to add as many badges to my left shirt sleeve as I could, I even entered a competition for excellence in translating German, only to come a cropper when the examiner floored me with a book on philosophy which I would not have understood even if it had been written in Russian.

By now almost two years had passed since the October Revolution, and Father, who had long predicted that "this crazy business cannot last" and that the Bolsheviks were going to be turned out of the Kremlin at any moment by their many enemies, had begun to give up hope. Odessa being in the grip of the Bolsheviks, like Moscow, there was no further point in keeping the family divided and dispersed. So Mother traveled to Odessa once again and brought Yuri and me back to Moscow by train.

Of this trip too I recall very little, beyond the fact that it took us two long weeks to cover those 980 miles, as we kept changing from one train to another, moving from Kharkov to Orël, from Orël to Tula, and from there on to Moscow. The conditions of travel were most uncomfortable and for part of the trip we even had to sit on bags and knapsacks in an open freight car. Mother had refused to be parted from her precious Amati, and during one tedious train stop, she pulled out her violin and treated the weary, unshaved soldiers to some unaccompanied Bach Sonatas.

Babushka's journey to Moscow, undertaken a little later, was even more trying. Not only did she have to shepherd little Irina with the help of Katya Rigert, but to her had been entrusted the delicate task of smuggling back a number of diamond brooches, earrings, and necklaces which Mother had deposited in Odessa for safekeeping. It was finally decided that the surest way of hiding this precious jewelry was to sew it inside a large pillow which Babushka was to carry with her. The Bolsheviks, ever on the lookout for thieves, spies, foreign agents, smugglers, disguised capitalists, and other "counterrevolutionary elements," had no respect for the privacy of luggage and did not hesitate to search the pockets of travelers who might seem better dressed or look suspiciously affluent. The pillow, into whose feathery entrails the jewels were carefully sewn, thus seemed the safest bet.

The local trains Grandmother had to use proved to be as slow as those on which Mother, Yuri, and I had traveled, and at one point she found herself sharing a compartment with some Red Army soldiers. Noticing that whenever she got out to stretch her legs, she took the pillow with her, as though it were already winter and this a warm sealskin muff, they began teasing her about it. "Now tell us, Granny, why are you so attached to that cushion you're holding? Why do you have to take it with you when you get out for a walk on the platform? Why not leave it here with us? We'll take good care of it . . ." and so on.

Alarmed by their needling curiosity, Grandmother got off at the next stop and had Katya Rigert and Irina follow her into the station. "Go into the ladies' room and stay there, and don't come out until after the train has left," she ordered the governess. "After it leaves the station, pretend that you and the child missed the train. I'll come back to pick you up as soon as I can."

Climbing back into the train compartment with her pillow, Grandmother sat alone among the soldiers, who resumed their teasing. "Now tell us, Babushka, what's so special about that pillow that you have to take it wherever you go? . . ." Grandmother pursed her lips and said nothing, but as soon as the train began to move she jumped up excitedly from her seat and began shouting: "What! The train's moving and they're not here! Oh, please, get the train to stop! Get the train to stop! Oh, I've lost my little granddaughter, I've lost my little Irina! What am I to do?"

She put on such a convincing act about her "little lost child" that the suspect pillow was completely forgotten in the general commotion. At the next stop the soldiers, taking pity on her plight, even helped her to unload all her bags and parcels, while the stationmaster, to whom she poured out her tale of woe, arranged to have her catch the next train traveling in the opposite direction so that she could join her "mislaid" granddaughter and the governess. The three of them were soon reunited, and after more tedious stops and changes Babushka was able to ride into Moscow still cradling the precious pillow in her arms.

Father had somehow found accommodations for both Grandmother and Grandfather in our apartment house on the Trubnikovsky Pereulok, and later Uncle Petya also moved into it with his young wife. Though the Luboshutz trio still occasionally performed in public, it was no longer the close-knit threesome it had once been. Aunt Anna had also married — a brilliant doctor named Sergei Adolfovich Shereshevsky, who had helped bring Irina into the world and who was now in charge of an important Moscow hospital. Being anything but a Bohemian in his prim and proper tastes, he clearly disapproved of Father, who had been married to another woman before he met Lea Luboshutz. Thus began an estrangement, which was soon to put a continent, and eventually an ocean, between the two sisters.

In Moscow Yuri and I resumed our school studies at the *gymnasium*. He had by now abandoned all thought of a musical career and was increasingly interested in science, while I was once again entrusted to the stern discipline and drill of Karl Avgustovich Kipp. Being young, irresponsible, and ignorant, we were less disturbed by what was going on about us than were our parents, and we tended to find all these upheavals and excitements something of a lark. But we too were in for a shock the day the police came to arrest Father, who was led off to the dread Lubyanka prison for interrogation. What occasioned this arrest I do not know. It may have been Father's connections with the German Embassy, for which he had been acting as a legal consultant. But fortunately for all of us, Father's period of detention was brief.

The most adroit in "getting around" during these troubled times was Uncle Petya, whose piano playing was much appreciated by the new regime's avant-garde society, now led by the revolutionary poets, Mayakovsky and Yesenin. The latter had embarked on a tempestuous affair with the American dancer Isadora Duncan, who had come to Russia to hail the "new dawn of socialism" and who, gaily trampling on all petty bourgeois conventions and outworn notions of morality, would not hesitate to strip at a party and dance around in almost totally unfettered nudity. Uncle Petya, who was sometimes called upon to provide a piano accompaniment for the cavortings of this scantily clad Botticellian Grace, managed to get us tickets for perhaps the most astounding of all her public exhibitions. This was an Isadora Duncan solo performed on the vast stage of the Bolshoy. And what a solo! Accompanying her in the pit was a full orchestra which played Tchaikovsky's Sixth (*Pathétique*) Symphony — from the first note to the last. For three quarters of an hour we sat in an elegant box spellbound by the extraordinary undulations of this High Priestess of the Dance, a somewhat fleshy, barefoot priestess in a kind of Arcadian garb who played with her seven veils like a Pre-Raphaelite Salome.

The following summer — that of 1921 — I spent a few privileged weeks at the dacha of Alexander Tikhonovich Grechaninov, one of Russia's most popular songwriters as well as the author of two operas and four symphonies, who undertook to tutor me in composition. Already, while taking my first piano lessons with Gelman, I had begun studying solfège and theory at a music school run by two Gnyessin sisters, whose establishment was located conveniently close to our Trubnikovsky Pereulok apartment. After returning from Odessa I had also been admitted to the Moscow Conservatory, where I studied theoretical subjects. But to be personally tutored by a well-known composer like Grechaninov was, of course, a supreme consecration for a thirteen-year-old youngster.

This, though I did not suspect it at the time, was destined to be my last summer in Russia. The food shortage was as grim as ever, and there were days when we had little more to sustain us than the cans of condensed milk which were then being distributed by Herbert Hoover's American Relief Administration. The taste of that creamy, oversweet liquid, which was such a boon to us children, is one I shall never forget, just as I shall never forget the wolflike avidity with which Yuri and I, after licking our plates clean, would watch to see if our little dark-haired sister was going to leave anything uneaten, thus giving us a chance to gobble up the scraps.

Not long after my return to Moscow from Grechaninov's place in the country, we were taken to a big fund-raising concert staged at the Blagorodnoye Sobranye (the Assembly Hall of the Nobility), now renamed Dom Soyuzov (the House of Unions). There were terrible stories of people in starving villages being reduced to eating human flesh, and many prominent actors, singers, and musicians — including Mother, Aunt Anna, and Uncle Petya — had accordingly agreed to stage a benefit performance to aid the destitute and hungry. A number of glass stands had been mounted in the colonnaded foyer, where photographs were exhibited of haggard, hollow-eyed skeletons, the clothes hanging from their emaciated frames like scarecrow rags. One of these display cases even contained something that looked like a piece of meat and which was apparently a morsel of cooked human flesh.

For once I can date this particular event. It occurred on August 2, 1921. For in the middle of the concert a man came on to the stage with a telegram in his hand. He told the hushed house that Caruso had just died. The consternation that this news produced among the audience is indescribable. Everyone present seemed instinctively to understand that this death marked the end of an epoch and that the world would never be quite the same again.

And so in a sense it did — at any rate for us. A few weeks later Mother and I left Moscow, headed for the West.

2

From Moscow to Berlin

THERE IS LITTLE I can recall of our trip to Petrograd, beyond the fact that it was made in a typically Russian, wide-gauge railway carriage. The steamer we then boarded was anything but large, and as we were met by a fierce Baltic wind shortly after clearing the mouth of the Neva estuary, we were rolled and tossed all the way to Stettin. It was my first sea voyage, and by the time we landed I was fervently hoping it would be the last. I had vomited up everything my heaving stomach had contained and felt as limp as jelly when I made my unsteady way across the creaking gangplank onto the motionless wharf. An hour or two later, after undergoing the inevitable passport and customs inspections, we boarded another solid-wheeled, though narrow-gauge carriage, in which we were soon being propelled across the potato- and beet-studded flatlands of Pomerania toward Berlin.

Though Frederick the Great's broad-boulevarded and airy capital had since been transformed into a bustling streetcar-, carriage-, and automobile-cluttered metropolis, Berlin was once again a haven for the persecuted and oppressed. The Huguenots, who had so profoundly marked it in the eighteenth century, had now been replaced by Russians, who had flooded into the western parts of the city and opened clubs, coffee houses, restaurants, and even publishing companies. The new émigrés from the East had also established a Russian school, in the residential Charlottenburg area, in which I was enrolled soon after we had rented two rather grubby rooms near the Potsdamer Strasse.

So many momentous things occurred during those first weeks in Berlin that I find it impossible to record them in exact chronological order. Mother had been allowed to leave the Soviet Union for a few concerts which she had been invited to give in several German cities, and I of course went along as her accompanist. Father may have helped to arrange these recitals through his German Embassy connections in Moscow. It had been agreed in any case that we were not to return to Russia, now in the throes of revolutionary turmoil, civil strife, and famine, and that Father would do his best to join us in Berlin as soon as possible with the other members of the family. But a bare week after our arrival in Berlin, Mother received a telegram from Moscow saying that Father had suffered a stroke and died. We later heard — though we had no way of knowing if this was true — that he had been informed he was going to be arrested. Having to climb five flights every day to the Trubnikovsky Pereulok apartment had already imposed a great strain on his heart, and this latest piece of bad news was not made to calm his nerves. Aunt Anna's doctor husband, Sergei Shereshevsky, was immediately summoned to the scene, but there was nothing he could do to save my father, who died shortly after being carried into the apartment.

Needless to say, this was a bitter blow for Mother and myself. If these had been normal times, she would have rushed back to Moscow to succor and console the not quite five-year-old Irina and Yuri. But under the circumstances, the only thing to do was wait, in the hope that the enterprising Uncle Petya and the resourceful Babushka could find some way of leaving the Soviet Union with the children.

In the meantime we had to struggle to survive in a city which, like the rest of Germany, was now in the throes of a galloping inflation. Prices kept rising by the day and eventually by the hour, so that the 500-mark note with which one had sallied forth in the morning to buy a pound of butter might not, by sunset, be able to buy more than half that much. Fortunately for both of us, Mother had left Russia with fifty American dollars — obtained I know not how — and these were our salvation. A single U.S. dollar, we were happy to discover, was enough to provide us room and board for an entire week. But that left little for luxuries or the possibly rainy days ahead.

Fortunately for us, too, Berlin was now full of Russian friends who had known Mother and Father in Moscow. One of them was a gentleman named Alexander Sher, and if I mention him it is because he had a lovely daughter named Nina with whom, since we were in the same class, I soon found myself walking every day to school. As deliciously plump as she was beautifully dark-haired, she was the very embodiment of desire: a desire she unconcernedly exacerbated in the thirteen-year-old adolescent I was by using an exquisite perfume which still makes my blood tingle when I think of it. Ah, those morning walks through the wintry streets of Berlin to our Charlottenburg school! At once ecstatic and desperately frustrating! For my adolescent passion, as so often happens in such cases, was not requited, and Nina, though so physically close and tempting, remained cool, untouched by the ardent flame her heavenly scent ignited.

Among the many Russians whom Mother befriended in Berlin was a lady who rather fancied her keyboard virtuosity. I have forgotten her name, but she it was, I believe, who persuaded Mother to take me to Leonid Kreutzer, a St. Petersburg Russian who had studied composition with Glazunov before moving to Berlin, where he had settled down for good and married a German lady. A well-known pianist as well as a composer, he gave lessons to gifted students in his elegant apartment near the Luisenplatz. He was apparently much flattered by Mother's visit and welcomed us with open arms. The fact that, though married, he had no children of his own may have helped, for after hearing me play a piece or two and listening to Mother's account of how I had accompanied her at public concerts, Kreutzer decided once and for all that I was a *Wunderkind,* a child prodigy who needed only the gentlest guidance and encouragement for his youthful genius to flower.

I, of course, was delighted by this unexpected burst of sunshine. To be freed at last from the mechanical drudgery of Hanon's patterns, Czerny's exercises, Kramer's studies, and Kuhlau's sonatinas was a treat I had not expected. With Ganymede-like ease I was suddenly lifted up to the higher realms of the piano-playing art and asked to learn Schumann's G Minor Sonata. It was sheer bliss, and I yielded to it with almost voluptuous rapture, little realizing what this "high road" to the empyrean was going to cost me in later years. For this was an act of madness Karl Avgustovich Kipp would never have committed. Schumann's G Minor Sonata is far too difficult a piece for a child of thirteen, and it is little wonder if I then played it like a pig.

But for Leonid Kreutzer I was the child genius who could do no wrong. No matter how sloppily I played, I was endowed with the magic touch. I was still young; time would iron out the imperfections.

Quite early on he asked me if I had ever played any of Chopin's Preludes. I told him I hadn't.

"Then bring them to the next lesson," he said, giving me a friendly pat on the back.

At the time I knew next to nothing about Chopin. When I inquired at the music store, I was told that there were twenty-four Chopin Preludes. Since my teacher had asked me to bring them along, I decided to learn the lot. Who was I to argue with the famous Leonid Kreutzer? So I turned up for the next lesson prepared to massacre all twenty-four Preludes — an act of idiocy if ever there was one. But instead of chiding my young foolishness, Kreutzer went into raptures.

"The darling boy!" he kept repeating, almost clapping his hands in delight. "Isn't he marvelous! My, what ambition! What industry! What talent!"

I should add, for the sake of accuracy, that these heady compliments were as much directed to my mother as myself. For if I was a *Wunderkind,* it was because I was my mother's son, the gifted child of a gifted *artiste.* To treat me as an ordinary pupil would be shocking; the very idea was blasphemous. No, I was an artist in my own right — just as was Lea Luboshutz and just as was Leonid Kreutzer, the pianist, composer, and conductor. Why keep so much talent concealed beneath a bushel when it was waiting to be revealed? So let them reveal it now! A small chamber-music recital? "Nonsense! It will be a full-scale concert. In the Beethoven-saal, what's more, and with the Philharmonic Orchestra!"

In those days the Berlin Philharmonic Orchestra could be hired for an astronomical sum of marks (almost worthless the next week) by any enterprising conductor. For a man of Kreutzer's prestige, hiring the orchestra was child's play. Since Berlin was now swamped with Russians, let it be a Russian soirée with an all-Russian program. As an hors d'oeuvre Kreutzer would conduct the overture to Glinka's *Russlan and Ludmila.* Then would come the first pièce de résistance, with Lea Luboshutz, the famous violinist, performing the concerto by Glazunov. This would be followed by a surprise entrée — a piano concerto by Liapunov played by the *Wunderkind* Goldovsky. And to crown this musical feast there would be another exhibition of exquisite bow work by Madame Luboshutz, playing the violin concerto by Tchaikovsky.

I spent the next few weeks memorizing the Liapunov concerto, which fortunately was not difficult to master. News meanwhile had gone out that the Berlin Philharmonic, under Leonid Kreutzer's direction, was going to give an evening of Russian music. When the event finally took place — in early January of 1922, if I rightly recall — the Beethoven-saal was as packed as a Russian church on the Eve of the Epiphany. All 1200 seats had been bought up, most of them by Russians, poor and rich, moved by nostalgia and a spirit of national solidarity. Mother fiddled beautifully, while Kreutzer, on his conductor's podium, beamed and swayed as he kept time. As for myself, I had not yet reached the age for wearing long trousers. So I came on stage dressed in a sailor suit, with short pants, white socks, and black patent-leather shoes.

I have no idea how well or badly I played. But I don't think it really mattered. Berlin's Russian colony, which had turned out in force that evening, would have cheered and clapped and cried even if I had missed half the notes. Backstage Mother was radiant and Kreutzer in seventh heaven. Even the reviews were good — which in a musically exacting city like Berlin meant a lot.

The spring of 1922 is associated in my mind with an extraordinary transaction I pulled off — with little doubt the most profitable of my entire career — and which was a dramatic illustration of the financial whirlwind in the midst of which we and 50 million Germans were trying to survive. The inflationary spiral had by now reached such stratospheric heights that an American dollar which might be worth 700,000 German marks on Monday could buy a million marks on Friday and perhaps double that amount the next time one went to the bank. The only thing to do with these huge quantities of marks was to convert them as fast as possible into rental payments, food, or usable commodities.

We had in the meantime been befriended by a gentleman named Frick, who was connected in some way with the League of Nations in Geneva. Very fond of music, he liked to invite me to his apartment and listen to me practice Schumann, Chopin, Debussy, or whatever new composer Kreutzer had decided to introduce me to. One day, after I had complained about the tinny tone of his upright piano, he said that if I could find him a decent grand piano he would gladly buy it and pay for it in American dollars.

Not far away, in a music store, I had seen a lovely Blüthner baby grand. Returning to the shop, I asked the owner how much he would charge if it were paid for in dollars. "Dollars?" he said, his eyes brightening. Yes, I explained, I knew someone who was ready to pay for the piano in genuine American dollars. Now how much would it be?

"Forty dollars," he finally said, after rapidly calculating in his head how many months' worth of meat, vegetables, and liquors this fantastic hoard of greenbacks could buy. Extracting that number of American dollars from somebody, even for something like a Blüthner baby grand, must have seemed to him a tall order, for he quickly added: "If you can persuade this gentleman to pay forty dollars for this piano, I'll give you a 10 percent commission."

I had no trouble inducing our League of Nations friend to part with $40, and several days later I found myself with four crisp dollar bills in my pocket. They did not stay there long. That same day I converted them into forty thick, brand-new volumes of the Peters edition, comprising the complete piano works of Bach, Mozart, Beethoven, Schubert, Brahms, and Liszt. It took me six trips, on the bicycle I had recently acquired, to lug those precious tomes back to the two rooms that Mother and I then occupied on the Bülowstrasse. They have remained to this day among my most treasured possessions.

Shortly after this extraordinary transaction, we moved to more comfortable quarters on the Hohenzollerndamm, so as to be closer to the Russian school I was attending. The matronly Frau Delbrück, who took us in as boarders, had, like so many other German women, lost her husband during the recent war. She was touched to discover that Mother too was a widow, and she did her best to make us feel at home in a city which only yesterday had been the "enemy's capital." In the living room there was a piano on which I could practice or accompany Mother, and as there was only one other paying guest — a tall Norwegian blonde named Astrid, who looked like a Valkyrie — I never had any trouble monopolizing the keyboard. Nor was I overly disturbed by the presence of the fair-haired siren, who was already in her twenties and thus beyond the predatory reach of an immature adolescent. We would meet regularly for breakfast at the dining room table, across which she would generously pass me slices of tasty brown *gjetost* cheese, specially sent to her from Norway.

Life in Berlin, even in those distinctly madcap early twenties, was not all milk and roses, even for those who were lucky enough to own a few dollars, as Mother was soon to discover. I was too young and innocent to be more than dimly aware of it, but Leonid Kreutzer must by this time have embarked on a hot and heavy affair with Mother. Romances of this kind are not easy to conceal, and Kreutzer was evidently less than expert in the art of amorous dissimulation. All I knew was that suddenly, without warning, my piano lessons with him were terminated. Why? There were embarrassed explanations. Frau Kreutzer, it seemed, had put her foot down. "No, you are *not* going to teach this boy any longer and you are *not* going to see that woman again!" That was the gist of the injunction, which the hen-pecked Leonid was forced to heed — or else! "That woman" of course was Mother, who in early 1922 was still a relatively young and attractive widow of thirty-seven years.

There were fortunately other eminent piano teachers in Berlin to whom I could be apprenticed. Foremost among them was Artur Schnabel, to whom Mother now took me. Schnabel was a very different kind of teacher from the easygoing Kreutzer. But unfortunately for my pianistic development, he too was easily persuaded that I was something special, a *Wunderkind* who didn't need to be drilled since he was already a master of digital technique. I was accordingly enrolled in the Staatsakademie für Musik — a meaningless formality, since it was at Schnabel's home, located on a street parallel to the fashionable Kurfürstendamm, that I went for my lessons.

Once again there was no question of payment. As the gifted son of a professional violinist, I was ipso facto an Honorary Member of the Guild of Virtuosi and thus entitled to free instruction. Thus it had been with Kipp, and thus it had been with Kreutzer.

Ordinary students were one thing, like the daily bread of life, but child geniuses were beings of a different order and on their precious heads no price could be set.

With Leonid Kreutzer I had already been abruptly dragged from the disciplinary swamp of Hanon and launched out onto the stormy seas of Schumann's sonatas, long before I knew how to sail or swim. With my new teacher this tendency was carried even further. Artur Schnabel could not be bothered with small unsophisticated pieces; he was only interested in *Meisterwerke* — exalted masterworks.

It was sheer madness now that I look back on it. Yet this is exactly what happened. Blithely overlooking the fact that I was barely fourteen years old, Schnabel had me prepare complex compositions like the Brahms F Minor Sonata, Schumann's *Kreisleriana,* and Beethoven's Opus 109 and 110, which were way over my head.

Though short of stature and somewhat potbellied, Schnabel was an enormously impressive gentleman. Entering his home was like entering a sanctum. One immediately felt that this was a temple of music. The walls of his living room, where I often had to wait till he and Frau Schnabel finished lunch, were lined with the complete Urtext editions of Beethoven, Brahms, Schumann, and other composers. But the central feature of the room was two grand pianos, placed side by side. Schnabel was not the kind of teacher who is there to listen to the pupil play and to correct him. This was not his way. The pupil was there to listen to him, and in so doing he was expected to absorb his particular philosophy and style.

This philosophy was summed up in a series of aphorisms, the most important of which was *"Das naheliegende ist immer falsch!"* The near-to-hand (and thus the obvious) is always wrong. What one might at first regard as the "normal" way of playing a piece was thus outlawed a priori. The "normal" way was the easy way, the superficial way, and thus to be rejected. To play a piece properly, to bring out its profundity, one had to analyze it carefully and then, after much study and meditation, find *the* way of playing it correctly, which is never the obvious way.

To claim that there was only *one* true and authentic way of interpreting every composition was a pretty arrogant assertion. But Schnabel's philosophy was expressed so unequivocally as the absolute truth that it carried conviction. He made you feel he had done this work of rigorous analysis ahead of time. He had studied the minutiae and subtleties of every score. He had solved all the problems, he had discovered all the truths. All you had to do was sit still, have him explain it all, listen to him play, and then imitate his playing on your own keyboard. And there it was, as simple as that — a sure-fire recipe for greatness.

It was all most convincing. Indeed, as I only realized later, it was all too convincing. And it was so because, when he played, he produced the most gorgeous sound. I find it difficult to describe just how I felt listening to him explain the profundities of a piece and then demonstrating them on the keyboard. It was majestic. It was sublime. The sounds that emanated from that grand piano, when he played it, were like a foretaste of paradise. No wonder I did my best to imitate him. To be able to play like Artur Schnabel at this still tender moment of my life seemed the apex and summum of ambition.

Throughout these months Mother had been corresponding with Babushka and Uncle Petya in Moscow, trying to find ways of getting them to Berlin. Our exit visas, issued in the Soviet Union, had long since expired, and she knew that we would be in serious trouble were we to return to Moscow. But the question remained: how could we survive in Berlin? Mother's concert engagements had been fulfilled, and there had been the glorious Berlin Philharmonic soirée with the all-Russian program. But Leonid Kreutzer's patronage was no longer available, and new engagements did not seem to be forthcoming.

There was a momentary diversion when we made a trip to Riga, where Mother played and I accompanied her in a violin recital. The trip gave us a chance to look up Katya Rigert, the Latvian governess who had taught Yuri and me to speak German. We found her living very poorly in her sister Erna's tiny flat and trying to make ends meet as a seamstress. In the "good old days," as she now called them, Mother had paid her thirty rubles a month, with room and board. Katya had sent half of those rubles to her sister, keeping the rest for her personal expenses. These could not have been too great, to judge by the excitement that had traditionally been associated with "new blouse day." For once a year — it was never more than that — we boys would sally forth with Katya Rigert to the dress shop, where she would buy herself a new white blouse to go with the black skirt she invariably wore. One new white blouse a year was all her meager allowance could afford. She had often felt that those were "hard times," but now, she told us, as she strained her eyes over her sewing, those thirty rubles a month seemed a princely salary.

When the time came to kiss her goodbye, I sensed that I would never be seeing dear Katya Rigert again. Yes, the happy moments we had once enjoyed together were now a thing of the past. Sorrowfully I remembered how she and Yuri had laughed because of something I had said during one of those annual blouse-buying expeditions in Moscow. Noticing a brassiere exhibited in a shop window, I wondered what it was, since I had never seen anything like it before. Finally, I explained triumphantly: "I know what they are — they must be bonnets for Siamese babies!" Long and loud had been the laughter this remark had provoked at home.

A few weeks after this trip to the Eastern Baltic, Irina joined us in Berlin. She had been smuggled out of Moscow by an attaché working for the German Embassy, who had pretended that she was his daughter. Mother was shocked by her appearance. In Moscow she had been kept alive, as I had, with the help of ARA condensed milk and also by the hot chicken soup Babushka made for her each time Uncle Petya managed to bring back a hen after a tiring foray in the country. Since the clothes shops were now bare, Babushka had made Irina a dress and a warm coat by removing the upholstery from the living room couch. Also, before leaving Moscow, Irina's hair had been carefully deloused with the aid of a fine-toothed comb and some kind of strong antiseptic. Mother, who went to the station to meet her, took one look at that mass of dark, deloused hair and whisked her daughter straight to the *Friseur,* where her long locks were shorn before she was taken home to our Hohenzollerndamm apartment.

Irina was subsequently entrusted to a nearby kindergarten, since Mother needed many daylight hours for her violin practicing. If she had been a "good girl" the previous day and had not pestered me too much, I would gallantly offer to carry her to school on the handlebar of my bicycle. The offer was brusquely withdrawn one morning when Irina carelessly let the toe of her shoe get caught between the spokes. The front wheel came to a sudden stop and we were both thrown to the ground. I administered a severe thrashing on the spot, there was a lot of tearful wailing, and for several days we had to walk to our respective schools while the wheel and spokes of my bicycle were straightened out.

Mother, of course, was overjoyed to have her daughter with her once again, though she would have been happier still if Yuri could have accompanied Irina to Berlin. But no way had yet been found of getting my brother out of Russia. Nor, from what we were soon to learn, did he seem much disposed to leave.

In the late autumn of 1922 there was a moment of panic for all of us when it almost looked as though Mother was going to follow Father to the grave. She began to cough convulsively and a doctor was summoned to deal with a case of incipient pneumonia. Heated suction cups were placed on her back to "draw out" the inflammation from the lungs, and the remedy, though old-fashioned, worked wonders, permitting Mother to recover soon afterward.

There was another moment of excitement when Babushka and

Grandfather reached Berlin in their turn. Mother decided to take them to Paris along with Irina. She apparently felt that there was no further hope of violin recitals in Germany and that she would have better luck in France. But since I was now completely under Schnabel's spell, I was permitted to stay on in Berlin and continue my lessons with the master.

A few weeks later I got an urgent telegram from Mother, saying I must come immediately to Paris. She was giving a concert and needed an accompanist. The thought of leaving my forty volumes of piano music behind (with friends) and of having to say goodbye to Artur Schnabel, even for a few weeks, was truly painful, but faced with such a peremptory summons I had no choice. Our livelihood depended on Mother's ability to give concerts. So reluctantly I packed my bags, and armed with a new Nansen passport (to replace my invalid Soviet papers), I boarded the train for Paris.

Mother, with her parents and Irina, had established residence in a fairly modern apartment building at 16, Rue Raynouard, not far from where Balzac had once lived, in Passy. Paris, like Berlin, had also succumbed to the new Russian diaspora, and the landscape was now dotted with Russian and Armenian *épiceries,* restaurants, and cabarets, where shashlik was served on flaming spits and booted dancers in black Circassian riding coats and *shapkas* projected teeth-held knives into banknotes casually strewn on the floor. Though I was too young and we were generally too poor to enjoy much of this exhilarating entertainment, some of the bygone imperial glamour and daredevil panache of *la vieille Russie* seemed to have infected Passy, which was gradually being "colonized" by dispossessed landlords, mustachioed army officers with or without families, and *artistes* of one kind or another. The apartment above our own was thus occupied by a legendary ballerina, Olga Preobrazhenskaya, who lived there with a hunchback woman servant, an old Scottie dog, a turtle, and a paramour named Labinsky, who was both pianist and composer.

What the French neighbors thought of Mother I have no idea.

She never adopted a title or tried to pass herself off as a princess, but with her straight back, upraised chin, and determined look, she was very much a *grande dame* in bearing and behavior. None of us looked or played the part of mad Russian musicians, though Grandfather's high hat — which was neither a top hat nor a bowler — looked distinctly exotic.

The only sign of absent-minded eccentricity any of us displayed came on the night of Mother's concert, which was to be given at the Salle Gaveau. Mother had had some trouble adjusting her evening dress and we were late reaching the hall. Clutching her precious Amati, she darted across the sidewalk and into the building, while I slammed the taxi door and scurried after her. But once inside we stopped and looked at each other in dismay. Where was the music from which I was to play the accompaniment? In our precipitation we had left the scores in the taxi.

Backstage there was consternation. The hall was packed and the fastidious *cognoscenti* were waiting restlessly for the concert to begin. Somebody was hastily dispatched in a taxi to the Rue Raynouard to pick up some Beethoven violin and piano sonatas so that we could at least play something, while a Salle Gaveau official went out onto the stage to tell the audience what had happened and to ask them to be patient. From the wings we could feel the public's simmering discontent, though no one had yet begun to boo or stamp his feet.

Then suddenly the most extraordinary thing happened. An usher came backstage with a gentleman who had, it seemed, hailed the very taxi we had traveled in. He had found the music on the back seat and — since he too was headed for the Salle Gaveau — had quick-wittedly guessed that the scores were destined for our recital.

The announcer came forward again to tell the audience that a "miracle" had occurred: the lost music had been found, and the concert could now at last begin. Those "mad Russian musicians" were apparently magicians as well.

*

The concert concluded, Mother could at last break the bad news. "My dear Boris," she said to me, "you are staying in Paris. I simply cannot afford to send you back to Berlin. I don't have the money. Here we have an apartment. Your sister is here, Babushka and Dedushka are here, and there is room enough in the apartment for you. So that's all there is to it — you are not going back."

I protested violently. I screamed bloody murder. I said that my musical career as a pianist was being wrecked, for without Schnabel I was nothing. All to no avail. Mother remained obdurate. Schnabel could wait. He was not going to die tomorrow, and in the meantime I needed something more substantial to live on than fresh air and "profound interpretations." There was a Russian school not too far away, it was probably as good as the one in Charlottenburg, and that was where I was going to continue my studies. So I had better forget about Berlin and my beloved Artur Schnabel. I was staying in Paris.

In Berlin I had had almost two years of schooling, and I needed two more to obtain my *Gymnasium* diploma. But when I went to report to the Russian school on the Rue du Dr. Blanche, on the western periphery of Passy, I made a heartening discovery. "We Berliners" were ahead of our Paris cousins in virtually every subject except mathematics. They had studied trigonometry; we had not. But in every other subject I was far enough advanced to be able to enter the senior class.

By this time it was May and the summer holidays were about to begin. I would thus have three full months in which to master the secrets of trigonometry before the start of the autumn term. Taking the advice offered me, I called on a Monsieur Dufour, an aged gentleman who taught mathematics. For a modest sum he agreed to give me three months' tutoring. He then handed me a copy of the trigonometry textbook that was used at the Russian school. I was told to go home and prepare the first lesson.

At the Rue Raynouard apartment I had a good look at it. Everything was so simply and lucidly explained that in no time at all I was on to the second lesson. From there I passed to the third, and then to the fourth. It was idiotically simple, like eating cake. And before I quite knew it, I had finished the entire book.

I should here add, by way of explanation, that I had long shown a special aptitude for mathematics and an interest in arithmetical puzzles. As a young boy in Moscow I had picked up a number of tricks with which I liked to "dazzle" grown-ups. There was, for example, a short-cut method for the squaring of numbers ending in a 5. If asked to multiply 25 by 25, I would answer in a flash: 625. How? The method (which I kept to myself) was simple. Taking the first digit — 2 — I would multiply it by the next digit in the numerical system (3), and that would give me 6. To this I would then append the basic number 25 — and arrive at 625. Forty-five × 45 thus gave me 4 times 5, equals 20; this, followed by 25, gave me 2025. Seventy-five × 75 could similarly be broken down to 7 × 8, equals 56, for a total of 5625. I had figured out similar short cuts for multiplying 24 by 26, 74 by 76, 83 by 87, and so on, with the certainty of obtaining lightning-quick answers. For a high-speed calculator like myself trigonometry was a push-over.

When I went back to see Monsieur Dufour, four or five days later, I had to tell him the truth. Seldom have I seen such a crest-fallen expression on a man's face. Instead of congratulating me, he looked utterly dejected. The three months of revenue he had been looking forward to had gone up in smoke, and all he could now expect to pocket was the price for one lesson.

Though there was an upright piano in the living room to practice on, it was soon apparent that Irina had not inherited the musical talent of her family. This realization caused her endless distress. Her fumbling efforts with the keyboard were pathetic and she cried her eyes out in frustration. To put an end to her misery Mother finally told her that music was not really a profession for a woman, even though she herself had been brought up to play the violin. Better things were in store for her and if she kept on crying like this, the tears running down her cheeks would ruin her lovely smooth skin. So Irina gave up the unequal struggle and turned her young mind to other things. She was luckier with her dancing, for which she displayed considerable aptitude. Madame Preobrazhenskaya, in whose apartment she liked to spend hours playing with the Scottie dog and contemplating the slow-motion turtle, even graciously admitted her to her ballet school.

Irina's main problem at this point was linguistic. She had begun to forget the German she had picked up in Berlin and was now desperately anxious to acquire a French vocabulary. The need for it became particularly acute in the autumn when she was enrolled at the Lycée Molière, while I began attending classes at the Russian school on the Rue du Dr. Blanche. At home we always conversed in Russian — the only language, outside of Yiddish, which the grandparents understood. Since I had been taught to speak French by a pre-Revolutionary mademoiselle in Moscow — a privilege denied my sister — Irina kept pestering me for the French equivalents of Russian words. "How does one say this? . . . How does one say that? . . ."

One day I said to her: "Look, it's simple. Take the word *sol'*" — which in Russian means *salt*. "In French it is *sel*. The *o* in the Russian word becomes an *e* in the French word. All Russian words with *o* vowel sounds can thus be changed into French words. There's nothing to it."

Poor Irina! She took her brother seriously and was enchanted by the sudden kinship discovered between two such differently sounding languages. The results were wonderfully comic. Thus the Russian word *stol* (table) was transformed into the French word *stèle* (upright slab). *Bok* (side) became *bec* (beak); *kot* (cat) was metamorphosed into *quête* (quest), *sok* (juice) into *sec* (dry). But the semantical havoc this caused was nothing compared to the glorious gibberish which resulted when other words, like *kon'* (steed), *lokot'* (elbow), or *khorosho* (well, fine), were transmuted into *quenne, lequette,* or the almost Persian-sounding *khèrèschè*. At the Lycée Molière Irina's *trouvailles* were greeted with hoots of derision, and it was days before she would speak to me again.

By all accounts — or at any rate by hers — I was not a particularly attractive adolescent. Like many boys of that age, I was covered with pimples. This embarrassing condition exacerbated the feeling I had long suffered from: being ugly. In the past I had tried to compensate for this by showing off my other than surface brilliance — that which lay behind the unappealing face — by improvising on the piano or doing mathematical tricks. But now in Paris, where I was forced to remain against my will, I often felt like doing nothing and letting myself drift. I was mulish, as adolescents tend to be during *l'âge ingrat,* and at times I was downright impossible. Once, while I was seated at the piano during some living room rehearsal, I so enraged Mother by my sloppy accompanying that she took off her shoe and flung it at me. It missed my head but smashed the vase on the piano into tiny pieces. Fortunately, like most of the other objects in this rented apartment, it was not something of great value.

Ours, I must admit, was a tumultuous household. In Moscow there had been a cook, a maid, and a governess to help Mother, while Father took care of the bills. In Odessa Babushka had run the roost, and her strong-willed daughter Lea had visited her only rarely. Now that Babushka and Mother found themselves under the same roof, the sparks never stopped flying. Though they loved each other dearly, they fought like cats and dogs. Grandmother was determined to have things *her* way no matter what her daughter might think; after all, she was twenty years her senior. She was not going to let Lea run the house while she was around, certainly not! Lea was a concert violinist, let her stick to her profession. But she, Babushka, would take care of the cooking and even do the shopping. Mother would protest, saying she hardly knew a word of French, but there was no stopping Babushka, who would march out with her shopping bag to the nearest market and proceed to haggle over the prices in an extraordinary Franco-Russian-Yiddish Esperanto. She counted every centime with the same gimlet-eyed care with which, in Russia, she had counted every kopeck, and even in this strange new land she never let herself be taken for a ride.

The kitchen, of course, was Babushka's domain and she ruled over it with a hand of iron. As the borscht bubbled away in its large stewpot the kitchen would begin to steam up, the walls would sweat, rivulets would run down the panes. But the window, looking out on a dingy inner court, would remain obstinately shut. For if anyone dared open it, there would be shouts of *"Ostorozhno ot zugwinda! Zakroy okno, zakroy okno!"* (Watch out for the draft! Close the window, close the window!) This fear of the *zugwind* — a word which haunted our daily lives like a leitmotif — was so obsessive that Babushka was usually to be seen, wrapped up in her shawls and mopping her moist brow beneath the soft gray hair heaped up in a bun upon her head.

Mother in her own way could be just as obstinate. Determined that Irina should be fashionably dressed, she had her wear short skirts all through the winter, no matter how cold it might be outside. As a result my poor sister seldom stopped sneezing, sniffling, coughing, and blowing her nose. But Mother didn't have the heart to send her straight to bed after Irina had finished supper and her ritual game of *durachki* with Grandfather, so she would be allowed to stretch out under a blanket on the living room couch while Mother and I practiced piano and violin sonatas.

From the musical point of view the year I spent in Paris was an almost total loss. Since there were no piano teachers who could be compared to Kreutzer or Schnabel, there was no point in my wasting time with lessons. My talent was allowed to go to seed, or so it seemed to me. This fitted my mood, which was one of unmitigated scorn for French music and musicians. In Berlin I had learned to look down my nose at the French as a race of musical amateurs. Even their pianos — their Pleyels, Erards, and Gaveaus — were inferior to the Steinways of Hamburg, the Bechsteins and Blüthners of Berlin. The same was true of their composers. Debussy, to be sure, was an interesting "experimenter" and "innovator," but he was not in the same league with the truly great. César Franck was known to Mother and myself only through his lovely sonata for violin and piano. But a man with just one symphony to his credit was not worth discussing, and in Berlin I had never seen his majestic D Minor Symphony advertised on a concert billboard.

As a super-Schnabelian I brought these prejudices to Paris and made little effort to conceal them. I spent a minimum of time practicing on the living room piano. Most of my energies were focused on completing my final year at school, and for a while I even pushed my studied uninterest in music to the point of toying with the idea of giving up music and of enrolling in the mathematics department of the Sorbonne.

Mother, who had more serious matters to worry about, paid little heed to these adolescent whims. She rightly suspected that I would "return to reason," as the French put it, once my final *lycée* year was over, and in the meantime there was no point in slowing down my classroom progress. Besides, she knew me well enough to be sure that I would never resist an invitation to perform in public. And of course she was right.

The first such occasion presented itself shortly after the start of the autumn term in October 1923. Mother, after graduating from the Moscow Conservatory at the age of eighteen, had spent a couple of summers in France studying with the eminent Belgian violinist Eugène Isaye. Now, some twenty years later, she resumed her friendship with her former teacher, who, wishing to be helpful to her in her exile, praised her highly to Queen Elizabeth of Belgium, who happened to be another of his violin-playing pupils. As a result of this intercession, there soon came a personal invitation from the Belgian queen asking Mother to come to Brussels in mid-October to give a private concert for the royal family. Mother wrote to ask the Queen if she could bring me along as her accompanist. The reply was extremely gracious, the Queen even going so far as to suggest that I play a few solo pieces. I immediately wrote to Isaye to ask if there were any composers of whom the Queen was particularly fond. The answer came back: I could play anything by Chopin and Her Majesty would be delighted.

Having been brought up on fairy tales but never having seen

a real-life monarch, I was understandably thrilled, and for several weeks I spent all of my free hours practicing Chopin Nocturnes and Preludes. Meanwhile Mother, with a small retinue of female friends, was making the rounds of the *salons de haute couture.* What concerned her at this point was not her violin playing, which she knew to be more than satisfactory and far above the Queen's own level, it was the kind of evening gown she would wear when in the royal presence.

The dress finally chosen, after what seemed like weeks of intensive search and consultation, was a white gown with the then fashionable hip-level waistline. It was embroidered in pink and covered from top to bottom with sequins, imitation pearls, and diamonds.

In Brussels a suite had been reserved for us at an elegant hotel, and on the evening of the performance Eugène Isaye drove up to the entrance in an enormous Hispano Suiza. He was all decked out for the occasion and there were almost as many medals dangling from his chest as there were sequins on Mother's gown.

Inside the palace we were ushered into a large chandelier-lit salon, where a number of privileged guests, in gala uniforms and trailing dresses, were already assembled. After a brief wait two liveried footmen opened the doors and announced: "Her Royal Majesty!" As Queen Elizabeth, followed by assorted princes and princesses, approached, Mother suddenly gripped my arm. "Look, look!" she whispered, as her face turned pale. In a flash I realized that the Queen was wearing the same dress as Mother's, identical down to the last pearl and sequin. This did not strike me as particularly unusual, since many of the gentlemen present were dressed exactly as I was. But the effect of this similitude in dress on Mother was so staggering that for a moment I thought she would faint.

When, in the middle of the bowing and scraping, it was our turn to be presented to her, the Queen bent forward and whispered to Mother, "Aren't fashions becoming this year?" But the comforting words had no effect and when the time came to start the concert, Mother had barely enough strength to tune her violin.

She played the opening number as best she could. Then she stopped. She was terribly sorry, she said, she had a blinding headache and asked Her Majesty's gracious permission to retire. The permission was graciously granted, and after more bowing and curtsying in an atmosphere of general consternation, we walked out. We were never asked to return, nor was I ever given another chance to charm the Queen of Belgium with my lovingly chosen Chopin pieces.

Some four months after this distressing episode Mother persuaded the manager of the Salle Gaveau to let me give a solo recital. The idea of being a star attraction was of course more than my young ego could resist, and for a few weeks I practiced furiously to refresh my memory and limber up my fingers. But the hours I spent at the keyboard were too few for a really satisfactory performance.

The main item on the program was Schumann's *Symphonic Etudes,* which I had already studied under Schnabel, and to these I added Prokofieff's *Visions fugitives* and several other pieces, the titles of which I have forgotten. What I most vividly recall about this concert is, oddly enough, the way I was dressed. Gone was the time when I could appear on stage as a *Wunderkind,* wearing a sailor suit and short pants. This time, instead of the rented outfit I had worn in Brussels, I sported a brand-new dinner jacket, complete with elegant shirt studs and patent-leather shoes.

The most curious reaction — not only to my playing, which was lackluster, but also to my attire — came in a roundabout way from distant Russia. It took the form of a letter from my brother, Yuri — the only letter, in fact, he ever wrote to me, or at least the only one I ever received. He had heard about my recital from a Soviet trade-mission official who happened to be in Paris at the time and who had gone to the Salle Gaveau to hear the young Goldovsky perform. The young Goldovsky had played very badly, it seemed. But what distressed Yuri even more was to learn from the same source that I had appeared on stage in a black bow tie, velvet-lapelled dinner jacket, and shiny pumps. I was really overdoing it. Instead of slaving away in hard, honest piano practice, learning to play properly, I had been wasting my time in fancy tailor shops and showing off in all this bourgeois finery in an effort to look "up-to-date" and "fashionable." In a word, I had succumbed to the lures of bourgeois culture and had sold out to a decadent capitalistic regime.

It would have been a funny letter to read from someone other than my own brother. And it made me sad to think that two more years of Soviet schooling had sufficed to turn the once easy-going Yuri into an antibourgeois Party-liner.

My own bourgeois-capitalistic schooling was successfully completed a few months later. I sailed smoothly through all the examinations except one — which sufficed to make me realize to what extent luck can govern the outcome of academic tests. During the final Latin exam I was summoned from my seat and made to stand in front of a panel of visiting inquisitors drawn from other Paris schools and faculties. One of them told me to listen carefully while he read off a sequence of eight or nine Latin words, after which I was to tell him how else this particular sentence could be organized. I listened quietly, not having the foggiest notion of what the uttered words really meant. Trying to hide my confusion — for I was hopelessly lost and certain that I was about to flunk the test — I slowly repeated the sentence the examiner had uttered. In so doing, I accidentally omitted the particle *ut*. "Very good!" the examiner commended me. "Bravo! *Ut* can be omitted. You may return to your seat." I walked back, as though in a dream, vaguely aware that I had not been flunked after all.

Eventually, I was awarded a certificate of matriculation, which was issued to me by the White Russian Embassy in Paris and solemnly signed by the President of the Examining Commission, Monsieur Gaston de Latours.

The existence of a White Russian Embassy in this early summer of 1924 may seem odd to us now, but it was taken pretty much for granted at the time. Though Georges Clemenceau had retired from public life, his cordon sanitaire philosophy still held sway. France, like the rest of Europe east of the Vistula and the Bug, had to be protected from the Bolshevik virus, and the stoutly bourgeois republic of Raymond Poincaré was not yet prepared to recognize the authority of the Red Commissars of Russia.

Sometime during the summer of 1924 Mother informed us that she was going to the United States. The year spent in Paris had been financially ruinous to her. The one or two recitals she had given had brought her applause but little else. The Parisians seemed to think that artists are born rich and need nothing but praise and flattering reviews to sustain them. This had confirmed me in my Germanic disdain for French music and musicians, and it had made Mother realize that she must look for recognition elsewhere. She could not go on forever selling the few jewels she still possessed — like the expensive sapphire-and-diamond brooch (one of the precious items Babushka had carried from Odessa to Moscow in her pillow) which she had been forced to sacrifice to keep us all from starving.

America, on the other hand, was a Promised Land, an El Dorado for musicians. Its streets were paved with gold. Here gifted artists were sure of being honored and respected and offered a place in the sun. How many Old World musicians had drunk the cup of bitterness to the dregs only to find wealth and recognition on the other side of the ocean! Even Richard Wagner had been tempted at one low ebb of his career by the idea of crossing the Atlantic. In the end he hadn't done so; he had been rescued in extremis from his misery. Wagner had been one of the lucky ones. Musicians who could survive in Europe obviously didn't hesitate a moment in choosing to stay on. Europe, after all, was the home of culture, whereas America was a wild, untamed land inhabited by Indians and barbarians. But the barbarians were rich, and, though uncouth, they seemed to appreciate good music. So there was nothing to do but stuff one's cultural pride in one's pocket and set sail for the West. It was as simple as that.

Mother, as it happened, had already crossed the Atlantic once before, during the winter season of 1907–1908 when Vassili Safonov, Director of the Moscow Conservatory of Music, had taken her on a concert tour with Feodor Chaliapin. I too had crossed the ocean — in her womb, as Mother liked to point out — for it was only after she had returned to Moscow in the spring of 1908 that she had given birth to her second son, Boris. But during that eventful visit she had established a firm friendship with a Mrs. Sidney Prince, an aspiring pianist who had married a wealthy Wall Street stockbroker. They had kept in touch ever since and had recently met again, this time in Paris. On hearing Mother's tale of woe and how difficult it was for an artist to survive in the French capital, her American friend Tessie — as Mrs. Prince was known to all who knew her well — had urged her to come to the United States. "There, you'll see, we'll get you more concerts than you can handle and you'll have nothing to worry about."

Babushka and Grandfather were to remain in the Rue Raynouard apartment with the almost eight-year-old Irina, who was to continue her studies at the Lycée Molière. But I was going to go to the United States with Mother. When I heard this, I dug in my adolescent heels and said no. I wasn't going to New York. I was going back to Berlin to study with Schnabel.

"My dear boy," said Mother, "you're talking like a child. I've already told you — I don't have the money to support you in Berlin. We'll find somebody just as good to give you piano lessons in the United States."

"There's nobody in the world like Schnabel," I insisted, with the petulance of youth. "If you don't let me go back to Berlin I'm going to commit suicide!"

I must have looked grimly determined, for Mother soon relented — partially at any rate.

"Nobody wants you to commit suicide, Boris, but what are you going to live on since I can't give you an allowance?"

"Never mind about that," I answered confidently. "I'll manage. I'll find something to keep me going. All I need is a railway ticket and enough money to cover my expenses in Berlin for the first week."

And so, eventually, it was decided. Mother bought the railway ticket and gave me enough money to tide me over for a couple of weeks. A number of family friends were living in Berlin, and I was told to look them up on arrival. They might be able to put me up for a while; they would probably invite me over for an occasional meal, and, being Berliners, they could offer me precious advice.

The two most helpful persons in this category were both diplomats whom Father had known in Moscow. One was a Herr Schlesinger, who was most kind to me, as was his wife, a very intellectual and art-conscious lady. They had let me store my forty volumes of piano music in the basement of their house in Grunewald, so they were not unduly surprised to see me back in Berlin. The other helpful person was Herr Hilger, the German Embassy attaché who had smuggled Irina out of Russia by claiming that she was his own daughter.

It was with the Hilgers that I spent my first few days in Berlin, before moving to an inexpensive room in a house near the Hallensee at the southwestern extremity of the Kurfürstendamm. Schnabel seemed pleased to have me back as a pupil, and his instruction once again was offered to me gratis. As for the piano I needed for practicing, it too was offered to me free of charge by the Blüthner company — this being a privileged dispensation granted to a Schnabel pupil who might some day become a successful keyboard virtuoso. In exchange for this generous favor I had to promise to use a Blüthner piano in any recitals I might give.

These problems solved, I cast around for a job. I visited several Russian restaurants and finally found a coffee house, near the Nollendorfplatz, where I was told that they could use the services of a pianist from 8:00 P.M. to one o'clock in the morning. I could play what I liked. It didn't necessarily have to be popular music, and if I wanted to practice something I was preparing for Schnabel, I was free to do so.

This happy arrangement lasted all of one month, at the end of which, having pocketed my salary, I felt as rich as a king. The coffee-house clients did not seem to mind my playing "serious" music along with the latest "hits," and one of them — Gregor Piatigorsky, who was then the first cellist of the Berlin Philharmonic orchestra — even took the trouble to congratulate me on my playing.

But then, suddenly, disaster struck. An official letter reached me at my Hallensee lodgings, informing me that I must leave Germany within twenty-four hours. I had broken some kind of regulation and was consequently being expelled.

This was not the first time I had had trouble with the German police. At the time of my arrival a local police sergeant had examined my papers with extreme suspicion before growling: "*Wieviel Mal wurden Sie geboren?*" How many times had I been born? Under other circumstances I would have been moved to laugh, but this, I sensed, was no laughing matter. According to my birth certificate, issued under the Tsarist regime and the old Julian calendar, I was born on May 25, but on my Nansen passport, filled out according to the reformed Gregorian calendar, the date was given as June 7. The police official could not understand the discrepancy, probably attributing it to the carelessness of a less than expert forger. I had had to do quite a bit of explaining to persuade the fellow that I was not a sinister crook.

I appealed at once to Herr Hilger, who kindly accompanied me to police headquarters. Here we were informed that I had violated the law: I had been admitted to Germany with a student visa which allowed me to study but not to be gainfully employed.

"Look at him, he's just a youngster!" Herr Hilger remonstrated with the officials. "He's not aware of these technicalities. Otherwise, he would never have taken a job. This young man didn't come here to make money. He came here to study the piano with the world-famous teacher, Professor Artur Schnabel. He is not trying to undermine our laws or take jobs away from others . . . We are very sorry for what has happened and we promise you that it will not be repeated."

Thanks to this persuasive intervention, the expulsion order was rescinded and I was allowed to stay on in Berlin. But I had to give up my job at the Russian coffee house, and this was a real blow.

To survive, there was only one thing left: I had to give private lessons, which did not have to be reported to the police. I was accordingly recommended by one of the diplomatic wives — I don't remember if it was Mrs. Schlesinger or Mrs. Hilger — to a Frau Grabowski, a middle-aged matron married to a wealthy industrialist. She was a not unattractive lady, generously endowed with a Rubens-like bosom which was sprayed with some exotic perfume. The apartment she inhabited was equally grand and a welcome relief from my small, piano-encumbered bedroom. In addition to the elegant furniture, the drawing room walls were lined with exquisitely bound and illustrated books. I had time to look at some of them while waiting for their owner to appear, and I particularly recall one, entitled *Geschichte der erotischen Kunst* — a history of erotic art lavishly illustrated with reproductions of naked men and women in the blissful abandon of amorous contortions.

Once a week I came here to give a lesson. Frau Grabowski did not seem to mind receiving piano instruction from an adolescent who could almost have been her son, and for a number of weeks all went well. I was able to leave each lesson the richer by five marks — worth about one dollar now that the inflationary genie had been caught and forced back into its bottle.

But alas, these lucrative sessions came to an all too quick and bitter end. As a new assignment, I had asked Frau Grabowski to learn a composition which began with both hands playing in the treble clef. Having always played the left hand in the bass clef, the good lady blithely misread the score and transposed the accompaniment an octave and a sixth lower than written. The resulting cacophony was so unexpected and grotesque that I nearly burst my sides with laughter.

Frau Grabowski stopped her playing immediately. Rising from her piano stool, her cheeks flushed with indignation, she told me that she did not pay me to laugh at her. She was sorry, but she was not putting up with any more of this. The lessons were terminated, here and now, and I need not return next week.

For a while I was left with just one student. He was an eleven-year-old boy who was staying with his mother in a kind of sanatorium, located some distance from Berlin. To reach it, I had to travel on the elevated *Stadt-bahn* train for three quarters of an hour and then walk for another twenty minutes. The boy I tutored cared little for music and even less for me. I detested him just as cordially as he detested me. But there was nothing either of us could do about this unpleasant situation. His mother was determined to make a pianist out of him, and I could not afford to lose the ten marks I desperately needed to survive.

Those were indeed hard times. I had to make do on the strictest minimum, eating meat only once a week. I had learned what it feels like to be hungry in post-Revolutionary Moscow, and the experience was now often repeated. To be able to attend an occasional concert — like a Philharmonic orchestra evening with Furtwängler or a piano recital by Edwin Fischer — I had to tighten my belt an additional notch and give up riding the streetcar. This last became my definition of poverty. One was poor, I decided, when one had to walk several miles rather than ride the tram.

Fortunately, I was popular with the girls and had a number of friends in the Russian colony who would invite me over to share their borscht, meat-stuffed pirozhki, marinated herring, and Russian salads. I even had a couple of girl friends — one named Tamara, another called Zhenia — with whom I vaguely flirted. But I was still too young and inexperienced and above all too penniless to start an affair with either one.

I had always been something of a showoff, and at parties I could be counted on to dazzle the assembled company with mathematical tricks of one kind or another. One evening I was taken to some kind of variety show, where a man with a turban wound round his head who claimed to have spent years in India studying yoga and Hindu magic had persons in the audience multiply quotients until an eleven- or twelve-digit number would result. The number was then inscribed on a blackboard. The "magician" gazed at it intently for a while before announcing the cube root, which he had extracted in his head.

I was so impressed by this performance that I went home and spent hours trying to figure out how he did it. I discovered that it was by no means as difficult as it seemed, and I was even able to improve on the bogus Hindu's "magic" by eliminating the blackboard rigmarole. Numbers, often fairly long ones, would be thrown at me, and in a matter of fifteen or twenty seconds I could extract the cube root.

Tricks like this turned me into a swollen-headed, "know-it-all" adolescent. But now that I was back studying the piano, mathematics could no longer make a serious claim on my future, as they had threatened to do in Paris. My soul, my mind, and my fingers belonged to Artur Schnabel.

One day — I don't now recall in exactly which month it was — I was granted a particularly pleasant surprise when Uncle Petya turned up in Berlin with his wife, Elena Mikhailovna. They too had somehow managed to get exit visas and leave the Soviet Union, and they were in no mood to return. Aunt Anna, however, had decided to stay on in Moscow with her doctor husband, who had apparently reconciled himself quite happily to the new regime. My brother, Yuri, whom they had more or less adopted after Father's death, was now engrossed in his science studies and so confident of the radiant future ahead of him in this land of revolutionary change and innovation that he too would not hear of abandoning the Soviet Union for the doomed as well as decadent West.

When we had all lived together in the Trubnikovsky Pereulok apartment house, I had often teased Uncle Petya's French poodle, which was then no more than a puppy, by seizing its lower jaw with my two hands and shaking it, while the little dog fought to free itself. It was a game which, I rashly assumed, we had both of us enjoyed.

The poodle too had been allowed to leave the Soviet Union, but I had trouble recognizing it, so much bigger had it grown in the intervening years.

"So this is Reggie?" I said, stretching out a welcoming hand. "Remember, Reggie, how I used to play with you?"

"I advise you not to get too close to Reggie," Uncle Petya warned.

"Oh, Reggie and I are friends," I answered confidently. "Didn't we always play this game together?"

I couldn't see from the shaggy hairs covering his eyes what Reggie thought about it all, but a moment later he made his feelings known by sinking his teeth into my thumb. I let out a yell, and fortunately the dog let go or I might have lost my thumb forever.

"Well, that should teach you a lesson," said Uncle Petya with a laugh.

It certainly did. My bloodied thumb was so deeply gashed that it was days before I could play the piano again. I even had to cancel my next lesson with Schnabel.

Uncle Petya was on his way to Paris. As a quick-witted *débrouillard* and man-about-town, he was sure he could land some piano-playing engagements, and he didn't like the idea of leaving Babushka and Dedushka to fend for themselves in a strange, foreign city.

I was sorry to see him go, but I did not feel a stranger in the cosmopolitan capital of Germany, where I had quite a few friends. Above all, I had Schnabel, whom I regarded with endless veneration. This of course was the way he wanted it to be. As his disciple, I was expected to tread *his* road and no other.

There was something thoroughly dogmatic, I am tempted to say Prussian, in Schnabel's attitude to his students. Even his apartment and the large room with the music library and the two Bechstein pianos seemed designed to induce a sentiment of awe. I knew he had a wife who was a singer, for I once heard them give a joint recital. But I can't recall having ever seen her when I came for my lessons. She was a distant, shadowy figure, like their son, who was also studying the piano and who later became quite a well-known pianist in his own right.

The same was true of Schnabel's other pupils. I knew they existed, but I had no idea who they were. Somehow our paths never crossed. Schnabel never mentioned them, just as he never talked about members of his family. He was a serious, tremendously concentrated person. And thus was created, unintentionally no doubt, a strange, Svengali-like relationship between master and apprentice to which, I must confess, I completely succumbed.

Schnabel, as I have said, was not interested in teaching digital technique, in one's ability to play the music being studied. He assumed — rashly in my case — that such problems had long since been disposed of, just as he had disposed of them in his own younger years. What interested him was the composition we happened to be working on, and this he had analyzed down to the very last detail. It had to be played exactly the way he played it, because that was what he, Schnabel, had discovered after prolonged meditation. *"Das naheliegende ist immer falsch!"* he would repeat, lest I be tempted to think that the composer had written something facile or superficial. The treasures of musical masterworks were always buried beneath the surface. They were like glittering pearls which only a well-trained diver could bring up from the depths.

Schnabel had a theory that music consists mostly of four-measure phrases, linked in certain ways and bearing special relationships to each other which have to be carefully observed. The result was a kind of musical geometry in which everything was worked out in advance. There could be no variation from this preordained scheme of things because upon it was stamped the static seal of perfection.

Only later did I begin to grasp how crippling this mode of instruction could be. For Schnabel, basically, was not interested in developing the musical insights and intuitions of his students. He wanted them to participate in music on his own exclusive terms. Any other were, by definition, inferior, second-rate, misleading. For he, once and for all, had discovered *the* truth. He was a kind of prophet, a Moses laying down the law and insisting that one learn the Ten Commandments.

Linked to this credo was the extraordinary notion that great composers were infallible. This was particularly true of Beethoven, whom he placed above all others. Beethoven, being a superhuman figure, could never commit an accidental error. Schnabel could not admit the possibility that Beethoven could make a slip of the pen.

No, indeed! The wrongly written note was simply the mark of Beethoven's unorthodox, tradition-breaking genius.

In the first movement of his *Hammerklavier* Sonata, for example, there is an obvious omission just before the recapitulation of the opening theme, where Beethoven forgot to place a natural sign before the *a*. Gustav Mahler, who, like other modern composers, readily experimented with new intervals and dissonances, used to put an asterisk next to such intervals, adding below: "This is not a misprint." But this was something Schnabel could not accept. And so, in annotating the *Hammerklavier* Sonata, he added a footnote in which those, i.e., the critics, the doubters, the blasphemers who called "the dogmatic propositions of Harmony to their aid," were told to bow down in repentance since they could not stand up against the greatness of a genius who dared to use an A sharp before an F natural. The man who composed the *Hammerklavier* Sonata was not an ordinary mortal, capable of human error. He was a demigod and thus infallible.

This, of course, is not a sensible point of view, as I later came to realize. But at the time I was ready to follow Schnabel down any road and to the extremes of any aberration. Though my piano technique was clumsy, I was a reasonably good imitator, and like all imitators, I found it easiest to ape the affectations and the mannerisms.

One of Schnabel's peculiarities was a tendency to grunt while playing. I don't think he himself was aware of it. In my infatuated innocence I convinced myself that this is what all great pianists have to do. These grunts were the outward manifestation of an intense, inner concentration. They were a mark of genius. Soon I began grunting too, like the master. If anything, I outgrunted Schnabel, as I think all of his students did. For it was the one thing we could all fairly easily achieve.

Only much later, after I had had a lot of experience teaching singers how to behave on stage and had studied muscular mechanics, did I understand the cause of this grunting. Piano playing requires considerable muscular effort — in one's fingers, arms, and shoulders — particularly when one has to play loud or difficult passages. Bit by bit, unless one has learned to relax them, other muscles begin to tighten. It is very easy to have the neck and throat tense up too, and then, without realizing it, one begins making grunting or moaning sounds which one may not hear oneself, but which are perfectly audible to others. These can be eliminated through special exercises and precautions — of which Artur Schnabel was sublimely ignorant, as he was of all questions of mechanical or muscular technique.

Schnabel, as I have said, was an utterly serious musician. He had no use for short, "entertaining" pieces. Once, when asked in what way his concert programs differed from those of other pianists, he answered gruffly: "My programs are boring — also after the intermission." There was nothing of the musical demagogue about him, and he was not going to compromise his own lofty ideals just to pander to the public taste. He was going to give his audiences the noblest, the finest, the deepest music, whether they liked it or not.

Not all of these "masterworks" were by Beethoven. For it is a great mistake to think that Schnabel neither played nor fancied anything else. Two of the great works he had me study and which he obviously loved were the B Minor sonatas of Chopin and Liszt. These were far beyond the reach of my limited technique, and though I sought to imitate him as best I could, I was never satisfied with the results. For some reason I could not get my Blüthner baby grand to behave as I wanted it to. I had the vision, but the reality was beyond my grasp.

Later on I will explain how these problems were finally solved. My "salvation" was accompanied by a belated reaction against everything Schnabel represented. I began to detest the god I had once adored.

In the early 1920s Schnabel had made a trip to the United States which left him much embittered. It was the "return to normalcy" period of Warren Harding, when Americans — most of them at any rate — wanted to turn their backs on Europe and the world. They had had their fill of Wilsonian idealism and were now interested in getting rich quick, by gambling on the stock market or digging like mad beavers for oil. Schnabel's "profound interpretations" did not appeal to American audiences, who wanted slick keyboard performances, and his trip to the United States was a resounding flop.

About America Schnabel never spoke to me save in the most critical and cynical terms. Americans, he would say, have no understanding of anything decent or profound, they are money-grubbers devoted to shallow and superficial pleasures. When I once asked him about the kinds of pianos they had over there, he replied: "Oh, the pianos are excellent," adding: "They are a lot better than the people who own them."

He also told me a story which he must have picked up from somebody else, since he himself was a performer rather than a lecturer. When Americans die, he said, the good ones move slowly up toward heaven, forming large, gregarious groups, like the tourists one often sees gaping at European monuments or clambering over venerable ruins. Finally the good Americans reach a point where there are two signs. One, pointing left, reads: "This way to Paradise." The other, pointing right, reads: "This way to a lecture on Paradise." Invariably, Schnabel claimed, the Americans choose the right-hand road.

Times change and so do tastes and prejudices. During the early Depression years Schnabel returned to the United States, probably expecting a chilly reception. Instead, his recitals touched off thunderous ovations and won him unprecedented acclaim. His "profound" way of playing seemed to appeal to people who had rediscovered the meaning of hardship, suffering, and despair. Suddenly there was nobody quite like him. He was unique, in a class of his own. He was the master of masters, the greatest Beethoven interpreter the world had ever seen.

My own enthusiasm, in the meantime, had waned. Though he came to cities where I lived and worked — like Philadelphia and Cleveland — I never once went to hear him play. I made no effort to meet the teacher I had once revered. I now look back on this attitude with shame. I realize how shabby my behavior was. When I think of all the hours of instruction he had given me free of charge!

Yet mine was an understandable reaction. When I began to realize how overpowering his influence on me had been, I developed a hatred for what he represented. I fought to free myself from a hypnotic influence which I felt had been crippling, which had robbed me of my artistic individuality. For years I could never play any piano piece I had studied with him without feeling that Schnabel was standing over me, telling me *exactly* how it must be interpreted. I had the feeling that these pieces were lost to me forever, that I would never make them truly my own.

In all fairness to Schnabel, I should add that other pianists and dedicated Schnabel students — like Victor Babin and his wife, Vitya Vronsky — with whom, much later, I discussed these questions, did not react as I had. Schnabel, they claimed, had let them express their own musical individualities. He had not struck them as being either overpowering, tyrannical, or dogmatic. But then they had studied under him when they were quite a bit older than I had been. Schnabel's methods, they suggested, were not appropriate for children. They were probably right.

3

With Dohnányi in Budapest

IN JUNE of 1925 Mother recrossed the Atlantic, this time in an easterly direction. I was still in Berlin when she got off the boat-train at the Gare Saint-Lazare in Paris, and I thus missed the tearful scene which ensued when Babushka, who was waiting on the platform to greet her with Irina, informed her that Grandfather had died a few months before of a heart attack. He had been given a proper Jewish funeral, with shiva mourners and the rest, but not wishing to upset Mother's vitally important concert engagements in the United States, Babushka had decided not to breathe a word about this tragedy until Mother was back in France. I too had been kept in the dark and only learned what had happened after my return to Paris a few days later.

It was only now, seeing her in mourning, that I realized how attached to her father Mother had always been. For years this sweet, soft-spoken, pious, somewhat scholarly and abominably henpecked husband had served as a kind of lightning rod for the electric storms touched off by Babushka's volatile temper. From now on Mother would have to bear the full brunt of these discharges. Irina too had been much affected, having lost her faithful partner for the evening game of *durachki*.

Fortunately for us all, the hopes Mother had placed in the United States had not been disappointed. She had given a number of successful recitals in different cities and was due to play in the autumn in New York City with the New York State Symphony Orchestra (originally created by Walter Damrosch). The immediate future seemed assured and there was even enough left over to finance a vacation. Leaving Babushka in Paris, where Uncle Petya could look after her, Mother followed the recommendation of a French friend and decided to spend the summer at Saint-Jean-de-Luz, not far from the Spanish border. The quaint seaside port was full of *pensions de famille* where the three of us could be lodged for several months for a reasonable sum. I suspect, however, that the deciding factor in the choice was less the bracing Bay of Biscay air or the picturesque Basque hinterland than the gambling casino, which Mother was soon to frequent. For, as we now discovered, Mother had a passion for gambling. Roulette — "that game made for Russians," as Dostoevsky once called it — she left to others. Her nemesis was chemin de fer.

On the whole it was a happy summer, unexpectedly enlivened by the arrival of Uncle Petya — or Uncle Pierre, as we now began calling him — who decided to journey down for a few weeks with Elena Mikhailovna. Irina, whose name had also been Gallicized at the Lycée Molière, where she was known as Irène, now spoke French fluently, so I could no longer play linguistic tricks on her. We splashed around in the surf, we played tennis, we did gymnastics on the beach, and I even persuaded our "monitor" to teach me a few wrestling holds.

Parts of Paris's Russian colony had also drifted south, and among them were a number of *artistes* — like the singer Maria Kurenko, who had come down with her little boy, and the famous soprano Nina Koshetz, who presided over a menage à trois with her businessman husband, who provided the money, and a tenor, who provided the entertainment. To judge by her descriptions, the latter was something of a bedroom virtuoso, for Madame was not above boasting of his prowess and would even compare his amorous crescendi with her husband's diminuendo performances.

Uncle Petya being ideally suited to accompany her on the piano, Nina Koshetz decided to give a recital. But there was a last-minute crisis when l'Oncle Pierre was urgently summoned back to Paris to accompany the violinist Paul Kochanski, with whom he had signed a one-year contract. Now "in all her states," as the French so graphically put it, Madame Koshetz would quite willingly have strangled her runaway partner for thus leaving her in the lurch. Once again I was called upon to fill the gap, as I had done in Moscow. It was the first time I had accompanied a singer, and it was a new experience. We practiced songs by Tchaikovsky and Rachmaninoff and after I had adjusted my playing to the particular demands of her voice, I found it less difficult than accompanying Mother, with her often disconcerting lapses of memory. The concert went off fairly well, and Nina Koshetz graciously complimented me on my piano playing, letting everyone know that I was a better accompanist than l'Oncle Pierre. But I am sure she said it to punish the "scoundrel" who had so unceremoniously decamped and almost sabotaged her concert.

The last weeks of these summer holidays were dominated by Prokofieff's First Violin Concerto, which Mother was due to play in New York in October. In preparation for this important event we spent many hours together going over the complicated score.

In September we returned to Paris, where Irina, who was not quite nine, was enrolled for another year at the Lycée Molière and entrusted to Babushka's vigilant care. The nine months I had spent in Berlin trying to keep body and soul together had made me a little wiser, and I was now ready to heed Mother's sensible suggestions about crossing the Atlantic. In the United States she had met and befriended Josef Hofmann, who, she said, was an even greater pianist than Schnabel, and she was pretty sure that he would agree to take me on as a pupil, just as others had done in the past.

A few days later we set sail from Cherbourg for the New World.

The voyage must have been uneventful, for I can remember nothing about it, not even the name of the liner on which we traveled. Like the others who were crossing the ocean for the first time, I had the steward wake me very early on the last morning so as to be able to see the bristling spires of Manhattan emerge through the mist into the rosy light of dawn. Skyscrapers were as yet unknown in Europe, and my first glimpse of this Cyclopean panorama was awe-inspiring.

Mother had reserved a suite for us at the Great Northern Hotel, which, being only half a block distant from Carnegie Hall on West 57th Street, was much favored by visiting musicians. An upright piano was installed in the sitting room, where we could practice together and where Mother could receive her New York friends. Though these were already quite numerous, my first weeks in Manhattan were anything but happy ones. I hardly spoke a word of English and felt very much like a fish out of water. Never before had I been in a country where all around me I heard people speaking a language I could not understand. It was a most frustrating experience. With Mother's Russian friends, of course, there was no problem. With one or two of the others I could speak French, and with others — like Mrs. Sidney Prince — I could converse in German. But they were like scattered islands, few and far between, in an ocean of mysteriously babbling tongues.

German was also the lingua franca used when Josef Hofmann came to call. Like Schnabel, he was on the shortish side, and he had the squat build of a mountaineer. With his light brown hair, turned-up nose, and a rather nondescript face, he did not look at all like a musician. The one thing about him that might have led one to suspect that he was an artist was a certain moodiness which would often descend on his brow and sit there like a cloud.

Just how they had met I do not now recall; it may have been on the ship which had first brought Mother to the United States. But by her violin playing Josef Hofmann had been much impressed. My piano playing, on the other hand, left him cold. The living room's upright piano, on which I boldly launched into Liszt's B Minor Sonata, could not stand comparison with the Bechsteins and Blüthners I had played in Berlin. But what was far more serious and less excusable to Hofmann was my slipshod way of handling the keyboard. The "profundity" of my playing, à la Artur Schnabel, did not impress him in the least. No matter how "deep" and "metaphysical" this particular style might claim to be, this to him was a sloppy way of playing the piano.

To have my talent brushed aside by somebody like Josef Hofmann, for whom Mother had an almost limitless admiration, was a humbling experience. But we were both too busy at that moment preparing for Mother's forthcoming performance with the State Symphony Orchestra to worry too much about it. The time for deciding what I should do would come after the concert was over. In the meantime, the man who was to conduct the orchestra — a Hungarian named Ernö Dohnányi, or Ernst von Dohnányi, as he was more generally known abroad — had telephoned, asking if he could call on Mother at the Great Northern Hotel to listen to her play the Prokofieff concerto.

For both of us Dohnányi, whom we had never met, was little more than a name. But we were soon to be agreeably surprised. A handsome, aristocratic gentleman of polished bearing and demeanor, with a high forehead, a fine straight nose, and a strong square chin, Dohnányi combined the informality of a country squire with the grace of a diplomat. We were both startled to hear that he was unfamiliar with the Prokofieff violin concerto which he was to conduct in less than two weeks. He had simply not had time to study it, he explained, and that was why he wished to become acquainted with it.

Mother took our her violin, I sat down at the piano, and we went through the entire thirty-minute-long concerto. Dohnányi sat quietly on the couch and did not utter a word until we had finished. But to judge by his faint, enigmatic smile, he seemed pleased. "Very good," he commented. "It is a fine piece, and I am particularly intrigued by the scherzo movement." Then, rising to his feet, he added: "Madame, would it trouble you too much to play this middle movement over, and this time I will accompany you?"

Mother said she would gladly oblige, while I thought to myself: "Oho, this is going to be really funny. We're going to see this fine gentleman fall flat on his face!" The middle movement he had volunteered to play was an exceedingly difficult one, full of tricky syncopations and unusual modulations which had to be handled at a breakneck pace. I had been practicing it for weeks and it still gave me trouble.

Chuckling inwardly, I took Dohnányi's place on the couch and waited. At the very first difficulty I was sure he would come a cropper. But without a trace of strain or effort Dohnányi proceeded to sight-read the intricate scherzo as though he had been playing it for years. There was not the slightest hitch or hesitation. By the time he was through, I realized that this stranger, who had never laid eyes on this music before, had played it better than I had after several months of practice. Not only was this somewhat dilettantish-looking man a keyboard virtuoso, he was a sight-reading magician!

This first surprise was soon followed by a second, which impressed me even more. At the conclusion of the New York State Symphony Orchestra's concert, which was a resounding success both for Dohnányi and my mother, Mr. and Mrs. Sidney Prince threw a big party in their magnificent apartment on Park Avenue. In the multitude of strange, incomprehensively chattering faces I felt completely lost, and I finally decided that the surest refuge was the buffet table. Here at least I could fill my tongue-tied mouth with food. I had seized a plate and was about to sink my teeth into a sandwich when suddenly I "heard a ghost." This is the only way I can describe the extraordinary sensation — half thrill, half shock — which gripped me as I listened to a familiar, haunting melody coming from the living room. There could be no doubt about it: it was the "Dream Waltz" of my Moscow youth being played by some stranger who had apparently learned it by heart. But how? How could he be playing something I had privately invented years before and which had never been publicly performed?

Clutching my plate of sandwiches, I made for the grand piano. Seated before the keyboard was Dohnányi, playing my waltz, and playing it beautifully, with a faint, dimpled smile on his contented face.

Using my dish of sandwiches as a ram, I forced my way through to the piano. I could hardly wait for Dohnányi to finish, so staggered and outraged did I feel.

The final chords were greeted with "Bravo!"s and some clapping from those whose hands were free.

"What is it? What was that you were just playing?" I almost shouted at Dohnányi in German.

"Why are you so excited?" he asked. "That was just a waltz I was playing. And how thoughtful of you to bring these sandwiches!"

"Yes," I exclaimed, "but that was *my* waltz!"

"*Your* waltz?" he laughed over the sandwich he was holding. "My dear boy, I wrote this when you were still a baby. I composed it for a pantomime called *Der Schleier der Pierrette*" — *The Veil of Pierrette* — which had its first performance almost fifteen years ago."

"But I remember playing that waltz when I was still in Moscow, before the Revolution," I insisted.

At this Dohnányi looked genuinely surprised. "In Moscow?" he repeated. "Before the Revolution? . . . How strange! . . . This pantomime of mine was performed quite a bit in Austria and Germany before the war . . . but in Russia? How curious! . . . Then there must have been some truth in what somebody once told me — that some amateur group had put it on in Russia before the war. But I was never paid any royalties and was unable to discover who those people were."

And thus, in the most unexpected way, was solved one of the great mysteries of my youth. In strict fact, I had invented nothing, either waking or asleep. Some member of the strange, enterprising troupe that had decided to perform this pantomime in Moscow must have been lodged in a neighboring apartment, and I must have heard him playing or practicing this waltz while I lay half asleep in the bedroom giving on to the inner court of the Trubnikovsky Pereulok. I was not the youthful "composer" I had, in my childish conceit, fancied myself to be.

I soon discovered that this lovely, lilting waltz, which I had used in Berlin to charm various girl friends, had also played a major role in Ernö Dohnányi's life. The actress who had been chosen, or, more exactly, who had decided to dance the leading role in the Viennese production of *The Veil of Pierrette,* Elsa Galafrés, had later become Dohnányi's wife. She had in fact accompanied him to the United States, and I was soon to meet her.

Dohnányi was obviously intrigued by the idea that I had heard his waltz played in distant Moscow, and this, combined with Mother's playing of the Prokofieff violin concerto, established a bond between us. In addition to conducting the New York State Symphony Orchestra, Dohnányi played two of his piano and string quintets at a special chamber music recital. I was allowed to sit next to him and turn the pages. Both quintets were charming pieces, and to hear the piano part played by their composer was a rare treat, for his playing was simply exquisite.

I finally screwed up my courage and asked him if I could come out to his Forest Hills hotel, explaining that I wanted his advice about my piano playing, which was not what it should be. He readily assented, and a day or two later I took the Long Island train to Forest Hills, where he and Madame Dohnányi were staying. I was ushered into an impressive suite, where the first thing I noticed was a Chickering concert grand. Affable as ever, Dohnányi invited me to sit down and play anything I liked.

At that time my *cheval de bataille* — the "battle-horse" on which I liked to pin my musical colors — was Liszt's B Minor Sonata, which I had carefully studied with Schnabel. I had vainly sought to impress Josef Hofmann by playing it. Now I hoped to have better luck.

I played the sonata, which has but one long movement, lasting a good half hour, from beginning to end. Dohnányi listened patiently, not once trying to stop me. Having finished, I looked at him questioningly.

"My dear boy," he said, "you have a musical gift, that is certain. But I will be frank with you. You do not know how to play the piano. You seem to know nothing about technique."

"Ah, Herr von Dohnányi," I said, "I am so happy to hear you say that. I know myself that there is something wrong with my technical equipment. But in Berlin, where I studied, neither Leonid Kreutzer nor Artur Schnabel ever discussed such matters. They were only interested in other things. They seemed to think that I played well enough. You have just told me the truth. Please teach me how to play correctly."

Dohnányi shook his head. "I'm sorry, but this I cannot do."

"Why not?" I asked. "You have analyzed my problem. Why can't you help me?"

"I will be honest with you. I do not know how to teach piano technique."

"What do you mean you do not know?" I insisted. "You play so beautifully yourself. Your fingers do exactly what you want them to do; you know how it is done."

"Yes, I play well," he agreed. "My fingers do what I want them to do, but just how they do it, I honestly do not know. It is all instinctive. It is not something I can teach to others."

At this point I began to get aggressive, for I was a pretty brash youth and I was not going to take no for an answer. "You have analyzed my problem, yet now you say you are not going to help me. You are the one person who can, who must help me! If you cannot teach me, then I would like to know who can!"

My vehemence evidently impressed him. At least I knew what I wanted.

"All right . . . I'll tell you . . . I do know somebody . . ." He paused for a moment of reflection. "I know somebody who might be able to help you. She is a woman and she lives in Budapest."

"What is she?" I asked. "One of your assistants, one of your students?"

"No, she's neither an assistant nor a student. In fact, I do not know her well at all."

"What do you mean — you do not know her well? Then how can you recommend her?"

"Let me explain," said Dohnányi. "I have had to listen to a great many students at the Franz Liszt Academy of Music in Budapest. Some played the piano fairly well, others not so well. But those who played the best, I soon discovered, had all been trained by this woman."

"What is her name?"

"Irèn Senn."

"Ah," I said. I don't know what I had expected, but I had never heard of her.

"It is a long way, I realize, but if you wish to go to Budapest, I feel sure she will be happy to teach you. And you will have no cause to regret it."

"All right," I said. "I'm ready to go to Budapest. Why not? But if I do, will you also teach me?"

Dohnányi smiled. My enthusiasm must have flattered as well as amused him. "Yes, I will help you. But you must first work with Miss Senn. After that you can study with me."

The malady had at last been diagnosed, but the remedy seemed hopelessly out of reach. When I returned to the Great Northern Hotel and told Mother of our conversation, she immediately lost patience.

"What kind of nonsense is this?" she cried. "You say Dohnányi thinks you should go to Budapest to learn how to play the piano! And you of course agree! And on what kind of money I would like to know? Have you given any thought to that? No, of course you haven't. You went to Berlin for eight months and were barely able to keep yourself alive, and now you want to go and starve to death in Budapest, which is even farther away. What on earth has got into you? In Berlin at least you had a few friends to fall back on. But in Budapest you don't know a blessed soul. You don't even speak the language. Why, you're out of your mind. This is nonsense. Forget it!"

A lot of arguing followed, because I could be stubborn when my mind was set on something. In fact, the arguing went on for days. The problem, as far as I was concerned, was not whether I should go to Budapest or not, it was how I was to get there.

The subject came up the next time we were invited to lunch with the Princes.

"You know what this crazy son of mine wants to do now?" said Mother. "He wants to go to Budapest! Yes, to Budapest, if you please! To learn to play the piano with some woman nobody has ever heard of but who's supposed to be a genius. I let him go to Berlin to study with Schnabel, but that apparently wasn't enough. Now it's got to be Budapest!"

Her friend Tessie Prince, being a pianist, listened sympathetically while I explained my problem. But once lunch was over, Sidney Prince drew me off to one side. Like his wife, he spoke tolerably good German. For some reason he had taken a liking to me and had decided that I was a bright boy. He and his wife were childless, having lost their only son in a terrible automobile accident when he was about eighteen years old. Probably, like most fathers, Sidney Prince had dreamed of having his son follow in his own affluent footsteps. Fate had decided otherwise. Now here, he must have thought, was a bright young lad who, though he didn't speak much English, could read, write, and speak three foreign languages; what was more, he could do complicated arithmetical calculations in his head in a matter of seconds. For a broker who had a seat on the New York Stock Exchange a fellow like myself might be a first-rate asset.

"I don't understand," he said to me when we were by ourselves. "What's the matter with you? You say you want to become a pianist, but what on earth for? Because your mother is a famous violinist? That makes no sense. Your father too could play the piano, but he knew better than to try to make a go of it as a professional musician. He became a lawyer and he ended up making quite a bit of money — enough to support his wife, to have a cook and a maid, and to bring up three children in style. He knew how to live. He had his feet on the ground. So why all this silly talk about becoming a musician? You're a bright boy and you're simply wasting your talents. I mean, there are much more interesting things for you to do than to make fancy noises on the keyboard. You can play the piano as a hobby, the way my wife does. But if you want to make money — and without it you can't hope to survive in this world — then take my advice: go into the brokerage business.

"In fact," he went on, "I'll make you a proposition. I'll be very happy to take you into our firm. I'll teach you the A.B.C.'s of buying and selling stocks and bonds, and before you know it, you'll be doing very well. Because I'm sure you have what it takes to become a successful businessman."

"Mr. Prince," I said, "this is very kind of you, but unfortunately I do not want to become a successful businessman. I have no particular desire to be wealthy. What I want to be is a musician. This is the only thing in the world that really interests me, that I absolutely want to be — a musician!"

"So you want to be a musician, and nothing else interests you?" asked Sidney Prince, slowly shaking his graying head while he fingered his mustache. "So that's how it is, hmm . . ." He realized he was getting nowhere with his Wall Street line.

I nodded vigorously. "A musician," I repeated. "A musician and nothing else."

"And you say you have to go to Budapest to learn how to play the piano correctly?"

"That's what Herr von Dohnányi thinks," I said. "He's listened to me and he knows what's wrong with my playing. He's done for me what no one else could do — point out what is wrong. So if he says I should go to Budapest, because he knows somebody there who can teach me, I think his advice is worth following."

"All right," said Sidney Prince, after a moment of silence. "I'll tell you what. I'll take the matter up with Dohnányi, and if he says you should go to Budapest, then I'll make it possible for you to go there. I'll take care of your passage over and back, and I'll have my secretary send you a monthly allowance — let's say a hundred dollars — to pay for your study and expenses."

I could hardly believe my ears. I felt like embracing him. This was American generosity beyond my wildest dreams. In Central Europe, in the mid-1920s, $100 was a small fortune. In Berlin I had actually managed to survive for a while on about eight dollars a month. This was twelve times as much!

Fortunately I had an ally in Mrs. Sidney Prince. She admired Dohnányi almost as much as I did. She considered him a great man. If he thought I should go to Budapest to study the piano, then by all means I should go.

And so, a week or two later, it was decided. My stay in Budapest would not cost me or Mother a penny. Of the $100 allowance I was to receive, half was to cover special tutoring expenses — with Miss Irèn Senn and others — the rest would take care of board and lodging. I would leave in February, when the Dohnányis left New York, and I would cross the ocean with them. That would give me a few weeks in which to pick up a bit of Hungarian. English, in the interim, could wait.

I would have had to cross the Atlantic in any case, for I had been admitted to the United States on a limited, six-month visa. But getting to Budapest on my Nansen passport was no simple matter.

For some reason I could not obtain a Hungarian visa in the United States; I would have to get it in some other country. So when our transatlantic liner put in to Cherbourg, I said goodbye to the Dohnányis, who were sailing on to Hamburg.

My stopover in Paris, where I stayed in the Rue Raynouard apartment, gave me a chance to see my sister Irène, now nine years and three months old and spouting volubly in French, Babushka, as bustling and domineering as ever, and Uncle Pierre, who had lifted part of the load from Mother's shoulders by agreeing to take care of Grandmother's expenses. Though I was delighted to see them all again, I soon grew fretful over the sluggishness of the Hungarian consular machine, which required not days but weeks to obtain the simplest bureaucratic response to any query or request. Day after day I had to stand in line, only to be informed, when I reached the counter, that the authorization for my visa had not yet arrived and that I would have to come back the next day. I spent the rest of my time, or most of it, studying Hungarian, and when I was finally informed, after what seemed like an eternity, that my visa permit had arrived, my Hungarian had noticeably improved and I could install myself and my bags in the Orient Express compartment with a sense of anticipation unclouded by linguistic apprehensions.

It must have been mid-March, or even later, when I finally reached Budapest. Spring was just around the corner and soon the city was a-flower with sweet-smelling acacia blossoms. The swiftly flowing Danube, lined on both banks with terraced hotels; the narrow, crescent-shaped old town of Buda, with its verdant, undulating hills and royal castle; the flat expanse of Pest, with its neo-Gothic parliament building and its fine, tree-lined avenues radiating north and east toward the great Hungarian plain beyond — everything about this gay, vital, exuberant city delighted me. The air seemed filled with an intense joie de vivre I have never felt equaled elsewhere, not even in Paris, a far more cerebral and calculating, if more beautiful, metropolis.

It was near the end of one of Pest's finest avenues, named after the famous nineteenth-century statesman Count Gyula Andrássy, that I first found lodgings in a small house located just beyond an eight-pointed roundabout known as the Octagon. I was taken there, as I recall, by one of Dohnányi's assistants, who explained to the landlady who I was and who provided me with the necessary explanations regarding the front-door key and the rest.

Having unpacked my suitcases and hung up my clothes, I went out for a stroll, which was interrupted by a sudden gastric attack. Hurrying back to the house, I opened the front door with my key and raced upstairs as fast as I could. Impatiently I rang the apartment bell. The door was opened by a maid, past whom I rushed, headed down the corridor for the toilet. She shouted something in Hungarian which I could not understand, but I was in too critical a state to stop. Wrenching open the door, I locked myself into the toilet with a feeling of desperate relief.

Outside I could hear an angry babble of voices, and then someone came up and began pounding on the door. I answered in German, asking for a little patience, whereupon the pounding grew more insistent. When I finally opened the door, I was afraid for a moment that I was going to be lynched. There were about eight people in the corridor, all glaring at me and shouting insults and abuses that I could not understand. My landlady was not among them. Only then did I realize that in my precipitation I had entered the wrong apartment.

My piano teacher, Irèn Senn, turned out to be a tall and energetic spinster with kindly gray eyes and a smiling and open countenance. She gave lessons in a large apartment which she shared with her bachelor brother.

Under Karl Avgustovich Kipp, in Moscow, I had developed the muscles in my hands and fingers by spending hours of excruciating practice going through the monotonous Hanon exercises. I had learned something of the "how" of piano playing, without understanding any of the "why." This Irèn Senn proceeded to explain to me, at any rate in part — for it was not until much later, when

I came across Arnold Schultz's *The Riddle of the Pianist's Finger,* that I finally understood what piano playing is really all about.

Reduced to essentials, piano playing consists of little more than pushing down keys. In this it resembles typing, which is also a method for pushing down keys, though the emphasis and aim — a more or less uniform speed — are of course quite different. To play the piano well, you have to learn how to push the keys down in different ways — sometimes hard and loud, at other times softly; sometimes very fast, at other times slowly.

Irèn Senn distinguished two different types of playing very sharply. She called the first — for loud, slow playing — "the Big technique," and the second — for fast, soft playing — "the Small technique." The Big technique involved the activities of one's arms and shoulders, and the angle of the spine and torso best suited to exert a maximum of effective muscular contractions. The Small technique involved the finger muscles of the hands, and in particular the fingertips, so important to the playing of very fast and very soft passages.

In order to master these two techniques Irèn Senn had developed a whole series of exercises which her students had to perform every day. She also taught me something else that was invaluable. One of the major problems in piano playing is that it is difficult to play loudly without having it sound harsh. We have all of us been exposed at one time or another to a brutal key-pounder, whose insensitive hammering causes the strings inside the box to reverberate and echo in the most jarring fashion. To get around this problem, Irèn Senn taught us what she called the "double touch." We were never supposed to strike a key directly. One had first to finger it before striking, so that the down-action, when it came, was more pushing than hitting. And this technique of pretouching, or double-touching, did not only hold for soft passages. We had to master it for all forms of playing, from the loudest and slowest to the softest and fastest.

*

After three months in Budapest I took the train back to Paris, where I found Mother once again installed in the Rue Raynouard apartment with Babushka and Irina. Her prestige as a concert violinist was now fairly solidly established in the United States thanks to the patronage of Josef Hofmann, who had taken her under his wing and agreed to play with her a number of piano and violin sonatas. There were, as I was soon to discover, special reasons for this extraordinary homage paid by a man whom many considered the greatest pianist alive to a violinist who, though very talented, was not quite in the same class. I shall explain what they were a little farther on, when I describe the summer months of 1927. But in June of 1926 all I knew was that Mother had traveled with Hofmann to London a few weeks before to give a joint sonata recital. More recitals were scheduled in the United States in the autumn, but in the meantime we — which is to say, Mother, Irina, and I — were going to spend another vacation together at Saint-Jean-de-Luz, while Babushka remained in Paris with Uncle Pierre.

In September we split up once again. Irina was left with Babushka in the Rue Raynouard apartment in Passy to begin her fourth year at the Lycée Molière. Mother sailed to New York, while I took the train to Budapest.

Here I resumed my piano lessons with Irèn Senn. Among her pupils was another young boy named Edward Kilényi, who had also come to study with her at Dohnányi's suggestion. His mother was a rather flamboyant American woman, who, after being separated from her husband, had chosen to settle down in Budapest with her son. The youthful Eddie was a year or so younger than myself, but he was already a most promising pianist and we soon became firm friends. At first we conversed in German until my Hungarian had improved to the point where I could carry on a rudimentary conversation in that language. Later still, we began to speak in English, a language in which he was fluent.

German, however, remained the linguistic mainstay of my existence, for it was used not only by Irèn Senn but also by Leo Weiner, a composer and music teacher with whom I now started to study harmony and orchestration. A small, live wire of a fellow, Weiner was an extremely gifted all-round musician who seemed to be able to teach any instrument — whether it was violin, flute, oboe, or trumpet. The teaching he dispensed was primarily theoretical, but it was highly prized and he himself was so popular that half of the Budapest Philharmonic Orchestra seemed, at some time or other, to have been tutored by him.

Not being on the staff of the Franz Liszt Academy of Music, Leo Weiner had to charge for the instruction he dispensed. Thanks to the $50 a month that Sidney Prince had generously provided for my tuition needs, this was a luxury I could easily afford. And a real treat it was, even though it was not always smooth sailing. To teach me harmony, Weiner had me study Bach's famous harmonizations — 350, all told — of chorale melodies used in German Lutheran services. While I sat in his score-cluttered room, he would give me a chorale melody for which, without further ado, I had to provide a four-part harmony. It was a fascinating challenge. Because Weiner was a gifted composer in his own right, one had the exhilarating feeling under his tutelage that what one was doing was creative and that by the end of the academic year one would have sprouted wings oneself and developed into a full-fledged composer.

Since we were expected to familiarize ourselves with Bach's harmonic procedures, I spent quite a bit of time at home studying his settings. In one of them I came across a passage that struck me as a rather daring departure from the normal, with an unusual voice-leading pattern bordering on the grotesque. Intrigued, I made a note of it. Several weeks later, we were seated in Weiner's room when he happened to give me this particular chorale melody to harmonize. I had not forgotten Bach's daring innovation, and so as I sat at the table, filling in the four parts, I included the unorthodox idea Bach had developed.

Weiner had either forgotten or overlooked this particular setting, for when I handed him my finished work, he got all red in the face. "What's the matter with you today? What kind of nonsense is this?" he exclaimed, pointing at the passage and crosshatching it with large red pencil strokes. "This is absurd, ridiculous!"

"*Meister,*" I said, "I seem to recall that Bach once did something similar."

"What! Like this? Nonsense! Nonsense!"

Getting up, I walked over to a bookshelf and pulled out the volume of Bach chorales. When I found the one I wanted, I handed him the opened book. Weiner stared at the unusual harmonization, at first in disbelief and then in growing wonderment. He began shaking his head as he mumbled: "Genius! Sheer genius!" Weiner, of course, was right. As the Romans used to say, "*Quod licet Jovi non licet bovi.*" What is permitted to Jupiter is not permitted to an ox.

By and large Leo Weiner was a remarkably vivacious and witty teacher from whom I learned many things. He taught me, for example, how to read orchestral scores. He also put me through a series of fascinating and at the same time exacting exercises by having me play string quartets on the piano. To be able to do this, one must first learn the various clefs fluently — the alto clef for the viola, the tenor clef for the cello — just as one learns the clefs used to transpose the clarinet, French horn, and trumpet lines in an orchestral score. Paradoxical as it may sound, it is easier to play a full orchestral score on the piano than it is to play a string quartet or quintet. Symphonies are usually written in a pianistic style. The dominant theme or themes and the harmonic structure are almost immediately apparent and can be reproduced on the piano without too much difficulty. But in the string quartets of Mozart, Beethoven, Schubert, and Brahms, which I studied with Weiner, there is so much counterpoint and the voice-leading is so tricky that it is maddeningly difficult to do justice to them on the piano. However, as the months passed and I grew more skilled, I found that I could turn string quartets and quintets into effective piano pieces, which even Leo Weiner was prepared to commend.

My piano playing, on the other hand, did not improve as rapidly as Dohnányi had hoped. The fault was not Irèn Senn's but mine. I have never much cared for piano practice, which is for the most part mechanical, muscular, and repetitive. Much of my spare time was now spent studying Hungarian, and for a while I went through an acute "Schopenhauer period." His *The World as Will and Idea* made an immense impression on me, as did *The Two Fundamental Problems of Ethics.*

When I think back on my years in Budapest, my memory clouds up and I find it almost impossible to recall exactly what happened when. So many things were going on at once. I was confronted with an embarrassment of cultural riches which, as a young man, I found irresistibly tempting.

One of these cultural temptations was chess. Many Hungarians, I discovered, were chess addicts, and they would think nothing of spending entire afternoons or evenings at the local Chess Club. I decided to become a member. This would give me an opportunity of meeting Hungarians who were not musicians, and it would also offer me precious hours of distraction. Chess is a game that appeals to many different kinds of people. I don't think that the hold it now came to have on me can simply be ascribed to my mathematical bent, since many nonmathematically inclined individuals — like the writer Vladimir Nabokov, for example — have felt the same attraction. My interest in chess, however, soon became all-absorbing. I found myself replaying chess games in my head in an effort to figure out what I had done wrong and what better moves I could have made. Chess, as I only realized later after I had "sobered up," is a dangerous hobby. It takes possession of you; it invades every nook and cranny of your mind until you can think of nothing else. Like a drug, it breeds an addiction and you end up obsessed.

That is what happened to me. So involved with chess did I

become that I began neglecting my piano playing, while spending ever longer hours at the Chess Club. Determined to improve my game, I paid one of my fellow members, an unusually brilliant player, to give me private tutoring. "Twice a week you will come to my room and we will play chess together," I proposed. "Every now and then, before I make a move, I shall tell you what I am planning, and you will criticize it and tell me what you would do in my place. In this way I shall learn to think the way you do and thus improve my playing."

He accepted my proposal. But even though he taught me a lot, it was never enough to enable me to catch up with him. He always kept surprising me with moves I had not anticipated. I particularly remember one game during which I found myself faced with three obvious choices for the next move. After pondering the situation for a long time, I explained my thinking to him: "There are three possible moves I'm considering. I can do this . . . or this . . . or that . . . Now which of these moves do you think is the best?"

"Oh, no, no, no," he said, shaking his head. "Frankly, I never even considered these possibilities. They never entered my mind. As far as I'm concerned, there are only two moves here that would be appropriate. There is this" — and he moved a piece across the board — "or this" — and he moved another. "Those are the only ones I would consider. And of the two, it is obvious enough that this one is the better move."

This incident impressed me greatly. I realized that my gifted tutor had developed some kind of chess-playing mechanism in his brain which acted like a filter. Thanks to this cerebral computer all mediocre or second-rate moves were eliminated in advance and only the highest grade were allowed to seep through to the chambers of creative combustion.

But more than this was needed to dampen my enthusiasm for chess. When it was announced that the Hungarian chess Grand Master, Géza Maróczy, would be visiting the Chess Club and would take on all comers in a simultaneous exhibition, I was one of the many members who immediately signed up. In the end there were so many of us that it was decided we would have to double up. I found myself paired off with an impressively taciturn, dark-haired player named Szabó who, being far more skilled than I was, kept overruling me.

Of the thirty-eight simultaneous matches Géza Maróczy played, thirty were easily won by the champion. Seven others, as I recall, were tied. But there was one game he lost — thanks to a wrong move he made which my dark-haired partner skillfully exploited.

The news was given a big play in the next morning's papers, where it was reported that the one match Géza Maróczy had lost had been fought against Goldovsky and Szabó (my name coming first as a matter of alphabetical order). It thus sounded like a Goldovsky rather than a Szabó victory.

The news was not long in reaching the ears of Ernö Dohnányi, who had been following my progress carefully and who had finally agreed to give me special piano lessons. The next time we were together, he said to me: "My dear boy, I have been wondering why you have not been playing well recently, and now I think I know the answer. You have not been practicing, you have not been preparing your lessons. Why? Because you are a chess player, and seemingly a good one." He paused, and then looking me straight in the eyes, he added: "You will have to make up your mind now what you want to be and do in life, whether you would rather play the piano or play chess. Because you cannot do both. If you wish to be a pianist, that is fine. But then I demand that you give up chess *entirely* and *immediately!*"

It was an ultimatum, a completely justified ultimatum, and I hastened to capitulate. I have never had reason to regret it. For when I removed myself from the running, the world was definitely not losing an Alekhine, a Bobby Fischer, or a Spassky.

*

The summer of 1927, which I again spent at Saint-Jean-de-Luz with Mother and Irina, was a particularly memorable one for several reasons. This time Babushka came with us, for Mother had decided to give up the Rue Raynouard apartment. Her patron and protector, Josef Hofmann, had recently been appointed director of the Curtis Institute of Music in Philadelphia, and he had offered her a job in the violin-teaching department. This was a real bonanza, for it guaranteed Mother steady employment. Though her recitals with Hofmann had been widely acclaimed, they had been too short-lived to assure her financially against the hazards of the future. Hofmann, furthermore, had all but retired from regular concertizing, having moodily decided that solo recitals, in the great Thalberg-Liszt-Rubinstein tradition, were doomed, since music lovers were increasingly drawn to symphonic performances and other group events. He had agreed to play with Mother for purely personal reasons that had nothing to do with music but a great deal to do with an attractive light-skinned blonde named Betty Sharp, to whom he had been giving piano lessons. When he realized that his fair-haired pupil was pregnant and that he was the father-to-be, he decided to take Betty to London so that the child could be born far from the eyes of inquisitive Americans. Mother, who had been invited to make the trip with them, made an admirable screen, and so often were she and Hofmann seen together in public that there was now no room for doubt: they were lovers. So at least it was believed by almost everybody, and those who knew the truth were not out to publicize it.

At a time when music teachers in Europe would consider themselves lucky to be able to earn one or two dollars for an hour of instruction, the teachers at the Curtis Institute — the most lavishly endowed musical institution in the world — were being paid a fabulous thirty dollars an hour. Mother was not yet rich, but for the first time in years she was beginning to feel financially secure. America having lived up to its mythical reputation as an

El Dorado for musicians, there was no point in maintaining a pied-à-terre in Paris. In September she was taking Irina with her to New York, and the understanding was that Babushka would soon be following with Uncle Pierre. I would be allowed to return to Budapest to complete my schooling with Dohnányi, but eventually I too would cross the ocean and try my luck in the New World.

Meanwhile there was plenty to keep us all busy. A Miss B., who had begun giving Irène (as she called her) lessons in English, came down from Paris to give her special, midsummer coaching in the language she would soon be using at school.

In September, when I returned to Budapest, I left the little apartment house I had inhabited up till then, near the Andrássy Avenue's Octagon circle, and transferred to the Buda side of the Danube. The comfortable house into which I moved was located in an area known as the Kis Sváab Hegy — the Little Swabian Hill. The owner was a *tábla biró,* or lower court judge, named Aladár Sándor, who occupied the third floor, along with his wife and eighteen-year-old daughter, Sári (Hungarian for Charlotte). The latter were singularly unappetizing members of their sex, and the mother had not only a bit of a mustache under her nose but a small thicket of hair which was to be seen sprouting unashamedly from her bosom each time she wore a décolleté evening dress.

I myself was lodged on the second floor with the judge's mother-in-law, a nondescript son of hers whose only apparent interest in life was in choral music, and the cook, affectionately known to us all as Téri Néni — Aunt Teresa. The dining room was also on this floor, and it was here that we took our meals together, at a table presided over by the small but imperious grandmother. I was treated as a member of the family and entitled to three meals a day. And what meals! The Hungarian cuisine — with a succulent gamut of meat and fish dishes, not to mention delicious layer cakes and tarts — is one of the finest in the world, and Téri Néni was in this respect a worthy specimen of her country and calling.

When she learned that I was paying the judge $50 a month for room and board — an unheard-of, a "scandalous" sum to be paying for one's food and lodgings, as my Hungarian friends kept telling me — she too was outraged; and being possessed of an instinctive sense of justice, she saw to it that I got my money's worth. No matter how many times a week I might be invited out to lunch or dinner — and as I was a popular young boy this happened fairly often — I would come home to find my fair share waiting to be consumed on a tray in my room. And so tempting did these generous portions always seem, even when stone cold, that I invariably gobbled them up. The lean, hungering adolescent who had studied under Schnabel in Berlin had ceased to be a beanstalk and was now as plump as a banana.

Because I had crossed the Atlantic with Dohnányi and was sustained by a monthly allowance from the United States, I was generally known to my friends — at the Liszt Academy and elsewhere — as "the American": a decidedly curious appellation for someone who still could hardly speak a word of English. At Eddie Kilényi's suggestion, I had started reading P. G. Wodehouse novels, and even reading them with relish, but I had to guess at the meaning of more than half the words as I followed Bertie Wooster's and Jeeves's hilarious adventures.

My Hungarian, however, had improved to the point where I could go to the theater and enjoy Hungarian plays. The Hungarians, theatrically as well as musically, are among the most gifted people I have known. The number of first-class singers, conductors, musicians, and particularly actors and actresses that this relatively small country has produced is astounding. In Budapest there was not a night on which one was not offered a choice of several really first-class plays. Among the many unforgettable evenings I spent at the theater I particularly remember two — both of them plays by Ferenc Molnár. One of them was called *Játék a kastélyban* — literally *Play in the Castle,* but which has been translated into English as *The Play's the Thing.* The other was *Az Ördög — The Devil* — a curious tale about a desperately enamored pair, a married woman and a painter, whose virtuous resistance to desire so enrages the Devil that he cooks up a complicated stratagem to induce them to fall into each other's arms. The part of the Devil was particularly impressive, played as it was by Hegedüs, then regarded as the finest actor in Hungary.

If I was able to enjoy so many of these plays, it was, I must admit, because I could read and thus familiarize myself in advance with the written texts. But when my Budapest friends took me to one of the city's political cabarets, where well-known comedians came out on stage to make fun of contemporary politics and politicians, I was lost. Their witty skits, which kept the audiences in stitches, were over my head, being full of clever puns and allusions which only somebody who had spent years in Budapest could properly appreciate.

Unlike Artur Schnabel, who had always enveloped his private life in a shroud of mystery, Dohnányi from the start had welcomed me into the family. And a curious family it was. For in addition to Mr. and Mrs. Dohnányi, it included two mothers-in-law and two sons from different fathers. This unusual circumstance, which one would normally have expected to be storm-inducing, had proved to be an unexpected boon a few years earlier, during the topsy-turvy months of Béla Kun's communist "republic." For when the "confidence comrade" appointed to supervise their urban district had come to inspect their house, with the idea of lodging other "boarders," he had thrown up his arms in horror on being informed by the quick-witted cook that under this one roof lived two shrieking children and two perpetually screaming mothers-in-law. "My God, that must be hell!" he had exclaimed, cutting short his inspection and disappearing into the street without another word.

The new house into which Ernö Dohnányi had recently moved with his family was as unusual as the persons inhabiting it. Located in the suburbs, on the Buda side of the Danube, it had a tall gabled roof and was built into a steep pine-studded hillside, which had once been part of a royal hunting preserve. If you entered from the small, upper-garden side, you found yourself on the floor where all the bedrooms were located and you had to descend the stairs to reach the main rooms. These, including a spacious dining room and the drawing room, which contained two Bösendorfer pianos, looked out on to a much larger garden, full of flowers, shrubbery, and evergreens.

Ernö Dohnányi's father, who had been a teacher by profession and a cello player in his spare time, had died long before, but his mother — now known as *Nagymama* (Little Grandmother) — was very much alive. Like her daughter, Mizzike (Ernö's younger sister), she had been forced to leave their home in Pozsony, when that Danubian town, renamed Bratislava, was incorporated into the newly created Czechoslovakian republic at the end of the First World War. A very small, alert Hungarian lady with the beaky features of a bird of prey, she had been a permanent fixture of the Dohnányi household for the past ten years. She tended to be short of speech, but her phrases, when she opened her mouth, were as short and sharp as her features. Her rare utterances were thus listened to with great respect. To be complimented by *Nagymama* was considered the height of praise.

Quite different was the second grandmother. Fairly tall and bosomy, like her daughter Elsa, she had gray eyes that were as soft and kindly as the name Oma by which she was universally known.

Dohnányi's wife, née Elsa Galafrés, was born and brought up in Berlin. Too flighty and undisciplined to become a really first-class pianist, she had found an outlet for her romantic and histrionic inclinations as an actress and a dancer. Her first husband, Bronislaw Huberman, was a famous Polish violinist who suffered agonies of anticipatory doubt and stage fright each time he had to give a public recital. She had borne him a son — a blond-haired boy, Johannes (better known as "Hally") — who had later become a bitter bone of contention when she decided that she could no longer live with her high-strung, insomniac, perpetually concert-touring husband. The resultant legal wrangle had become a prewar cause célèbre, but she had managed to retain custody of her child even after the start of her liaison with Ernö Dohnányi, as fascinated by her theatrical performance in the Viennese production of his musical pantomime, *The Veil of Pierrette,* as she was by his calm, confident, intelligent conducting.

At the time Ernö Dohnányi was no freer than she, being married to a somewhat demure German girl who had borne him two children. But this marital complication had not kept him from having a third child with Elsa, not long after they had moved from Berlin to Budapest, where she had reluctantly agreed to sacrifice her stage career in order to become a dutiful home-keeper and mother. This child, named Mátyás, was about ten years old when I first got to know him in Budapest, and in the congenial and somewhat Bohemian atmosphere of the Dohnányi household he did not seem to suffer from the realization that he was born out of wedlock. He may not even have been aware of the fact that it was not until two years after he was born — during the short-lived Béla Kun regime and thanks to a liberal divorce law that had been prepared by one of their friends who had been named Minister of Justice (and who referred to it jokingly as the Lex Dohnányi) — that his parents could "regularize" their union with a civil wedding ceremony.

Madame Dohnányi, as often happens with ladies who have an unconventional past to live down, had since turned into a model of marital respectability. She stressed duty and discipline, extolled law and order, and had no use for manifestations of revolutionary *laisser-aller* and license.

Dohnányi himself was a reserved rather than an outgoing personality. The enigmatic smile that flitted about his lips expressed an ironic appreciation of life, but it was also a kind of screen behind which he hid his innermost thoughts and inclinations. He was essentially a tolerant person and, as a well-bred Austro-Hungarian aristocrat, he seldom raised his voice or expressed violent opinions. He left such expressions of vehemence to others — like his sister Mizzi's husband, Professor Ferencz Kovács, who was as vociferous as Dohnányi was soft-spoken.

The name Kovács — the Hungarian equivalent of Smith — was an exceedingly common one in Budapest. In the Dohnányi household no one ever addressed the professor as "Kovács Ur" (Mr. Kovacs). He was always referred to as "Ferencz Bácsi" (Uncle Francis) or more simply, as Ferry. Because of his thick black beard, Ferencz Bácsi never wore a tie. There was something more Bohemian than professorial about this political science instructor who had once studied the cello under Dohnányi's father, and this nonacademic impression was fortified by the prejudiced enormities that kept issuing from his hairy mouth. Like many other Hungarians, he was outspokenly anti-Jewish, getting off remarks in my presence which apparently did not concern me, because I had been accepted by the Dohnányi family and was thus persona grata. This latent anti-Semitism was part of the cultural tradition, or maybe I should say the cultural disdain, of Hungary's upper classes, and since it was not accompanied by any overt animosity, I quietly disregarded it.

Far more surprising, to me at any rate, were Ferencz Bácsi's anti-French sentiments. As a Hungarian super-patriot who had been forced to abandon his home town of Pozsony, he could not forgive the French for having helped to dismember the Austro-Hungarian Empire by distributing bits of what had once been "Greater Hungary" to Czechoslovakia, Romania, and Yugoslavia. But instead of expending his xenophobic ire on Clemenceau and the other "cannibals" who had drafted the Treaty of Saint-Germain, he damned the French people as a whole, terming them an inferior, runtish, second-rate nation. They were a race of immoral degenerates and depraved syphilitics. Their language was stilted, their philosophers and poets were fundamentally shallow, and, as for their music, it was beneath contempt — the triviality of Offenbach and Bizet compared to the sublime profundity of Bach, Beethoven, Brahms, and Wagner.

As someone who had spent a year in Paris and who had studied French, I was flabbergasted by these sentiments. They echoed the contempt for French music I had already encountered in Berlin. In Budapest too Beethoven — the hundredth anniversary of whose death Dohnányi had helped to celebrate in the spring of 1927 by giving thirty-five concerts in twenty-two different Hungarian localities — was treated as a god; Gounod, Debussy, and Franck, on the other hand, were relegated to oblivion.

The prejudice was so pronounced that it even affected a composer like Chopin, the hybrid offspring of a French father and a Polish mother. Chopin was generally regarded as a kind of charming salon composer, of limited scope and genius, who was simply not in the same league with the giants of the German-speaking world. It was thus something of an event when a Hungarian pianist named Kéri-Szánto undertook to defy this prejudice by staging an all-Chopin recital in Budapest. Unfortunately his playing was not up to his temerity, and where his fingers should have danced and rippled, they thumped. In the cafés and drawing rooms of Budapest, where every educated individual spoke German, Kéri-Szánto was henceforth known as *der ungarische Chopinhauer* (the Hungarian Chopin-hacker) — a designation I have always treasured as a prize specimen of musico-philosophical punning.

Of all the summers we spent at Saint-Jean-de-Luz, the last — in 1928 — was far and away the most eventful and exciting. This time we were lodged in a villa rather than in a *pension de famille,* for in addition to Babushka, Uncle Petya, Aunt Elena Mikhailovna, and my sister Irène, Mother had crossed the ocean with four of her violin students from the Curtis Institute — Celia and

Robert Gomberg, Ethel Stark, and Judith Poska — as well as Edwin Bachmann, who was to join the Curtis faculty in the autumn. Josef Hofmann was intent on having his institute develop a first-class string quartet. Being a soloist, Mother knew little about ensemble playing, whereas Bachmann, who had played second fiddle with many leading quartet organizations, knew all of the standard works of this genre inside out.

At the Franz Liszt Academy of Music in Budapest, I had attended a few chamber-music classes with a teacher named Imre Waldbauer, but I had soon given them up, dissatisfied by the poor performance of the student string players. Now, however, I had two first-class violinists to accompany, and they — that is, Mother and Eddie Bachmann — were delighted to have the viola and cello parts filled in by a pianist who had acquired considerable skill in this kind of score reading, thanks to Leo Weiner's expert instruction. The practicing we did that summer was one of the most fruitful musical experiences I have ever encountered, and I doubt that there are many pianists alive today who have been put through such an intensive course of string quartet training with two such gifted violinists.

Eddie Bachmann, as it happened, was only the first of an impressive retinue of great musicians whom Mother had somehow managed to lure to the Basque coast. Another was the violinist Mischa Elman, who arrived with his wife and three sisters. A small, balding, self-infatuated egocentric, Elman talked compulsively and nonstop about himself, never missing an opportunity to denigrate rivals like Jascha Heifetz, whose virtuosity was unforgivable and unforgiven.

One of the star visitors to Saint-Jean-de-Luz was Josef Hofmann, who turned up with his new wife, Betty. Two other talented musicians also joined us that summer. One of them was the violinist Toscha Seidel, who, like Elman and Heifetz, had studied under Leopold Auer in prewar Petersburg. The other was Harry Kaufman, a very fine pianist who had been appointed head of the accompanying department at the Curtis Institute of Music. His wife, Lillian, who had a mind and a tongue of her own — one she used frequently on her "lesser half" — had elected to remain in Paris, preferring to spend her husband's money in the dress shops. But she too soon joined us as the result of a tragicomic incident, which threw us all into a momentary panic.

As Saint-Jean-de-Luz was conveniently close to the Spanish border, Josef Hofmann invited Mother, Toscha Seidel, and Harry Kaufman to accompany him to San Sebastián to see the Sunday afternoon bullfights. On the way back, the bus in which they were traveling along the sinuous Pyrenean coast was involved in a collision with another vehicle. Mother and the others suffered bruises and cuts from bits of flying glass, but the injuries were minor. In Paris Mrs. Kaufman was informed by telegram that her husband had been involved in a road accident. Imagining the worst, she boarded the train and spent a sleepless night computing what to do with the life insurance money she would receive as a result of her husband's death. Having a wonderful sense of humor, she told us all this after reaching Saint-Jean-de-Luz, where she was jarred back to reality by the sight of her husband, who had strips of adhesive on his hands and forehead but who otherwise was in one hale and hearty piece.

More readily accessible than the San Sebastián corridas were the games of *pelote basque* (or jai alai) which we often went to watch at a nearby *frontón.* The chief attraction was a powerfully built Basque called Chiquito de Cambo, so named because he was on the shortish side and hailed from the town of Cambo, in the rising uplands of the Pyrenees. He was as lithe and agile as a monkey as he bounded around the court in his white trousers and espadrilles with his two teammates, scooping up the ball in his curved wicker basket and hurling it back against the whitewashed wall. Yet invariably toward the middle of the game his strength would sag and the opposing threesome would add point after point. Sometimes the lead would reach seven full points, standing at a perilous 16 to 9, and moving on from there to a no less dangerous 17 to 11. At 17 to 12 there would be cheers, and at 18 to 12 groans and exclamations of dismay from the bystanders. *"Mais c'est inimaginable, le Chiquito va perdre! On a jamais vu ça!"* But the unthinkable catastrophe would somehow be averted, and suddenly, as though galvanized by the onrushing disaster, the Chiquito and his teammates would spring furiously to life, retrieving the most impossible shots and hurling back the ball with an unerring aim and speed which left their flatfooted opponents breathlessly outpaced. The score would soon be equaled, and a minute or two later the onlookers, worked up to a fever pitch of anxiety, could relax and shout their heads off in delight at the realization that the world's most invincible *pelote* player had just come from behind to win another hairbreadth victory.

The local casino, of course, continued to exercise its fateful magnetism on Mother, who was readier than ever to succumb to its hypnotic spell now that her financial future was assured by her Curtis Institute job. Nor, as it happened, was she the only loser among us. One evening I accompanied her, Toscha Seidel, Harry Kaufman, Mischa Elman and his wife and sisters to the Biarritz casino, some fifteen kilometers up the coast. The purpose of this trip was not to gamble but to listen to a Polish pianist named Artur Rubinstein give a Chopin recital. I had heard him perform during my year in Paris and had been much impressed by his playing. But to the other members of the party he was quite unknown. "Oh, you must hear him!" I kept repeating. "He's terrific!"

I don't remember what other compliments I paid him, but I must have laid it on pretty thick, for I managed to persuade everyone that he was a pianist worth listening to. Nor can I recall exactly what Rubinstein played when we finally took our seats in the casino's auditorium. But it was a dismal performance. I could hardly believe my ears. This was not the superior artist I had heard in Paris, but some kind of flustered musician whose fingers kept tripping over each other as he slipped and slobbered his way through Preludes and Polonaises.

I later discovered the reason. Rubinstein, like Mother, had caught the local "bug" — to such an extent that he kept rushing back to the gambling rooms between each group and during each inordinately long intermission. But the explanation came too late to save me from the avalanche of reproaches which descended on me as we were returning home that night. "So that's the *brilliant* pianist you wanted us to hear! The greatest thing to come out of Poland since Paderewski, eh? . . . Now what kind of idiots do you take us for anyway?"

That night, as the French say, I was in my smallest shoes. I really felt like a fool. It was years before I dared breathe the name of Artur Rubinstein again.

On returning to Budapest, in the autumn of this same year, I was one of four privileged students to be admitted to Dohnányi's piano master class in the Franz Liszt Academy of Music. Dohnányi had just been named co-director of the academy to take some of the administrative burden off the shoulders of the ailing composer-violinist Jenö Hubay, who had just turned seventy.

Many years later, when I was a member of a question-answering panel in the United States, I received an urgent telephone call from one of the quiz master's assistants, asking me if by any chance I could tell her who had written the opera *Anna Karenina*. She had been unable to find the composer's name in any reference book and had drawn a blank with all the experts she had questioned on the subject. Yet such an opera apparently existed. "*Anna Karenina?*" I answered, as though this were something every teen-aged child should know. "Now what's so mysterious about that? Of course it exists. It was composed by a violinist named Jenö — or Eugene, if you prefer — Hubay." I spelled the name out for her, then added: "He was a great violin teacher, being for Hungary and the Hungarians roughly what Leopold Auer was for Russia and the Russians before the Revolution."

This answer helped to establish my reputation as a musicologist of encyclopedic scope, a reputation due to the accidental fact that I had spent some years in Budapest. No one outside of Hungary need feel particularly ashamed for not knowing that Hubay composed an opera called *Anna Karenina,* for Hubay was unquestionably a better violin teacher than a composer.

Almost twenty years younger than Hubay, Dohnányi had been offered the directorship of the Franz Liszt Academy at the end of the First World War, when he was barely forty. Characteristically, he had turned the offer down, having no taste for administrative work and no need of an official post or title to bolster his soaring prestige as Hungary's foremost musician. His first major composition — a Piano Quintet in C Minor, which he wrote when he was only seventeen — was praised by Brahms, who exclaimed after hearing the performance: "I couldn't have done better myself." Since then, between love affairs and concert tours which won him international acclaim, Dohnányi had managed to compose a number of major works. In 1927 he was appointed permanent director of the Budapest Philharmonic Orchestra, and by the time I came to know him, he was the uncontested as well as uncrowned king of Hungarian music. Budapest had seen nothing like it since the declining years of Franz Liszt, and if the present is any criterion for estimating the future, it will not see the like of him again.

I feel the need to say this because Ernö Dohnányi is not particularly well known in the United States today. His fame as a piano player has sunk into oblivion, while his renown as a composer has been overshadowed by the achievements of his slightly younger contemporaries Béla Bartók and Zoltán Kodály. When I was in Budapest, both were considered to be rabid "modernists" and much appreciated as impassioned collectors of Hungarian folk music. Though they respected Dohnányi as a musician — Bartók had even taken piano lessons from him for a while — both men and even more their followers, tended to look down on Dohnányi's post-Romantic, post-Brahmsian style of composing as much too "sentimental" and old-fashioned for their avant garde tastes. Dohnányi might be the Tsar of Hungarian music, but he represented the ancien régime, which the young rebels wanted to replace with something newer and better. Dohnányi, for his part, felt little sympathy for the harsh dissonances and orchestral complications which Bartók and Kodály boldly indulged in. He was even ready to disparage their passion for Hungarian folk music, seeing in it a deliberate return to primitivism. "Primitivism stands at the beginning of a culture, and to return to it after a culture has developed is to display the impotence and senility of 'second youth.' "

At the time I was not much concerned by these musical fads and feuds, any more than was Dohnányi, who was not a person to lose sleep over the comments of rivals or the condemnations of detractors. Indeed, with a self-assurance which some found much too patronizing, he purposely threw away all laudatory articles, keeping only unflattering reviews, which were retained more for the sake of amusement and as a commentary on the authors than for their relevance to his playing or conducting. Nor did his feelings about Bartók amount to anything like a tàboo, for when I once brought a set of mildly modernistic Bartók dances to one of our regular piano lessons, he willingly played them for me. But he also made it clear that this was not really his "cup of tea."

As a protégé of Dohnányi's, I was virtually treated as a member of the family and allowed to attend the Budapest Philharmonic Orchestra's Sunday afternoon performances, held in the main auditorium of the Franz Liszt Academy, where Madame Dohnányi and her sons and relatives had a row of reserved seats at their disposal. I could also, as a well-heeled "American" with money to burn, have spent many evenings at the opera. But as I had little taste for it, much preferring the less-stilted vitality of the theater stage, I limited my visits to a few Wagnerian operas.

Here too I learned a lesson from Dohnányi I have never forgotten. I had gone to a performance of *Tristan und Isolde,* which I had never seen before, and though enormously impressed and overwhelmed by the grandeur and richness of the music, my powers of concentration began to wilt during the long last act. At our next lesson I told Dohnányi that I had seen *Tristan* performed at the Royal Opera House, that the first two acts had seemed to me marvelous but that the third had struck me as much inferior, too long, and even boring in its interminable repetitions. Dohnányi did not look painted or outraged by this observation; on the contrary, he seemed to appreciate its frankness. "Now you must promise that you will do something for me," he said, as though he were asking a favor of me rather than issuing a gentle reprimand. "You have a pass to the Opera House?" I nodded. "Well, the next time they perform *Tristan,* find out when the final act begins. Don't go to hear the first two acts, but go in for the last act only. Then tell me if you still feel the same way."

I followed this sage advice and was greatly surprised by the result. The third act of *Tristan,* unpreceded by the two others, now seemed like a revelation. I realized then that there is a limit to what a music lover can reasonably absorb in one evening. Four hours of music are tiring even for those who are the best disposed or the most intent in listening. There is a lot more to be said about the peculiarly hypnotic effect of Wagner's music later on, but the truth that Dohnányi had helped me to discover applies in general to all music, just as it does to all long operas. Even today I rarely sit through an entire opera. I prefer to see and hear one act at a time. In this way I can give it the maximum of intelligent attention and derive the greatest satisfaction from the performance. Long operas — let us be honest about it — are very difficult to take. One gets tired as the performance proceeds, no matter how wonderfully the singers may sing or the orchestra may play. This is only human. It is not something one need be ashamed of, but it is something all opera conductors and producers should remember. For I am convinced, on the basis of long experience, that most people feel that way.

The reason I had a pass granting me free admission to the Royal Opera House was simple. The year after I entered the Franz Liszt Academy in the autumn of 1928, Dohnányi recommended that I take lessons in conducting. He did not want me to become a narrow specialist; he was more interested in having me develop into an all-round musician, like himself. All students in the conducting class were given a pass to the Royal Opera House. This entitled them to a free seat in one of the two "cuckoo boxes" that were located on the topmost balcony overlooking the orchestra pit. The one on the left, looking at the stage, was reserved for male vocalists and fledgling conductors like myself; the one on the right was reserved for female singers.

On the whole, I made little use of my Opera House pass, since I had little taste for opera, and even less appetite for operas which, from the lofty perch of our allotted cuckoo box, we could hear sung but not see played, as the operatic stars and choruses came into view only when they were standing or moving about on the opposite side of the stage. I thus missed a "scandal" which took place during a performance of Hubay's *The Violin-Maker of Cremona* and created quite an uproar. One of the Liszt Academy's girl singers, seated in the fifth-tier cuckoo box, was leaning out over the velvet balustrade while she sucked a piece of hard candy. In the middle of a pianissimo passage, it accidentally fell out of her mouth and landed on a kettledrum, setting off a mighty "Boom!" which exploded like a thunderclap over the soft piping and fiddling. Hubay was incensed. That one of the academy's vocalists should be disrespectful enough to suck candy through one of his operas was bad enough, but that she should add carelessness to disrespect was unforgivable. And so for more than a week apprentice conductors and student-singers were, on orders from Hubay, denied access to their cuckoo-boxes.

I also missed another and far more serious operatic scandal, which occurred during the last winter of my stay in Budapest. By the late 1920s the recording of human voices, which had actually begun around 1904, was already a big and profitable business.

While Bartók and Kodály spent a lot of time roaming through the provinces and recording local folk tunes, many other Hungarians had begun collecting records of famous opera stars. One of these was Amelita Galli-Curci, whose recordings enjoyed an immense vogue among Hungarians who had never seen her on the stage. When, in the course of a European tour, it was announced that she was coming to sing the roles of Violetta, Gilda, and Rosina in Budapest, the local opera lovers went wild. Here was the chance of a lifetime for the thousands, indeed for the tens of thousands of Hungarians who had been unable to cross the Atlantic to hear her sing at the Metropolitan Opera House in New York. The box offices and theater agencies were literally stormed, and within forty-eight hours there was not a seat to be had for either *La Traviata, Rigoletto,* or *The Barber of Seville*.

I did not attend the great diva's opening night, which turned out to be her first and last performance in Budapest. The shortage of tickets by this time was so great that many of these first-nighters had arranged to go in for just one act, turning over their tickets to friends or relatives during the first or second intermissions so that others could partake of this rare musical treat. Their expectations, however, received a rude jolt when the curtain lifted on *La Traviata* and Galli-Curci came out on stage. She was no longer the singer she had been a year or two before. Her voice began wobbling and she could not sustain the highest notes. Even her most fanatical admirers were appalled by the glaring disparity between the unsteady, real-life voice and the strong, pure, full-throated sounds that had gushed forth from her recordings. The operatic star they had paid sky-high prices to admire had quite simply lost her voice. There were howls of indignation from irate connoisseurs, and the resultant clamor was so great that the rest of Galli-Curci's scheduled performances had to be canceled on the spot.

The whole wretched business was most embarrassing, not least of all for me. Though I had not gone to listen to her, it had been assumed that as an "American" I knew all that was worth knowing about Galli-Curci. I should have warned my friends that she had lost her voice! Instead I had said nothing and let them pay exorbitant sums of money for the privilege of listening to a fading star.

Quite different from this musical fiasco was the première of Dohnányi's opera *The Tenor,* which he completed in 1929. Some fifteen years earlier, when he was living and teaching in Berlin, Dohnányi had amused himself by composing a deliberately comic work for piano and orchestra entitled *Variations on a Nursery Song,* in which different instruments were given the most unexpected passages to play — to the vast delight of the musicians of the academy, who enjoyed this game as much as stuffier members of the audience resented it. *The Tenor* was composed in the same humorous vein. It was the story of an amateur vocal quartet suddenly reduced to a trio through the death of one of its members. To replace the deceased first tenor, a competition is staged. The winner, however, belongs to a lower class of society, and this creates a whole series of embarrassing as well as amusing situations. I personally found it a most entertaining opera, which deserved the success it enjoyed not only in Budapest but in Austria and Germany, where it was subsequently performed. The subject, with its subtle social nuances, was, however, too quintessentially Hungarian, or at any rate Central European, to gain worldwide appeal, and this expains why it has never, as far as I know, been professionally performed in the United States.

Ernö Dohnányi may not have been one of the greatest composers of this century, but as a pianist and teacher he was — at least as far as I am concerned — incomparable. Whereas Artur Schnabel could achieve his results only through intense analysis, Dohnányi seemed to soar effortlessly. His piano playing was magical — I cannot find another word for it — yet he himself almost never practiced. He even believed that too much preparation could do as much harm as good, and, as he once advised his fellow pianist Josef Lhevinne, who had always suffered agonies of stage fright: "On concert days, Joseph, cut out the practicing altogether. Eat a good meal before the concert, and then forget the audience completely."

Because he never practiced, Dohnányi occasionally misplayed difficult passages. But in slow movements, where there were no technical problems to overcome, his playing was subtle and most moving. Try as I might, I could never figure out just how he achieved the effects he did. In Berlin I had found Schnabel fairly easy to imitate. I could listen to what he was doing and then proceed to copy him. But with Dohnányi I found myself baffled by the ineffable charm, by the infinite grace of his phrasing. It was simply uncanny.

Once, I recall, I brought Schumann's A Minor Concerto to one of my lessons. In this work, after a few opening measures played by the orchestra, the piano launches into a long and most beautiful passage.

"*Meister,*" I said, "would you mind playing this opening theme for me?"

"But of course," he answered.

Under Dohnányi's magic touch, Schumann's music took wing, like a skylark. Crouched over the keyboard, I watched his fingers to see if I could catch the secret of his exquisite phrasing. But somehow the principle governing these subtle pianistic inflections escaped me, even though I had him repeat this passage three times. There was an impalpable quality about his playing — like the soft scent of a flower one can inhale, but which eludes one's grasp.

This gift was obviously innate. Music, in the most literal sense, was Dohnányi's native tongue. Indeed, the impression he made on me was at once kindly, mysterious, and remote, as though he were not made of flesh and bones. He was music incarnate, and precisely because of this he could be relaxed about it. Virtuosity per se did not interest him. It was a form of exhibitionism which he deplored as unworthy of the genuine artist. This is not to say that he advocated carelessness in performance. He demanded clean passage work from his students, but excessive concentration on neatness was eyed with suspicion. It was all right for American audiences who admired surface polish, but truly gifted musicians were or should be interested in other facets of performance, more basic but also more elusive and difficult to explain. Hidden as these musical matters were, they became elementary, not to say self-evident, when he played for us, demonstrating a Brahms intermezzo or the slow movement of a Beethoven sonata.

On such occasions his playing was breathtaking in its obvious "rightness" and simplicity, yet impossible to imitate. Each of his fingers seemed to know, by some kind of preestablished harmony, exactly how hard or softly each note should be played. The music did not sound as though it were being read from a score. It didn't even sound like a composition. It sounded like something Dohnányi was inventing on the spot, that he was improvising before one's eyes. There was nothing calculated about his playing. It was a gift of grace, bestowed on a human being who did not have to make the slightest effort to attain perfection.

In addition to my friend Edward Kilényi, the piano master class consisted of a gifted German-Hungarian named Ludwig Heimlich and a tall and gangling fellow named George Ferenczy, who for some obscure reason always referred to himself as "the great white angel." He was not a particularly talented performer, and it was rumored that Dohnányi agreed to accept him into the master class only because Ferenczy desperately needed a music degree. To compensate for his pianistic deficiencies the great white angel had a remarkable flair for card playing. His virtuosity at the contract bridge table was uncanny and his ability to predict the distribution of cards in the hands of his opponents never ceased to astonish me. Every Wednesday afternoon the four of us would climb on the streetcar and ride out to the suburbs of Buda to reach Dohnányi's hillside house on the Szeher Ut. As privileged members of the academy's piano master class, we could also, if we wished, turn up on Sunday afternoons, when the Dohnányis held a kind of "open house" reception for their friends.

When I think back on the many instructive hours I spent in his living room with the two fine Bösendorfer pianos, one incident in particular stands out in my mind as characteristic of his quiet but effective manner of teaching. Among the many Beethoven compositions he had me study was the *Hammerklavier* Sonata. The third, slow movement of this work is a magnificent piece of music but it happens to be unusually long. When the time came for me to play it in Dohnányi's presence, he listened patiently without interrupting. Dohnányi rarely stopped us, even when we made silly errors or suffered lapses of memory. He would merely sit back, quietly smoking a cigarette; often a faint air of amusement would come over his face, as much as to say: "Ah, now let's see how he's going to get out of this mess." But Dohnányi's comments were all the more precious for being so rare.

After letting me finish the third section of the sonata, he said: "Tell me, do you think this is the right tempo at which to play this movement?"

"Well, I realize it should go quite a bit slower, but this is a terribly long piece. Do you know how long this movement lasts if one treats it as a true adagio sostenuto, the way it is marked?"

"No," he said. "Do *you?*"

"Yes, I have timed it," I proudly replied. "It takes sixteen and a half minutes."

"And how long does it take when played your way?"

"Just about fifteen minutes," I answered, as though this were a real accomplishment.

"Tell me," he said quietly, "do you think it is better to play a piece wrongly for fifteen minutes than to play it right for sixteen and a half minutes?"

That single sentence has remained engraved in my memory. Dohnányi, in uttering these few simple words cured me forever of the itch to "improve" musical compositions by simply stepping on the gas; and his ability to express a basic musical truth in such plain terms has remained a guiding light for me in dealing with my own students.

There was another important respect in which his mode of teaching differed sharply from Schnabel's. Whereas Schnabel expected me to polish up each piece to a point of absolute perfection, Dohnányi never gave me time to polish up anything. Hardly had I begun to master one Beethoven sonata than he would shift me to another.

One day I complained about this method of instruction. *"Meister,"* I said, "I'm troubled and also a bit confused. I often find myself at parties where I am asked to play. Since I'm one of your pupils, they expect something special, and I'm most embarrassed because I have nothing that I've had time to refine and polish."

"Oh, but that's no problem," said Dohnányi. "We don't have to study the pieces you may want to play for your friends. Just review a few things you have studied before, and keep them ready for such occasions."

I thanked him for the suggestion but said that I was still puzzled by the pace at which we were going through these Beethoven sonatas. "You give me little more than one week to go through an entire Beethoven sonata. Once you've listened to it, you seldom have me bring it back for the next lesson. As a result I never have time to perfect any of them."

"Let me be honest with you," he replied. "You are very musical and I am pleased with the progress you are making. But let's face it — you are not mature enough to master all the problems to be found in Beethoven. No matter how hard you practiced, you wouldn't be able to play these great compositions in any truly adequate fashion. But in the meantime you are learning them.

And what is more important, you are gradually steeping yourself in Beethoven's style. Maybe what I am saying to you now is a bit disappointing, but believe me, one day you will be grateful. For when you have played all thirty-two sonatas, you will have a better idea of what Beethoven is all about."

Ernö Dohnányi felt no need to exploit his students' talents for purposes of self-aggrandizement. He wanted them to develop as all-round musicians and artists so that what they had learned when young would pay dividends in adult life.

Later, when I came back to the sonatas I had studied with Dohnányi in Budapest, I found that I could "perfect" them very quickly. Thanks to his teaching I had acquired a far better understanding of Beethoven, not only of his sonatas but of his symphonies and string quartets as well. I had built a solid foundation, which is all that a young boy of twenty can hope to achieve, but without which he can be musically handicapped or even crippled forever.

During my last two years in Hungary I made the acquaintance of a German-Hungarian family named Donner, who lived in a large town house on the Pest side of the Danube. Donner Ur — or Herr Donner, as the Germans would have called him — was a well-to-do business consultant and broker, while his wife, notwithstanding her short, plump figure, was a finely dressed lady and a most imposing hostess. The older of their two daughters — Gertrude, or Trudi, as she was more generally known — was married to a gentleman named Kovács, and they occupied one wing of this lovely mansion, which was built around an inner patio or cortile. The younger, unmarried daughter was named Marianne and must have been around nineteen years old — about a year younger than I — when we were first introduced to each other. She had large, almost doll-like greenish brown eyes, auburn hair, and was — at least for me — something of a beauty.

It was at the Donners' house, one day in 1929 or possibly 1930, that I heard a radio broadcast for the very first time. My hosts, being relatively wealthy, had bought a small receiving set which functioned with the aid of crystals and to which one could listen through earphones. We each took turns listening to what was being broadcast — a violin concerto being played by someone in Vienna — and though there was more static to be heard than music, we all considered it something of a miracle.

Having acquired the aura of a salon entertainer who could enliven evenings with mathematical puzzles, amusing anecdotes, and exuberant keyboard demonstrations, I was welcomed into the Donner household as a friend and soon became a regular visitor. There was a fine grand piano in their spacious drawing room which I enjoyed playing as much as my kind hosts seemed to enjoy listening to me. Although one of the daughters sang — in a rather amateurish fashion — neither of them played the piano, which made my performances particularly appreciated.

Here, as in so many Budapest households, German and Hungarian were spoken interchangeably. But the two daughters, who had been offered a better-than-average education, also spoke French and English, which in those days in Budapest was rare. This made for an unusually cosmopolitan and congenial atmosphere for a polyglot like myself who, not content with Hungarian, was now trying to learn English. Marianne, as it happened, loved the language and in particular its Romantic poets, including Burns, Byron, and Swinburne.

It was not long before I realized that I was in love with Marianne and she with me. We went to concerts together, we took long walks through Pest and even longer strolls over the wooded hills of Buda. As the months passed and the winter snows gave way to crocuses, primroses, fragrant hyacinths, and the vernal exuberance of May and June, we went to play tennis on Saint Margaret's Island, in the middle of the Danube, and we plunged into the cold river water from its beaches or splashed around in the luxuriously heated swimming pool on the terrace of the Gellert Hotel. Often, in the evening after dinner, when her parents and Trudi and her husband had retired for the night, Marianne and I would linger in the drawing room to hold hands and exchange furtive kisses.

The hot Hungarian summer inevitably stoked the fires of an obsessive, all-consuming passion. Mother, in this year of 1929, had decided to go to California with Babushka, Irene, and several of her Curtis Institute pupils, while I remained in Budapest. Though I continued my piano practicing, I was under less academic pressure during these holiday months and consequently freer to see Marianne. Our disappearances into the hillside woods of Buda grew more frequent and prolonged, until Marianne's parents began to be alarmed. What had started out as an innocent flirtation was assuming the sultry aspect of a *grande passion*. She was asked to see me less frequently and to pay more attention to other suitors who, being older and better established financially, were more reliable prospects as potential spouses. For Herr Donner, who was no fool, knew perfectly well that my relative wealth as an "American" was a purely transient phenomenon and that but for the stipend I received from the generous Sidney Prince I would have been a pauper.

But Marianne by now had eyes only for me. The more her parents insisted, remonstrated, and reproved, the more stubbornly, heatedly, passionately she became attached. The obstacles placed between us merely fanned the flames of our mutual passion. Like all persons desperately in love, we resorted to the usual subterfuges, arranging furtive rendevous and "accidental" meetings, which were too frequent to disarm parental suspicions. Yet our trysts, notwithstanding the ecstasy of shared embraces, remained platonic, as we both struggled to contain our longing within respectable bounds.

Like all repressed lovers, we were wracked by feelings of guilt and plunged into abysses of despair. We suffered torments at the thought of not being able to see each other for one or two days, and we were tortured by the nagging realization that one day — when the time came for me to leave Budapest — we would be parted. There was even a particularly anguished period, lasting several weeks, during which Marianne was forbidden by her parents from seeing me at all. We fumed and fretted vainly, cursing the iron-hearted conventions that kept us cruelly separated, and were miserably unhappy. Then one evening, at a concert, we glimpsed each other from a distance and our hearts began beating wildly. Marianne's parents must have been struck by her distressed condition, for they finally relented to the point of allowing us to meet once a week.

If music be the food of love, it is also a welcome balm for the emotionally frustrated. With the resumption of the academic year in the autumn of 1929 I found myself more immersed in music than ever. I continued to receive piano tutoring from Dohnányi and composition lessons from Leo Weiner. I did not continue my studies in chamber music given by Imre Waldbauer, feeling that the other students were woefuly inferior to the level which I, obviously a pampered adolescent, had grown accustomed to at Saint-Jean-de-Luz, in the summer of 1928, thanks to the combined talents of my mother and Eddie Bachman.

I experienced something of the same dissatisfaction in the orchestral conducting class, for which I had signed up in the fall of 1929, at Dohnányi's suggestion. Learning how to conduct is probably, of all musical activities, the most inherently frustrating, for the simple reason that the student cannot be given a full-scale orchestra with which to practice. Professional orchestras are prohibitively expensive to hire and student orchestras are anything but eager to serve as guinea pigs for inexperienced beginners. Student conductors are thus obliged to master the basic rudiments of the art — how to decipher an orchestral score, how to hold the baton, beat time in varying metric patterns, start and stop the players, and give cues to different instruments — in a kind of artistic vacuum, by conducting an imaginary orchestra or having a colleague play the score on a piano as a monochrome substitute for the real thing.

There were several other pianists in the conducting class at the

Franz Liszt Academy, but none of them could sight-read orchestral scores anywhere near as well as I could — thanks to the fine training I had received in this field from the ebullient Leo Weiner. I was thus repeatedly called upon to impersonate the orchestra for the benefit of my grateful fellow students.

I cannot recall the name of the person who presided over our conducting class. He was a relatively young, colorless individual who did, however, have one remarkable gift. He could whistle the most involved flute or violin passages with startling accuracy. There were thus usually two of us to simulate an entire symphonic ensemble.

The long-awaited chance of leading a real-life orchestra finally loomed toward the end of the year, when we were scheduled to conduct a concert with the Liszt Academy's ensemble of instrumentalists. I found the prospect exhilarating, for by this time I had caught the conductor's "bug" and was thrilled by the idea of being able to lift my hand and elicit gusts of gorgeous sound through the waving of a magic wand. It made one feel like a celestial sculptor, carving melodies from cerulean depths of silence, like Jupiter releasing his thunderbolts from the heights or Neptune stilling the agitated waters his unleashed winds had aroused. In particular the idea of being able to conduct Liszt's *Faust* Symphony, which I had studied with Leo Weiner, struck me as being the greatest boon that could be granted to a human being, and I would gladly have signed away five years of my life in a pact with Mephistopheles if that Prince of Darkness could have made it possible for me to conduct a first-rate orchestra, like the Budapest Philharmonic, through five preparatory rehearsals and one public performance.

My soaring daydreams were rudely brought to earth when I discovered the nature of the piece that had been chosen for me. Whereas the other students of the class had been assigned separate movements from Haydn and Mozart symphonies, I was to prepare Mendelssohn's *Infelice,* a concert aria for soprano and orchestra.

I felt slighted, the victim of a base discrimination. Why should I have been singled out for this humiliating role, virtually that of an accompanist for a singer who would be the natural center of attraction, the focus of listening ears and watching eyes? Our teacher immediately set me right: I should feel honored rather than upset by this assignment. A concert aria, and particularly one in which there were recitatives and several contrasting sections with tricky changes of pace and varying meters, was much more difficult to conduct than a classical symphony movement. Not only would I have to coordinate the vocal part and the orchestral accompaniment, I would also have to train the singer.

This explanation, made to me in the presence of my fellow students, reconciled me to the assignment. I was not one to run away from difficulties, if such they really were. So I went to work studying the score until I knew virtually every line by heart. I was ready to recite any instrumental part verbatim to any student rash enough to challenge my knowledge of the score, and soon I was walking the streets and avenues of Budapest, throwing cues to the invisible soloist and urging different players in the imaginary orchestra to correct their intolerable mistakes.

The soloist did not remain invisible for long. The soprano chosen for the part bore the euphonious Magyar-Slavic name of Ilonka Horvatovich. She was a good-natured girl, robust and extensive in circumference with a correspondingly robust and extensive voice. She was not particularly musical, but I refused to be discouraged. After all, it was up to me to train her, and train her I did — every syllable and note, every pause and every breath. We got along well. She had a deep, almost cringing respect for anyone who could play a score on the piano. As far as she was concerned, I was a *maestro,* an oracle whose most trivial remarks were to be treated as inspired revelations.

Everything seemed to be going beautifully when suddenly, in mid-April, a bare month before our one and only full orchestra rehearsal, the young girl came to me to say that I would have to find someone else to sing the *Infelice*. It was not her fault, she had not intended it that way, but the Academy's Opera School, to which she belonged, was leaving in early May for a two-week tour of the Hungarian provinces with a production of Weber's *Der Freischütz*. She had been chosen to sing the leading role of Agathe.

I was stunned by the news. The Opera School troupe was due to return to Budapest on a Tuesday afternoon, one day after the full rehearsal with singer and orchestra that had been scheduled for that Monday, and one day before the final examination-concert, which we were to give in the main hall of the Academy, where Dohnányi conducted the weekly concerts of the Budapest Philharmonic Orchestra. To start all over from scratch at this late date and to train another soprano struck me as an impossible task, and I very much doubted that I could find another student soloist who could do justice to the part, since the best available voices had now been recruited for the Weber opera.

"Look," I finally said to her, "this is what we'll do. There's not time enough now for me to find somebody to replace you. But since you know the *Infelice* inside out, there won't be any problem. I'll take the orchestra through the dress rehearsal on Monday without you, and I'll have them play the score exactly as I've played it to you on the piano. Wednesday morning, after you're back, we'll have an hour's practice session to refresh your memory, and in the afternoon everything will go perfectly."

The young lady did not take easily to this proposal. She didn't like the idea of having to sing in public at an important Budapest concert without attending a single orchestra rehearsal and after two weeks of absence from her maestro. But I finally managed to overcome her misgivings by promising to give her a daily coaching lesson right up to the day of her departure for the provinces.

The orchestral rehearsal, held a few weeks later, went without a problem. Under the watchful eye of our teacher, the student instrumentalists played surprisingly well. I substituted for the absent prima donna in the recitatives, while the instructor whistled her part in the cantilenas and exciting allegro sections, when I had to focus all of my attention on the subtleties of the orchestral score. The rehearsal finished, everyone felt satisfied and relieved. We need have no worries about the Wednesday afternoon performance.

Wednesday morning, however, I got a most unpleasant shock. The telephone rang and over the wire came the familiar soprano voice of Ilonka Horvatovich, mournfully informing me that she had returned very late on Tuesday night and was in no condition to sing in the afternoon concert. I told her she couldn't let me down like this. We had had a very successful dress rehearsal without her, and all we needed was her presence for a definitive performance in public. No, she kept repeating, she just couldn't do it, she couldn't bear the thought of singing badly in public.

Finally, after a lot of desperate pleading on my part, she agreed to meet me at the academy building in the early afternoon. But not to sing, she said, just to explain her condition. I spent the rest of the morning wondering what on earth had happened. I had heard cases of singers suddenly losing their voices and being unable to sing a note, but her voice over the telephone, though tearful and unhappy, did not sound hoarse or faint in any way.

Shortly after lunch she turned up at the academy, looking more robust than ever. Her tour of the provinces even seemed to have added color to her cheeks. Oh no, she assured me, she was not feeling unwell. That wasn't the trouble at all. The reason she couldn't sing Mendelssohn's concert aria was simply that she had forgotten it. For the past two weeks she had been singing Agathe and the music had taken over so completely that she could no longer recall anything of the *Infelice*.

This was more than my patience could endure. The thought that I would have to forgo my long-awaited opportunity to conduct the academy's student orchestra because of this featherbrained, forgetful, fat half-wit of a soprano filled me with fury.

"No," I screamed at her. "It is not possible! You have *not* forgotten it! You *could not* have forgotten it after all the rehearsing we did together! Sing it to me! Sing it this very instant — or else I am not responsible for what may happen! You don't know us Russians! When provoked beyond reason we are ready to kill!"

My outburst had an immediate, surprising effect on the poor girl. She stood before me, trembling, pale, too frightened to move. Her eyes seemed to be beseeching mercy, as though I really were a mad, homicidal Russian capable of strangling her in a fit of uncontrollable rage.

Realizing that her life might still be spared, she agreed to go through the *Infelice* with me. It was quickly apparent that she had not been exaggerating; she had forgotten the aria rather thoroughly. Fortunately, there was still an hour to go before the concert began in the main auditorium. We could also count on another hour of grace while my colleagues conducted their assignments from the Haydn and Mozart symphonies. Thank heaven we were last on the program.

Bit by bit I managed to clear the cobwebs from the soloist's head. After going through the aria five or six times, she began to remember the words and musical phrases with increasing facility. What she had forgotten, it became apparent, was not so much *what* she should sing as *when* she should sing it. The aria's orchestral interludes had disappeared into the remoter reaches of her brain, and there seemed no quick way of retrieving them from the impenetrable fog in which they were now enveloped. She would attack her phrases entire measures ahead of time or, just as disastrously, wait for several beats after the proper entrance cue. The minute hand on the clock was meanwhile advancing inexorably.

"Listen!" I finally said to her. "Listen carefully! You do exactly as I tell you and no harm will come to you." It sounded like a sentence out of a third-rate mystery novel, but there was no time for verbal subtleties and this seemed to be the language most likely to get results. "When we are on the stage, watch me every second of the time. Stare at me! Don't take your eyes off me! As long as I shake my head from right to left and left to right and back again, you have nothing to worry about. Just stand there and keep quiet! When I stop shaking my head, that means take a breath and watch for my cue. I will give it to you every single time."

I felt like Svengali. I may even have looked like him, for I noticed that the soprano's eyes were now shining with excitement. She was involved in some kind of strange adventure, which was already sending romantic shivers up and down her spine. She was both frightened and elated, and her voice had never sounded better.

Finally the moment came for us to walk out onto the stage. Before launching into the *Infelice,* I wanted to give my soloist a reassuring smile, just to cheer her up, but I caught myself just in time. A smile at this critical moment might break the demonic spell. Instead, I scowled, while she gazed at me with bright-eyed intensity, as though afraid to blink her eyes. I looked at her and began slowly shaking my head. She nodded at me — we were in complete rapport — and with that I waved the orchestra into action.

It was an eerie performance, but it worked. The student ensemble played well and Ilonka Horvatovich's singing earned long and merited applause.

Later, backstage, I saw Dohnányi talking to the teacher of our conducting class. Both seemed pleased with the way things had gone. I couldn't wait to hear my mentor's opinion about my performance.

"Meister," I inquired, almost breathlessly, "how did it go? Was it all right?"

"My boy," he replied, "I must compliment you. You have a real gift for conducting. For someone who has never conducted before, you did remarkably well. There's just one thing," he added in a lower voice, drawing me gently off to one side. "You have a strange habit — it's most peculiar. I don't think I've ever seen this mannerism before, and you may not even be aware of it — but you must get rid of it as soon as possible."

4

Josef Hofmann and the Curtis Institute of Music

A DAY OR TWO after our final examinations — which had included a concerto played with the student orchestra conducted by Dohnányi, a solo recital, and nerve-racking inquisitions before a jury composed of all the members of the academy's piano faculty — the three other students of the piano master class and I were invited to Dohnányi's suburban house for a final word of instruction. We reached his home on the Szeher Ut much puzzled by this unexpected summons and wondering what kind of parting message lay in store for us. We were even more surprised to be ushered into our illustrious mentor's bedroom rather than downstairs to the salon, with the juxtaposed Bösendorfer pianos. Dohnányi was waiting for us with a more than usually dimpled smile on his face.

"My dear young friends," he said, "during the last two years we have had many discussions concerning musical and pianistic matters, but now I want to show you something that may prove even more valuable in your careers as concert artists." Pulling a black cutaway and trousers from his closet, he spread them out on the bed and then showed us how to fold them into a suitcase in such a way that they could be removed after a lengthy train trip without looking so hideously creased that they had to be sent to the cleaners to be pressed. This was Dohnányi's very special manner of indicating that we had now made the grade and could sally forth into the world, armed with impressive-looking diplomas from the Franz Liszt Academy of Music. And as I look back on this late spring of 1930, I think I can honestly say that this final clothes-folding lecture has proved more valuable to me in my subsequent travels than the elegant Hungarian scroll we were given at the graduation ceremonies.

It was as a budding pianist and not as an incipient orchestra conductor that I finally graduated from the academy in early June. I had taken the trouble to polish up a number of compositions I had studied with Dohnányi. They included several Beethoven sonatas, Busoni transcriptions of Bach's Organ Choral Preludes, various pieces by Liszt, Bartók, and Dohnányi, and my pièce de résistance — Schumann's Fantasia in C Major. My performance was considered good enough to warrant a brief concert tour to the provinces, which took me to Szeged and Debreczen.

My playing of Beethoven's *Hammerklavier* Sonata at the graduation recital in Budapest aroused much interest and comment, and I cannot resist quoting at length from one particular review, written after the event by some Magyar super-patriot:

> Yet another first-class pianist from Dohnányi's Master School! Named Boris Goldovsky, he came to us from Russia, learned to speak Hungarian and to "play Hungarian," that is, to play the piano in a way in which a young musician today can only learn to play here, in Dohnányi's realm. To sit down before the keyboard without any outward pose, without any prior "stylistic attitude," to give oneself up unreservedly to the essence of the work, to say simply and without artifice what has to be said and neither more nor less than what comes from the soul — that is a piano-playing esthetic of the very highest class. This kind of piano playing seems to have died out completely in foreign piano schools, so that we can calmly declare that today in the competing technical and stylistic specialties of the present peda-

gogical world, Hungary — Dohnányi's classroom — is the last refuge of pure, natural, esthetic culture.

When someone from this training school presents himself on the podium with the *Hammerklavier* Sonata, we can be certain that he does not do so from swollen-headedness or cultural snobbishness. And so, when we saw the *Hammerklavier* Sonata inscribed on Goldovsky's program, we knew in advance that we were dealing with an artist, with a reliable guide capable of leading us over the steepest and most dangerous paths of Beethovenite poetry, and who, even if he does not show us everything, will not divert our attention from great things to petty details. We therefore expected a lot, for to follow the course of Beethoven's greatest thoughts, even if only in the main lines, is a mighty test of talent. It became clear from Goldovsky's playing that this barely twenty-two-year-old artist knew how to give us a generally speaking correct rendition of Beethoven's greatest piano work, and that he could plunge into depths which only the fantasy of outstanding Beethoven players dares to penetrate. Marvelous, for example, was the way in which he rendered the volcanic passion of the gigantic, sorrow-drenched adagio, revealing the dark, ominous visions that haunt the heads of dream-immersed poets. Goldovsky demonstrated the heavy, exhaustive, declamatory way of playing that mixture of *parlando rubato* and *arioso* which is the sine qua non of a proper interpretation of the *Hammerklavier* Sonata. Goldovsky exaggerates and forces here and there, but only where such things actually exist in the composition . . . one of the ablest Beethoven interpreters of the younger generation. Great knowledge, a serious musician, a powerful, convincing temperament . . .

These overblown and exaggeratedly flattering words helped to mitigate the sorrow I felt at having to leave a city and a people I had grown to love. I was taking my brain and my piano-playing fingers to the West, but my heart remained behind. For in bidding farewell to Budapest, I was also saying goodbye to Marianne. It was a painful parting for both of us, but there was nothing we could do about it. I had to return to the United States and embark on my musical career, if only to prove to Sidney Prince that the close to $4000 he had invested in me had not been money thrown down the drain, while Marianne had no choice but to remain in Budapest. All we could do was promise to write to each other, pending the day when we would somehow, miraculously, be reunited.

Four years had passed since I had last crossed the Atlantic, and in the interval a great deal had happened. Assured of a fairly permanent teaching post at the Curtis Institute of Music, Mother had moved from New York to Philadelphia, where she and Babushka occupied an apartment in a building known as the "Town House," at 1832 Spruce Street, just one block away from Rittenhouse Square. Irene, who was also living with them, now spoke English fluently — which was a good deal more than could be said for the rest of us, since Babushka spoke not a word, I was a hesitant beginner, and Mother had a way of speaking the language that was uniquely hers (and about which I shall have more to say anon). But if Irene had learned English, she had learned little else. A Philadelphia friend of Mother's, a certain Emma Loeb, had had the unfortunate idea of enrolling my sister in the Oak Lane Country Day School, a "progressive" institution from which classroom grades had been eliminated as potentially damaging to tender adolescent egos, which were allowed to romp at will and sow their wild oats with raucous and often ruffianlike impunity.

From Philadelphia, where I was barely given enough time to embrace Irene and Babushka, I was whisked away by Mother to Atlantic City, where Josef Hofmann, who liked to stroll up and down its then fashionable boardwalk, was enjoying the sea air. Like Uncle Pierre, who had finally settled down in New York with his wife, Mother considered Hofmann the greatest pianist alive, and it was her hope that he would now at last agree to take me under his wing, recommend me to his manager, and thus help speed me on my way as a young piano virtuoso and concert soloist.

Hofmann was not unfriendly, and he seemed to appreciate the fact that I could converse in German — a language which he, like Mother, spoke better than he did English. But he refused to be impressed by my recently acquired credentials as a graduate of the Franz Liszt Academy of Music in Budapest. In the autumn of 1925, when I was still a bright-eyed Schnabelite, I had played the piano for him and he had found my playing sloppy. Under the guidance of Irèn Senn and Ernö Dohnányi I had acquired a different, technically more proficient style of playing, but this too failed to find favor in his eyes. I played well enough, he intimated, to accompany Mother on her concert tours, but as a solo pianist I didn't stand a chance.

I cannot describe the shattering effect of this negative opinion on me. I felt crushed, annihilated. In Budapest, as a member of Dohnányi's master class, I had been somebody. I had been asked to perform at private parties and at public concerts, and my playing had been praised by discerning critics. But now, suddenly, I was nobody — at any rate in the eyes of Josef Hofmann which, as far as Mother was concerned, were the only eyes or ears that mattered. If Hofmann, the king of pianists, felt that I could never become a successful concert pianist, like himself, then that was that. The oracle had spoken and there could be no question of challenging his imperious pronouncement.

Only much later, when I read *The Amazing Marriage** and particularly fragments from the diary of Marie Eustis (Hofmann's first wife), did I realize how personally colored and prejudiced was his negative view of my playing. Josef Hofmann may not have ap-

---

* N. S. Graydon and M. D. Sizemore, *The Amazing Marriage of Marie Eustis & Josef Hofmann* (Columbia, S.C.: University of South Carolina Press, 1965).

preciated Schnabel's "sloppy" way of playing the piano, but he harbored a real hatred for Dohnányi. They had met in Russia some years before the First World War, and Hofmann had apparently developed an intense dislike for the smooth, unruffled gentleman-pianist-conductor who could seemingly do everything, even compose, with such effortless grace. Although he too was an immensely gifted pianist and with little doubt the greatest keyboard virtuoso Europe had seen since Anton Rubinstein, Hofmann wanted to be more than just a pianist. He longed to be a composer, like Ignace Paderewski, who was also a Pole, and his craving for recognition in this respect had led him to invent a pseudonym, Michael Dvorsky, derived from *dvor,* the Slavic equivalent of the German *Hof,* meaning "court." But Michael Dvorsky's compositions had by and large left the critics cold, and he was not one who could, like Dohnányi, count Johannes Brahms among his many admirers. Whence, I suspect, a lurking sense of jealousy and inferiority, which drew its nourishment from the rotting compost of a thwarted ambition.

There were other reasons, as I was also to discover later. Josef Hofmann, in this watershed year of 1930, may already have sensed that the great vogue for solo pianists that had swept over Europe with the Romantic revolution of 1830 and been epitomized by Thalberg, Liszt, and Anton Rubinstein had spent its force. What music lovers now wanted was less solo recitals than ensemble performances — by ballet companies or symphony orchestras. Hofmann's own playing was in less demand, he was giving a smaller number of annual recitals, and this realization may have led him to the gloomy conclusion that the piano-playing soloist was a dying breed. He was thus doing his friend Lea Luboshutz a favor in recommending that her son find some other outlet for his talents.

The weeks and months of holiday idleness that followed were for me singularly dismal. They were spent at Rockport, Maine, where Mother had been offered a summerhouse to live in by

Mary Louise Curtis Bok, who had founded the Curtis Institute of Music in 1924 with the active assistance of her wealthy father, Cyrus Curtis, and her enterprising husband, Edward Bok. I suspect, though I have no means of knowing this for sure, that it was Josef Hofmann who had given Mrs. Bok the idea of turning the little fishermen's town of Rockport into a summer colony for musicians, perhaps remembering what a happy summer he, Mischa Elman, Toscha Seidel, Harry Kaufman, Eddie Bachmann, and Mother had spent together at Saint-Jean-de-Luz in 1928.

The Curtis Institute of Music, Josef Hofmann felt, should be a training ground for musical geniuses, brought to Philadelphia from all over the world and offered full, year-round scholarships. The teaching, to be effective, had to be intensive and uninterrupted. There was to be no long, three- to four-month break in the hot summer months, during which the unemployed and possibly indolent students could neglect their studies and forget everything they had learned over the previous eight or nine months. Contact between teacher and pupil was to be unbroken — which meant that the students had to follow their instructor if he or she chose to go off somewhere on vacation. Mother, in keeping with this philosophy, had brought four of her pupils to Saint-Jean-de-Luz in the summer of 1928, and she had been accompanied by three others when she had gone to Carmel, California, in 1929.

The idea of setting up a summer colony in the United States had many things to commend it. It reduced traveling expenses considerably and made for a concentration of artistic talent which would have been virtually impossible to provide in some distant European community. As it happened, Cyrus Curtis had a seaside mansion in Camden, overlooking Penobscot Bay. Her husband, who had succeeded the sea-loving "Commodore" as head of the Curtis Publishing Company empire, had subsequently built a second seaside mansion for them to live in. All Mary Louise Bok now had to do — and with the Curtis fortune this was easy — was to buy up a score of houses in neighboring Rockport, let the various teachers of the institute inhabit them during the hot summer months, and the artist colony was born.

The clapboard house which Mother had been offered by Mrs. Bok was situated on the promontory overlooking Penobscot Bay. Not far away was a "Community House" where singers and other Curtis students had their quarters and ate their meals in a common dining room. Another house along this same Beauchamp Avenue lodged the English cellist Felix Salmond. The violinist Efrem Zimbalist lived nearby. Josef Hofmann, who was by now being paid a princely salary of $50,000 to direct the Curtis Institute and who earned another $50,000 a year giving piano lessons to a few privileged students — to say nothing of what he earned with each of his piano recitals — had bought himself a far grander edifice made of stone and known as "The Rock." It was virtually an estate, composed of gardens, lawns, shrubbery, and a tennis court much frequented by the Curtis Institute students.

It was only later, after I had become reconciled to my lot, that I came to appreciate the beauties of this stretch of sheltered coastline, such a refreshingly cool, tranquil, and unpolluted change from the nervous, sweltering heat of midsummer Philadelphia. But at this point in my life I was in an unhappy and rebellious mood and little prepared to lavish love on neighbors or surroundings. Irene, who was now thirteen and a half, had developed a youthful infatuation for Josef Hofmann, who appealed to her both as a man and a musician, but for me he was Satan incarnate and Private Enemy Number One.

In September we took the train back to Philadelphia for the start of the new academic year. Since he could not claim that I was totally ungifted or deny all value to the musical diploma I had obtained in Budapest, Josef Hofmann had finally agreed with Mother that the best thing for me to do — since I was not destined to be a great piano virtuoso — was continue my studies in orchestra conducting.

The person who then directed the Curtis student orchestra and who gave lessons in conducting was Emil Mlynarski — the same gifted violinist who had taught Mother in Odessa and under whose direction she had later played in Warsaw, which before the First World War was part of the Tsar's empire. Now a sexagenarian, Mlynarski was a charming Polish gentleman whose head was almost bald save for patches of white hair above the ears and neck. Why he had been chosen to direct the Curtis student orchestra I do not know, but it must have been a Polish plot. Leopold Stokowski, who had helped Mary Louise Bok set up the Curtis Institute in 1924, may have had something to do with it. So probably did Artur Rodzinski, who had succeeded Stokowski as the institute's orchestra director and who had once been a protégé of Mlynarski's in the early 1920s in Warsaw. The choice of Mlynarski to succeed Rodzinski in 1929 must also have appealed to Josef Hofmann, since he too was of Polish origin. Whatever the reason, it was a catastrophic choice, for this old Polish gentleman, already half crippled by arthritis, did not have the slightest idea of how to deal with obstreperous young Americans. In Poland Mlynarski had apparently conducted the Warsaw Opera with some degree of success. But at the Curtis Institute his benign and somewhat sagging Old World manner induced nothing but the most blatant indifference.

The first orchestra rehearsals that I attended in the institute's Casimir Hall (so named after Josef Hofmann's father) left me open-mouthed and appalled. Seldom in my life have I seen anything more heartbreaking than the sight of Emil Mlynarski standing in front of the student instrumentalists and vainly trying to enlist their cooperation. They were the most undisciplined bunch of players I think I have ever seen. None of them paid the slightest heed to the white-haired old gentleman. Some went right on talking to their neighbors, others continued to tune their instruments or practice unrelated passages, while some even read newspapers right under his nose. Finally, when the chaos and the noise rose to a cacophonic *fortissimo,* the old man would wave his arms and cry, "Shtop! Shtop!" in a voice which sent titters through the orchestra.

As a teacher of conducting Mlynarski was no better. Since he was not a pianist, he could not illustrate particular passages on the keyboard, which is what a good conducting teacher should be able to do in the absence of an orchestra. Even worse, he could not sight-read a score with any degree of proficiency, which meant that he had only the haziest notion of what the nonstring instruments were playing.

More irritated than ever against Hofmann, whom I blamed for this scandalous state of affairs, I finally stopped attending Mlynarski's orchestra rehearsals and conducting classes altogether. Instead, I enrolled in a special class in the sight-reading of symphonic scores, the students of which were eventually given a chance to conduct the Curtis orchestra.

After weeks of waiting, I was informed that the long-expected moment was near. I would be granted the rare privilege of conducting the student orchestra. I had only to name the piece I wished to practice with them. I chose the first movement of Liszt's *Faust* Symphony. At the time it was virtually unknown in the United States. I, on the other hand, had studied it meticulously with Leo Weiner in Budapest. I knew virtually every note played by every instrument and if asked to, I could play from memory the entire movement from start to finish.

Although I had seen how the students were capable of behaving under Mlynarski's ineffective direction, I had rashly assumed that when I raised the baton things would be different and this student ensemble would play as well as the orchestra I had been given to conduct at the Liszt Academy. But I was in for a disagreeable surprise. From the opening measures it was clear that few of the players intended to do justice to the score. Virtually all of them began playing wrong notes. I stood there, baffled, feeling increasingly helpless in the face of this musical debacle. When one instrument plays the wrong notes, one can single out the trouble and have it corrected. But when just about every player in an orchestra is playing incorrectly on purpose, there is not much one can do about it.

Finally, in a rage, I stopped the orchestra and turned angrily to the trombones. "In what key do you transpose?" I demanded. My question provoked a mocking retort: "Don't you know that trombones don't transpose?" There were hoots of laughter from the trombone players and other members of the orchestra, who were overjoyed by this serious faux pas. I could almost hear them muttering, "What a swollen-headed ninny, this Goldovsky fellow! As conceited as hell, yet he doesn't even know that trombones don't transpose."

In reality, I knew perfectly well that trombones were not transposing instruments, but in my frustrated fury I had made a stupid slip of the tongue. It was too late now to repair the damage. Since I was such a ninny, the student instrumentalists were going to treat me as they treated Mlynarski, by playing as they pleased.

I soon realized that there was no point in continuing. The whole thing was a shambles. I stopped the orchestra and said, "Okay. Enough. There's no use going on." The rehearsal I had so much looked forward to had lasted less than ten of the forty minutes allotted to me.

This spectacular fiasco did nothing to improve my already dubious reputation at the Curtis Institute of Music. Gossip had it that Mother had been and might still be Josef Hofmann's mistress, and many of my fellow students were convinced that I had only managed to muscle my way into the school because I was the red-haired Lea Luboshutz's son. Few of them had ever heard me play the piano, and they knew nothing of my past training and achievements with Kreutzer, Schnabel, and Dohnányi. In short, I had no right to be at the Curtis Institute at all. I was an interloper, an intruder who concealed his lack of genuine talent behind the mask of a know-it-all arrogance.

Mother had meanwhile contracted for several concert appearances — the first with the Cincinnati Symphony Orchestra, the others on the West Coast. She asked me to accompany her, and I was only too happy to accept. In Cincinnati I was introduced to Fritz Reiner, a stocky, dark-haired man with a typically swarthy, Hungarian complexion, who reminded me a bit of Leo Weiner. At a party given after one of the concerts I was allowed to play the piano, and unlike Hofmann, Reiner seemed to like what he heard, for he commended me on my playing.

In Los Angeles the same cordiality was shown to Mother and me by Artur Rodzinski, who was then in charge of its symphony orchestra. Still relatively young — he was only thirty-six — Rodzinski looked like a windblown product of the Polish plains, with a protruding *menton en galoche* and a shock of tousled brown hair which would rise and fall in waves as he became more animated in conversations or conducting. There was something warm and impulsive about the shy, almost boyish grin that kept creasing his oblong face, but it betrayed a certain insecurity and a craving to please, which were totally missing in Reiner, who ruled his orchestra with a rod of iron.

The Rodzinskis — Artur and his German-born wife, Ilse — could not have been more friendly and hospitable. While Mother journeyed on to Seattle, where she was engaged to play with the local symphony orchestra, I was invited to stay on in Beverly Hills in the Rodzinskis' Spanish-style villa, in a wonderfully fragrant setting of orange blossoms, palm trees, and flowering shrubs. Mrs. Rodzinski, who had first met Rodzinski in Vienna at a time when they were both studying music at the conservatory, was, like her husband, a pianist. She frequently accompanied singers at recitals, and I believe that she had often helped her husband in the past by playing the piano for him while he was studying new orchestral scores. It was thus a very musical household, even though their ten-year-old son, Witold, had not inherited the musical gifts of his parents.

One day, before Mother's return from Seattle, I had myself driven in to Los Angeles to attend a Philharmonic Symphony concert. Why I didn't drive in with Rodzinski I don't now recall. What I do most vividly remember is the unusually long wait to which we were subjected before the concert could begin. Rodzinski finally hurried out onto the stage, looking distinctly flustered, three quarters of an hour after the scheduled starting time — something that had given rise to a lot of muttering and grumbling in the audience. That evening, as we drove back to his Beverly Hills home, I learned what had happened. He had left his house on time, but then as he was driving into Los Angeles, it had suddenly occurred to him that he had left something vital behind: the pistol he always carried on him when conducting. So he had turned around and driven back to get it, even though he knew this would delay the concert's start by many, many minutes. As it happened, though I could not have guessed it at the time, this odd experience was simply a foretaste of other curious, preconcert superstitions Rodzinski was to reveal to me when I came to know him better.

After we had returned to Philadelphia I found myself once again adrift, not quite knowing what to do, as dissatisfied and unhappy as ever. I had long since decided that further study with Mlynarski was a waste of time. I let myself be talked into going to see a production of Verdi's *Aida,* which he put on with the Philadelphia Grand Opera Association, which was linked to the Curtis Institute and which Mary Louise Bok was then helping to finance.

I found the music — and Chief Caupolican, a full-blooded American Indian who sang the role of Aida's father, King Amonasro, with lifelike ferocity — most impressive. As it was the first time I had ever seen *Aida,* I was in no position to judge Mlynarski's proficiency as an opera conductor. But others better qualified to judge it assured me that it was the slowest and longest — and by that they meant the most tedious — *Aida* they had ever heard.

For lack of anything better to do I studied English diction and music history. I also decided to sample other courses since the Curtis Institute, under Josef Hofmann's direction, was now officially dedicated to attracting the world's most brilliant performers to teach America's most gifted students. Although the idea of getting an older generation of geniuses to teach a younger generation of geniuses is not a sure-fire recipe for success — simply because the greatest performers do not necessarily make the finest teachers — the fabulous salaries that were being offered to the Curtis Institute's teaching staff had already attracted a small cluster of luminaries — like Leopold Auer and Efrem Zimbalist for the violin, Marcella Sembrich and Emilio de Gogorza for the voice students, Felix Salmond for the cello, and Carlos Salzedo for the harp. And no wonder! The head of a department, for example, was paid $100 for an hour-long lesson. Being a genius — for this was a school run by and for geniuses — it did not matter if he actually filled his allotted quota of ten hours of instruction per week. If he only completed seven or eight hours with particularly gifted pupils, this was considered quite all right and he could count on receiving $1000 a week — which at a time when the income tax was less steeply graduated than it is today was enough to make one rich.

Among the instrumental teachers at the institute were several woodwind players from the Philadelphia Orchestra: the flutist, William Kincaid, the French hornist, Anton Horner, and several others. The most eminent among them was the oboe virtuoso, Marcel Tabuteau. So great was the prestige of this balding, bon vivant Frenchman that he had been entrusted with the task of training the Curtis Institute's woodwind ensembles. Inasmuch as my interest in conducting was as lively as ever, nothwithstanding my disappointing experiences with Mlynarski and the institute's student orchestra, I asked to be allowed to attend a few of Tabuteau's classes so that I could see how a professional wind-instrument player goes about the task of coordinating a wind-instrument ensemble. The permission was granted to me, but I was warned to be discreet since Monsieur Tabuteau did not like to have outsiders eavesdropping on his rehearsals.

Taking a seat in a remote corner of his rehearsal room, I strained my ears to follow what Tabuteau was saying to the students. I could not make out the meaning of his words, but from their intonation I realized he was speaking French. This struck me as distinctly odd — we were after all in the United States. I decided to leave my distant corner and move a little closer. I now discovered that my first impression was mistaken. He was speaking English, all right, but it was an English the likes of which I don't believe I have ever heard elsewhere. Though he was using English words, every syllable was emitted in the brittle, precise, undiphthonged manner in which it would have been pronounced in French. "You most not poot de notes befor de ouind. You most poot de ouind behind de notes," and so on.

Tabuteau's method of teaching was every bit as original as his mode of English speech. With a Cartesian sense of precision he had invented a scale for measuring the loudness and, consequently, the exact degree of importance in the sequence of tones in any melodic phrase. The range varied from 1 (softest) to 9 (loudest), so that the correct manner of playing could be expressed mathematically by a simple series of numbers — like, let us say, 5 7 3 8 4 2 9 1 — each number corresponding to a different note.

I have never had occasion to determine the real efficacy of such a system, but the idea appealed to me as I had long been interested in mathematical problems. Even Dohnányi's subtle phrasing, which had struck me in Budapest as so inherently mysterious, inimitable, and uniquely his, might after all be analyzed in this way and thus made to yield its secrets through a system of numerical notation.

After the fiascos I had witnessed at Mlynarski's orchestra rehearsals, it was a real pleasure to watch a consummate professional at work. Marcel Tabuteau was a master educator — and not simply in the realm of oboe playing. He was a great connoisseur of all the woodwinds, as well as of horns and other brasses, and the way he taught his students to attack and mold a phrase was a marvel to behold as well as hear.

Among the students at the Curtis Institute of Music I had made at least one friend. Of Russian Jewish origin like myself, he was named Jascha Brodsky and played the violin. For some reason — it may have been because of Josef Hofmann's incommunicative nature, his brooding manner and the way he had of walking down corridors and across the foyer with his eyes focused on the floor so as to avoid having to greet passers-by — Brodsky had also developed an intense dislike for the director of the Curtis Institute. This helped to cement the bond between us. Our feelings may be judged by the term which in our conversations replaced the detested name of Josef Hofmann, which we refused to utter. The unmentionable was known to us as *govnó sobatchoye* — Dogshit.

It was thanks to Brodsky, who was interested in chamber music and who was soon to become the first violinist of the Curtis String Quartet, that I was allowed to audit the chamber-music classes of another Frenchman named Louis Bailly. Smaller and somewhat paunchier than Tabuteau, but with the same tendency to baldness, Bailly was a viola player who for years had been a member of the world-famous Flonzaley Quartet. His studio, situated on the third floor of the main Curtis Institute building, had been specially equipped to suit his curious pedagogic fancies. Possessed of a passion for conducting — which in chamber music is quite unnecessary — he sat behind a desk at one end of the room with a baton in his hand, while the string quartet players, two to the left, two others to the right, faced each other at the opposite end. Since they sat in profile to him, Bailly had had a red bulb installed on each of the two walls facing the performers, and whenever he wanted them to stop so that he could explain something, he would press a button on his desk and the two red bulbs would flash on. His little lecture finished, the bulbs would go out.

I was even more amused by the blue bulb he had placed next to one of the red bulbs for the benefit of the pianist, when there was one. Thus, in a quintet, whenever the piano threatened to drown out the strings — and for Bailly this seemed to be the case most of the time — the blue bulb would flash on and the fellow at the keyboard was expected to play more softly, if not pianissimo.

Toward the end of the academic year, Louis Bailly decided, with Josef Hofmann's blessing, to put on a performance of Gabriel Fauré's *Requiem* as part of a series of concerts that were being given at the Philadelphia Museum of Art. Two Curtis vocal students — a soprano named Natalia Bodanskaya (who was later to marry Jascha Brodsky) and a baritone named Conrad Thibault — were chosen to be the soloists, but as the institute had no standing choir, other students — instrumentalists as well as singers — were commandeered to make a chorus. Having nothing better to do, I gladly added my puny tenor voice to this collective effort.

It turned out to be a most diverting enterprise. Whereas Mlynarski as a conductor of a large ensemble had been pathetic, Louis Bailly was comic. On the podium his body performed the most extraordinary gyrations, the significance of which nobody tried to understand. For the instrumentalists and choristers kept their eyes glued to the music. The only singer who held his score at chest level, so that he could watch Bailly's astonishing contortions, was myself. He obviously appreciated this rapt attention, and I soon became the sole recipient of his cues and the privileged target toward which those Laocoon-like convolutions were almost exclusively directed.

Shortly after this Fauré *Requiem* performance, in mid-April of 1931, I had to leave the United States. The entry visa I had been granted was valid for only six months, and I now discovered what so many other immigrants have learned to their sorrow; to get this visa extended, I had to leave the country and stage an official reentry. Why? I doubt that there is a single bureaucrat in the U.S. Department of Immigration who could answer that question. So it has been, ever since this sorry regulation was first established in some misguided piece of congressional legislation, and so it is likely to remain for years and decades to come, a blemish on the face of Uncle Sam which the powers that be seem bent on preserving.

Not knowing what to do, Mother and I called on one of Mrs. Bok's sons, a distinguished member of the Philadelphia bench. "It's simple," said the judge. "We'll send the boy to Canada, and there he'll get another visa from the U.S. consular officials and be allowed to reenter the country."

I accordingly boarded the Montreal express. But when the train reached the border, the Canadian passport examiners took one look at my Nansen certificate and said, "Sorry, but we don't recognize this document. We cannot let you into Canada."

There was nothing I could do but return to Philadelphia. There was a lot of nervous hand-wringing and cursing, now aimed at the Canadians as well as the obtusely bureaucratic immigration authorities in Washington. We soon realized that there was no alternative. I would have to go back to Europe and obtain another U.S. entry visa in a country which recognized the validity of Nansen passports.

In New York I boarded a liner headed for Hamburg. I persuaded Mother that I would have less trouble with my Nansen passport in Germany and that it would be easier for me to get a U.S. quota visa there than in Paris. The truth of the matter was that Berlin was closer to Budapest and to Marianne, with whom I had been exchanging letters ever since I had left Hungary twelve months before.

I had not been in Berlin long when Marianne turned up with her sister, Trudi Kovács, who had been sent along as a chaperone by their understandably uneasy parents. Marianne must have displayed a hundred signs of terrible distress to have succeeded in extracting this extraordinary concession from her father and mother. And, indeed, it was obvious from the moment we saw each other again that she was still desperately in love.

For some reason I find it difficult to explain, I soon discovered to my dismay that I could no longer feel or express the same sense of rapture. In Budapest I had done the courting, and our romance had been nourished and embellished by that wonderful city's joie de vivre and the background entertainment of Tzigane orchestras. But here in Berlin I was being courted by a young lady who had chosen to stay with her sister in the same hotel as I, not far from the Kurfürstendamm. The romance had been transported to this completely different, colder, less-spontaneous northern city, and in the process of uprooting it had lost its bloom. The spell was broken and there was nothing I could do to restore it. I simply was not in love with her anymore.

It was a most painful moment when it finally dawned on both of us that something had snapped. I was no longer the same carefree, insouciant, supremely confident Boris she had known in Budapest. I had just spent a miserable year more or less marking time, and I had no idea what the future might hold in store for me. I was not a person on whom someone like Marianne could reasonably pin her hopes now that my own had been so cruelly dashed. Budapest, with all the wonderful experiences it had contained, belonged to the radiant past, but, as the Germans say, *das war alles vorbei!* It was now over and done with, and there was no bringing it back. For good or ill I was going to have to make my mark in the United States and perhaps overcome my discontent by sowing a few wild oats. There was no place for someone as delicate and tender as Marianne in this rough, uncertain, disorderly scheme.

Our second parting, being unsustained by hope — at any rate on my side — was even sadder than our first, a year before. Marianne returned dolefully to Budapest in a state of profound dejection. She continued to write to me — letters that were full of love and desperate expectation which made me feel like a cad. But I was no longer able to reciprocate. I had surrendered to other tides, which were carrying me remorselessly in other directions.

Four years later Mother happened to cross the Atlantic once again, this time on a European concert tour. One of her stops was Budapest. After her first recital a twenty-five-year-old Hungarian girl came backstage to call on her. She introduced herself: Marianne Donner, once a friend of her son, Boris. It was immediately clear to my mother from the light in her gray green eyes and the tremble in her voice that Marianne had been unable to tear me, or at least the remembered image of me, from her heart. Mother was sufficiently impressed to speak to me about this unexpected visit after she had returned to Philadelphia, adding rather uncharitably, "That's the girl you should have married!"

What would have happened if Mother had met Marianne earlier and said this to me in 1931 I do not know. It is by no means certain that she would have said it. Mothers are not always easy to deal with, and particularly a mother who has lost her husband and wants nothing but the very best for her remaining "child genius."

Having obtained a new permanent reentry visa, I sailed back from Bremen on the *Europa*. Mother was waiting on the Manhattan pier to greet me, but my problems as an immigrant were far from over. After my luggage had been carried off the ship and the needed papers, signed by various U.S. citizens who were willing to attest that I was a responsible, law-abiding individual who was not likely to run amuck, set fire to public buildings, or be a financial burden to American society, had been produced, we were informed that I still had to be "processed" and that this could only be done on Ellis Island. However, as it was only a short boat ride to the island, the whole procedure probably wouldn't take more than an hour or two.

Leaving Mother on the dock with my bags, I joined the throng of immigrants who were bound for Ellis Island. To keep myself occupied during the boat trip there and back, I brought along an attaché case containing the score of Richard Strauss's opera *Ariadne auf Naxos,* which I wanted to study.

By the time we reached Ellis Island, it was already the middle of Friday afternoon. Soon after we had disembarked, we were informed that there were so many people ahead of us that they couldn't possibly take care of everyone that afternoon. President Hoover had just laid down a new ruling for federal employees, who were no longer to work on Saturdays. "So we're going to close shop right now. Sorry, but you'll have to stick around here until Monday morning."

Ellis Island in those days bore a grim resemblance to a penitentiary. Criminals, prostitutes, and derelicts of very kind were confined there prior to being expelled or repatriated to less moral lands. We too now suffered the same fate and were herded into cell-like dormitories, where the lights were abruptly extinguished at 8:00 P.M.

The next morning they flashed on again at five o'clock. After being offered a miserable breakfast of tepid oatmeal and watered-down coffee, we were herded into a large hall where we rubbed shoulders with the pimps, prostitutes, and pickpockets who were waiting to be deported. On one side of the hall, on a little platform, as luck would have it, was an upright piano. Since we were being condemned to idleness for the next forty-eight hours, I persuaded one of the guards to unlock the piano. Sitting down at the keyboard, I began playing *Ariadne auf Naxos.* The hours passed and I could feel an aching void in my stomach. Then, suddenly, the doors were flung open and a number of guards appeared with trays covered with glasses of milk. Gratefully I made a rush for the nearest tray, only to be rebuffed. "This ain't for you, buddy!" I was told. "This here milk is for women and children only."

I returned to the piano with a watering mouth and an even

hollower feeling in my stomach. I could joyfully have strangled those guards, but it would merely have assured my expulsion from God's Own Country. So I sat down again before the keyboard and swore that if ever I was lucky enough to conduct *Ariadne auf Naxos* in the United States, I would donate the proceeds to a special fund destined to provide the unfortunate males on Ellis Island with a glass of morning milk. (I did indeed get an opportunity to conduct this Strauss opera, years later, but by that time Ellis Island, as a purgatory for criminals, streetwalkers, Nansen passport holders, and other forms of social vermin, had ceased to exist.)

Two days later I was at last able to tread the terra firma of the New World without being arrested or turned back as an unwanted alien. After a brief stopover in Philadelphia, we headed northeast once again for Rockport, Maine, where we were to spend the summer with Irene and Babushka.

On the whole this was for me a more pleasant summer than the previous one, even though my detestation of Josef Hofmann remained as vigorous as ever. But I was now much more at home in English, and this made me feel less of a stranger in this little seaside community.

Of all the gifted musicians we now numbered among our neighbors, none, I think, was as congenial to me as Felix Salmond. This lanky, spare, slightly walleyed Englishman, with his long arms and legs, looked, when playing the cello, like an octopus devouring an oyster. His prestige as a teacher was so great that he was the only member of the Curtis faculty who also taught at the Juilliard School of Music in New York. Although quite a few of the contemporary world's most celebrated cellists received instruction from him, Salmond himself was not really a virtuoso cello player. He never managed to get rid of a faint rasping sound as he drew his bow across the strings. But aside from being a most delightful companion, Salmond was a consummate musician. His mother, a tiny but vibrant woman who once came to Rockport to visit him, was an accomplished pianist, and from her Salmond had inherited an extraordinary appreciation of pianistic subtleties.

There was not, I think, an important piece of chamber music with piano that Felix Salmond did not know inside out. With Mother we played many trios together, and these were most instructive as well as pleasant experiences. I now began to understand why performers consider chamber music to be the highest of all forms of music. The reason is that in a chamber-music ensemble one is playing for the most expert and sophisticated audience imaginable: one's own partners. This is not true of symphony orchestras, where there are so many instruments and so much "doubling" that it is virtually impossible for one instrumentalist to know how well or badly his neighbors may be playing. But in a chamber-music trio, foursome, or quintet, each instrument is clearly audible to all the players involved.

With Salmond, I always had the impression that he was not playing so much as listening to how his partners played. Whenever I managed to phrase a passage with particular delicacy, I would hear Salmond whispering under his breath, just audibly enough for me to hear it, "Bravo, Boree!" I cannot describe the pleasure those two words gave me. They were among the greatest compliments I have ever received and were all the more precious for being proffered at a time when it had been decreed — from on high — that my career as a pianist was finished.

However, if there was something Salmond did not like about one's playing, he made no bones about it. Sometimes my place at the keyboard would be taken by Isabella Vengerova, a famous Russian piano teacher who was also on the faculty of the Curtis Institute. If she played a passage in some way Salmond disapproved of, he would jump up from his chair, as though stung by a nettle, and wave his bow at her: "But, Isabella, how can you, how can you?" Mother, Irene, and I used to laugh over these agitated interruptions after Salmond and the others had left the house. But it was no joking matter to be taken to task by this sharp-eared and sharp-tongued cellist, for he could be as cutting in his criticism as he was generous in his praise.

Everything Felix Salmond did, he did with the most extraordinary zest. He was the very opposite of the stereotypical inhibited, buttoned-up Englishman. If you told him a funny story, he would double up with mirth, rise from his chair, and lean against the wall, holding his head against his forearm while he howled with laughter until the tears came running down his cheeks.

He applied the same infectious enthusiasm to his long-armed and long-legged Ping-Ponging, whooping with delight or rage each time he scored a smash or drove the ball into the net. It was the same with golf, which he tried to teach me, albeit in vain. I never could develop the patience and muscular control to hit those tiny balls in just the right way with just the right implement. But I don't believe anyone but Salmond could have persuaded me to follow him around the links, as I did time and again, with a kind of docile, doglike contentment.

Although Mother did her best to improve relations by helping to organize benefit recitals for one local cause or another, I think that many of the fishermen and yacht owners who frequented this sheltered bay must have looked askance at this unorthodox artistic invasion. Not all of these musicians, beginning with Hofmann, were of the long-haired type, but some were distinctly odd. There was, for example, the world-famous harpist Carlos Salzedo, a small, monkeylike man of Spanish extraction. His Curtis students, all girls, were lodged near the house which Mrs. Bok had found for him in nearby Camden, and to judge by what we could hear or see of the goings-on there, he watched over his flock of string-plucking damsels like an Argus, forcing them to adhere to an almost conventual discipline.

We would occasionally see them when they were invited to take part in one of Mother's musical soirées, for somehow, probably because she was the most eminent of the lady teachers from the Curtis Institute and very much a *grande dame* in her manner of speaking and dressing, Mother and her summerhouse had become the social center of this musical community. Though she herself was not a really great violinist — in a class with an Elman, a Heifetz, or a Menuhin — she was an excellent performer and practiced a great deal. Her own tiny roost was popularly referred to as the "Seven-to-Eleven Club," for her students had strict orders to get up at six in the morning and practice strenuously from seven to eleven, after which they could relax and amuse themselves as they saw fit. But as privileged inhabitants of our birch- and fir-surrounded community, they were of course expected to be present whenever Mother gave one of her musical evenings.

Whether Mother had anything to do with it I honestly don't know, though Josef Hofmann may well have consulted her about it, but in the autumn of 1931, when we returned to Philadelphia, there was a major change at the Curtis Institute of Music. In the place of the charmingly ineffectual Emil Mlynarski, who was quietly dismissed, the Curtis student orchestra acquired a drillmaster of the first order. He was Fritz Reiner, the same Fritz Reiner who had commended me on my piano playing when Mother had taken me to Cincinnati.

Reiner's move to Philadelphia was for us a major stroke of luck, for the Curtis Institute thus acquired one of the finest living conductors. Normally he would have stayed at his regular post. But not long before Mother and I had made our trip to Cincinnati, a troupe of traveling actors had come to perform in that city. Among them was a lively and uninhibited actress named Carlotta Irwin, to whose bright eyes and strong voice Reiner took an immediate fancy. Neglecting his wife, Berta — a daughter of the great Hungarian soprano Etelka Gerster — he began publicly courting the flamboyant Carlotta. Soon the city's high society was a-buzz with gossip. The symphony orchestra's board of directors were outraged, and even more their august spouses, who held the dignified and popular Mrs. Reiner in high esteem. Such shocking behavior was judged inadmissible on the part of the resident conductor, who was expected to be a model of civic respectability. His contract was accordingly terminated, and Reiner was informed that he would have to look for a job elsewhere.

American high society in those days was still strictly puritanical, and other cities with symphony orchestras were no readier to pardon a sinner who had overstepped the bounds. But the director of the Curtis Institute felt differently. His own behavior, though more discreet, had not been exactly impeccable, for he had flouted convention by first seducing and then marrying one of his piano students. Mother, who had acted as a more or less willing shield for this particular peccadillo, must have felt much the same way, and, besides, she regarded Fritz Reiner as a friend. Cincinnati's loss could thus prove the Curtis Institute's gain.

A gain it unquestionably was — for the institute as a whole and for Boris Goldovsky in particular. From the moment Reiner mounted the podium and faced the student orchestra, there was a silence in that hall such as I had never heard before. The man's look was terrifying. He had a gimlet eye that could pierce you like a dagger, even when he was looking at you from the side, and he had a tongue to match. He had a way of rolling his tongue around inside his mouth and behind the bulging cheeks which was particularly unnerving, for it created a kind of anxious suspense as one waited for the climax of this critical rumination to erupt like a whiplash. But on the occasion of this first encounter with the Curtis student orchestra he didn't even have to raise his voice for everyone present to understand that the musical recreation they had enjoyed under the benign Mlynarski was over. The man before them was a taskmaster. He wasn't going to stand for any nonsense or shoddy playing from anybody, and if necessary he would drill them until they were all purple in the face.

Later, when the time comes to discuss his deficiencies, I shall add the necessary reservations. But the impression he first made on us was devastating. Reiner had everything Mlynarski lacked.

He was not only a great conductor, he was also a great teacher. He made this immediately clear to the four of us who had been admitted to his orchestra-conducting class. They included Saul Cohen, a virtuoso trumpeter, and Willie Van den Burg, a consummate cellist, both of whom at that time were leaders of their respective sections in the Philadelphia Symphony Orchestra. (Saul Cohen, who later changed his name to Caston, eventually became the resident conductor of the Denver Symphony Orchestra, while Van den Burg moved to California to pursue his career as cellist and leader of various orchestras.) The fourth member of the class was Louis Vyner, a talented viola player who had been Mlynarski's favored pupil.

"Conducting," Reiner told us at our very first lesson, "is basically a simple business as long as the tempo doesn't change. Anyone can beat time evenly and it's nothing to be proud of, because any fool can do it. And I'm not going to waste your time and mine teaching you easy things. What I'm going to do first is teach you how to conduct operatic recitatives. Because until you've conducted opera, you don't know what conducting really is."

He then asked each of us in turn what we knew about opera. When my turn came to answer, I brashly told him that I knew nothing about opera. In fact, I didn't like it, I wasn't interested in it, I wanted to have nothing to do with it.

"I don't care whether you are interested in opera or not," said Reiner crisply. "You are going to learn it whether you like it or not. And if you don't know anything about it, then that's too bad. You're just going to have to study it."

Having put me in my place, he added a little later: "Since you sight-read well and know a few languages, I know what I'll do with you. I'm going to make you a repertoire coach. You'll give twelve hours of operatic instruction every week, and that way you'll find out what opera is all about."

Since these coaching lessons were paid at the rate of six dollars an hour, I soon found myself earning the princely sum of seventy-two dollars a week. The satisfaction I derived from this new emolument would have been greater if I had felt that the money earned was really deserved. But I couldn't honestly feel that it was. Although I sat up at night feverishly studying operatic scores, my ignorance for the first few months was appalling and only matched by my basic dislike for this musical art form. My students couldn't help sensing it, and it did not take them long to realize that they were dealing with an ignoramus, and with an opinionated ignoramus at that.

As someone who had been trained to be an instrumentalist, I did not realize that the musical phrasing of singers is substantially different from that of pianists. A singer would turn up with a score for his or her hour of instruction and say, "Maestro, I'm supposed to learn this, can you help me?" I would look at the music, hoping I could identify the opera from which the particular aria came, but as often as not I was in the dark about this too. Often the text was in Italian, a language which at that time I neither understood nor knew how to pronounce correctly. Not realizing that the words of an aria are every bit as important as the melodic line, I would insist that the student respect the exact timing indicated in the score, as though I were dealing with an instrument rather than with a human being who not only has to take a breath every now and then, but who is meant to utter sounds that are meaningful and intelligible.

It was months before I began to understand that in singing the language value of a phrase is every bit as important as the musical mathematics. This is one of the many things a good repertoire coach must know. Another thing I did not know is that one can speak a language well, as I spoke German, and yet be ignorant of the technicalities of its pronunciation. I insisted that my students double a consonant in a word like *Donner* (thunder) — thus rendering it *Don-ner* — much as in Italian one elongates the two juxtaposed consonants in a word like *donna* (*don-na*), meaning lady. The word, I insisted, had to be pronounced *my* way.

The harassed student would then run to the German teacher, who would listen to each new tale of woe with mounting exasperation before exploding: "How dare Goldovsky teach you to mispronounce words? This is none of his business. Let him stick to music. It's my job to teach you to pronounce German correctly." Not only was I wrong, I was even aggressive in my wrongness.

One of my unfortunate charges, a soprano with long, light brown hair and sparkling brown eyes named Margaret Codd, was so exasperated by this aggressive ignorance of mine that, after two or three lessons, she went to complain to Josef Hofmann, saying that I knew less than nothing about opera and that it was a sheer waste of her time to be taught by a smart aleck who was much too big for his breeches. Hofmann never breathed a word to me about this incident, and it was only later that I found out why Margaret Codd had been transferred to Sylvan Levin, who, fortunately for her, knew considerably more about opera than I did. But at this time I could not have cared less what a singer felt or thought about me. I had been forced into coaching against my will, and I took it the way one takes castor oil. It had certainly not reconciled me to opera, which I still regarded as a misshapen hybrid not really worthy of serious musical attention.

But it did not take me long to realize that Fritz Reiner meant business. He was not a man to lavish pity on anybody, and if there was one thing he really relished it was to humiliate publicly a student who had failed to do his homework. I had apparently muffed my potential career as a concert pianist. I could not risk another shattering fiasco by being ruled out as a conductor. If Reiner decided that I had to know every major opera in the repertoire — and there are at least sixty of them — then I just had to burn the midnight oil and learn them.

To improve my woefully limited knowledge, I decided to get a backstage job with the Philadelphia Grand Opera Company, which Mrs. Curtis Bok was then helping to finance. Her reasons for supporting this company were closely linked to her desire to develop a first-class vocal department at the Curtis Institute of Music. The opera company's instrumentalists came from Leopold Stokowski's Philadelphia Orchestra, the leading singers were brought in from outside, and the secondary roles were sung by the students from the Curtis Institute.

Since Mother was by now a good friend of Mrs. Bok's, I had little trouble getting hired. The opera company's leading baritone at this time was John Charles Thomas. Though he had a lovely, honey-colored voice, he was basically an indolent Don Juan with a burning itch to chase any skirt that passed his way. Since there was no telling in advance just where or how hotly he might be pursuing this extracurricular activity, I was assigned the job of warning him ten or sometimes fifteen minutes in advance of his next stage entrance. If I was lucky I found him in his dressing room, but there were also times when, after some hectic searching, I would find him enveloped with some chorister or dancer in the folds of a black curtain leading to the wings, and it would require some insistence to pry him away from his latest victim.

When the moment finally came for him to go on stage, Thomas always managed to hover near the prompter's box. Careless as well as lazy, he could never bother to learn his roles with the necessary thoroughness.

I particularly remember a performance of Massenet's *Thaïs,* which almost ended in disaster as a result of his deplorable insouciance. In this opera, based on the novel by Anatole France, the monk Athanaël undertakes to save the soul of a beautiful Alexandrian courtesan named Thaïs who has been living a life of pagan wantonness. The luscious, luxury-loving courtesan finally yields to the holy man's entreaties and agrees to devote the rest of her days to God, but she asks to be allowed to take along a little statuette of Eros, which is most dear to her. Annoyed by this reversion to idolatry, the monk seizes the earthenware statuette and flings it to the ground, where it breaks into little fragments.

Because this animated tête-à-tête is followed in the opera by a barefoot ballet, the stage director had urged John Charles Thomas (who was playing the part of the monk) to throw the statuette upstage, leaving the downstage area free of broken fragments for the ballerinas to dance on. The choreography for the ballet had been entrusted to two sisters, Catherine and Dorothy Littlefield, and I happened to be standing in the wings next to the latter when to our horror we saw Thomas throw the statuette down in front of him, littering the front of the stage with pieces of terra cotta.

Dorothy Littlefield was appalled. "I'm not going to let my dancers go out there and slash their feet," she told me firmly. I pleaded with her: "Come now, please, the opera has to go on." But she was adamant: "No, I tell you, no. I will not permit it."

Fortunately for us, Massenet had introduced a brief chorus interlude between the statue-breaking scene and the ballet. Accompanied by several stagehands, I moved out behind the chorus, gently pushing the singers forward as close to the footlights as possible while we bent down and picked up the debris behind their backs.

I was quite proud of this operatic rescue, but I had no time to rest on my laurels. For John Charles Thomas was soon to cause me more trouble in the final act, where Athanaël leads the repented courtesan Thaïs to a nunnery in the desert. This last act begins with a fairly long orchestral prelude; then the nuns come out of their convent carrying urns, which they fill with water before carrying them back inside. After giving the curtain cue, I hurried to Thomas's dressing room to warn him that fairly soon he would be making his stage entrance. But Thomas was not there. When I returned to the wings I was horrified to see that he was already on stage. He and Thaïs had apparently been surprised by the rising curtain, and, realizing that they had no business being there, they shuffled laboriously, as though totally exhausted, across the stage to a distant corner, where they sat down, trying to look as inconspicuous as possible. It was the slowest and, I think, the most catastrophic crossing of a stage that I have ever witnessed.

John Charles Thomas also sang the lead role of the hunchback jester in Verdi's *Rigoletto,* under the direction of Cesare Sodero. I remember the first performance vividly because to my amazement Thomas sang half the opera in Italian and the other half in French. He had spent many years in Brussels, singing at the Théâtre de la Monnaie, where French versions of Italian operas were invariably used, and since returning to the United States he had only managed to master half the original text.

Since I was a backstage assistant, it was assumed that I knew a great deal about opera — which was anything but the case. Singing in this opera with Thomas was a young tenor named Nino Martini who was making his operatic debut as the Duke of Mantua. He had come to Philadelphia with his voice teacher, former opera star Giovanni Zenatello, husband of the famous Spanish contralto Maria Gay.

In the last act of *Rigoletto* there is a tavern scene where the Duke, after flirting with Maddalena, decides to climax his amorous affair by spending the night in her brother Sparafucile's inn. The Duke goes upstairs to the bedroom, where he can be heard through a window opening on to the stage. Since he cannot see the conductor from this upstairs room, the tenor singing this role needs special backstage assistance. Nowadays this is handled by means of a closed-circuit television monitor. But in the early 1930s an assistant was needed to transmit the conductor's tempo to the singer, which he did by peering through a hole in the scenery.

The last act was well under way when suddenly Giovanni Zenatello buttonholed me backstage and said, "Maestro, please help Nino here. He has never done this role before. This is his debut, and he is very unsure of himself." I nodded, to give him the impression that I understood what he wanted me to do. But in truth I didn't have a clue as to what was needed at this point. I was still leafing frantically through the score trying to locate the scene when I realized it was already too late. I never did discover how Martini managed to come in on time, but after the performance was over I felt very bad about it. Far from being the expert backstage technician I was supposed to be, I was a hopeless bungler.

Conducting classes with Fritz Reiner were not exclusively devoted to opera, but from the start that was where the emphasis was placed. I remember that he had us study Beethoven's First Symphony, and not long afterward he assigned us the introduction to the last movement of his Ninth, which is notorious for its difficulty and complexity.

Preparing for one of Reiner's conducting sessions was an arduous business. One had to know the piece of music being studied meticulously so as to be able to say, whenever he chose to question us: "At this point the two bassoons play these notes, and then they are joined by a clarinet, which plays . . . ," etc. Woe to the person who resorted to guesswork to cover up his ignorance. Reiner would descend on the poor fellow like an eagle and make mincemeat of his pretenses. Not only was he ignorant, he was a liar to boot! It was better to say one did not know, at the risk of being told that one was *total unbegabt* (totally untalented), which was one of Reiner's favorite and most withering expressions.

Since he was always trying to trip us with trick questions, the four of us got together over the Christmas holidays of 1931 and spent hours cross-examining each other to check our knowledge of the last movement of Beethoven's Ninth Symphony. "Which instrument plays this? . . . Which instruments play that? . . . Start conducting four measures before the letter A," and so on. We carried the whole business to exaggerated extremes, for once determined not to be defeated by unexpected queries and made to look like dolts.

Reiner held his conducting classes in a large room which contained two grand pianos. When we turned up for the next scheduled lesson, shortly after New Year's, we found him seated in front of one of the pianos looking more than usually grim. We stood there, waiting for him to select one of us and say, "You were assigned the last movement of the Ninth Symphony, were you not? Well, take the stick and start it out!" The stick was Reiner's, an elegant baton with a distinctive cork handle with which we tried to imitate his precise, subtle, extremely spare style of conducting.

Instead, Reiner said, "Goldovsky, come here!" There was a thundercloud over his head. A storm was clearly brewing, but why, I had no idea.

I came up to the piano, while my colleagues sat down to wait their turn. On the rack was a thick score. But before I could see what it was, Reiner opened it brusquely, pointed to a spot on the page, and asked, "Who plays this?"

I stared at the page and realized that it had nothing to do with the last movement of Beethoven's Ninth Symphony, which we were supposed to have studied. It was obviously the piano vocal score of some Wagnerian opera. But I had not the faintest idea which opera it might be, still less which particular instrument or instruments played this particular passage.

"But, *Meister,*" I began.

"Please don't argue with me," interrupted Reiner. "Do you know it or don't you know it? Who plays this?"

It would have been folly to hazard a guess. "I don't know," I answered.

"Van den Burg," he called, summoning the next victim, while I went back to sit with the others.

"Who plays this?"

Van den Burg stared at the score as I had, shrugged his shoulders helplessly, and said, "I don't know."

It was Saul Cohen's turn next, and then Louis Vyner's. They were no wiser than I and had to confess that they didn't know.

That was all Reiner needed. He stood up. "You are a bunch of ignorants!" he exploded, and then marched out of the room.

After he had left, we crowded round the piano. The passage he had pointed to was from the first act of Wagner's *Die Walküre*. We looked at each other in bewilderment. Hadn't he assigned us the last movement of Beethoven's Ninth Symphony? He most certainly had! We wouldn't have slaved over it for hours, trying to memorize every note and measure, played by every instrument, if he hadn't. Then what was the meaning of it all?

Only later, quite by accident, did I discover the reason for this extraordinary behavior. Reiner wanted to go to some kind of party, and our weekly lesson happened to conflict with it. So instead of simply postponing our class, he preferred to surprise us with a Wagner score we hadn't been told to study. This was Reiner's way of killing two birds with one stone. He got out of an irksome duty and at the same time succeeded in exposing his students' "ignorance."

As the months went by I found myself, unwillingly, more and more absorbed in opera. Remorselessly, relentlessly Reiner drilled us, taking us from the orchestral recitatives of *The Marriage of Figaro* and *Carmen* through Beckmesser's serenade from *Die Meistersinger* (which is full of "stop" and "go" signals) and the Sprecher scene from *The Magic Flute*. My basic dislike of opera remained as keen as ever, but I was beginning to know something about this complex form of art.

Although Reiner's main job at Curtis was training the institute's student orchestra, he decided to follow Emil Mlynarski's example by putting on a number of operas with the Philadelphia Grand Opera Association.

The opera Reiner chose to begin with was Richard Strauss's *Elektra*, which had been neglected by New York's Metropolitan Opera Company and not performed anywhere in the United States for years. The reason may have been that Strauss's operas are extremely difficult to produce. The orchestral texture is most involved, with contrapuntal passages, dissonances, and strange sound effects introduced by additional instruments. Keeping singers and orchestra together when so many complicated things are going on requires a truly magisterial control, but this Reiner had. Indeed, if he was such an outstanding Strauss conductor, it was precisely because operas like *Elektra, Der Rosenkavalier,* and *Salome,* which he later conducted in New York, kept him really busy. When Reiner conducted a Mozart symphony, he had a tendency to get bored, and it looked at times as though he were half asleep. It was too simple, too easy; there was too little for him to do.

Richard Strauss's *Elektra* was something else again. The same Nelson Eddy who later became a famous Hollywood star was chosen for the important baritone role of Orestes, and when it was announced that the great Hungarian mezzo-soprano Margaret Matzenauer would be singing the part of Klytemnestra, the news was a national event, attracting the attention of music fans and critics all over the eastern seaboard. Though fifty, she still had an extraordinary voice and such perfect pitch that it was commonly said that she could give the *A* to the orchestra to tune by — something that is generally done by an oboe.

This may well be legend, for I myself never saw her do it. But Margaret Matzenauer's portrayal of Klytemnestra, as a woman devoured by pangs of conscience and fear of her son and daughter, was simply magnificent. With her face hideously made up, she looked like a creature that was rotting alive.

For this production too I acted as a backstage assistant. The stage director, who also taught opera staging and dramatic acting at the Curtis Institute, was a gentleman named Wilhelm von Wymetal, whose father had been a famous stage director in Vienna. I had watched him teach dramatic action to Curtis Institute vocal students, and the conclusion I had come to was that, unlike his father, who may have been gifted, Wilhelm von Wymetal was *total unbegabt*. Everything he had the students do looked stilted and artificial; it lacked the spontaneity and breath of life I had so enjoyed at Stanislavsky's Art Theatre in Moscow and on the Budapest stage. It was bogus, unconvincing drama, and it gave me one more reason for not liking opera.

From the point of view of the stage director, *Elektra* is a rather static work. It consists for the most part of duet scenes, where Elektra is on stage with her mother, Klytemnestra, her sister, Chrysothemis, or her brother, Orestes. In the 1930s such scenes required little stage directing and the singers were left pretty much to their own devices. It was in the handling of group ensembles that a good director was expected to make his mark. Now in *Elektra,* as it happens, there is no chorus. The opera opens with a brief sequence in which five girls are shown gathered around a well, but it lasts only a couple of minutes before the main protagonists appear.

The only truly exciting scene from the stage director's viewpoint occurs later on, after the long and frightening duet in which Elektra tells her mother that she is going to be butchered by her son, Orestes. Immediately thereafter two of Klytemnestra's confidantes appear and whisper something into the terrorized mother's ears. Just what they tell her is not immediately apparent to the spectators, but it is illustrated scenically by the appearance of female attendants who come in bearing torches and take up positions around the stage to form a harmonious tableau. The purpose of this group pantomime, which moves from the hectic to the static and is marvelously underlined in the orchestral accompaniment, is to suggest the waves of conflicting emotion that sweep over Klytemnestra when she is told that Orestes is dead. The first shock and sense of maternal loss soon give way to a feeling of intense relief, tinged of course by guilt, at the news that her vengeful son has died and that she has nothing further to fear from him.

Since it was the only place in the opera where he could display his *maestría* as a stage director, Wymetal gave this pantomime sequence a lot of attention in rehearsals. The torch-bearing attendants were divided into groups of two or three dancers who were taught how to dart out onto the stage from inside the palace. Wymetal trained them to bounce off the left or the right side of the portal as they ran out and then to skip to their appointed positions in crisscrossing patterns as they shuttled light-footedly past each other with their burning brands.

To coordinate this choreographic ensemble, the various contingents were each given a number and instructed to run out on stage only as it was called. The job of calling out these numbers had been given to one of my colleagues who was acting as senior backstage assistant. As I had nothing to do during this particular episode, I left the wings with Willy von Wymetal and went to the back of the auditorium of the Academy of Music to see how the ballet-pantomime looked to the audience. We were standing there watching the first torch-bearing dancers make their complex, ricocheting entrances, when it suddenly became apparent that something had gone wrong. The second and third groups collided as they reached the portal simultaneously, jamming the gateway. Soon dancers were leaping this way and that to avoid hitting one another. The delicate shuttlework of flaming brands and sandaled feet abruptly dissolved into a kind of *sauve-qui-peut* scramble.

Wondering what had happened, I turned to look at Wymetal. But he was already heading backstage. I ran after him. By the time I reached the wings, it was too late. The dancers were all on stage, settling uneasily into their preassigned positions. I had no time to watch them from between the curtains, for at that moment I caught sight of Wymetal. He was standing next to a red brick wall, methodically pounding his head against it. Blood was beginning to run down his temple and cheek. He had clearly lost his mind, or, it suddenly dawned on me, he was trying to commit suicide.

Grabbing hold of two stagehands, I said, "Quick! We must stop him!" We rushed up, seized Wymetal by the arms, and pulled him away from the wall. But we did not have an easy time of it. He struggled to break loose for another ramlike assault on those red bricks, while we kept pulling him back and away before he could do himself irreparable damage. He kept muttering and moaning in the most dreadful way as the blood trickled down his nose and chin. But finally he stopped struggling and went limp and we were able to drag him over to a chair.

The truly ironic thing about this *suicide manqué* was that it was totally unnecessary. In his single-minded concentration, Wymetal had persuaded himself that this particular torch-bearing scene was the most important in the opera. It was the dramatic climax toward which everything built up, and it had ended in catastrophe. As a stage director he was finished, his career was at an end. Nobody would ever want to hire him again, after a fiasco like this, which every critic present was certain to excoriate.

In fact, the music critics present made no mention of the mix-up. They may not even have noticed the confusion, and, not having attended the rehearsals, there was no need for them to get too upset about it. They had come to watch Fritz Reiner conduct and to hear Margaret Matzenauer sing, and the results were superlative. Reiner, as a conducter of a Richard Strauss opera, had proved himself *total begabt,* while Margaret Matzenauer had emerged as a great actress as well as a great singer, on a par with Chaliapin. The rest, for the critics — who for once were right — was of secondary importance.

The summer of 1932 was again spent at Rockport, but it was marred by an unexpected and tragic blow. One morning in early June, when I made my usual visit to the local post office to pick up the daily mail, I found a letter from the Soviet Union addressed to Mother in an unfamiliar hand, with the name Natalya Goldovskaya on the back of the envelope. This was a totally unexpected event. I knew that in the middle 1920s Mother, as well as Uncle Pierre, had tried to start a correspondence with my brother, Yuri, and with Aunt Anna. There had been no response, except for a single postcard in which Mother was told that Yuri had married a fellow student named Natalya Levy from the mathematics faculty of the University of Moscow. A couple of years later we received a reprint from a scientific Soviet journal containing an article by Yuri devoted to what was described as an "elegant" solution to some complicated mathematical theorem. After that there was neither news nor answers to Mother's letters. Having read that communications with relatives living in capitalist countries were frowned upon in the U.S.S.R., Mother decided not to embarrass and endanger Yuri and her sister by any further attempts to get in touch with them. Receiving a letter from Natalya was therefore very startling and even somewhat ominous. Right then and there I unsealed the envelope and read to my horror that Yuri was dead. His widow told of having given birth to a healthy boy named Dimitry; shortly thereafter — she wrote — Yuri had left Moscow to go on a skiing holiday in the Caucasus. From this expedition he and his companions had never returned, and later she was informed that they had all perished in an avalanche. Having to convey the contents of this letter to Mother and Babushka was a most difficult and painful task. Mother was grief-stricken and wrote to her daughter-in-law asking for more details about her and the child. For a long time we heard nothing. Then, about a year later, another envelope came containing a small picture of a lovely looking baby and a few words from the mother. Lubo — as we now called Mother — and I made several démarches trying to discover the whereabouts of my brother's widow and her son, but we were not able to trace their address or discover anything at all about them.

Mother's main consolation during that summer was the first car she had ever owned — a little Chevrolet which made it possible for us to abandon train travel for the novel thrills of automobile driving. The idea had gathered irresistible force in Philadelphia because we had decided to move from the crowded center out to the suburban community of Cynwyd, where Mrs. Bok had offered Mother a house which had once been inhabited by her butler. An automobile now seemed indispensable for her commuting to the Curtis Institute and back.

The vehicle chosen was a convertible with a rumble seat. It was painted bright green, and Mother was so proud of its glossy appearance that when setting out for a drive she would carefully choose a dress that went well with her beautifully dyed red hair and her little convertible's green *carrosserie*.

Mother was also very proud of having learned to drive her Chevrolet over the country roads of Maine. Everything was just wonderful, she told us one day over the lunch table as she described her latest drive. The car was working beautifully, and — "You know, the Americans are quite extraordinary people. I was a bit nervous and tense while driving, but then suddenly I see a sign which says, 'Soft Shoulders!' Now I ask you, who else would think of something like that? How thoughtful of them to put up a sign reminding people to relax their shoulders. I did just that and immediately felt and drove much better."

But several days later she returned very upset from another drive in her green Chevrolet. "I must get rid of this car!" she declared irritably. "It's no good! I tell you it's no good!"

Irene and I were sitting in the living room with some friends. We both got up to reason with her. "But, Mother dear, it's a brand-new car. You've only just bought it. Why do you want to get rid of it now?"

"No, no, no," she insisted. "I tell you it's no good. It made me very unhappy today."

We asked her what had happened.

"Well," she said, "there was a red traffic light and so I stopped. But the motor also stopped, and I couldn't start it again. There were a lot of people behind me, and they began honking their horns, but the car woudn't start and I got nervous, and I tell you, the car's no good. I'm going to get rid of it."

"But, Mother," I protested, "you got back here all right, so the motor must still work. All it probably needs is a little adjusting. Probably there's nothing wrong with it at all, except that the mixture is too lean."

"The mixture is too lean?" repeated Mother in a kind of dreamy voice. "Yes, yes, you are probably right, Boris. That must be the trouble — the mixture is too lean."

There was something in the tone of her voice which made me have my doubts. "Lubo, darling, do you know what it's a mixture of?"

"Certainly I do. It's a mixture of oil and water."

I felt like laughing. "But, Mother dear, what makes you say that?"

"Well, when you are driving and we stop to buy gasoline, you always say to the man, 'Check the oil and water.' "

Mother's knowledge of English may have left something to be desired, but there was no denying its quaintness. When the time came to return to Philadelphia, we decided that we would avoid the shortest, shoreline roads and instead make a long detour through the White Mountains. We were not in a hurry and the drive back took us two leisurely days.

At one point during the trip, while Irene was up front with Mother, who was at the wheel, I found myself seated in the back with one of Mother's violin pupils. He was a young fellow named Jimmy Bloom, about twenty-three years old and very much a scholarly type. I told him of the trouble I was having trying to learn to speak English correctly. The verb forms were very odd, and as for pronunciation, it was crazy; there were simply no rules, you just about had to learn each individual word by ear.

"Boys," Mother suddenly addressed us. "Vot you talking about?"

"You see, Jimmy," I said to the young violinist, "there is Lubo and she says, 'Boys, vot you talking about?' This is not a possible English sentence. This is very poor English. Now how would you say it, I mean in really good English?"

We discussed the possibilities for several minutes, and finally Jimmy suggested that in really elegant English the question would have been, "Gentlemen, may I inquire as to the topic of your conversation?"

Mother heard the phrase and fell in love with it immediately. "How lovely!" she kept repeating. " 'May I inkvire as to the topic of your conversation?' Beautiful! Oh, vot a *beau*-tiful sentence!"

As we approached Philadelphia, Mother decided that we had better stop somewhere and telephone Babushka to say that we would be arriving in time for dinner. We pulled up to a drugstore and went in. Walking up to the counter, Mother addressed the pharmacist in her most impressive Grand Duchess manner: "May I inkvire as to the topic of your telephone?"

The man looked at her open-mouthed, while Irene and I hooted with delight.

At Rockport, Mother's seaside house was more than ever the center of musical attention now that we could number the members of the Curtis Quartet among our neighbors. In 1927, when the quartet had first been formed, its student members had decided to call themselves the Swastika Quartet. The Indian motif had been recommended to Mrs. Curtis Bok by her friend Rudyard Kipling, and it figured prominently in the wall decorations of her summerhouse at Camden and of her suburban home at Merion (just outside of Philadelphia), where she spent the rest of each year. Though the bent spokes of the Indian motif faced right rather than left, the name "Swastika" was abandoned when Hitler made it a symbol for mass hatred and hysteria, and the student players were allowed by Josef Hofmann to rename themselves the Curtis Quartet.

The first violinist at this time was my friend Jascha Brodsky — a deceptively frail and emaciated person who often looked as though his last hour was at hand, but who was too much interested in wooing the fair sex to be in any mood to kick the bucket.

He was seconded by Ben Sharlip. The violist was Max Aronoff, and the cellist was Orlando Cole.

The presence of these young virtuosos added a considerable luster to Mother's musical soirées, which had by now become a standard feature of Rockport's summer entertainment. Every Sunday, anybody in the neighborhood who wished could drop in for an informal, "open house" concert, which was offered as a kind of cultural sop to the staider members of the community, who had at first been a bit perturbed by this Tzigane-like invasion of musicians, most of whom spoke English with thick foreign accents.

In this respect Mother was a typical offender, even though with her expensive Paris-style dresses and Shalimar perfume no one could have mistaken her for a Gypsy. But her sketchy knowledge of English pronunciation often led her to utter the most incredible enormities. She seemed to think that English, because of its partly Saxon origin, should be pronounced like German, and Irene and I had a lot of trouble explaining to her that the word "worm," for example, had to be pronounced *wurm* and not *vorm*.

On one of these Sunday evening concerts the living room was already well filled with sedate ladies and gentlemen who were waiting for the music to begin when Mother decided to close the curtains. Beyond the broad picture window a thick mist hid everything and one could not even see the water.

"My, vot a fok! Vot a fok!" exclaimed Mother, as she drew the curtain across the misty glass. In a small, adjacent room, where the four members of the Curtis Quartet were waiting, as it were, "off stage," Jascha Brodsky and his companions almost split their sides trying not to laugh, while the ladies in the living room looked this way and that pretending they hadn't heard.

In her generous desire to make the Curtis Institute into something special, not to say unique, Mrs. Bok had purchased a number of valuable violins, violas, and cellos made by famous Italian craftsmen. The collection included two Stradivari violins, an Amati viola, and a Montagnana cello which, as a special mark of favor, the members of the Curtis Quartet were allowed to play.

Later, when they undertook concert tours, they were permitted to take these precious instruments with them. The instruments even became a major attraction. Acting as spokesman for the others, since he was the only one among them who did not sound like a foreigner, Orlando Cole would preface each recital with a speech, saying that anyone in the audience who wanted could come backstage after the concert to admire their instruments, "made by the greatest violin-makers of all time."

One day a little old lady came to the green room to look at the fabulous instruments. Obligingly Jascha showed her his precious violin, let her admire its exquisite design and proportions, its beautifully lacquered wood. Then he pointed out the date: "Stradivari 1698."

"$16.98!" the old lady repeated, her eyes opening wide. "Why say, that's quite a bargain, isn't it!"

Not all our time, of course, was devoted to serious or informal musicmaking. Many of our neighbors, beginning with Felix Salmond, were rabid poker players. Normally we played a version known as Dealer's Choice. But one summer when our circle was joined by Leopold Auer's widow and one of Salmond's friends, a cellist from Cleveland named Victor de Gomez, we developed an extraordinary brand of poker known as the "Auer-de Gomez" variety, in which red sevens and one-eyed jacks were wild.

Another poker lover was Josef Hofmann, who was now practically a habitué at Mother's house. He spent increasingly long periods away from "The Rock," the sumptuous estate by the seashore located a mile or so away from Rockport, where he lived with his wife, Betty, her parents, two of her sisters, and their husbands. As though this were not company enough, Hofmann had to play host to a young man who made no effort to hide or to temper his assiduous advances to his hostess.

Although I still detested Hofmann heartily — he had hurt me too deeply to be easily forgiven — I now began to feel a certain pity for him. His first marriage might have been unhappy, but his second was clearly a disaster, and it left him much embittered about everything. To get away from the poisonous atmosphere of The Rock, he would spend hours puttering around in his workshop garage, where a mechanic named Mikla was employed on a year-round basis to help him with his automotive experiments. For Hofmann, among other things, was an inventor, or so at least he fancied. At one point in his life he had developed and patented some kind of shock absorber. How much of an innovation it really was I do not know. But I distinctly recall his latest "brain wave" in the early 1930s. Loudspeakers had recently appeared on the scene, and Hofmann decided that they should be exploited for piano-playing purposes. "What's the use of having to travel around with a nine-foot Steinway concert grand," he used to say, "when all you need is a small, reliable speaker that can be attached to the lid of a baby grand to amplify the sound?" Nothing ever came of this particular idea, but it kept Hofmann's mind and fingers occupied for many summers.

Though generally morose and incommunicative, he liked to talk about mechanical things and problems. On the other hand, he almost never discussed music. One even got the impression that music bored him, notwithstanding his prestige as one of the greatest pianists of all time. The real, profound reason for this, I believe, was his lack of success as a composer, to which I have previously alluded. For whenever Michael Dvorsky's compositions were performed, it was more as a personal favor shown to the Director of the Curtis Institute than because of their intrinsic merits. Hofmann, who was no fool, was keenly aware of the fact.

Even his piano playing was not all it was supposed to be. I do not mean by this that Hofmann couldn't hit the heights. When he really wanted to, he could. I remember one day hearing him play at The Rock. In fact, it was the only time I ever heard him practicing. It happened during an interlude on the tennis court, when somebody had taken my place behind the net. Hearing the sound of a piano coming from an open ground floor window of the large stone house, I wandered up through the grounds and hid behind some bushes. It was Hofmann all right, and what a performance! He was playing Chopin's magnificent Fourth Ballade in F Minor, and it was uncannily beautiful. I realized then that Mother's and Uncle Pierre's exalted opinion of him was justified.

I must add, however, that Hofmann's recitals in the Curtis Institute's Casimir Hall never particularly impressed me. I never felt then, as I did on that one occasion at The Rock, that the man behind the keyboard had a right to be considered the greatest of the great. It was all too mechanical. The inspiration, the fire were no longer there.

The reason, as I have suggested, is that Hofmann was increasingly bored with music. It had not brought him the rewards and recognition he had secretly craved as a composer. He would often sleep through student recitals — though I vividly recall one occasion when I happened to be sitting next to him. Half opening an eyelid in the direction of one of Felix Salmond's pupils, a particularly luscious female specimen who was stroking her trembling instrument between parted legs, Hofmann turned to me and whispered, "This is the first time in my life I am sorry I am not a cello." But it took something as unusual as that to arouse him from his customary apathy. He even manifested his disinterest in music in the most curious way, by stuffing cotton wool into his ears before his own recitals, as much as to say, "You see, I don't even like my own playing."

The basic trouble, I think, was that Hofmann was bored by the limited range of his repertoire. Unlike other successful pianists, he could not sight-read at all well. Once, when I questioned him about this, he admitted it quite candidly: "Well, you see, I hardly ever had to read music when I was young, because when studying with Anton Rubinstein my memory was so good that if he played something through once or twice I could remember it all and play it back to him by ear."

This sounds incredible, coming from a world-famous pianist

who had been chosen to direct the most prestigious school of music in the United States, but to me at least it has the ring of truth. Of course Hofmann could read a score, but it cost him a lot of effort. As often happens with people who are immensely talented, he took the easy way out. Having mastered a repertoire of sixty or seventy piano pieces, he played them over and over. He couldn't be bothered to enlarge it by learning other pieces, to which, had he but made the effort, he could have brought a new and luminous interpretation.

It is always dangerous for a musician to become pigeonholed as being exclusively a "Chopin player," or a "Beethoven interpreter," or "a master of Debussy and Ravel." The novelty of his recitals begins to wear off, not only for the audience but also and more seriously for the performer. This is what happened to Josef Hofmann. Increasingly bored by his standard repertory pieces, he began tinkering with them, much as he tinkered with the machines in his garage. In order to create new effects, he introduced unexpected innovations, began emphasizing the accompaniment or unduly stressing the secondary voices. The result was bizarre, but that was all it was.

Not far from Mother's birch-shaded house on Beauchamp Road there was a house, somewhat larger than its neighbors, which was known as the "Community House." It contained a dining room where most of the Curtis Institute students who came up to Rockport for the summer took their meals. A number of bedrooms on its upper floors were inhabited by singers, often referred to (by the name of their teacher) as "van Emden's girls." A large room, located over the garage, had been turned into a separate apartment for two particularly gifted students of composition who were to achieve international fame in later years: Gian-Carlo Menotti and Samuel Barber.

During our first summers at Rockport anyone staying in Mother's house who wanted to go for a dip in the ocean would have to walk down Beauchamp Road with a towel and bathing suit and use the steps and the wooden raft behind the Community House. There was thus a constant coming and going between the Community House and our own, and since van Emden's girls were often invited over to sing at Mother's soirées, we had plenty of opportunity to meet them.

Now one of them, as it happened, was the same Margaret Codd whom I had briefly tried to coach in singing in the autumn of 1931 and who had asked to be transferred to a less ignorant teacher. I had been too preoccupied by other problems at the time to be much concerned by this loss, and by the early summer of 1932 she was little more than a vague memory. But one day, while I was enjoying the midday sun seated on a rock overlooking the water behind Mother's house, I happened to look up from the orchestral score I was studying as a little rowboat passed. It was being rowed by a light-brown-haired siren in a bathing suit. There was some sheet music on the wooden traverse in front of her, which made me realize that this was one of van Emden's girls. As I was admiring the cataract of light brown hair that tumbled down her back, she suddenly glanced up at me and our eyes met. It was Margaret Codd. But instead of scowling at me, which she had every right to do, she said "Hello" in a gay, singsong voice, adding a charming smile as she rowed on.

There was something too inviting about that cheery smile and greeting for me to be able to resist. That same evening I walked over to the Community House to call on the brown-eyed mermaid with the long, nut-brown hair. She had once felt a positive loathing for that "stuck-up Goldovsky fellow," but now, through some kind of midsummer magic, all trace of it had disappeared. We were both drawn to each other by a strange, instinctive impulse, and during the casual stroll we took under the trees our lips suddenly met in a breathless embrace.

It did not take me long to discover that this siren and I had a number of things in common. In addition to our love of music, we were both born in the same year, in a country other than the United States, and into a musical family. Her father, Alfred Arthur Codd, had been a *basso cantante* in his Victoria, British Columbia church choir. Her mother, Winnifred Sarah Nelson, had been a famous Canadian concert singer, and like her sister, Ethel, who had a lovely soprano voice, Margaret Codd had been taught to play the piano at an early age. Her mother had died of pneumonia and her father of cancer, leaving her an orphan before she was seven years old, and the rest of her youthful years had been full of unhappiness, as she was shunted back and forth between various aunts, who vainly sought to discipline her poetic and wayward disposition.

Poetry, play acting, and singing had been her consolations, and already at a high school in the town of Prince Albert, Saskatchewan, she had won a first prize for the quality of her voice. She had run away from school when she was only fifteen, had put on high heels and a pair of rakish silk stockings (adorned with blue and purple butterflies) in order to seem older than she really was, and had worked for a while as a salesgirl in a dry-goods store. Finally, after many other vicissitudes, she had enlisted the support of the noted concert singer Claire Dux, who had recommended her for a scholarship at the Eastman School of Music, to which her sister, Ethel, had already been admitted.

Since her scholarship only took care of tuition, she had had to take odd jobs — training the church choir, working at the chain store on Saturdays, ushering at the theater, or singing during movie intermissions — to pay for her food. At the Eastman School her acting ability had attracted as much attention as her singing. After a particularly harrowing portrayal of Madame Butterfly, in which real tears had poured down her cheeks while she simulated suicide, a well-known Rochester critic named Stewart Sabin had written her a private note to say that, though he was not allowed to review student performances, her rendition had been the closest to Geraldine Farrar's he had ever seen.

Ernst Lert, who converted me to opera.

Fritz Reiner, who taught me operatic conducting.

Father in Moscow.

Uncle Petya in Moscow.

Mother and Aunt Anna in Moscow.

Aunt Anna in Moscow.

Sister Irene with me in Berlin, 1922.

Grandfather in Paris, 1924.

Grandmother in Philadelphia, 1933.

Artur Schnabel.

Sidney Prince in New York.

A portrait of Tess Prince.

Irèn Senn and Eddy Kilényi with me in Budapest.

Ernö Dohnányi in Budapest.

Mother.

Carnegie Hall Program

FIRE NOTICE
Look around NOW and choose the nearest Exit to your seat. In case of fire walk (not run) to THAT Exit. Do not try to beat your neighbor to the street.
JOHN J. DORMAN, Fire Commissioner.

CARNEGIE HALL
Sunday Afternoon, January 30th, at 3:00

LEA LUBOSHUTZ

and

JOSEF HOFMANN

VIOLIN AND PIANOFORTE CONCERT

PROGRAMME:

Sonata in G major.............. Brahms

Vivace ma non troppo

Adagio

Allegro molto moderato

Program Concluded on Second Page Following

Carnegie Hall program (first part), New York, 1927.

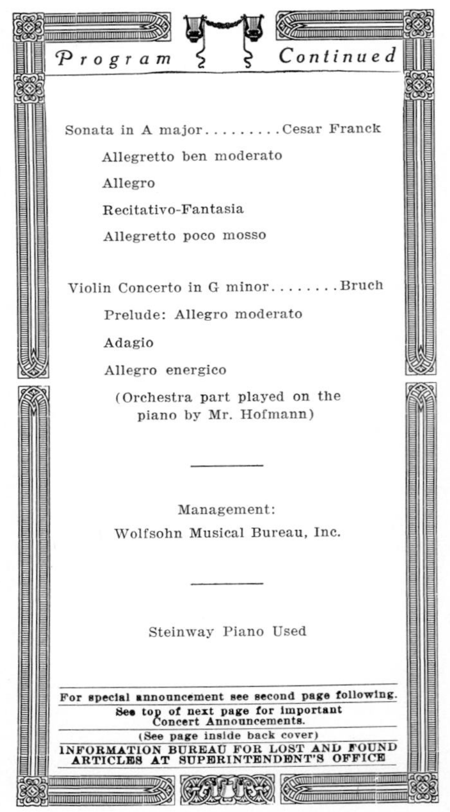

Program Continued

Sonata in A major......... Cesar Franck

Allegretto ben moderato

Allegro

Recitativo-Fantasia

Allegretto poco mosso

Violin Concerto in G minor........ Bruch

Prelude: Allegro moderato

Adagio

Allegro energico

(Orchestra part played on the piano by Mr. Hofmann)

Management:
Wolfsohn Musical Bureau, Inc.

Steinway Piano Used

For special announcement see second page following.
See top of next page for important Concert Announcements.
(See page inside back cover)
INFORMATION BUREAU FOR LOST AND FOUND ARTICLES AT SUPERINTENDENT'S OFFICE

Carnegie Hall program (second part), New York, 1927.

Josef Hofmann.

Irene and Billy Wolf on their honeymoon, 1933.

Mother and Felix Salmond in Maine.

Mother in her Chevrolet in Rockport, Maine.

Mother and Josef Lhevinne in Rockport, Maine.

Mother with me in Rockport, Maine.

Operatic extravaganza at Rodzinski's home, Cleveland, 1936.

Margaret and Michael, Cleveland, 1938.

Sarah Winifred Codd, Margaret's mother.

Alfred Arthur Codd, Margaret's father.

Margaret with Serge Koussevitzky in Boston.

Mother and Marina, Cleveland, 1942.

Uncle Pierre and Aunt Genia, with me in New York, 1956.

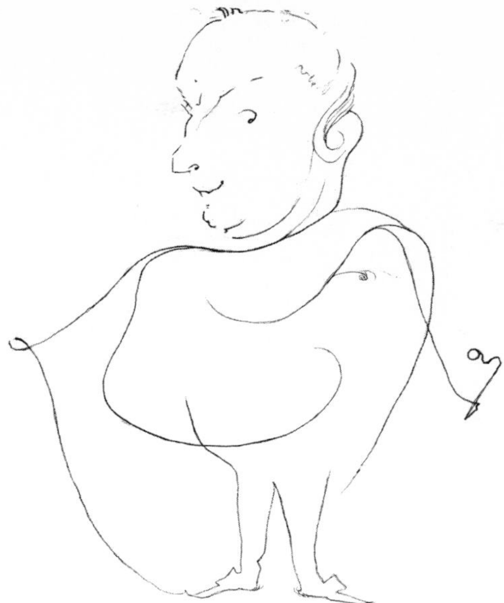

Caricature of me by Olga Koussevitzky,
Tanglewood, 1947.

Serge Koussevitzky.

Mother, Koussevitzky, Margaret, and I, after the premiere of *The Marriage of Figaro*, Boston, 1946.

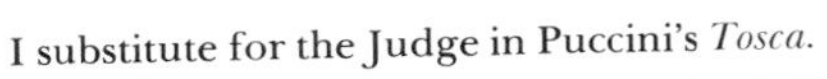
I substitute for the Judge in Puccini's *Tosca.*

Margaret as Susanna in *The Marriage of Figaro*, Boston, 1946.

Cast of *The Marriage of Figaro* in our living room, Brookline, 1946.

Mozart's *Idomeneo* (Finale of Act 1), Tanglewood, 1947.

Later, the famous Scottish-born soprano Mary Garden had come to the Eastman School to sing *Carmen,* and she had picked her out from the other members of the student chorus to be her adversary in the cigarette girls' scene. During the subsequent tussle on stage, the visiting soprano had seized her by the hair and given it such a violent tug that she, in turn, had angrily gripped Mary Garden's hair and practically yanked it out of her head — only to be complimented during the intermission: "Bravo, darling, how talented you are!" For in addition to her gifts as an actress and singer, "Coddie" — as she was known to her fellow students — was a gifted mimic with a fine ear for imitating other people's accents.

I had had my Sidney Prince; she had found a generous benefactor in a Miss Myra Smith, an unmarried lady from Palmyra, New York, who, after hearing her sing at an Eastman recital, had offered her a monthly allowance of $100 so that she could concentrate on her music studies without having to work in the supermarket or usher at the theater.

It took time, of course, to find all this out. But by now I was definitely "bitten." I called on Margaret every day, and in the evenings, when she and the other vocal students were officially confined inside the Community House, she would crawl out of her bedroom window, slide down the drainpipe, and tumble into my waiting arms. We went for moonlit and other strolls, and during the day, when it was warm, we would even meet while swimming, exchanging furtive kisses under the wooden platform on which my unsuspecting mother liked to sunbathe.

As one of "van Emden's girls," Margaret at this time was most unhappy. Her first voice teacher at the Curtis Institute had been the great operatic soprano Marcella Sembrich, to whom she had written one day at a time when she was living in Manhattan with her sister, who was now married to a talented composer and conductor named Otto Luening. Her request for an audition had been granted, she had gone to the famous diva's apartment and had sung for her, but the only comment at the end had been a noncommittal "Thank you, dearie!" which had left Margaret completely crushed. She had returned to her sister's apartment and cried her eyes out for the next twenty-four hours wondering what on earth she was going to do next. But then the telephone had rung: it was Marcella Sembrich's secretary, lady companion, and general factotum on the line, saying, "Madame would like to see you again."

"I was a nervous wreck," so Coddie described this second encounter to me, "but of course I went back. She had me sing again — what, I can't remember. Then she looked me over carefully, 'Now, dearie, you stand up straight, you turn around, you pull up skirts, hmm . . . Vary nice, vary nice!' She said something in Polish to her factotum and they exchanged some words I didn't understand. Finally, while I was still standing there and wondering what to do with myself, the factotum spoke: 'Madame has decided to give you a foohl scholarsheep!' I almost fainted dead away."

As a special mark of her esteem Marcella Sembrich had invited Margaret to spend the summer of 1930 in a country house she owned on the shores of Lake George, in Upper New York State, along with several other voice students and Sylvan Levin, who provided the piano accompaniment whenever they sang. The famous diva had insisted that her new protégée try on a number of her operatic costumes, occasionally getting down on her hands and knees to tug at a hem or rearrange some ruffles. She had by this time completely lost her voice, and she wanted to bestow these gifts on one who seemed destined to succeed her as a leading coloratura singer.

The summer had been marred by a momentary misunderstanding when Margaret had asked for permission to sing at a nearby hotel, where they were offering her the enormous sum of $10 for an evening of concert entertainment. Permission was indignantly denied by Marcella Sembrich, who was being paid $100 by the Curtis Institute for each hour of instruction. No, absolutely not! She was not going to sing at that hotel! Why, the idea of it — allowing one of her students to be paid a pauper's wage for an hour of her singing! Margaret was so upset that she cried. So, to cheer her up, the old lady had her sing Zerlina's part in the famous *"Là ci darem la mano"* duet, while she herself paced up and down the living room singing Don Giovanni's lines in a cracked, croaking voice.

The lesson completed, Marcella Sembrich had said to her, "Dearie, now ve vawk, ve vawk!" Taking Margaret by the arm, she had led her out for a walk around the garden, in the course of which the old lady had said to her in her strange shorthand mode of speech, "Not now . . . Later you — me!" meaning that her pupil was not yet a diva, but that one day she would follow in her footsteps.

This was Marcella Sembrich's way of saying farewell to the youngest of her pupils. She was seventy-two years old and the time was fast approaching when she would have to give up teaching, just as twenty years before she had had to abandon the operatic stage. And sure enough, she had only been able to complete one more academic year at Curtis. A former pupil of hers named Queena Mario, who was now singing with the Metropolitan Opera in New York, had been brought in to replace her. She had taken over the teaching of all of Marcella Sembrich's students, with the single exception of the youngest — Margaret Codd — who was turned over to another voice teacher named Harriet van Emden. Margaret detested her, as heartily as she had once detested me, and her one burning desire now was to find some way of escaping from her uncomfortably Sapphic clutches.

When Margaret requested a change of teachers from Harriet van Emden to Queena Mario, Hofmann explained to her that the latter had all the students she could handle, as it was, and that she would have to wait.

Margaret was so unhappy about this situation that before the school year was over, she took the train to New York and went to see the well-known voice teacher Estelle Liebling, who introduced her to several agents. She was offered a contract by the Shubert Theatre people as well as a chance to understudy Kitty Carlyle's roles on Broadway. But Margaret finally decided that she would be behaving like a ninny and ruining all her chances for an operatic career if she were to give up her scholarship at the Curtis Institute. And so, dutifully if a bit dispiritedly, she returned to Philadelphia.

Margaret then had a small apartment of her own not far from the Curtis Institute. Here I would often join her for lunch and listen to her pour out her grievances against Harriet van Emden. In her operatic acting class Margaret was known as an eager beaver because she was just about the only one of the girl vocalists who bothered to prepare the assignments given to the students by Wilhelm von Wymetal. With the bass-baritone Leonard Treash, who was her eager beaver counterpart on the male side, she would act out the *Là ci darem la mano* duet. When this weekly routine was over, Wymetal would ask what other scenes had been memorized. As a rule, none of the students would volunteer, and there would come the inevitable query: "Codd, how is your Philine?" Margaret's eagerness to act out this role from Thomas's *Mignon* was habitually frustrated by the lack of preparation and the general indiscipline of her classmates, who tended to behave with Wymetal much as the student instrumentalists had behaved with Mlynarski. I was called upon quite often to be the accompanist for these acting sessions, and the sorry spectacle I was offered did nothing to alter my prejudice against opera as a form of musical drama.

The following summer — that of 1933 — Margaret did not come to Rockport. Her hopes had been unexpectedly fulfilled at the end of the Curtis Institute's academic year when Queena Mario had one day hailed her in the foyer of the school and said, "Coddie, Pelly and I have been thinking about you and we would like you to come and stay with us for the summer, so that you can study with me." Queena Mario's husband, Wilfred Pelletier — or Pelly, as he was known to his friends — was a Metropolitan Opera conductor.

Overjoyed at her good luck, Margaret spent a blissful summer in Pennsylvania's Pocono Mountains, where the Pelletiers had a summerhouse, studying with her new voice teacher. They had her sing at local concerts with her friend Rose Bampton, who was also a Curtis student, and at night, to cheer her up, her charming hosts would sit on Margaret's bed and tell her how a future prima donna should dress, the sort of persons she should or should not consort with, and offer her other social pointers of that kind.

Our own summer — the one I spent with Mother, first in Philadelphia, and later in Rockport — was eventful for other reasons. A few months before, Irene had met an attractive young Philadelphian named Walter Wolf and had peremptorily decided that this was the man she was going to marry. Although Irene was astonishingly mature for her age, she was still only sixteen years old, and Mother was rightfully a bit surprised. In fact, we were all startled, for Irene had not yet graduated from high school. "Well, and what of it?" said Irene defiantly. If necessary, she would finish school *after* she was married; there would be plenty of time to complete her education before she had her first child!

Her astounding self-assurance swept everything before it. Mother, who on the whole was a domineering personality — except when Babushka expressed a strong dislike to something she was wearing and would order her to go upstairs and change her dress immediately (for yes, this too occasionally happened) — now suddenly capitulated. If this was the man her strong-willed daughter wanted for a husband, then let her have him. Walter Wolf's mother, for her part, was enchanted. Highly intellectual and interested in music, she had never expected her younger son, hitherto mostly interested in football and girls, to marry into a famous musical family. The prospect thrilled her, and since Irene was a fully grown young lady, as far as she was concerned let them be married by all means, and the sooner the better!

As a kind of wedding present, the young couple were offered a two-month honeymoon in Europe, while Mother outdid herself assembling a fabulous trousseau. After all, one only gets married (for the first time) once in a lifetime, and for her one and only daughter nothing but the very best would do. Irene, who up till then had worn simple cotton panties, was suddenly deluged with silk chemises and fancy lingerie, all exquisitely embroidered. The towels too had to be embroidered, and so did the dozens of sheets that she was given, enough to last her through two or three decades. In fact, the sheets had to be of such absolutely top-notch quality that there could be no question of their all being purchased in America. A select few, it was decreed (before the spoiled pair embarked on their honeymoon), would have to be bought and embroidered in Vienna.

Just how much these elaborate gifts cost Mother, I have no idea, but they must just about have emptied her bank account. Quite a bit of the finery, personally packed by Mother into huge steamer trunks with a fantastic quantity of tissue paper, actually preceded the bridal pair across the ocean — that is, before they themselves embarked on the *Majestic*. Irene later told me that when she and her husband finally began unpacking those trunks in their Paris hotel suite, so much paper came floating out with the precious lingerie and dresses that they were soon knee-deep in a ground fog of tissue.

In Rockport, the "hole" made by Irene's absence was filled to some extent by two new poker-loving musicians — Josef Lhevinne and his wife, Rosina. A Russian who had studied in St. Petersburg under the great Anton Rubinstein, Lhevinne now taught the piano at the Juilliard School of Music, as did his wife. I had heard him play magnificently at a recital he had given in Budapest. He must have been close to sixty, and to disguise the fact that he was bald, he wore a wig, or more exactly three wigs, which were changed at regular fortnightly intervals. The first simulated a fairly close-cropped head of hair, the second a head of hair in the intermediate stage, and the third a crop that was on the distinctly longish side. "I could do with a haircut," he would say as the date for the changeover approached, and a day or two later he would appear with his ears cleanly disengaged and a neat hairline across his nape.

Margaret, as I have said, was off in the Poconos staying with the Pelletiers. But I occasionally put in a telephone call to be sure that all was well and to say how much I missed our nocturnal escapades, the drainpipe gymnastics and the stealthy climbing back up into the second floor of the Community House.

In September, when we returned to Philadelphia, I decided to treat Margaret to a little surprise. I rang up some friends with whom she was due to stay on her return and found out exactly when she was expected to be back. I then drove over to their house, parked the car out of sight, and ducked into the coat closet in the front hall when we saw the headlights of a car turn into the driveway.

Margaret, as I later found out, had been driven back from the Poconos by a Canadian cellist named Tommy. After her bags had been taken out of the car and brought in, there was a lot of mysterious whispering on the front doorstep. They seemed to be taking an extraordinarily long time to say goodbye to each other. My suspicions were soon dramatically confirmed. "Oh, I'm so in love, I'm so in love!" I heard Margaret tell her friends in a dreamy voice. "Oh, I'm so in love! . . . With whom? But with Tommy, of course, who drove me here. He's so wonderful, you don't know him . . . but he's just divine, divine."

It was all I could take. The pleasant surprise I had prepared for Margaret had boomeranged disastrously. Opening the closet door, I stepped out into the hall, gave Margaret an angry look, and left the house without a word.

Several days passed before we saw each other again. They were unhappy days for me, but even unhappier for Margaret, who was overcome by remorse. Later she told me that after I had walked out, the sky had exploded. In a flash she had realized that it was a stupid summer romance, no more.

Nothing enhances a love affair more than adversity. Once we had made up and promised to forget this silly interlude, we began seeing each other more frequently than ever. In the evening, after driving Mother home from the Curtis Institute to our suburban house in Cynwyd, I would invent some pretext for taking the car out to "see some friends" or for any other reason I could think of at that moment.

Mother's suspicions had already been aroused the previous summer, at Rockport, by my frequent after-supper disappearances. She had tried to sound out one or two Curtis students to find out which of the van Emden girls her son was courting. But though it was a fairly open secret among the inmates of the Community House, nobody tattled. I had made no effort to introduce Margaret, who in any case was intimidated by Mother's somewhat distant straight-backed, almost haughty bearing. On the few occasion when she had been invited over with other Curtis students to sing at one of Mother's soirées, Margaret had been so tongue-tied in her presence that she had hardly uttered three words.

In the autumn of 1933, more than a year had passed and Margaret and I were closer than ever. Mother's suspicions were again aroused, but nobody betrayed our little secret — until one evening I inadvertently let the cat out of the bag. I was supposed to be driving Mother home from the Curtis Institute, as I did regularly at the end of the school day, when I absent-mindedly drove the car to the apartment house where Margaret was living. Before I could proceed, Mother pounced on me: "So, Boris, this is where you come in the evenings! Don't try to deny it! It's one of those van Emden girls you're after, isn't it? It started last summer in Rockport and it's been going on ever since, hasn't it? Now I want you to tell me who it is — right here this minute!"

I told her that it was Margaret Codd. Mother said nothing, but I could tell from her look and her silence that she was anything but pleased. It would have been difficult in any case to find somebody capable of living up to the exalted expectations Mother harbored for her "genius child," Boris.

Now that the secret was out, there was no use resorting to further subterfuges. I continued to see Margaret regularly, much to Mother's annoyance. But there was little she could do about it. Margaret, for her part, was more intimidated than ever, and whenever she smelled a whiff of Shalimar perfume in a Curtis corridor or caught sight of one of Mother's expensive dresses and a head of brightly dyed red hair, she turned and ran the other way.

For the Christmas holidays Margaret was invited to New York to continue her voice lessons with Queena Mario. Mother also decided to spend Christmas week in New York and I went with her. Once again we stayed at the Great Northern Hotel. This gave me a chance to call on the Pelletiers at their 72nd Street apartment and to see Margaret.

Three days after Christmas, Margaret and I had a trivial row over something, and that evening she told Queena Mario and "Pelly" that she was through with Boris Goldovsky for good! "Thank God!" they said. "Now we can get down to business! It's about time you got rid of him!" There was unanimous agreement that that Goldovsky fellow had been a great drain on her time and emotions, and as a future diva she'd better cut him right out of her life.

That same afternoon Mother decided to have it out with me at last.

"Boris," she demanded, "do you really love that Margaret Codd female?"

I answered, "Yes."

"Then, for God's sake, marry her!"

Without wasting time I hurried over to the Pelletiers' apartment to see Margaret. They must have been startled to see that detestable Goldovsky fellow darkening their threshold once again.

But opening her arms, Margaret generously forgave me. Without any further ado we decided to get married.

The next morning, a Friday, Margaret came over to the Great Northern Hotel, and from there we all went to Fritz Reiner's apartment.

"Fritz, vat you think?" said Mother, once her luxurious fur coat and suede gloves had been removed. "Margaret and Boris are going to be married!"

"Oh?" said Reiner, raising his dark eyebrows slightly. "But everybody at Curtis thought they were married a year ago."

The marriage, it was finally decided, would take place the next day, Saturday, December 30. Fritz Reiner agreed to be best man. Since I was still relatively penniless, Mother hurried off to buy a wedding ring, and later on this same Friday Margaret was introduced to Uncle Pierre and Aunt Genia, whom she had never met before.

The next morning we all descended into the subway and rode down to New York's City Hall. Reiner was accompanied by his wife, Carlotta, Uncle Pierre by Genia, I by Margaret, and Mother by the wedding ring she had bought for us.

Unfortunately we were not the only ones who had decided to get married on this last Saturday of the year. Dozens of other hopefuls and their kin were already lined up outside the registration office. The sight of this long queue was too much for Uncle Pierre. "Just leave it to me," he said. Walking boldly up to the head of the line, he approached the clerk sitting behind a desk and waved a ten-dollar bill under his nose. The clerk gave it a cross-eyed look and began shouting, "Hey, what do you take me for anyway? Where do you think you are? Get the hell back there in line, where you belong!"

Uncle Pierre came back to where we were standing, looking unusually crestfallen. For once his charm had failed to work. It even boomeranged badly, for the outraged clerk saw to it that we were the last to be married.

The ceremony completed, we repaired for a late lunch to the Russian Tea Room, next to Carnegie Hall, where Mother had reserved a table. We were seated there, all seven of us, and had just finished the first course when Mischa Elman walked in.

"Ah, Mischa," said Mother, pointing to the bride, "let me introduce my daughter-in-law. This is Margaret, who has just married *Barees.*"

Elman's eyes almost popped out of his head. "Vat!" he cried, "a vedding party? And vy vasn't I invited?"

There was a lot of laughter. But shortly afterward I suddenly felt violently sick and had to excuse myself. Margaret accompanied me back to the Great Northern Hotel, where Mother had booked a room for us, and I was put to bed.

It took me twenty-four hours to recover from my stomach upset. Meanwhile Mother left for Philadelphia, saying she didn't want to leave Babushka alone any longer. The next day she called us on the telephone. We must hurry back to Philadelphia immediately. She had arranged a big reception for that very evening so that Margaret could be formally introduced to Irene's husband, Walter, his mother, brother, and all the other members of the Wolf clan living in or near Philadelphia.

We had no choice but to obey. And that was the end of our "honeymoon."

5

Fritz Reiner's Great Opera Season

FOR THE FIRST MONTHS of our married life Margaret and I lived on the third floor of the Cynwyd house above the floor where Mother and Babushka had their rooms. It was not a very satisfactory arrangement for either of us, since we had to take the train to the Curtis Institute every morning and return the same way in the evening. Also, the atmosphere at home was not always congenial, as we discovered the very first morning when we came downstairs in our dressing gowns for breakfast. Seeing me appear with my arm around Margaret's waist, Lubo sternly rebuked us: "This is *not* a bedroom!"

With Babushka, Margaret had little trouble. They managed to communicate in a strange mixture of German (of which Margaret knew a few words) and Yiddish, and, generally speaking, there were few problems. Babushka doted on her daughter just as Mother doted on me, and she did not have particularly strong views as to the sort of person her grandson should have married.

With Lubo, of course, it was quite another matter. Though she had rushed us into marriage, she did not approve of Margaret and made little effort to conceal it. Margaret tried desperately hard to please her, but it was uphill work and the effort often showed.

We had only been married a few weeks when Mother decided to throw a small dinner party in our honor. It was a very elegant, black-tie-and-evening-dress affair, attended by Mrs. Curtis Bok, Josef Hofmann and his wife, and several other notables from the Curtis Institute. At the dinner table, where Mother had pointedly seated her daughter-in-law close to her, Margaret once again sought to please her by telling her what a genius her son was, this being the sort of thing Lubo loved to hear. "You know," she said, "it's so fantastic how musical Boris is! It's really extraordinary! Often I wake up in the middle of the night and see him conducting in his sleep."

The conversation had momentarily petered out at the other end of the table, so that everyone was listening when Lubo replied, "Oh, but dat is nothing, Margaret. How often do I vake in the middle of the night and find myself fingering my passages!"

There was a moment of dreadful silence, hastily broken by Mrs. Bok, who turned to Mother and said, "My dear, I think we're going to have an early spring, don't you? What a lovely afternoon it was today!" Mother innocently agreed, not realizing that she had just added another gem to our anthology of Luboisms.

A few weeks later, in May of 1934, Margaret and I were graduated from the Curtis Institute of Music. Shortly afterward we left for Rockport. Now that we were married, Margaret no longer needed to slide down the drainpipe of the Community House, for we had a room upstairs in Mother's house. But though we spent many carefree hours playing poker with Felix Salmond, Josef Lhevinne, and others, this was not a happy summer for Margaret, who was appalled by the spitefulness of the gossip and the pettiness of the intrigue, as different teachers, and even more their wives and relatives, indulged in various forms of character assassination.

Although Lubo never listened to gossip — a quality that had endeared her to many a musician — she was a forbidding mother-in-law as far as Margaret was concerned. To conceal her dismay and her feeling of being an outsider, Margaret would retire upstairs and spend hours in her room alone. She was so miserable and upset that finally she went to see a country doctor, a sort of homespun psychiatrist who advised her, after hearing her tale of woe, "to get out of that household — and fast!"

A day or two later she received a telegram from the Steel Pier Opera Company asking if she could come to Atlantic City to sing the part of Olympia, the doll, in *The Tales of Hoffmann* — a role Margaret had already filled, in September of the previous year, with the San Carlo Opera Company. (Queena Mario had even wanted her to go on tour with the San Carlo group to gain some valuable firsthand opera experience, but Margaret had preferred to return to the Curtis Institute, and, incidentally, to me.) This invitation from Atlantic City was followed almost immediately by a second, made by Alexander Smallens, who had been acting as Leopold Stokowski's assistant with the Philadelphia Orchestra. Smallens also was planning to put on *Hoffmann* as part of a series of open-air concerts held in the Robin Hood Dell amphitheater of Fairmount Park in central Philadelphia, and he too wanted Margaret to sing Olympia. She accepted both invitations with alacrity.

Fritz Reiner had meanwhile asked me to stay on at the Curtis Institute as a coach and as a special assistant for opera productions — a job for which I was to be paid an additional $50 a week. His electrifying *Elektra* production had been followed, during the previous academic season, by a performance of Mussorgsky's *Boris Godunov,* in which I was dressed up as a Russian nobleman in order to direct some of the on-stage choruses. Two months later (in February 1932) I had to appear on stage again, during a performance of Wagner's *Lohengrin,* sneaking out behind the backs of King Henry's four trumpeters in order to give them advance warning of their musical cues. In April Reiner squeezed in two more operas — *Carmen* and *Aida* — but with this final flourish the Philadelphia Grand Opera Association quietly gave up the ghost. Even the wealthy and generous Mrs. Bok could no longer cover its ever-mounting debts.

As part of a belt-tightening regime imposed by the Depression, New York's Metropolitan Opera Company had also seen fit to forgo its regular Tuesday-night excursions to Philadelphia. To fill the cultural void thus opened, the trustees of the Philadelphia Orchestra decided on a bold innovation. Since neither the Met nor the city's now defunct opera company could provide this kind of entertainment, the orchestra would step into the breach, embellishing the forthcoming concert season (1934–1935) with a series of special opera performances, to be put on in the Academy of Music's main auditorium. The schedule called for a total of ten operas, which were to be interlarded into the normal concert season. A new opera was to be presented every third week — the first performance being given on a Thursday afternoon, followed by a second performance on Saturday evening, and a third and final showing three nights later.

The idea had not appealed to everyone, beginning with the Philadelphia Orchestra's resident conductor, Leopold Stokowski, who would have nothing to do with it. Since his assistant, Alexander Smallens, could not handle more than five operas himself, Fritz Reiner was asked to conduct the rest. Even though stage rehearsals would have to be held on Sundays — the only day on which the Academy of Music's main auditorium was available — Fritz Reiner was in no mood to refuse this unexpected chance to direct an absolutely first-class ensemble.

The Philadelphia Orchestra was then probably the finest in the world. I realize that this statement may sound a bit extreme to those who were not alive at the time or who were too young to remember its extraordinary quality and renown. By 1934 close to half of its instrumentalists were graduates of the Curtis Institute — having studied there with men like Marcel Tabuteau, the oboist; William Kincaid, the flutist; Saul Caston, the trumpeter; and Anton Horner, master teacher of the French horn.

The bane of all orchestras is a tendency to sloppiness, which sets in as a result of repetitive routine. Since all orchestra conductors have their strengths and weaknesses, and since there are a limited number of things that they can really teach well-trained players, it is rare for an orchestral ensemble to play at its very best under the same conductor for more than a few years. Under Stokowski, certain sections of the Philadelphia Orchestra, particularly the woodwinds and the brasses, had reached a state of remarkable excellence as early as 1925. I can still remember the sound of three muted trumpets in Debussy's *Fêtes* (as orchestrated by Ravel) which I was fortunate enough to hear in the autumn of that year, when I had accompanied Mother to a Philadelphia concert. It was a sound such as I have never heard (before or since) — hauntingly beautiful, like some foretaste of paradise.

Part of the credit for such breathtaking effects undoubtedly belonged to "Stokie," as he was popularly known. But much of it was also due to the proximity of the Curtis Institute of Music and its great teachers. For the graduates who joined the Philadelphia Orchestra were not only playing for the conductor, whether it was Stokowski or Smallens, they were sitting next to their peers; and — what was even more important — were being judged by their teachers in a more or less permanent examination.

No one knew this better than Fritz Reiner. After his Cincinnati setback this was the chance of a lifetime. Now he could really display his conducting talents in opera, that most difficult and challenging of musical fields.

In early September, when I returned to Philadelphia, Reiner thrust a score into my hand, saying, "This is a new Shostakovich opera. Since you know Russian, I want you to study it thoroughly and give me a detailed report on it in exactly three weeks' time. I have to discuss the possibilities with Herbert Graf, who is coming from Vienna to help us with the staging, and I cannot delay the decision much longer."

This new Shostakovich opera, based on a story by Nikolai Leskov, carried the tongue-twisting title (in English) of *Lady Macbeth of Mtsensk*. It was the tale of an unfaithful wife named Katerina Ismailova, who wantonly invites her lover to share her bed while her husband is away from home, and who later poisons her father-in-law and helps her lover to murder her husband.

Though the opera was marked by three brutal murders, Shostakovich's Lady Macbeth was really less interested in power than she was in sex. Leaving nothing to the imagination, the composer had even included a scene in an upstairs bedroom in which Katerina Ismailova and her paramour go to it behind a drawn curtain, while the instruments in the pit, in an elaborate orchestral interlude, provide a symphonic background of unmistakably erotic rasps and gasps.

Knowing what a stickler Reiner was for accuracy, I went through the Shostakovich score with a fine-toothed comb and nearly memorized the words and the music to familiarize myself with the scenic, orchestral, and vocal problems and to be able to describe the plot in complete detail.

When we finally got together with Herbert Graf, three weeks later, Reiner explained that he was planning to give Wagner's *Tristan und Isolde* and Richard Strauss's *Der Rosenkavalier* in German. On the other hand, he wanted to present an English version of Mozart's *Marriage of Figaro* so that everyone in the audience could appreciate its sprightly gaiety and humor. "Now what about this one?" he asked me, pointing to the Shostakovich score. "Do you think it too could be translated and presented in English?"

My answer was frankly negative. The patrons of the Philadelphia Orchestra were a distinctly conservative breed, and to expose them to something as brazen as this seemed to me very risky, to say the least. The libretto included all sorts of down-to-earth expressions that would be extremely offensive to people if they could understand them. At one point, for example, the workmen in the Ismailovs' yard try to squeeze a serving girl into a barrel. As they do so, they pinch her and make ribald remarks about her breasts, saying that they are going to squeeze some milk out of them. Some of the stage actions are extremely violent. A man is mercilessly flogged in full view of the audience. "There's also an on-stage bedroom scene," I added, "where the curtain is drawn to hide the bed and the goings-on, but the orchestra plays music that suggests sexual intercourse, and it's presented in rather obvious and occasionally vulgar terms. Frankly, if this is to be done at all, I think it should be done in Russian. Otherwise, many of your listeners are going to be shocked right out of their seats."

"Hmm," said Reiner, pursing his lips, "I guess you're right." He didn't even bother to check on my report by having me point out these various passages in the score. My recommendation apparently sufficed. His own amorous shenanigans in Cincinnati had provoked a lot of indignation and had cost him his job. He wasn't going to queer the pitch for himself in Philadelphia by precipitating another uproar. "This opera is not for us," he said, turning to Herbert Graf. "I don't want to perform it. We'll have to find something else."

The opera finally chosen to plug the gap was Verdi's *Falstaff*. Since the composer had borrowed his story from Shakespeare, it seemed fitting that it should be sung in English. But as we were soon to discover, this was not the last that Philadelphia was to hear of Shostakovich's provincial murderess.

Meticulous as ever, Fritz Reiner made frequent journeys to New York to hire the finest voices he could obtain for the major roles and to audition promising young singers for the secondary parts. He was not going to spoil this unique chance of conducting a superlative orchestra by lining up a second-rate cast of singers. But he was quite prepared to give a chance to talented beginners who had yet to make their mark. One of them — chosen for the important roles of Kurwenal in *Tristan und Isolde,* of Count Almaviva in *The Marriage of Figaro,* of Faninal in *Der Rosenkavalier,* of Falstaff, and finally of Kothner in Wagner's *Die Meistersinger* — was a young baritone from the Juilliard School of Music named Julius Huehn. He could not have been much more than twenty-three years old, and he had had very little opera experience before Reiner undertook to coach him.

Another talented beginner he was willing to promote was Margaret, whom he picked for the role of Cherubino in *The Marriage of Figaro.* Reiner also asked her to understudy Elizabeth Schumann's role of Sophie in *Der Rosenkavalier.* Nor were these the only operatic plums that were dropped into her lap. Impressed by her performance as Olympia in his open-air production of *The Tales of Hoffmann,* Alexander Smallens asked her to sing the role of Gretel in Humperdinck's *Hansel and Gretel.*

Since both Margaret and I were now often on call for afternoon or evening rehearsals, we decided to move out of Mother's suburban house and closer to the center of Philadelphia. The additional $50 a week I was now earning as one of Reiner's opera assistants, added to the $72 a week I was still earning as a coach at the Curtis Institute, made it possible for us to rent an apartment in the same "Town House" building, near Rittenhouse Square, where Mother had first lived with Babushka and Irene. We could now breakfast in our dressing gowns as often as we wanted without running the risk of offending Lubo's sense of domestic proprieties.

For the first of the scheduled season's operatic offerings Fritz Reiner had chosen one of Richard Wagner's grandest works, *Tristan und Isolde.* He had decided, furthermore, to present it in its entirety — something no opera company in the United States had ever dreamed of doing — and to add to the unprecedented splendor of the occasion, he had asked one of America's foremost scenic designers, Donald Oenslager, who was then teaching at Yale, to design the sets.

The results were memorable, particularly for the opera's first act, which takes place on board the ship that is carrying Tristan and Isolde from Ireland to Cornwall. This act has always posed scenic problems, since the focus of acting and singing keeps shifting back and forth from the quarters occupied by Isolde and her personal maid, Brangäne, to the deck, reserved for Tristan and the sailors. Oenslager's solution to this problem was dramatic in the extreme. He designed a ship with the bow pointed upstage into the open sea (to right and left). Forecastle and bowsprit were hidden by a huge saillike drape. But when the drape was opened, like a moving sail, the spectators could see Tristan seated high up by the prow, next to some sailors.

Viewed from the orchestra seats and the boxes, the result was a striking visual experience. But I soon discovered, when I went upstairs during one of the first stage rehearsals, that the bowsprit was placed so high that nothing but Tristan's boots could be seen from the second balcony of the Academy of Music.

The scenery's other peculiarity affected nobody but myself. As the conductor's chief assistant, I had to find a spot from which I could follow Reiner's beat and transmit it to the backstage chorus. But the ship Oenslager had devised was so solid and impenetrable that I could not find a crack or a chink through which to see Reiner. I was finally forced to lie down on my stomach near the bow and twist my neck in such a way that I could see Reiner on his podium, while I transmitted his sober beat with my left hand. Such, before the introduction of closed-circuit TV hookups, were the challenges that assistant opera conductors then had to face and overcome.

The Thursday matinee première was an unforgettable experience. The performance began at one o'clock in the afternoon and it must have ended around seven-fifteen in the evening, with but two relatively short, twenty-minute intermissions. The first uncut *Tristan* in American history had attracted so much attention that Eleanor Roosevelt came up specially from Washington to see it. I believe she left after the second act, and one can hardly blame her. Reiner conducted in a particularly majestic manner, and the first F in the cellos was so long drawn out that I thought it would never end.

Finally, when it was all over and the players began emerging from the orchestra pit, I caught sight of Marcel Tabuteau, tottering toward me. He looked utterly exhausted, but there was a faint gleam of recognition in his eyes as he asked, "Tell me, *mon cher,* is Roosevelt still President?"

That memorable matinee performance was not only the first, it was also the last uncut version of *Tristan und Isolde* to be staged in the United States. Having tried it once, Reiner prudently decided not to flaunt tradition a second time, and the next two performances — on the following Saturday and Tuesday nights — were given in the customary version, which is a good thirty minutes shorter.

Quite different were the problems encountered in the production of *The Marriage of Figaro,* which followed. In this opera orchestrally accompanied numbers are separated by so-called *secco* recitatives, which are half sung and half spoken to the accompaniment of a keyboard instrument. Some of these recitatives are rather long, and to keep from boring the audience, most conductors shorten them considerably. Such surgical operations require a certain skill, for one cannot simply cut in the middle of a sentence, ruining the verbal logic of the text, nor can one destroy the continuity of the music by joltingly shifting from one key to another. In other words, the cuts must make sense semantically as well as musically.

Reiner, like other opera conductors, had devised his own cuts in places where he felt that the least violence was done to the underlying intentions of composer and librettist. His scores were marked with the letter F where the cut began and with the letter R where the cut ended, a method I later copied with my own initials when I too started producing operas.

Before we began rehearsing *Figaro,* I brought my piano vocal score to Reiner, who marked it up with F and R. I thus knew, well in advance of our first stage rehearsal, exactly what was to be played and what was to be omitted. Much of the preliminary coaching had already been done by Reiner in New York, but when the time came for the ensemble rehearsals the singers moved to Philadelphia.

To help him with these rehearsals, Reiner had two assistants: myself and Sylvan Levin. Reiner would sit on a chair in one corner of a large room, quietly beating time, occasionally stopping the singers to make needed corrections, while I played the piano, which was placed off to one side in such a way that I could see conductor and singers.

At our first *Figaro* rehearsal, which began in the middle of the morning, I got up after an hour and a half of playing and asked Sylvan Levin to take over. Sylvan took my place at the piano, with his score open at the page where we had stopped. He then launched into a recitative section that Reiner wanted cut. Reiner immediately exploded. "What's going on here?" he cried. "Don't you know the opera?"

That was Reiner's way. Instead of asking Levin, "What's the matter with your score? Haven't you got the indicated cuts?" he had to browbeat and insult his assistant. But by this time Levin was fed up. He wasn't going to be humiliated by Reiner's offensive behavior.

"I know this opera very well," he retorted.

"Why are you playing something we are not going to do?" demanded Reiner angrily.

"You didn't give me the cuts."

"But Goldovsky had the cuts."

"You gave Goldovsky the cuts, but you didn't give the cuts to me!" said Sylvan, as much as to say, "you've only yourself to blame for being so careless."

This was too much for Reiner.

"You are fired!" he shouted, jumping up from his chair.

"I'm *not* fired!" answered Levin. "I have just resigned!" With that he picked up his hat and coat and walked out.

I had witnessed the scene, and now it was too late for me to make a quiet getaway.

"Hey there, Goldovsky, come back and sit down at the piano," cried Reiner. "We are going to go on with this rehearsal."

Obediently I returned to my post. Gone was all hope of an early lunch, as I played on and on without relief.

Accompanying singers for hours on end during opera rehearsals is a tiring business. It was more than one person could cope with, as Reiner well knew. But it was several days before he could find a substitute for Sylvan Levin.

The first replacement was a gentleman from Boston named Alexander Steinert, who prudently insisted on obtaining a two-week written contract before agreeing to come down to Philadelphia. This particular assistant did not last long. We were rehearsing the third act when the moment came for him to spell me. Sitting down at the piano, Steinert proceeded to play the duet of the two peasant maidens a shade more slowly than we had rehearsed it the day before. Reiner immediately lost his temper.

"Out!" he cried, pointing imperiously at the offender. "Out! Away! I never want to see you again! Goldovsky! . . . Goldovsky! Where is that fellow anyway? Oh, there you are. Sit down at the piano and start playing. We've lost enough time as it is!"

It was no use trying to argue with Reiner. Once his mind was made up, there was no changing it. If he didn't like someone's way of playing the piano, then that was too bad. He wasn't going to give the fellow a second chance, he was through with him forever. In this case, however, he had partly met his match. For the gentleman from Boston, having been hired for two weeks, refused to remove himself from Reiner's sight entirely. Instead, he stretched out on the luxurious four-poster bed which Herbert Graf was using as an elegant prop for the Countess's boudoir in the second act, and proceeded to sleep through my playing for hours at a time. It was possibly the most handsomely rewarded rest anyone has ever enjoyed.

Fortunately for me, as I was beginning to feel the strain, the next substitute was a talented young pianist named Fritz Kitzinger, who caused us no further trouble.

Not all the singers were happy, however, over Reiner's intensive drilling, just as not all of them were impressed by Herbert Graf's stage directing. One of them was Margaret, whose acting ability so impressed Graf that the only thing he could find to say to her during rehearsals was, "Just get out there and act, my dear, you've got all the talent it takes!"

Reiner's drillwork, on the other hand, tended to be ruthless and at times deliberately sadistic. He liked to play with his singers, much as a cat plays with a mouse, by unexpectedly changing the tempo from time to time. This was Reiner's way of keeping the singers on their toes, of forcing them to heed his sober beat. He, not the singer, was the boss, and save for the exceptional star, whom he could not browbeat in this way, he wanted the singers to know it.

Margaret, who was familiar with his ways, would watch him out of the corner of her eye, while continuing to act and sing, and she would never let him trick her. She even enjoyed these little games and could almost sense in advance just when Reiner was going to accelerate or decelerate the tempo. The musical rapport she thus established with Reiner was as satisfying as it was stimulating for them both. In the three public performances Margaret was an adorable Cherubino. This is not just my own, naturally prejudiced, feeling. It was also the opinion of the noted British musicologist Edward Dent, whose English translation we were using and who, after seeing one of her performances, wrote that Margaret Codd was the most charming Cherubino he had ever seen.

It was, however, with the third of this extraordinary season's operas — *Der Rosenkavalier* — that Reiner was really in his element. I have already remarked on his particular affinity for Richard Strauss, whose complicated scores were a perfect foil for his conducting talents. His *Rosenkavalier* was every bit as memorable as the *Elektra* he had conducted earlier and the *Salome* he later produced in New York. Indeed, of all the Richard Strauss opera conductors I have seen, and I have seen quite a few, Fritz Reiner was undoubtedly the finest.

As luck would have it, the great star of the Vienna Opera, Lotte Lehmann, was then in the United States so she could play the role of the Marschallin, which had made her world famous. The person Reiner chose for the role of Sophie (which Margaret was asked to understudy) was another darling of the Viennese named Elisabeth Schumann. At the first piano rehearsal her voice struck me as being much too weak for the part. I couldn't understand why Reiner had hired her. Though audible above my piano accompaniment, her fragile voice, I felt sure, would be completely drowned out by Strauss's sonorous orchestral textures. I asked Reiner how he could possibly have made such a choice.

He looked at me for a moment, then said, "You wait." I waited. On the afternoon of the first orchestra rehearsal, I got the surprise of my life. Elisabeth Schumann's seemingly tiny, light voice sailed out from the stage like a silver arrow. It cut through the orchestra with the greatest of ease and filled the auditorium with the most delicious sound. That taught me a lesson I was never to forget. It is not the volume or loudness of a voice that counts but the way it is pointed. Elisabeth Schumann's lyric soprano voice was beautifully projected, and her three renditions of the role of Sophie were in their own way as memorable as Lotte Lehmann's Marschallin.

The part of Octavian was sung by Eva Hadrabova, whom Reiner had imported from Prague. She was neither strikingly good nor strikingly bad. The leading male role, on the other hand — that of the fatuously bovine and lecherous Baron Ochs — was impersonated by Emanuel List.

This famous, Vienna-born basso, who had sung the role innumerable times in Europe and at the Metropolitan in New York, did not have to display any particular acting ability. With his puffy face and his big, bloated body, he was type-cast for this crude role. But it was not until he appeared for the first piano rehearsal that Reiner realized what a poor musician he was. At the time this was not unusual, and even today there are singers who, though they have beautiful voices, are musically inferior. The orchestral portions of the score mean very little to them. They succeed in memorizing their vocal lines, but the moment they stop singing, they enter a dark tunnel and have no clear idea when they are to emerge into the daylight and again burst into song. They look desperately at the prompter or at the conductor, waiting for one or the other to give them their next cue.

Emanual List was such a singer. Many of the entrances in *Der Rosenkavalier* are tricky ones, quite unexpectedly occurring between beats. List knew this well. To disguise his nervousness when the time for his next difficult entrance neared, he would start overacting. At the last moment he would stop dead in his tracks and rivet his gaze on the prompter or conductor, but even so he would often miss important cues.

After a few of List's mistakes the familiar thundercloud began to form on Reiner's brow. The pressure was building up inside him and he was ready to explode. He would have liked to tell List off as a no-good, know-nothing musician; he would have liked to shout at him and say that he should have chosen to be a cobbler or a tinsmith rather than a singer. But Reiner didn't dare. There was no one else around who could substitute for List should the latter take offense at Reiner's cutting remarks and tell him to go to hell. Reiner had to keep his feelings to himself, for if List walked out on him, that was the end of his *Rosenkavalier*.

I was playing the piano on one side of the stage, as usual, alternately looking at the score, Reiner, and the singers, when suddenly Reiner swiveled slightly on his chair so that I could no longer see his baton or follow his beat. This was not the first time such a thing had happened. When Reiner did this, I usually played more loudly so that the singers could hear me clearly, even if Reiner had stopped conducting for a moment. But this time he had not stopped, he had simply made it impossible for me to see his beat, which he now deliberately slowed. The singers followed his lead, and within a few seconds we were a measure apart.

Reiner now had a reason for blowing up. And did he blow up. "This is terrible!" he shouted. "This is disgraceful! There is nobody here who knows how to play this opera on the piano. I'm going to have to do everything myself. This is terrible, terrible! What are we going to do? What's the matter with this country? Why can't we find anyone in it who knows anything about Richard Strauss?" And on he went, spewing lava in all directions.

It was a ridiculous scene, of course. Although he was ostensibly bawling me out, calling me a dunderhead and every name in the book, his rage was really directed at Emanuel List. I was simply a scapegoat, an excuse for letting off steam. Knowing Reiner's ways, I sat at the keyboard in silence, waiting for the storm to abate. Suddenly the thunder subsided, and he announced a five-minute break.

When the rehearsal resumed, I was told to take my usual place at the piano. Reiner made no effort to replace me. We continued the rehearsal as though nothing had happened. But after it was finished, Reiner came over and said to me, "Come on, I'll treat you to a good dinner."

That was his way of apologizing. He could never bring himself to say, "I'm sorry, I lost my temper. I insulted you in front of all these people. But you must understand the state I'm in, how burned up I am by all this sloppy singing," or anything like that. No, never! Such a statement from Reiner was unthinkable. But knowing well how much he had offended me — unjustly and in public — he made up in his own way, by taking me out to a first-class restaurant.

The staging of this *Rosenkavalier* production, like that of most of the operas that were put on during this 1934–1935 season — was entrusted to Herbert Graf, whom Reiner had managed to lure away from Vienna. A short, intense-looking Austrian, with thin lips, blue black hair, and black eyes, Graf had the swarthy complexion of a gypsy. His somewhat saturnine appearance — enhanced by his habit of whispering his directions to each singer, as though they were part of a secret to be shared *à deux* — invested him with a certain aura of Old World mystery and fascination. The impression was a bit deceptive, for there was less there than met the eye and I personally found his acting instructions too casual for my dramatic taste, but there was no denying the technical competence of a man whose father had been a famous music critic and who had spent most of his life working on the opera stage.

In Vienna Graf had had ample opportunity to study the pitfalls inherent in a production of *Der Rosenkavalier.* This doubtless explained his insistence that I go out on stage to play the part of the flutist who accompanies the Italian tenor during the levee scene in the first act. He wanted to be sure that the actor chosen for this insignificant role knew enough about the score to be able to put on a convincing act imitating the musician in the pit who was actually playing the flute.

I accepted this on-stage assignment readily enough, but I balked when Graf proposed to add my name to the program as the flutist. I told him that I was to be identified as Reiner's assistant and as nothing else. Graf then changed my last name, and it was as Boris Hilfreich (Boris the Very Helpful) that I was officially listed. It was a graceful *trouvaille,* a pseudonym I was later to combine with all sorts of other first names — like Agnes, David, Harry, etc. — in my own opera productions whenever there was some doubt as to just who was to sing a particular minor role.

Herbert Graf's most spectacular contribution to this unusual opera season was a revolving stage, which had to be specially built in New York and then trucked to Philadelphia in forty different segments. It was used with notable effect during the last act of *Der Rosenkavalier,* which is set in the *chambre séparée* of a disreputable Viennese inn the lecherous Baron Ochs has hired for a secret tryst, complete with supper, with the Marschallin's maid. The conclusion of this act, after the Marschallin appears to bestow her blessing on Octavian and Sophie, is climaxed musically by a magnificent trio and a celestial duet. To highlight this sudden transfiguration, Graf had the felicitous idea of having the stage revolve so that the dénouement could take place in a lovely garden, so much more in keeping with the music and the dramatic situation than the sordid bedroom suite in which the third act begins.

The same technique was used, but for quite different reasons, in Herbert Graf's staging of *Carmen* — one of the operas that Alexander Smallens had chosen to conduct. For the start of the second act, set in Lillas Pastia's tavern, the full stage was used for the noisy entrance of the toreador Escamillo and his numerous admirers. But later, for Carmen's meeting with the smugglers and the seductive dance she puts on for the benefit of Don José, the stage was made to rotate so that both sequences took place in a private bedroom, which was both secretive and erotically suggestive. The stage then rotated back to show the main tavern hall for the final tumultuous scenes in which the soldier Don José battles with his captain, Zuniga. It was the only time I have ever seen *Carmen* so performed, and it was much to the credit of Herbert Graf's sense of theatrical fitness.

The same could not, alas, be said of Graf's staging of *The Barber of Seville*. This rollicking Rossini opera was not part of the Philadelphia Orchestra's operatic program, but deciding to make the most of Graf's presence in Philadelphia, Reiner had him train the Curtis vocalists for a performance of this opera with the institute's orchestra. Though she had already graduated from the Curtis Institute, Margaret was offered the role of Rosina, which she sang and acted fully as well as she had that of Cherubino. But she was more than a little annoyed, as were most of the other performers, by the heavy-handed symbolism Graf imposed on them, as each protagonist had to wear a costume intended to represent some allegorical figure. For some unfathomable reason Margaret was costumed as Alice in Wonderland, in a short white dress, blue silk sash with a bow in the back, white half-length socks, and patent leather shoes. To top it off, she wore a blond wig with long curls falling down over her shoulders.

First put on by the Curtis singers and orchestra in Philadelphia's Academy of Music in January 1935, this Reiner-Graf production of *Barber* was later presented at New York City's Juilliard School of Music in March of the same year. Though both performances were much applauded and did credit to the musicianship of Fritz Reiner and his well-drilled students, this experiment in gimmick-ridden staging did nothing to warm my still tepid feelings about opera as a form of "art."

From the purely scenic point of view, I think there can be no doubt that the most impressive of all the operas performed in Philadelphia during this extraordinary season was Gluck's *Iphigénie en Aulide.* Alexander Smallens had deliberately selected this fairly obscure opera because it is full of moving, stately music. Not to be outdone by Oenslager's dramatic scenery for *Tristan,* Smallens asked another famous American stage designer, Norman Bel Geddes, to create the sets for *Iphigénie.*

The result — an enormous conic structure with outjutting platforms spiraling up toward an altarlike summit — was even more breathtaking than Oenslager's ship. The rest of the stage was absolutely bare, but it was framed by a cyclorama and by hanging drapes, on to which differently colored spotlights were aimed to suggest the arrival and presence of Agamemnon's fleet in the little port of Aulis. The duets and trios — with Agamemnon and the high priest, Calchas (who tells him that he must sacrifice his daughter Iphigénie to placate Artemis and persuade her to give his becalmed ships the wind they need to carry them to Troy), with Iphigénie and her mother, Clytemnestre, or with Achilles, her betrothed — took place on one or another of the cone's outjutting platforms. The opera thus moved with slow, but relentless momentum up toward the tragic, sacrificial dénouement at the summit of the cone, each platform scene being dramatized and pinpointed through the use of multicolored spotlights.

The paraphernalia that Norman Bel Geddes brought to Philadelphia for this production had to be seen to be believed. He had not scores, but hundreds of electric lamps and instruments, which were suspended from balconies, hidden in the wings and flies, mounted on proscenium booms, and trained from every conceivable angle in every imaginable direction. The "light plot" needed to coordinate this elaborate machinery — with precise instructions for turning on different spotlights and giving them various intensities (one quarter up, half up, three quarters up, full up) — was the most complicated I have ever laid eyes on. For it fell to me, as one of Smallens' assistants, to coordinate these luminous effects with the music. The number of light cues I had to inscribe in my copy of the score — "Cue 62 half ready, Cue 47 three quarters ready, Cue 33 out" — was staggering and ran into the hundreds.

Bel Geddes, as we soon learned to our cost, was a rigorous perfectionist. While the scenery was being mounted, he noticed that one of the backdrops did not fall smoothly to the ground but was marred by surface wrinkles.

"I told you I wanted those wrinkles removed," said he sternly to the chief carpenter.

"Yes, sir," the chief carpenter assured him. "It will be done by this evening."

But when evening came, the wrinkles were still there. "Yes, Mr. Bel Geddes," said the carpenter, "we'll have it done for you tomorrow." But on the morrow, the work was still not done.

"The drape comes off!" Bel Geddes brusquely ordered. "Take it away! The whole effect is canceled!"

This was a mild prelude to what was to follow. To stress the theme of inexorable destiny on which Gluck's opera (like Racine's play) is based, Bel Geddes decided to impose a total blackout on the stage as the curtain rose at the conclusion of the overture. The impenetrable darkness, lasting for about fifteen seconds, was then, suddenly and dramatically, to be rent by a piercing shaft of light descending from above and hitting the top of the cone. The visual effect could not have been more startling.

When the time came for the final dress rehearsal, Bel Geddes stationed himself some distance up one of the auditorium aisles, while Smallens took his place in the orchestra pit. As soon as the final chord of the overture was played, I gave the "Curtain up" cue.

A moment later there was a shout from the auditorium: "Goldovsky! Goldovsky!"

I ran out onto the dark stage. "Yes, Mr. Bel Geddes, is there anything wrong?"

"Do you call that a blackout?" Bel Geddes demanded.

I looked around and saw that the base of the cone and a patch of floor next to it were bathed in a faint flood of light.

"Just a moment, Mr. Bel Geddes, I'm going to check."

I hurried back to the electricians in the wings and asked if by any chance one of the lights had been left on. But they had not. Even the orchestra lights had been completely dimmed and the master switch momentarily disconnected.

I returned to the stage, completely baffled. The light spill was there, there was no doubt about it, but I couldn't determine its source.

"Mr. Bel Geddes," I called, "the electricians have turned off everything. This is a complete blackout."

"What do you mean, a *complete blackout?* Haven't you got eyes? Don't you see that spill there, on the stage?"

I had to admit I did. But I had no idea where it came from.

"Well, you've got to find it!" roared Bel Geddes.

In the lightless pit Smallens and the musicians waited while we bustled around with the electricians trying to find the source of the "leak."

"Look," cried one of them, pointing to an illuminated clock face on one of the backstage walls. "It must come from there."

"Mr. Bel Geddes, Mr. Bel Geddes," I cried, hurrying back out onto the stage, "I think we've found the trouble. It must come from the clock in the wings."

"All right," he shouted back, "take it away, remove it!"

"I'll try to find some way of doing it," I said, anxious to have the rehearsal resume.

"No!" shouted Bel Geddes. "Have it removed — *immediately*."

Removing an illuminated wall clock is not an easy matter, but one of the stagehands climbed up on a ladder and covered the face with a piece of dark cloth.

As soon as he was through I had the curtain lowered. The orchestra lights came on, and Smallens had his players repeat the last few bars of the overture. After that, I again gave the cue for the curtain to be raised.

"Goldovsky!" came a shout from the auditorium.

With a sinking feeling I hurried back out onto the stage, and, sure enough, the light spill was still there.

We scurried around, while from the pitch-black orchestra pit came the sound of mutterings and curses. A stagehand finally spotted the source of the leak. It was a slanted skylight, located high up in the flies, which admitted just enough daylight to bathe the foot of the cone in a kind of ghostly pallor.

"Mr. Bel Geddes," I called, coming back out onto the stage, "we now know what the trouble is. The spill comes from a skylight in the roof. So you don't have to worry about it. We'll have the skylight painted black in time for the first performance."

"No!" thundered Bel Geddes. "You'll do nothing of the sort! It is going to be painted black *now!*"

Smallens was fit to be tied. This was going to cost thousands of dollars in overtime for the musicians. But there was nothing he could do. It had been his idea to commission Bel Geddes, and he had to bear with the great man's idiosyncrasies. So while conductor and musicians fumed and fretted, a stagehand climbed up and painted the skylight black. But it was almost an hour before the rehearsal could be resumed.

What Alexander Smallens thought of Fritz Reiner I do not know, but there was almost certainly an element of jealousy involved. This is generally the rule with orchestra conductors, who can be as prejudiced and temperamental as prima donnas. Reiner had a withering contempt for all conductors other than himself, while Smallens had not made himself particularly liked at the start of this operatic season by the airs he gave himself.

I vividly recall a cocktail party that I attended along with the other members of Reiner's conducting class. Smallens was sounding off about conductors who didn't know how to rehearse efficiently, who didn't know how to do this or that, and who, generally speaking, wasted the musicians' time — whereas he, Smallens, was so skillful that he could prepare all four operas of Wagner's *Ring* with a single orchestra rehearsal. The remark left us open-mouthed.

A day or two later, when we were gathered in Reiner's classroom for a conference, one of us said that he had heard Mr. Smallens make an extraordinary statement and that he would like to get Reiner's reaction.

"Well, what was it?"

"Mr. Smallens said that he could prepare the entire *Ring* cycle with a single orchestra rehearsal. What do you think, sir, is that possible?"

"With Smallens? But of course it's possible," answered Reiner. "Why, he wouldn't know what to say at the second rehearsal."

I have no idea if the remark ever got back to Smallens, who subsequently developed quite a liking for me. My piano playing so impressed him that he generously invited me to play Mozart's D Minor Concerto with the Philadelphia Orchestra, which he was now conducting on an almost full-time basis while Leopold Stokowski enjoyed a sabbatical half year. It was a wonderful tonic to my wounded ego, and I couldn't help relishing the flattering comments made on my playing by my friend and Curtis classmate Gama Gilbert in the Philadelphia *Record* and by Samuel Laciar in the *Public Ledger.* "His tone was beautiful," wrote Laciar, "especially in the second theme of the slow movement, which is played in single notes with the right hand and is perhaps the supreme test of piano playing." Aha! I thought to myself, what must that old sourpuss (*govnó sobatchye*) (Josef Hofmann) have thought after reading a sentence like that?

Smallens was also impressed by the fact that I knew Russian. Though he too was Russian-born (St. Petersburg, 1889), he had come to the United States while still a child and he did not speak the language at all well. But here was somebody who could read Pushkin in the original without the slightest difficulty. I was exactly the person needed to help him with *Mavra,* a one-act comic opera by Stravinsky (based on a humorous Pushkin poem) which he wanted to pair off with Humperdinck's *Hansel and Gretel* to make a full opera evening. "Since we're going to do it in Russian," he told me, "and you're the only person around who can speak it, I'm going to make you the *souffleur.*" So, for the first and I can add, thankfully, the last time in my life, I had to squeeze myself into the prompter's box, and anticipate possible memory slips on the part of the naughty Parasha and her hussar boyfriend, the bogus cook "Mavra," to make sure that they would not muff their lines.

Mavra, of course, was an entertaining lark, but not enough to compete with the major operatic works Fritz Reiner was presenting. Smallens' and Bel Geddes' *Iphigénie en Aulide* could stand comparison with Reiner's *Tristan und Isolde,* but *Hansel and Gretel* was a bit tinselly when set against *Der Rosenkavalier.* To fill out his own five-opera quota, Smallens needed something sensational, a full-length opera nobody in Philadelphia had ever seen before.

The work he finally chose was the very one that Reiner, on my recommendation, had previously rejected: Shostakovich's *Lady Macbeth of Mtsensk.* It had in the meantime been successfully produced by Artur Rodzinski, who had had the bright idea of hiring a group of New York *émigré* singers who called themselves "Art of Russia, Incorporated." They may not have been the greatest singers in the world, but a number of them had either studied under Stanislavsky or been much influenced by his Moscow Art Theatre, and most of them were unusually fine actors. Their performance in Cleveland was a stunning hit, and later in New York they played and sang to a completely sold-out Metropolitan Opera house and were applauded by a gala turnout of the world's musical elite, led by Igor Stravinsky, George Gershwin, Arturo Toscanini, Bruno Walter, and Serge Koussevitsky. Smallens too had seen this memorable performance, and on the spot he had decided to hire the Russian singers as well as the scenery, designed by a talented and imaginative Czech named Richard Rychtarik.

The stage director chosen for the Philadelphia première of this lusty Shostakovich opera was the same Wilhelm von Wymetal whom I had one day saved from a backstage self-destruction during Reiner's performance of *Elektra.* He had left the Curtis Institute at the time that Margaret and I had been graduated in May 1934 and had gone to Cleveland to stage a few operas. Since I knew Russian and had already helped Smallens with *Mavra,* I was hired as Wymetal's assistant.

The Shostakovich opera that Rodzinski had produced, and which Smallens had inherited, was not quite the same *Lady Macbeth of Mtsensk* I had studied for Reiner. It had been considerably cleaned up and some of the salacious music played by the orchestra during the upstairs fornication scene had been omitted, though enough remained to make it clear to everyone just what was going on behind that drawn bedroom curtain. But by the time the opera reached Philadelphia, it was fairly common knowledge that it was on the bawdy side.

Shortly after we had begun rehearsals, I was awakened one night by an unexpected telephone call. Still half asleep, I lifted the receiver, wondering who on earth could be calling me at three-thirty in the morning.

"Uh . . . uh, are you Mr. Goldovsky?" a rather breathless voice inquired.

"Yes," I answered. "Who is it?"

"Oh, Mr. Goldovsky, this is —" I have forgotten the name, but it was somebody working for a Philadelphia newspaper. "Mr. Goldovsky, you . . . you must help me. I've . . . I've been told you are the only one who has the score of the . . . opera that's being given by the Philadelphia Orchestra, this Shos-ta-ko-vich, is that right? Yes, this Shostakovich opera, *Lady Macbeth of something*, or something like that?"

"Yes, yes," I said impatiently. "But why are you calling me like this in the middle of the night? What can I do for you?"

"Oh, oh, because — this is very important — because, you see, I understand there's some music there, in this opera, that's very obscene, and there are some sections that have been removed, yes, some sections have been removed, it seems, because they're much too, much too . . . suggestive. Yes, much too suggestive . . . Hello, Mr. Goldovsky?"

"Yes," I said, in an increasingly cross voice.

"You see, Mr. Goldovsky, er — how can I put it? We're very sorry, we realize it's very early in the morning, but we're wondering if we couldn't come to your house, Mr. Goldovsky — yes, to your house to er — photo — photograph the obscene passages of music in your score?"

The major cut that Smallens had made concerned some trombone "slides," which sounded a bit like foghorn whoops and which Shostakovich had introduced into his score to suggest the climax of sexual passion in the upstairs bedroom scene. Even if I had had the score at home, which was not the case, the photographing of this "obscene music" would have been a far cry from the kind of "filthy pictures" that this harassed photographer wanted to offer to his sensation-seeking paper. But it was several minutes before I could shake him off and resume my interrupted slumber.

I have no idea if this pornographic smuthound subsequently attended the first performance. If so, he must have been sorely disappointed, for during the upstairs bedroom scene, the curtain that was supposed to hide the amorous disportments of Katerina and Sergei collapsed and the two exposed "lovers," not knowing what to do, sat quietly side by side listening to the sounds of rapturous passion welling up from the orchestra pit.

A day or two before, Wilhelm von Wymetal had stopped me in the wings of the Academy of Music with a worried look on his face.

"Boris," he said to me, "I don't know what to do. I'm frankly in a jam. Something quite unexpected has turned up and next week I've got to leave for San Francisco. This means that I can be here for the Thursday matinee première, and also for next Saturday evening's performance. But I won't be here Tuesday for the last performance. This is a brand-new opera, nobody here knows it, and I just don't know what will happen."

"Mr. von Wymetal," I said, "why don't we try something? I will watch very carefully how you handle things on Thursday afternoon. Then on Saturday I will repeat everything you did — supervise all the backstage stuff, conduct all the choruses, give all entrances, curtain and light cues. If I make any mistakes, you'll be here to correct me, and that way on Tuesday I'll know exactly how you want it done."

Wymetal looked at me dubiously. He obviously thought me out of my mind: "You're trying to bite off more than you can chew. I mean, this is a new piece. It isn't that simple. It has complicated music, it has a lot of very involved backstage work, and I don't see how you can handle it all properly on the basis of two performances."

"Well, give me a chance," I said. I didn't feel the need to tell Wymetal how meticulously I had studied Shostakovich's opera for Fritz Reiner.

When the time came for the Thursday matinee première, I watched Wymetal closely. To his surprise I did not follow him around with a score, as I knew it well enough to be able to dispense with it. Saturday evening, I took over and did everything he had done without a score and without a hitch. Wymetal was flabbergasted. He had expected me to run around, getting a bit panicky here and there as I tried to figure out exactly when I should be giving this cue or that. But nothing of the sort happened. He did not need to correct me once, and, what was more amazing, I did his job without once referring to the music.

After the performance he thanked me profusely. "I don't know how you did it!" he congratulated me. "I wouldn't have thought it possible — familiarizing yourself with an opera like that on the basis of one rehearsal and performance . . . But anyway, many, many thanks. I'm tremendously relieved. Now I know I can leave for San Francisco without having to worry about what's going to happen Tuesday night.

Little did I guess, as he thanked me, that my successful understudying of his stage director's job was soon to alter my life and musical career completely.

For the fourth of the five operas he was due to conduct, Fritz Reiner had chosen Verdi's *Falstaff*. This opera is based on *The Merry Wives of Windsor,* which is not Shakespeare's greatest play. Nor is it Verdi's greatest opera. It lacks the element of passion and dramatic tension that characterize *La Traviata, Rigoletto, Aida, Otello,* and so many other Verdi operas, while the musical subtleties pass by so swiftly that they are lost on the audience. Still, it was something of a miracle that Verdi could compose such a work in his eightieth year, when many men are already in their dotage.

Once again I was impressed by Reiner's meticulous rehearsing, and in particular by the extraordinary pains he took with the final episode, when the ten principal singers mingle their voices in a joyous culminating fugue. The handling of this section is a very tricky business, for it requires split-second timing as each new voice joins the tumultuous melee. Reiner had his singers stand in line and watch him like hawks, giving each of them his or her cue in succession. Even so, mistakes were made during rehearsals right up to the eve of the first performance.

Unwilling to take chances, Reiner subjected them all to a final runthrough during the intermission preceding the last act in the academy's green room — not only for the first, but for the second and third performances as well. Thanks to this painstaking preparation, the three *Falstaff* performances went off without a hitch and received the acclaim they deserved.

Reiner had begun his opera cycle with Wagner's *Tristan und Isolde,* and it was with another Wagner opera, *Die Meistersinger,* that he closed this extraordinary season. It was the short-lived opera company's majestic swan song as well as another memorable example of what a great conductor can do with a great orchestra.

Once again, as Reiner's chief assistant, I was kept busy and not simply during rehearsals and backstage. Reiner even had me costumed as one of the apprentices, who play such an important role in the opera. I could thus appear on stage and, unnoticed by the audience, supervise the singing and the actions of the various ensemble groups.

In the meantime, Wilhelm von Wymetal had returned to Cleveland, after his brief trip to California, to help Artur Rodzinski prepare the next opera season: 1935–1936. As a one-time pupil and protégé of Emil Mlynarski, who had taught him the rudiments of conducting in Warsaw, Rodzinski had inherited a passion for producing operas, which he had contagiously communicated to the music lovers of Cleveland. During the 1934–1935 season he had managed, with the help of an Italian assistant named

Spadoni, to cram six opera productions into the full orchestral schedule. Spadoni, however, was not familiar with German opera. Accordingly Rodzinski consulted Wymetal, who had been acting as his stage director. Did he know of anybody who was well versed in German and who could help him put on Wagner and Richard Strauss operas?

"As a matter of fact," Wymetal told him, "I do know of somebody who could help you — that is, if you can lure him way from Philadelphia. He's a student of Reiner's, and you know what that means. He recently assisted Reiner with *Tristan* and also *Rosenkavalier,* and before that he helped him with *Elektra,* which I stage-directed. He's still pretty young — I don't think he can be much more than twenty-six or twenty-seven years old — but he's incredible. I saw him do something in Smallens' production of *Lady Mabeth of Mtsensk* that I would never have believed possible if I hadn't seen it with my own eyes . . ."

Rodzinski was so impressed by Wymetal's account of how I had substituted for him at our second Shostakovich performance that he decided to make a special trip to Philadelphia. He arrived in time to see the last, or it may have been the penultimate, performance of Wagner's *Die Meistersinger.* But his eyes were not trained on the conductor, they were trained on a certain apprentice who had been pointed out to him and who, as he could see through his opera glasses, moved from one group to another, giving cues and conducting choruses.

I had no idea I was being so closely scrutinized until several days later, when a Mr. Carl Vosburgh came to the Curtis Institute to see me. He told me that, as business manager of the Cleveland Orchestra, he had been sent to Philadelphia by Dr. Rodzinski, who was anxious to hire me as his assistant. Dr. Rodzinski was planning to put on five operas during the next season, and he needed someone to help him with several German operas. It would be my job to train the minor roles, the choruses, and play the piano at rehearsals. For the preparation of each opera Dr. Rodzinski was willing to pay me $1000. I could thus look forward to a total remuneration of $5000.

For me this was a staggering offer. As Reiner's assistant I had been earning $50 a week, for an annual total of $1500. What Rodzinski was offering me was more than three times that amount.

"Mr. Vosburgh," I said, "this is a very tempting offer, and I am very flattered by it. But you see, I owe it to Mr. Reiner to consult him first. However, I will let you have my decision as soon as possible."

On that understanding Carl Vosburgh returned to Cleveland while I went to see Reiner. Reiner immediately hit the roof.

"What!" he said. "You're thinking of going to work for that ignorant, uneducated, impossible, illiterate peasant! Come now, Boris, how can you demean yourself by associating with a man like that? Why, he doesn't know anything! I tell you, it's shameful, a real comedown for a talented fellow like you to get involved with such a clown. It would be the end of your musical career! Besides," he went on, "I have plans for you next year. We're going to have another great season and there will be plenty for you to do. If it's your salary that's troubling you, don't worry. I can give you a lot more money, and you can train the choruses and even conduct some of the rehearsals."

Much as I admired Reiner, I was exasperated by this deliberate deceit. My mother, being a close friend of Mrs. Bok's, had already been told that there was not going to be a second opera season for the Philadelphia Orchestra. Mrs. Bok's son, Curtis, who was now chairman of the orchestra's board of directors, had told his mother the bad news. The cost of producing ten lavishly staged operas had nearly bankrupted the orchestra, whose financial reserves — $250,000, carefully accumulated over the preceding two decades — had evaporated like a puddle of water on a hot summer day. All that was left was a glorious hollow on which the dust was already beginning to settle. The board of directors had regretfully come to the conclusion that Leopold Stokowski was right in opposing the idea of a special opera season. The country was now in the throes of a profound economic depression, and this was no time for extravagance.

Fritz Reiner, as a matter of course, had been informed of this decision. Yet here he was, building castles in Spain and trying to tempt me with fabulous expectations, just to keep me from going to work for someone as *total unbegabt* as Rodzinski.

A day or two later I informed Carl Vosburgh that I was accepting Dr. Rodzinski's kind offer.

(6)

My First Years with Rodzinski

OUR DECISION to move to Cleveland was not made immediately. Although Reiner was furious with me for agreeing to work for an "ignorant, uneducated . . . peasant," he wanted to retain my services as his personal assistant and repertoire coach at the Curtis Institute. For my part, I felt that Reiner could still teach me a great deal more. It was accordingly agreed with Josef Hofmann, who also took a dim view of my Cleveland job, that I would continue working at the Curtis Institute while commuting to Cleveland for several days each week to help Rodzinski with his operas.

Once again we spent the hot summer months at Rockport, where we shared Mother's house with Irene and her husband, Walter Wolf. For much of the vacation we were left to our own devices, while Mother went off to Europe on a long concert tour. But the poker games in the living room were as animated as ever, as were our music sessions with our friends from the Curtis Quartet, Felix Salmond, Josef Lhevinne, and his wife, Rosina.

Like my Uncle Pierre, who during one of his trips to Paris had begun flirting with a charming keyboard artist named Genia Nemenoff, whom he had later made his second wife, Josef Lhevinne had married a talented pianist, who, like himself, taught at the Juilliard School. Why they chose to spend their summers on this particular stretch of Maine coastline I do not know, for they were not formally a part of the Curtis Institute's music colony. But like the harpist Carlos Salzedo, the Lhevinnes had succeeded in housing a small flock of music students near the large house they had rented in Camden.

Although a magnificent pianist, Josef Lhevinne had great difficulty memorizing music and he experienced frequent "black-outs." This made him extremely nervous, and he suffered agonies each time he performed in public. I was all too familiar with this particular fear-of-forgetting syndrome. Already as a young boy and as Mother's accompanist, I had been dismayed by the intense nervousness she would display before every public performance, and the conclusion I had reached was that if this debilitating weakness could not be overcome by some means or other, then solo recitals were not worth the anticipatory agony they occasioned. With Mother the dreaded moment would approach with the implacable force of an impending execution, as though she were about to be dragged off to the guillotine. Holding her head high, she nevertheless managed to conceal her intense anxiety when she actually stepped onto the stage. Not so Lhevinne. He would get so panicky that at the last moment he would balk and refuse to come on stage. Not unfrequently his manager would have to push him bodily from the wings, sometimes with a kick in the pants that would make him stagger out into public view in a rather undignified manner.

One day, while we were sitting on the porch, I told Rosina Lhevinne that I had given this matter of memory blanks a lot of thought and had developed a way of handling it. It was brash of me to be offering advice to a famous teacher who was almost thirty years my senior, but I offered it anyway.

Many artists, I told her, whether pianists or violinists, suffer from this agonizing fear of forgetting. Usually all the performer can do when experiencing a severe memory lapse, is to go back to the beginning and start the piece all over. But — and this was the essential question — what makes this possible? Why should a musician always be able to recall the beginning of a composition? The answer quite obviously is that the opening section is the only one he knows with absolute certainty.

Having thus analyzed the problem, I had reached the following conclusion. Because anybody can suffer a memory blank, it is important to regard it as a natural occurrence rather than as something dreadful and paralyzing. Such a feeling of doom can only add to the nervousness and anxiety, thus helping to precipitate the very catastrophe one is anxious to avoid. Instead of running away from the problem, it should be faced and handled as a rather trivial incident. The best way of dealing with such mishaps is to select a series of places in every composition and to memorize them as if each were a "beginning." From then on, these special passages will function as life buoys to which the performer moves instinctively when he or she begins to founder. The player's memory may stumble, but balance can quickly be regained by jumping ahead, as though nothing had happened, to the next "starting place." As one "practices" for accidents of this kind, they cease to be traumatic experiences and become a commonplace aspect of performing technique.

There are, of course, other ways of dealing with memory lapses. I had once heard Dohnányi play the Mendelssohn Fugue in E Minor, which I happened to know well. Not long after the start he got lost, but instead of going back to the beginning, he went on improvising a new and completely different fugue. For this, of course, an artist needs a very superior gift.

I don't believe that my system for curing nervousness did much to alleviate Josef Lhevinne's particular trouble, for he was too set in his ways. But my powers of analysis seem to have made a great impression on his wife. A few days later she said to me, "Boris, I have an idea. As you know, we've got quite a few of our Juilliard pupils studying with us this summer. They know a lot about piano music, but not much else. So why don't you come over and tell them something about opera?"

"What do you mean — 'tell them something about opera'?"

"Well, you know a lot about it," she insisted. "After all, you helped Fritz Reiner put on those Philadelphia operas, didn't you? You even married an opera singer, so don't try to pretend you know nothing about it."

"All right," I said. "If you think they'd be interested, I'll talk to them. But which opera did you have in mind?"

"Well, what about *Rosenkavalier*?"

A couple of evenings later, Margaret and I drove over to Camden in Mother's green Chevrolet convertible. A good twenty students, girls as well as boys, had assembled in the spacious living room to hear me. The lucky ones got armchairs, the less lucky had to make do with hard-seat dining room chairs, sit four abreast on the sofa, or sprawl on the floor.

Sitting down at the piano, I said that I was going to tell them the story of Richard Strauss's and Hugo von Hofmannsthal's *Der Rosenkavalier,* illustrating some of the major points on the keyboard as I went along. I picked out several important themes, explained their significance, and then launched into a partly verbal, partly musical description of the opera. If I had had to stand behind a lectern and deliver a formal address, the results would probably have been disastrous, but having a piano to help me when words began to fail was a tremendous asset and gave me a great deal of self-confidence.

I had no trouble getting through my lecture, except toward the end, when to emphasize the grotesque disparity in age between the lecherous Baron Ochs and the girl he intends to seduce, I mentioned the fact that at one point Ochs takes off his wig, revealing his completely bald pate. With a feeling of acute embarrassment I suddenly remembered the stories I had heard about Josef Lhevinne's wig. To make matters worse, Rosina also wore a wig — which in those days was an unusual thing for a woman to do. I had discovered it quite accidentally during a poker-playing session when, moving round the table after throwing in my hand, one of my shirt-sleeve buttons got caught in her hair and suddenly I had seen everything start moving. The hair would have left her head completely had she not caught it with both hands and kept it firmly in place, while I disengaged the button.

All of their students must have known that their teachers wore wigs, but fortunately no one smiled or giggled, and I completed my account of Baron Och's discomfiture to the general satisfaction of the assembled company. My lecture was warmly applauded, as though I had just given a piano recital. I felt agreeably surprised, not least of all by Rosina Lhevinne's complimentary words: "You know, Boris, you make an excellent speaker. You must come back soon and do another opera for us." It had never occurred to me that I might have a talent for lecturing, still less that I was destined to give hundreds of such opera talks in later years.

This particular summer did not end as happily as it had begun. After returning from her concert tour in Europe, Mother described to me in detail how, in Budapest, she had made the acquaintance of my former *grande passion*, Marianne. "That's the girl you should have married!" she added pointedly in Russian.

The upshot of this rather brutal candor was probably a bit different from what Lubo had expected. Even though we were no longer living in the Cynwyd house, Margaret and I decided that it would be better for everyone in the autumn if we left Philadelphia and moved to Cleveland. I could see Mother during the Tuesdays and Wednesdays I spent at the Curtis Institute, while Margaret would remain at a safe distance in Cleveland, beyond the range of upsetting confrontations.

The first months in Cleveland were singularly pleasant, though my commuting back and forth to Philadelphia was to create some problems for me. Margaret and I rented a small apartment not far from Severance Hall, where the relatively young Cleveland Orchestra — barely fifteen years old — now had its home. Artur Rodzinski could not have been kinder and more complimentary, as he introduced me to the members of the orchestra. Although he was only fourteen years older than myself, Rodzinski displayed an almost paternal affection and was soon calling me "Borischikov." He seemed enormously impressed by the fact that I had worked with Reiner, and, unlike Josef Hofmann, who had virtually written me off as a total keyboard loss, he appreciated the quality of my piano playing. He was equally delighted by my sight-reading proficiency, which he exploited almost shamelessly by having me sing *all* the parts of *Der Rosenkavalier* during the initial orchestral rehearsals.

To be carried like this on a velvet pillow was for me a new and somewhat heady experience after the many rough rides I had had with Fritz Reiner. Rodzinski's confidence in me during those early weeks in Cleveland seemed just about boundless. When the time came to rehearse the principal singers, who had been specially hired for the three performances in Cleveland, he called me in and said, "Borischikov, I'm too tied down here to be able to go to New York. So I'm sending you there alone to take care of the rehearsing. There's a runthrough of *Rosenkavalier* with the six main singers scheduled for next Monday morning. Check them out and see to it that everything is the way we have planned it. Then they'll know what to expect when they come here for the final orchestra and stage rehearsals."

I was frankly astounded and not a little overawed. Here was I, a youngster of twenty-seven who had never conducted an opera in his life, being asked to check out world-famous singers, most of whom had been singing *Rosenkavalier* for years. Emanuel List, who had again been chosen for the role of the lascivious Baron Ochs, posed no problem. I had already taken his measure during that tense piano rehearsal with Reiner in Philadelphia. But Grete Stückgold, who had been chosen for the role of Octavian, was an unknown quantity who might easily take offense if I found fault with her interpretation of the role. The most formidable of them all, however, was Lotte Lehmann, who had sung the Marschallin so many times that she had just about made it her exclusive property.

When I reached the rehearsal room in the Steinway Building in

New York, I found the six principal singers waiting for the conductor to appear. I brought them Dr. Rodzinski's greetings as well as his apologies for being unexpectedly detained in Cleveland, explaining that he had asked me to go through the opera with them in his absence. The singers probably raised their eyebrows and exchanged glances behind my back, but I decided that the best thing to do was to get down to business immediately so that they wouldn't feel that their time was being completely wasted.

At first everything went well. Madame Lehmann was seated to the left of me, while the others took up positions around the piano. All of them were experienced singers, they knew their roles well, and there was nothing for me to correct.

But then, toward the end of the first act, we came to the two Hofmannsthal verses:

> *Und wen von der Verwandtschaft haben Euer Liebden*
> *für dieses Ehrenamt ausersehen?*

which Lotte Lehmann sang with pitches and rhythms quite unlike those that were indicated in the score.

I stopped, wondering what to do. I couldn't conceivably say to this great lady of the operatic stage, "I am sorry, Madame, I am afraid that you have made a mistake." My tongue refused to utter anything so bold. Besides, I had a gnawing suspicion that Richard Strauss might have changed the music of these two lines especially for her, in a version I should have been acquainted with. In drawing attention to a mistake on her part, I might be revealing my own ignorance and inviting a stern rebuke, which would make me look like a monkey in front of the other singers. I had to think fast.

"Liebe, gnädige Frau," I said, "something happened here. Would you mind if we did it over again?"

Madame Lehmann gave me a long, searching look.

"My dear young man," she began — as though she were addressing a naughty adolescent — *"mein lieber Knabe,* you know I have sung this role under most of the great conductors of our time — under Klemperer, under Bruno Walter, under Furtwängler, under Knappertsbusch, Kleiber, and Reiner. I was coached in this role by them all, and even, as you probably know, by Richard Strauss himself!" She paused for a dramatic moment, and I thought to myself, "Ah, here comes the slap!" But then, with adorable simplicity, she added, "You know, as far as this sentence is concerned, never mind. It's no use. I will never learn it right."

I heaved a sigh of relief. My impertinence in pointing out a variation between the score and her singing could have culminated in a most embarrassing *Krawall* — that wonderfully gritty German word for "row." Instead, she had paid gracious homage to my knowledge of the score. Her way of singing those two verses, as a matter of fact, was probably better than it would have been had she sung the phrase correctly.

Later, at the final rehearsal in Cleveland, she again sang the lines incorrectly, though with infinite charm, glancing at me archly, as much as to say, *"Sehen Sie!"* She could glance at me, I might add, because one of the four lackeys present on stage at the end of the first act had happened to fall ill and I had had to replace him at all the dress rehearsals.

I thought nothing of it at the time; it was just one of those things, one more of an opera assistant's normal chores. But my performance as a substitute seems to have made a profound impression on Marks Levine, who then headed the NCAC (National Concert and Artists Corporation) and who happened to be present at one of these rehearsals. Years later, when my Uncle Pierre approached him, suggesting that he should manage my lectures and piano recitals, his eyes lit up when he heard the name Boris Goldovsky. Ah yes, it struck a distant bell — that young fellow, Artur Rodzinski's assistant, who went out on stage and sang and played a lackey's role? Why of course, a fellow capable of doing that was somebody worth backing.

Our second operatic production for this season was Bizet's *Carmen*. During the rehearsal period Margaret and I were quietly approached by Rodzinski's wife, Halina, to help arrange a surprise party for her husband. With her captivating, apple-cheeked smile, Halina was a social charmer and thus the very opposite of her bearish husband, who found it difficult to communicate with the members of the Musical Arts Association and the board of directors who controlled the Cleveland Orchestra's operating budget. Rodzinski, who was too ulcer-prone to be able to drink wine and who normally bolted his food like the high-strung individual he was, hated formal dinner parties, and the idea of having to bandy small talk with the influential ladies who might be seated to his left and right was enough to make him squirm. To overcome this social disability, the sprightly Halina decided to organize an evening of burlesque entertainment — the sort of Bohemian or artistic soirée her husband loved — for the benefit of Cleveland's music-loving upper crust.

The opera singers who had come to Cleveland to perform in *Carmen* were accordingly recruited into Halina Rodzinski's "Barnstorming Grand Opera Company, of Buckeye State," and were called upon to act and sing a multiheader entitled "The Secret of *Lady Carmen* of Seville, or The Tragic Adventure of La Tosca and Barber Tristan, the Master Singer of Nuremberg, with the Silver Rose." So read the placards that were readied for the occasion by Richard Rychtarik, who had been entrusted with the job of designing sets for all of the operas put on in Severance Hall. In addition to the posters he also fashioned some rudimentary scenery for this amateur stage show, while I had to invent a story line and write a crazy libretto for a mishmash or potpourri of opera themes and arias in which everything was deliberately mixed up.

This operatic burlesque was finally presented to one hundred top-drawer Clevelanders at an evening party given on December 1, 1935, in the Rodzinskis' graystone Tudor-style mansion. The sunken living room, next to a higher-level dining room (which thus became the stage), made a perfect "pit" or parterre for the select diamond-studded and boiled-shirted audience. Five female members from our *Carmen* chorus were dressed up in scarlet tunics, with lambswool Cossack *shapkas* and boots, to act as a kind of heel-clicking chorus line, while the Barnstorming Company's ringmaster, Halina Rodzinski, strutted around in a red riding coat, white breeches, and a black topper, cracking her long whip. Margaret, being the supposedly clandestine offspring of a love affair between the rose-bearing Octavian and the irresistibly seductive Carmen, was dressed to look like a child in a white dress with a blue satin sash around her waist.

But the hit of the evening, beyond any doubt, was John Severance, the septuagenarian philanthropist and chairman of the board of directors, who had financed the building of the orchestra's hall. Disguised as the Marschallin, he appeared in a curled wig, which hid his white hair though not his Vandyke beard. He could not keep a straight face when Margaret sat on his lap and sang some of the "Papa, Papa!" lines, inspired by the brood of supposedly illegitimate children who bedevil Baron Ochs in the last act of *Der Rosenkavalier.* His laugh was so infectious that Margaret's silvery voice broke into trills and roulades of high-pitched merriment, which I had some trouble accompanying on the piano. Even the most sedate dowagers and millionaires in the audience laughed or guffawed their heads off, some slapping their thighs in unashamed delight.

The production of *Carmen,* which coincided more or less with this hilarious evening, was unfortunately not as successful from our personal point of view — for reasons I should have foreseen. In operatic matters I was still something of a novice, so when Rodzinski, who did this to please me, generously offered Margaret the role of Micaëla (Don José's rustic sweetheart) both of us were delighted. Unfortunately, this soprano role was not really suited to Margaret's *leggiero,* or lyric coloratura voice, though neither of us realized it at the time.

As Micaëla, Margaret was not at her best, and in the next day's Cleveland *Plain Dealer* she was raked over the coals by the paper's music critic, Herbert Elwell.

I did my best to console her, reminding her of what Ernö Dohnányi used to say about the difference between music critics and performers. "A good musician is someone who is totally familiar with the furniture and contents of his artistic dwelling. He knows every nook and cranny, he inhabits it, he is completely at home in it. But people who write about music are strangers. They are 'outsiders.' They peer in through the windows to see what is going on inside, and they say, 'Ah, look, he is opening a drawer. Now what does that mean? What is he looking for?' Or they see him going to a shelf to take out a book, and they say, 'What book do you think it is?' They then resort to conjectures and fanciful interpretations. But since they do not really know what we are, it is silly to pay any attention to them." The simile, though apt, did little to relieve Margaret's distress.

I myself had been profoundly hurt by Josef Hofmann's cavalier treatment of my piano playing, and though Elwell was no Hofmann, Margaret's self-confidence as a singer was momentarily shattered by his withering critique. Now that I was married to a singer, I was better able to appreciate the immense psychological harm that can be inflicted by a single unfavorable review. The damage thus wrought can last for months and develop into a paralyzing trauma unless vigorously combated by the kind of therapy Dohnányi so sagaciously recommended.

Although Margaret soon redeemed herself in another opera, her setback in the role of Micaëla was a source of great embarrassment to both of us. Inevitably, word began to spread that she had only been offered the role in this *Carmen* production because she was the wife of the conductor's favorite assistant. Those who accepted this spiteful gossip were in every sense "outsiders," musical illiterates who did not have the slightest inkling of what was wrong. It even took us, the "insiders," time to understand the root of the trouble. Only now, when it was too late to repair the damage done, did Margaret begin to suspect the truth — which was that Marcella Sembrich, whom she had once idolized and in whose diva footsteps she had hoped to tread, had done her voice irreparable harm by teaching her to reach the highest coloratura notes through a special effort of vocal projection, not unlike a hoot, which had caused her throat muscles to contract. Where once she had been able to sing up to the G above high C, now she had difficulty sustaining a steady D.

Learning which muscles to contract and which to relax is one of the secrets of good singing. But this was something of which, in this winter of 1935–1936, I knew but little, even though I had now been listening to singers for four years. Although I was fast becoming an "opera expert," it was more from necessity than choice, and what I knew already was pitifully little compared to what I still had to learn. This was equally true in other areas. Paradoxical though it may sound, I, who over the years have mastered six languages and many dozens of musical and operatic scores, have never had a memory for faces. I can remember names, but connecting them with the corresponding faces is a gift I have not been able to develop.

During our first months in Cleveland, Margaret and I were positively overwhelmed by the kindness shown to us by local music lovers. Some of them would invite us to spend an entire Sunday at their homes, where we would play the piano, sing songs, and swap amusing stories.

Since I had to spend two days of every week in Philadelphia, I would take the Monday evening train to get there, returning two nights later to Cleveland. On one of these Wednesday evenings, when I felt worn out after a particularly full day of teaching sessions and orchestra rehearsals, I boarded the night train at Philadelphia's North Station and found that my berth had not yet been made up. The Pullman attendant, one of those affable black porters travelers used to meet on American trains before the country was overtaken by the aviation age, flashed an apologetic smile at me, asking if I wouldn't mind "waiting up ahead in the club car" while he prepared the bedding for the upper and lower berths.

Moving on to the club car, I sat down in gloomy impatience. Several conductors passed by, and one of them stopped to punch my ticket. Just behind him came another man, whom I also took for an official.

"Good evening," he addressed me.

"Good evening," I answered curtly, feeling in no mood to strike up a conversation with this railway official, no matter how friendly he might try to be.

"What's the matter? Don't you feel well?" asked the stranger. "You act as if you didn't know me."

I looked up at him and noticed that he wore an ordinary felt hat instead of a ticket collector's cap. Ah, another passenger, like myself. He wore a coat and had nice clean-cut features, but otherwise there was nothing remarkable about him. His was the kind of anonymous face one so often sees above a Brooks Brothers shirt and striped necktie on commuter trains. But I was still in no mood to reciprocate his greeting.

"I'm sorry," I said. "You must be mistaking me for somebody else. I don't believe we've ever met."

"Now isn't that peculiar?" said the stranger in an altered tone of voice. "I'm Whiting Williams, and you and your wife spent the whole of last Sunday at our house in Cleveland."

I jumped up from my seat as if stung by a bee, grasped his hand, and began apologizing. "Oh, Mr. Williams, please forgive me. It must be" — I was about to put the blame on an imaginary shortsightedness, when I remembered that the previous Sunday I had mentioned my excellent eyesight — "it must be that hat you're wearing, which makes you look different. And the lights here are a bit weak. Please forgive me, Mr. Williams, for seeming so rude."

He sat down on the next chair and we had a pleasant chat over a couple of drinks.

"Since our berths are in the same Pullman car," he said to me as we rose to leave, "why don't you let me give you a lift home when we reach Cleveland? My automobile's parked just beyond the station."

"That's awfully kind of you," I answered, and we bade each other good night.

I gave the matter no further thought until the following morning, when I climbed out of my berth and stumbled along the dark aisle toward the washroom. All six wash basins were occupied — by six men, all of them in undershirts. Several were lathering up, one or two of them were brushing their teeth or wiping their wet faces with towels. I looked from one face to the next with a feeling of sudden anxiety. What if one of them belonged to Whiting Williams? Would I be able to recognize it? Probably not. All six men looked pretty much the same — average age, average height, average face. I expected one of the faces to brighten and to smile at me in the mirror, but they all remained expressionless.

After one of the shavers had slipped on his shirt, I took his place at the basin and started shaving. Surreptitiously I glanced to the left, then to the right. The razors continued their scraping, the toothbrushes their scrubbing, the towels their wiping without their owners evincing a flicker of recognition. Several newcomers stepped up as the others moved back. Was one of them by any chance Whiting Williams? I found it impossible to say. I couldn't remember what he looked like. I still had a grip on his name, but his face was lost, as if in a morning fog.

When the train pulled into Cleveland, I decided that my only hope was to let the other passengers in the Pullman car pass me by as we walked up the platform. If Whiting Williams came abreast, he would surely hail me and then I would be saved. But the others all bustled past me on their busy, businesslike ways. Even their hats and coats looked astonishingly alike, and there were none that I could ascribe with any certainty to my host of the previous Sunday.

Emerging from the station, I hopped into a taxi to spare myself further embarrassment. As I was driven home, I found myself wondering what Whiting Williams must have thought of my bizarre behavior. I could almost hear him saying to his wife, "Just think, dear, we had him out here for the whole of Sunday, we met again in the club car and then again in the washroom, and he couldn't even be bothered to utter a civil 'good morning.' "

I never did have a chance to find out what he told his wife, for neither Margaret nor I ever saw the Williamses again. A few days later we invited them to come over to our place for a meal, but the invitation was chillingly refused. We ourselves were never invited to their home again. "That Goldovsky man," he must have told his friends, "is the rudest, most arrogant fellow I think I've ever met."

I realized with a helpless feeling that years of training with Schnabel, Dohnányi, and Fritz Reiner had not been enough, and that to complete my education I should have taken a course in Advanced Sociability with Dale Carnegie.

Whatever Whiting Williams may have thought of Boris Goldovsky, Artur Rodzinski continued to hold him in almost embarrassingly high esteem. He did everything he could to show me off as a kind of wonderboy assistant, and as a special mark of favor he invited me to play Richard Strauss's *Burleske* — a very showy piano concerto in one movement — with the Cleveland Orchestra.

This extraordinary privilege was soon followed by another, which pleased me far less. The third opera scheduled for this season was Johann Strauss's *Die Fledermaus* — which, like its predecessors, was due to be presented three times: in this case on

Thursday, February 27, on Saturday, February 29 (this being the leap year of 1936), and on Monday, March 2. But a few days before the first *Fledermaus* performance, Rodzinski summoned me to his office to inform me that he was not going to conduct it. He didn't feel well, he explained, adding, "Since you've been training the singers and know what it's all about, you conduct it!"

This sudden command — it was not an invitation — left me a bit nonplussed. To be sure, I had by now worked for Rodzinski long enough to be familiar with his hyper-nervous ways and curious idiosyncrasies. He was among other things a bundle of superstitions. In addition to the pistol, which he had to carry under his cutaway jacket in one of his trouser pockets, he never went out on stage without first kissing a photograph of his father, which he carried in another pocket. If his wife Halina was present, she would have to give him a ritual kiss on the forehead, accompanied by a Polish blessing. When George Higgins, the stage manager of Severance Hall, was not around to do it, I would be called upon to give his left arm a savage pinch — enough to leave one more mark on a limb that was black and blue with bruises before the concert season was even half completed. Apparently this bit of self-inflicted torture acted like a "shot in the arm" or a last-minute injection of adrenalin, galvanizing his faculties for the ordeal ahead. Rodzinski even wore a Chinese ring, whose "face" — a frog carved in ivory — had to be turned in a certain way on his finger, presumably to frighten away the demons and evil spirits who might be conspiring to sow chaos and confusion among his instrumentalists.

I was by now familiar with all these rituals and superstitions, just as I was with his periodic fits of pleasure and displeasure. Still, his sudden backing away from our scheduled *Fledermaus* production took me completely by surprise. He made it clear, however, that he would have nothing further to do with it. It was now my "baby," and I was left to finish the rehearsals and conduct the performances.

In Europe, Strauss's *Die Fledermaus* is often the first opera that apprentice conductors are given to direct. Its popular tunes are so well known to instrumentalists and singers that when the time comes for the matinee, the regular conductor often delegates the job to his concert master or assistant. But with the Cleveland Orchestra, as I discovered, it was quite another matter, for the operetta was as new to most of the players as it was to the singers.

Fortunately for all concerned, the performances went off well. Margaret sang and acted charmingly in the role of Adele, which was perfectly suited to her lyric coloratura voice.

There was one brief moment of crisis during the first performance, but it was more hilarious than tragic. Though we were using an English text, we had retained the services of our regular German prompter, an aged gentleman named Herr Schüller, who had helped us with the *Rosenkavalier* and *Carmen* performances. In the last act, during a dialogue between the jailer, Frank, and the banker, Eisenstein, both singers forgot their lines and began improvising madly. In the prompter's box Herr Schüller started shouting the words in his broken English. In his frantic desire to help, he got so worked up that his false teeth were ejected from his mouth and fell onto the stage. The spectacle was outrageously funny, and the actors on the stage couldn't keep from laughing, even as they spoke their wobbly lines. Since *Die Fledermaus* is a lighthearted farce, the incident was anything but catastrophic, and it gave us a lot to chuckle over after the curtain calls had all been taken and we could retire to our dressing rooms.

My final and in many ways most challenging assignment as Rodzinski's assistant was to help him prepare a special Holy Week production of Richard Wagner's last opera *Parsifal,* which is based on the medieval legend of the Holy Grail. Like *Die Meistersinger,* which I had helped Reiner put on in Philadelphia, *Parsifal* requires the participation of a considerable number of male choristers. To assemble the needed number, I was advised to get in touch with the Singers Club, a choral group made up of about one hundred businessmen, bankers, doctors, lawyers, and architects who sang "for the fun of it."

It was from this choral group that I finally selected the twenty-four male voices we needed for *Parsifal*. Training them for a kind of singing they had never before attempted proved quite a task. Among other things, I had to teach them how to pronounce the unfamiliar German words, since almost all of the singing they had undertaken up until then had been in English.

The three performances — the first given on Holy Thursday (April 9, 1936) — were sold out far in advance, as word spread that the famous basso Ludwig Hofmann, who had often performed at Bayreuth, was crossing the Atlantic to sing the role of Gurnemanz, while the German soprano Gertrude Kappel was coming from New York (where she had been singing with the Met) to play the role of the half-sorceress, half-temptress Kundry. Rodzinski, who had a passion for Wagner and was more at home with his works than he was with Richard Strauss's, conducted in a kind of trance, which rose to a state of almost religious rapture when the voices of an angelic choir seemed to descend from heaven over the enchanted hall. They were the voices of a number of handpicked young boys and girls whom I had carefully trained and whom I had placed in a (luckily available) hollow space above the ceiling of the auditorium.

The opera season was drawing to a close when the director of the Cleveland Institute of Music, Beryl Rubinstein, who was an accomplished pianist and something of a composer, asked me to come to his office.

"Mr. Goldovsky," he said, "you know, you have made quite an impression here in Cleveland. I've been getting very favorable reports that you have a real knack for teaching opera to young people. This has given me an idea. We have a number of good singing teachers here at the institute and quite a few promising vocal and instrumental students. What we need is somebody to bring them all together. How would you like to organize an opera department for us so that we could include it in next fall's curriculum?"

"Mr. Rubinstein," I said, "this is a fascinating proposition. Nothing could please me more. But . . . but just how is this going to work? I mean, I'll be glad to coach the singers and I can train and conduct the orchestra. But what about the dramatic side of it? Whom do you have in mind to teach operatic acting and to be the stage director?"

At this Beryl Rubinstein looked genuinely surprised. "But Mr. Goldovsky, you must understand. The institute couldn't possibly afford to hire two experts. We're not that rich. If you take this job — as I very much hope you will — you will have to take care of both — the theatrical as well as the musical side of things."

I protested that I knew nothing about acting and staging. I was a musician. I could coach singers, yes. I could train an orchestra, yes. I could train a chorus, yes. I could conduct. But teaching singers how to act was something I had never done. It was outside my field.

Rubinstein did not seem impressed: "You've worked with stage directors, haven't you?"

"Of course. As a pianist for stage rehearsals and as a conductor's assistant, I had to. That was part of my job."

"Well, and what are your feelings on the subject? Do you think the stage directors you've worked with were all that hot? That they really knew what they were doing?"

"Frankly, no," I answered. "I've seen some pretty dreadful staging. In fact, Mr. Rubinstein, this is one of the things that has long bothered me about opera. The music and the acting seem to have very little to do with each other. But how this trouble can be overcome I don't honestly know, because, as I've said, I have no experience of this type."

"You may not have any experience in staging," said Rubinstein, "but, you see, you've got some ideas about it, which is a good sign. Here's your chance to learn something. Why not? And who knows? You'll probably do no worse, and you might even do a lot better than a professional stage director. So how about it?"

"All right," I said, "but I'll need a week or so to think this over." And on that inconclusive, but by no means negative, note we parted.

The more I thought about Rubinstein's offer, the more tantalizing it became. Although I had never had much use for opera as an art form, I had seen enough fine singing and acting to realize what it could be at its best. Feodor Chaliapin as Tsar Boris or as the crazy old miller in Dargomizhsky's *Russalka,* Margaret Matzenauer as Klytemnestra in *Elektra,* Lotte Lehmann as the Marschallin in *Der Rosenkavalier* — those were great dramatic performances, examples of what opera could be when superbly acted and superbly sung. Even my Margaret had been from the dramatic as well as vocal point of view a wonderfully vital and plausible Cherubino in *The Marriage of Figaro.*

By this time we had left our little apartment on Cornell Road and had moved into a pleasant house on the St. James Parkway. Here I told Margaret about Beryl Rubinstein's offer.

"Oh, Boris!" she exclaimed, almost clapping her hands in delight. "An opera department at the Cleveland Institute of Music? And you running it? Oh, I think that's terrific, terrific!"

"Yes, Maggie," I said, "but just think what it's going to involve. The amount of work, the amount of studying. I haven't the faintest idea how to stage-direct an opera. I will have to learn everything from scratch. I don't even know where to start. I wish I had Herbert Graf's experience."

"Herbert Graf!" she cried. "Herbert Graf's experience! For Heaven's sake, Boris, what are you talking about? Do you remember how he directed me in *The Marriage of Figaro* and in *The Barber of Seville,* whispering in my ear just before I went on stage, 'Just get out there and *act,* my dear, you've got all the talent it takes.' Now what kind of experience does one need to give that kind of advice?"

"All right," I said. "But what about Willy von Wymetal? How does he strike you as a stage director?"

Margaret made a face. Wymetal obviously found no more favor in her eyes than did Herbert Graf.

"By the way," I went on, "when you were studying opera dramatics, what basic textbooks did you use?"

"Basic textbooks! Are you kidding? We never used any textbooks. All we had to learn were the words and the music. Wymetal took care of the rest by giving us some general ideas about posturing, gesturing, and the like."

I stared at Margaret in amazement. Up till now I had been so immersed in the musical side of opera that I had paid scant attention to its dramatic aspects. I had trusted the "professionals," who presumably knew what they were doing, though I certainly did not admire the results. But it had never occurred to me that the dramatic side of opera might have been left to chance, to the whim or fancy of the stage director, and that it might virtually be virgin land, waiting to be plowed and sown.

I spent the next couple of weeks going through opera scores to see what stage and acting directions they contained. The German librettists, beginning with Richard Wagner, were quite helpful, though even here there were long stretches of music with no specific pointers as to movements on the stage. Among the Italians, only the scores of Puccini and the later Verdi had any practical guidance to offer. In the case of Mozart's operas the stage directions were virtually nonexistent. The setting for the opening scene of *Così fan tutte,* for example, was described in exactly three words: *Bottega di caffè* — a coffee house. Nothing more. For the entire scene, consisting of three lively terzettos separated by two elaborate recitatives, I could find only six descriptive notations. Three of them — "with fire," "placidly," "jokingly" — indicated the kind of expression with which certain lines were to be sung. Two of them — "aside" and "to Ferrando" — specified to whom the words were to be addressed. The only stage direction that described a definite action — "they put their hands on their swords" — was hardly needed, for the text made it quite clear that such a gesture was intended.

The setting for the next scene was described even more succinctly. "A garden by the seashore" was the only indication given, and there were even fewer hints concerning actions than in the opening scene.

From the many scores I examined it became apparent that the few directions given referred only to the persons who happen to be singing at that moment. The other characters disappear into a kind of limbo, their continuing presence being left to the imagination.

The statuesque idleness resulting from this lack of precise indications was the very thing that had bothered me so much in most of the opera performances I had so far witnessed. When not singing, the actors tended to behave like orchestra musicians who, when not playing, sit quietly on their chairs counting measures and waiting for their cue. Whence the static quality of opera productions, as opposed to the vibrant theater performances I had enjoyed in Moscow and Budapest, where each character was acting to the hilt, as it were, all the time he was on stage. If opera was to be musical drama, as I instinctively felt it should be, then it had to be living, uninterrupted theater, which meant that the characters on the stage could not be reduced to a purely intermittent existence, coming to life only when they sang.

In the course of my research I finally came upon a little booklet which contained pictures of "standard" positions and gestures for opera singers. But the text and illustrations were even more ludicrous than most of the staging I had actually witnessed. The procedures that a stage director like Wilhelm von Wymetal passed on to his pupils were obviously derived from traditional habits. These the stage directors had picked up when relatively young from their elders, either by watching them at work or by listening to the advice and the suggestions made by retiring or faded "stars." The result was a body of conventional "wisdom," essentially transmitted by word of mouth, which was fundamentally wooden, lifeless, and unimaginative.

"You know," I finally said to Margaret, "I think there's only one solution. I'm going to have to get hold of Ernst Lert — you know, the fellow I was telling you about who made such an impression on me recently in Philadelphia."

Dr. Ernst Lert was a stocky, muscular Viennese, with a pair of close-set, almost foxlike eyes, who had taken over the teaching of operatic acting at the Curtis Institute. Exceedingly vital and intense, he was as different as could be imagined from the vague, indecisive Wilhelm von Wymetal, who had probably never had a truly original idea in his life. During one of my regular trips to Philadelphia, Lert's accompanist had fallen ill and I had been asked to substitute for him. Lert was teaching the singers a scene from Puccini's *La Bohème.* What I saw while sitting at the keyboard was a revelation. Lert induced each of them to act in a completely natural, unaffected manner, while at the same time controlling their movements in such a way that they followed the flow of the music. He had no more use for static, statutesque posturing than he did for overacting and the kind of mincing danciness I had always found so artificial and offensive in run-of-the-mill opera productions. The singers were taught to emphasize the subtlest nuances in the music through their motions, gestures, and expressions, but to do it in such a way as to make it all seem spontaneous and unrehearsed.

If there was one person who could help me in my new predicament, it was clearly Ernst Lert. Picking up the receiver, I put in a long-distance call to Manhattan, where he was then living. I explained how Beryl Rubinstein had asked me to set up an opera department for the Cleveland Institute of Music, but without the help of an extra stage director. "This means I'm going to have to teach opera dramatics, when I know next to nothing about it. So what I'm wondering, Dr. Lert, is if you couldn't give me some private coaching this summer. I don't know how much I would need, but at least if you could give me some pointers for one or two operas, then perhaps I could accept Mr. Rubinstein's offer."

Lert, on the other end of the line, was positively enthusiastic. "Take it, Mr. Goldovsky," he said to me. "Accept this offer, this position. Don't hesitate. I can give you all the instruction you'll need in July and August, if you can come here to New York. We'll have two sessions a week for a period of six weeks, and that should be sufficient for your purposes. Now how does that sound?"

I told him it sounded fine and that I would move to Manhattan in July and August for this badly needed six-week cram course in operatic staging.

In July Margaret and I moved to New York, taking up residence at the Ansonia Hotel, not far from where Lert lived, on the corner of 72nd Street and Riverside Drive. Margaret, who had always had trouble with her breathing, had decided to undergo an operation on her nose in order to straighten a deviated septum. She was still recovering from the operation when she discovered that she was pregnant. Though this meant that she would have to give up her opera appearances until our child was born, it was happy news for both of us.

When I turned up for my first lesson with Lert, he told me that he was going to have to charge me $35 a lesson. I remember having been quite flabbergasted by this unforeseen expense — proof of what an exceptionally privileged life I had led as a piano-playing *Wunderkind* — for Kipp, Kreutzer, Schnabel, and Dohnányi had never charged me a penny for instruction. But I had no reason to begrudge the $420 Lert charged me, as this was the best personal investment I have ever made.

What I learned from those twelve lessons surpassed my expectations. It was as though I had just discovered opera, a mysterious land I had so far hazily overflown or through which I had vaguely strayed with my eyes half blindfolded. Although he was not a professional musician, being neither an instrumentalist nor a singer, Lert had a remarkably fine ear for the dramatic meaning of music. He made me aware of many musical subtleties in opera scores that I had not noticed and which, particularly in Mozart operas, I now like to think of as "goodies" — delicate nuances indicating, for example, exactly how a caress of consolation is to be performed or a mustache is to be twirled.

No less eye-opening for me was Lert's insistence — one I have since made my own — that opera, like good theater, *must make sense.* Ever since the days of Dr. Johnson, who defined it as "an exotic and irrational entertainment," it has been fashionable to consider opera as a deliberately foolish form of art. I too had been unwittingly influenced by this ironic attitude, so common among opera lovers, who seem to think that the senselessness of opera confers on it a special glamour, comparable to the chaotic formlessness of so many contemporary canvases, which are prized by snobs because they are so intrinsically meaningless. But Lert had no use for this cult of foolishness. If opera did not make sense, it was because the people who conducted, stage-directed, and performed it did not make sense. Not only must the gestures match the words and the musical inflections of the phrase, but scenery, costumes, lights, instrumental passages, and everything else in opera had to be integrated into an artistic whole that was as real as the everyday happenings of our lives. He could identify with operatic characters to such an extent that he knew exactly how they felt and what they were thinking not only when they were singing and acting but even when they were not present on stage.

When I asked Lert to help me with the staging of Mozart's *Così fan tutte,* he frowned and shook his head.

"You don't need me for that," he said. "You should be able to figure that out by yourself on the basis of the indications in the libretto."

"I've studied the libretto," I pointed out, "but there was nothing there for me to go by."

"What do you mean 'Nothing'? Let's begin with the setting. How is that described?"

"Described?" I stared at him. "But there is no description. It simply says 'a coffee house.' "

"Exactly," said Lert. "A coffee house. Now didn't you tell me you spent some years in Budapest and Berlin and Paris? You should know all about coffee houses."

"Yes, I've been in lots of coffee houses."

"Fine. Now tell me everything you can remember about a coffee house: what it looks like, what goes on there — everything. Take your time. I'm not in a hurry."

I began describing my idea of a typical coffee house. A large room filled with small tables, surrounded by chairs. A main entrance with at least one door leading to a kind of kitchen or pantry. A lot of hustling and bustling about of waiters carrying trays, while the customers drink, smoke, play chess or checkers, or read newspapers. That was about all I could think of.

"Nonsense," said Lert. "You can think of a lot more. For example, imagine yourself walking into a coffee house and tell me everything you'd do once you were inside."

I began to enumerate the things I would do. Obviously I would begin by looking for an empty table. Then, having found one, I would take off my coat — that is, if I had one on — and I would try to find a peg to hang it on or sling it over the back of a chair. Next I would try to catch the waiter's eye to order a drink or, if I was hungry, I would ask for a menu and order a dish of something. And so on and so forth, until the time came for me to pay the bill, get up, retrieve my coat, and leave.

Lert laughed.

"What's wrong?" I asked. "Have I forgotten something?"

"Not that I know of," he answered. "But you have just staged the opening scene of *Così*."

"You mean that Ferrando, Gugliemo, and Don Alfonso can do all those things? But when? They have to sing, don't they?"

"You are very hard to please," said Lert, shaking his head with another laugh. "First you complain because the nonsinging characters stand still without having anything to do, and now you are worried because there is too much for them to do and no time in which to do it. But now think for a moment: who in this scene has the least to sing?"

"Don Alfonso. Of course," I exclaimed, as the light began to dawn. "He's the one who should study the menu and order something to eat for all three of them . . . and then . . ." Suddenly my mind was crowded with possibilities: "Yes, why not? Couldn't he order a leg of lamb or a chunk of ham, so that when he sings of fighting duels he can brandish a carving knife? And then, at the end, when they all sing and toast the God of Love, they could drink champagne and clink glasses."

"But wait," I said to Lert, who had been watching my mounting enthusiasm with considerable amusement. "What about the other customers? It would look a little peculiar if the coffee house was empty. But if we bring in more customers, wouldn't that be distracting for the audience?"

"You must not expect to solve all your problems in five minutes," Lert reminded me. "You must have visited coffee houses which were nearly empty. But that's not what really matters. The important thing is this: before you try to stage something, begin by consulting the score. The mood of the music is all-important, and not every staging idea can be squeezed into the time made available by the composer. You will save yourself a lot of trouble if you first analyze every aspect of the music and then decide which of your various coffee-house notions fits inside the musical framework and can be utilized to best advantage."

One of the first problems I was given to solve was how best to organize the staging of the opening scene of Verdi's *La Forza del Destino*. We were in the middle of the discussion when Lert suddenly said: "By the way, there is something Leonora wears under her skirt that she is hiding from her father. Do you know what it is?"

The question gave me quite a jolt. What could she possibly be wearing under her skirt if not petticoats?

"I don't know what sort of underclothing Spanish girls wore in those days, but it was probably not so much different from what they wear today. I don't see why her father would care one way or the other."

"Forget her underclothing!" said Lert with a forceful gesture. "She is wearing riding boots. She is about to elope. Don Alvaro is coming to fetch her with saddled horses, and they expect to ride through the night for many hours, to Seville and beyond. Riding boots are essential. Her father, of course, thinks she is about to retire for the night, and if he should ever notice that she's wearing riding boots, the game would be up. Obviously," he went on, "this is not the only reason for Leonora's nervousness, but those boots she is wearing serve to remind her painfully and continually of her tragic conflict of emotions."

I was profoundly impressed. Here was a seemingly unimportant detail, something that the people in the audience might not even notice. Yet it illuminated an approach to opera that was radically different from anything I had so far encountered. In thinking of Leonora's role in this scene, I had mainly been concerned with how well she was going to interpret her duet with the tenor, how much expression she was going to put into her sorrow at the thought of leaving her Spanish homeland, how sincerely she should portray her fear and guilt at deceiving her father. These were all important considerations, but so were those riding boots, which necessarily affected everything Leonora sang and did. I could feel myself, as Leonora, standing there in my gown while my feet, instead of being enveloped in soft slippers, were encased in hard-heeled boots. She was no longer merely thinking of eloping, she was already living its hardships.

Years later, when I had to stage this opening scene of *La Forza del Destino,* I went Lert one better by having Leonora wear an entire masculine riding habit underneath her dress so that she was ready to elope when Alvaro arrived. I found that the sudden transformation, when she removes her dress, heightened the element of urgency in the lovers' duet, as well as presenting other advantages for the subsequent development of the action. Lert by this time was long since dead, but I believe that he would have been pleased to see how his riding boots idea had sprouted.

What Ernst Lert taught me, among many other things, was to look for the tangible object that can give an operatic scene an even greater credibility. He made me understand that opera is not incidentally, but primordially a dramatic play in which the characters sing with instrumental accompaniment. It has to be approached initially from the dramatic, not from the musical, point of view. All the great opera composers — beginning with Mozart, Verdi, and Wagner — understood this instinctively, but unfortunately this has not generally been the case with opera conductors.

"The great tragedy in our field," Lert remarked to me one day, "is that opera conductors fail to realize the fundamental interdependence of musical and dramatic nuances. It will be a great day for opera when all conductors are made to study stage directing and all dramatic directors are required to master the essentials of music."

His own departure from the Metropolitan Opera Company had been occasioned by an opera conductor's bland disregard for the dramatic exigencies of the text. It had happened while he was staging the same Verdi opera he had assigned me to study: *La Forza del Destino.* In the third act of this opera there is a battlefield scene in which the itinerant Spanish friar Fra Melitone finds himself caught between Italian and Spanish soldiers. The Italians want to attack the friar, who has just preached a sermon accusing the whole world of iniquity, whereas the Spaniards, realizing that he is a fellow countryman, wish to protect him.

"Togone infame!" ("Cursed beetle," because he is wearing a black surplice), cry the Italians.

"Segui pur, padruccio!" ("Carry on, Little Father"), answer the Spaniards.

"Dallì, dallì!" ("Hit him, hit him"), shout the Italians.

"Scappa, scappa!" ("Run for it, escape"), the friar's fellow Spaniards urge.

When the time came to block this scene, Lert addressed the chorus, saying, "All right, which of you are the Italian soldiers and which of you are Spaniards?"

"We've learned both parts," the members of the chorus answered. "So you divide us up."

"Well, how nice of the chorus director!" said Lert, deciding to be tactful. "But where is the chorus director? I would like to have a word with him."

Summoned from the wings, the chorus director came out onto the stage.

"Will you please," Lert requested, "point out those who are to sing the Italians and those who are to sing the Spanish soldiers, since, as you know, they sing different words. I would rather you divide them up since you know these singers better than I do."

"It really doesn't matter how they're divided up," answered the chorus director, a gentleman by the name of Giulio Setti, "because they all sing all the words."

"What do you mean — all of them sing all the words?" demanded Lert. "You know the score as well as I do, and it's quite clear what happens. Half of the soldiers sing *'Dallì, dallì'* while the other half sing *'Scappa, scappa.'* They can't possibly sing both."

"Oh yes they do," replied Setti. "They *all* sing *all* the words."

"But that makes no sense," protested Lert.

"It has to be that way," the chorus director explained. "The music is divided, so if you take half the chorus, with a three-part division here and only three top tenors on each side to sing the highest notes, it doesn't sound full enough. So we always have everyone singing everything. It makes a much fuller sound."

"Look, I can't stage it on that basis," said Lert. "It's a dramatic contradiction. It inconceivable that they should all sing the same words."

"Well, I'm sorry," said Setti, "but that's the way we've always done it. I don't have the authority to make any changes. This is a musical matter, and if this is going to be changed, we'll have to see the conductor about it."

They went to see the conductor, Vincenzo Bellezza, who said, "No, no, Mr. Lert, Mr. Setti is right. We can't divide the voices because half the chorus would then have to sing in three-part harmony, and in this opera house it just won't sound right. They must all of them sing both parts."

"If that's the case, then somebody else is going to have to stage this opera," said Lert. And with that he walked out of the opera house.

"I just couldn't face the prospect of seeing that scene butchered and rendered totally meaningless," Lert explained to me, "simply because the conductor was only interested in the volume of sound produced by those top tenors. So I quit. On the spot. They'll never see me again, unless they start to change their ways. But I have no regrets. Now I can devote myself full-time to my students at the Curtis Institute."

When we returned to Cleveland in the autumn of 1936, Artur Rodzinski informed me that the forthcoming opera season was being drastically curtailed for lack of funds. John Severance, the white-haired chairman of the board who had contributed so much to the jollity of our "Secret of Lady Carmen of Seville" burlesque, had died a few weeks after that hilarious evening, in January 1936, and though he had been succeeded by another music-loving Maecenas named Dudley Blossom (who had also contributed financially to the construction of Severance Hall), Rodzinski's relations with the symphony orchestra's financial backers were no longer as cordial as they had once been. Toscanini had recently resigned as conductor of the New York Philharmonic Symphony Orchestra, and it was an open secret that Rodzinski coveted this post: an ambition that did not exactly endear him to his patrons in Cleveland.

There were of course other reasons. Like the Philadelphians before them, the Clevelanders were now discovering the hard way that producing opera is an expensive business. Rodzinski was thus obliged to limit the new season's operatic offerings to two productions: Wagner's *Tannhäuser* and Richard Strauss's *Elektra.* Since he had been paying me $1000 for each opera production, this sharply reduced schedule involved a considerable loss of income for me, but Rodzinski generously filled most of the resulting gap by giving me a new job — that of organizing a Philharmonic Chorus, made up of some 250 singers, who were to appear in two major choral productions per orchestral season. The two works chosen for the current 1936–1937 season were Beethoven's Ninth Symphony and Verdi's *Requiem.*

Training vocal ensembles was something I was familiar with, but only up to a point. Immediately following my arrival in Cleveland in the fall of 1935 I had assembled a group of choristers consisting of about thirty women and twenty men who had performed quite admirably in the important ensemble sections of *Carmen* and *Die Fledermaus.* The girls had also done a fine job in the very difficult Flower Maiden scene of *Parsifal.* Even so, to train the two hundred and fifty singers of the Philharmonic Chorus was a new opportunity and a new challenge. My immediate vocal ensemble problems, however, were related to the forthcoming production of *Tannhäuser.* The opening scene of this opera contains a chorus of women — the Venusberg nymphs — who must be trained to sing off stage while keeping in time with the orchestra, and to sing in such a way that their voices would at first sound ethereal, as though coming from very far away. To make this possible, I installed a microphone in the orchestra pit and hooked it up to several loudspeakers located far off stage. This is now a routine procedure, but in those days it was an almost revolutionary innovation. I then placed the women singers on several staircases connecting the stage to the rest of the building. By gradually opening and closing the doors leading to these staircases, I was able to obtain a most impressive crescendo and diminuendo effect, suggesting the nimble-footed approach and withdrawal of these invisible nymphs. The effect was spectacular, as the voices could be heard approaching and then receding, as though the nymphs were actually wandering through the distant caverns of the Venusberg. Rodzinski was beside himself with joy, for this experiment in off-stage dynamics surpassed his expectations.

This *Tannhäuser* production was noteworthy for another most successful innovation, for which Rodzinski deserves the credit. During the second scene of the first act a number of pilgrims bound for Rome file across the stage. To emphasize the ascetic nature of their quest, compared to Venusberg's sensuous delights, Wagner has them sing without orchestral accompaniment. The many changes of harmony make it very difficult for these choristers to keep on pitch during this long unaccompanied passage, and this was particularly true of the amateurs from the Singers Club whom I had to train. We therefore decided to introduce three clarinetists among the cowled and hooded pilgrims to keep the singers from going flat. The instruments were hidden by the long robes they wore, and though the clarinetists played loud enough to be heard by the singers, they were completely inaudible to the audience.

Even so, our production almost came to grief during the second performance, given on October 31. At the very end of the opera the same pilgrims rushed back to the stage with burning torches in their hands. As the last pilgrim made his entrance from the left, one of the stage drapes caught on fire. Having just given the entrance cue to the chorus, I was standing nearby and saw the flames leap up with surprising and frightening speed. Fortunately there was a fire extinguisher handy, and with the help of several stagehands we were able to tear down the drape and extinguish the flames. Rodzinski and the orchestra were unaware of what had happened, and the only persons in the audience who saw it were those who happened to be seated in the boxes on the opposite side. One of them was Margaret, who was seated next to Mrs. Adella Prentiss Hughes (the "Mother of the Cleveland Orchestra," as she was known for the help she had given to its establishment). Together they managed to calm their neighbors, who were about to panic.

Not long after this successful *Tannhäuser* production, Josef Hofmann came to Cleveland to play Beethoven's *Emperor* Concerto with Rodzinski and the Cleveland Orchestra. Naturally, I went to Severance Hall to say hello and shake Hofmann's hand. But he seemed anything but pleased to see me.

"Oh, so there you are!" he said in a curt, indeed almost cutting tone. "And what are you doing here? I thought you were going to live in Philadelphia."

He was obviously annoyed, and though he didn't actually say so, the implication was that I had broken my word and somehow double-crossed him. To be treated like this by my old director, for whose institute I was still working, was most upsetting. So instead of staying on for the rehearsal, I went back home to have lunch with Margaret. We were in the middle of eating when the telephone rang. It was Artur Rodzinski's secretary on the line. "Mr. Goldovsky," she said, "Dr. Rodzinski is very anxious to see you immediately. He wants you to come to Severance Hall at once."

"Oho!" I thought to myself. "Now I'm in real trouble. One of my bosses, the one in Philadelphia, is angry with me, and now he's complained to my second boss in Cleveland, and together they're going to rake me over the coals, and, who knows, I'm probably going to lose both jobs."

Without bothering to finish lunch, I climbed hurriedly into our white Packard roadster. Although it couldn't compete in length with the 16-cylinder black Cadillac convertible in which Fritz Reiner used to roll up to the Curtis Institute in Philadelphia, Margaret and I were very proud of our elegant open-air machine, which was considerably larger than Lubo's bright green Chevrolet. We had bought it on the strength of the two salaries I was now earning in Philadelphia and Cleveland. Indeed, I don't think I have ever felt quite as affluent in my entire life as I did during that year. Margaret and I had no children, and our living expenses were relatively modest. The result was this cocky display of conspicuous consumption: a gleaming white Packard, which it was a joy to contemplate and an even headier joy to drive, with one hand on the large steering wheel and the other on the rubber-bulb Klaxon.

After parking this glorious machine behind Severance Hall, I hurried to Rodzinski's office for what I feared might be a major dressing-down.

"Ah, Borischikov!" he exclaimed, his worried face creasing into a nervous smile. "Thank God you are here! I need your help. You must save my life."

I was greatly relieved to hear this. So it wasn't my life that needed saving.

"Dr. Rodzinski," I said, "what's wrong? What can I do to help you?"

"Are you familiar with the *Emperor* Concerto?"

"Yes, I studied it with Dohnányi."

"Well, you know that cadenzalike passage at the very end?"

"Of course I do."

"Then come, come with me," said Rodzinski, seizing me by the arm and propelling me out of his office. Walking briskly along the corridor, he took me down the stairs to the chamber-music auditorium, a small hall which could seat about 350 people.

"Here," he said, pointing to the piano. "Sit down and play it."

I started playing the cadenza.

"No, no!" Rodzinski stopped me. "Don't play it that way. You're playing it the way it is written."

"How else do you want me to play it?" I protested.

"Play it wrong, play it crazy!"

I had never seen him in such a state. He was a bundle of nerves. There was a muscular twitch near the left lens of his horn-rimmed glasses, and his husky voice had an almost hysterical quality to it.

Rodzinski then explained that he wanted me to distort the passage, as Josef Hofmann might decide to do during the evening performance. I knew that Hofmann enjoyed playing tricks on conductors, often playing certain passages in a deliberately topsy-turvy manner, unexpectedly accelerating the pace or slowing the tempo so that conductors would have trouble following him.

I was sufficiently familiar with Hofmann's rather warped sense of humor to realize that there were solid grounds for Rodzinski's preconcert panic. On one of the rare occasions when he had been willing to talk about music, Hofmann, in Rockport, had told me how, at a rehearsal held before the First World War where he was to play Schumann's Piano Concerto with the Boston Symphony Orchestra, he had been rather haughtily addressed by the famous German conductor Karl Muck: "Now what about the last movement? Do you play it straight, or do you do crazy things, such as some people like to do?" Hofmann had been so nettled by Muck's brusqueness that he had decided to teach him a lesson: "When we came to the last movement, I started changing the tempo and doing all sort of silly tricks, hoping I could throw him off. But I couldn't unseat him. He kept shooting angry glances at me, but he remained in the saddle. From then on we never spoke to one another. I even remember how once, when I saw him in the street, I crossed over to the other side so as not to have to say hello to him."

This unusually candid confession had reinforced my private detestation of Josef Hofmann. And now here he was, apparently out to trip Rodzinski, just as years before he had tried to "throw" Karl Muck. So for a full hour I was made to play that particular passage in every conceivable manner, suddenly racing up the scale to the high E-flat, abruptly slowing down, or slowing down and then accelerating again, so that Rodzinski's ear could familiarize itself with these malicious distortions.

Intrigued to know the outcome of this musical rodeo, I decided to attend the performance. Sure enough, when he reached the passage in question, Hofmann deliberately muddied up his playing, bunching up some notes and slowing down others, while Rodzinski, with beads of sweat pearling on his forehead, stared at him through his steel-rimmed glasses waiting for that last rising scale. But when he gave the signal with his baton, it was already too late. Hofmann, in a last-second burst of speed, managed to reach his high E-flat before the conductor could catch him.

While this battle of wits did nothing to enhance Josef Hofmann in my eyes, it sowed the first seeds of doubt in me about Artur Rodzinski's talents as a conductor. I couldn't help thinking that Hofmann could never have done to Reiner what he had just done to Rodzinski. When it came to rhythmic flexibility, the supreme quality needed in an opera conductor, Fritz Reiner was in a class by himself.

After our first collective effort for the Holy Week production of *Parsifal,* I had been approached by several members of the Singers Club of Cleveland, who told me that they were looking for a new conductor for their group. Although I was much younger than their previous leaders, they had decided that there was nobody else in Cleveland better fitted for the job. I had never worked before with an all-male chorus, and the idea appealed to me.

Before selecting a program for the coming autumn and winter, I went through the repertoire the club had sung in preceding years. Noticing the absence of operatic excerpts, I suggested that the Singers Club break new ground by undertaking one or two choral numbers from famous operas. The club's directors agreed, but to make sure that the evening was a success, they proposed that the popular Italian tenor Tito Schipa, who had performed with them before and who was a great favorite with Cleveland audiences, be invited to participate. Hitherto he had always sung two groups of solo numbers, but I saw no reason why he shouldn't sing some opera selection in conjunction with the members of the club.

It occurred to me that the third act of Verdi's *Rigoletto* contains exactly the combination I was looking for. This scene opens with a famous solo aria generally known by the first words of its introductory recitative — *"Ella mi fu rapita"* — in which the Duke of Mantua laments the disappearance of his beloved. His courtiers then burst in, and in a stirring chorus tell the Duke that they have succeeded in abducting the mistress of the court jester, Rigoletto. The courtiers, who detest the hunchbacked jester and his mocking tongue, sing with great gusto of their vengeful exploit. When he realizes that the kidnapped girl is none other than his beloved Gilda (in reality Rigoletto's daughter) and that she has been hidden away in a nearby room, the Duke gives vent to his delighted relief in a second aria, which takes the form of an "aside." The courtiers, intrigued by the Duke's sudden change of mood, begin to whisper among themselves, and as the scene closes, the Duke's soliloquy and the speculations of the courtiers gain in pace and loudness, culminating in several exclamatory high A's, which the tenor sings to the full-throated accompaniment of the chorus.

The role of the Duke was one in which Tito Schipa had been applauded at the New York Metropolitan Opera and elsewhere, and the sequence of dramatic recitative, melancholy aria, stirring choral singing, and rousing finale was a perfect combination for the Singers Club concert.

I was troubled, however, by a disturbing thought: would Schipa agree to sing the second aria, the one with the choral accompaniment? Even today, when producers and conductors have grown more adventurous, this D Major aria is rarely sung. In 1936 this portion of the scene was for all practical purposes nonexistent. From the dramatic point of view, of course, it is absurd to have a leading character leave the stage without reacting to the exciting news he has just heard. The origins of such omissions are usually obscure, but once the altered version has become "traditional," it tends to be treated with almost religious veneration. However, I knew that Toscanini was violently opposed to such blind adherence to conventional procedures, and it was just possible that

Schipa had sung this aria with the great Arturo or some other enterprising conductor.

Since Schipa, after his 1935 season at the Met, had returned to Italy, I wrote a polite letter to his Italian address, outlining the program we were planning and asking if he would agree to sing the complete *Rigoletto* sequence. Six weeks went by without an answer. I then wrote him a second letter, mailing a copy of it to the New York agency that had booked Schipa with the Singers Club.

By early November, there was still no word from Schipa and I was beginning to feel jittery. The members of the club were learning the music and mastering the unfamiliar Italian words, but without Schipa's cooperation the whole thing would collapse like a house of cards. I was beginning to suffer sleepless nights when at last I received a letter from the great tenor's booking agents in New York. They regretted being unable to answer my query regarding Signor Schipa's attitude to the D Major aria. However, they suggested that I discuss the problem with Signor Egidio Prandicelli, Signor Schipa's personal representative, who was going to stop in Cleveland on his way to Canada, where he was to organize a concert tour for the tenor in 1938.

Having been given a telephone number where I could reach Prandicelli, I lost no time calling him on the following Monday morning. But certainly, he said, he would with great pleasure dine with me that evening at Luigi Luccioni's.

Luccioni, aside from running an excellent Italian restaurant, happened to be a rabid opera lover. When I telephoned to tell him that I was coming that evening with Tito Schipa's personal representative, Luccioni began bubbling all over in anticipation, assuring me that for me and Signor Prandicelli there would be reserved the very best table, the very best antipasto and meat dishes, and *vini superiori* from the homeland across the sea.

I arrived a little ahead of the appointed time and was greeted by a beaming *padrone,* who led me over to a carefully reserved table. Not long afterward, Egidio Prandicelli was ushered in and we shook hands. He was a jovial, potbellied gentleman, quite elegantly dressed, with a pair of sparkling cuff links and well-manicured hands, which were always in motion. An irrepressible vitality seemed to radiate from every part of him, and particularly from his mouth, which emitted a surprisingly rapid and fluent flow of English. It was, of course, a heavily sunburned kind of English, but it was spoken with a relish made to carry everything before it.

After studying the menu and ordering the meal, we exchanged the usual amenities concerning the weather, the differences between American and Italian cooking, and traveling conditions. Ah, those terrible storms he and his ship had encountered during their recent transatlantic crossing. Terribile, terribile! But before his description could work itself up to full gale force, it was becalmed by the arrival of the antipasti. I saw my opening and took it, for I felt that there was not a moment to be lost. If Tito Schipa didn't know that D Major aria, then I was going to have to find some way of persuading him to learn it, and for this my guest's help might prove invaluable.

"I might as well tell you, Signor Prandicelli," I began, "that I have a special problem with the Singers Club concert we are planning for December. I have written two letters to Signor Schipa, but I have received no reply to either one of them."

To Prandicelli this must have sounded like an old, familiar tale. "O, you know how it is," he said. "Tito is-a great-a *tenore, è un gran artista* but is not a great-a *scrittore!* He do not-a write letters, not even to me . . . He sing-a, but he do not-a write-a!" He laughed heartily before filling his mouth with more prosciutto.

"You see, Mr. Prandicelli," I hastened to explain, "this is my first season with the Singers Club, and so it is most fortunate that we were able to secure the services of an artist who is so popular with audiences."

"Yes-a, that was-a very clever, very clever," said Prandicelli, helping himself to more olives. "I must-a congratulate you, young-a Maestro. With Tito Schipa you always have-a *gran successo,* with audience-a, with press-a, with . . . with . . . what-a you call it? . . . box . . . boxafeece-a? *Bene.*" He paused to take another bite of celery. "I hope you receive-a all the necessary publicity materials and the peectures?"

"No problem there at all, Signor Prandicelli, none at all. My letters to Signor Schipa were concerned with the program, particularly with the main group which is to come just before the intermission. Here I would like Signor Schipa to do a sequence from *Rigoletto.*"

"Rigoletto!" Prandicelli raised his eyes to the ceiling. "It is wonderful idea to have Schipa sing-a *Rigoletto. Una vera ispirazione!* Schipa, he sing-a il Duca di Mantova everywhere-a with the most greatest *successo!* In the last-a two year, he sing Duca in Roma, alla Scala in Milano, al San Carlo in Napoli, alla Fenice, in Venezia, he also sing Duca in Bologna, in Parma, Pisa, Firenze, and Genova."

I was about to say something, but he stopped me. "No, esacuse me, please, Genova, that was-a three year before, but Milano, Roma, Napoli, Venezia, Bologna, Firenze, Pisa, that was all-a in the last two year."

"Yes, I know, of course," I began, as the waiter leaned over to remove the empty antipasto dishes.

"And-a Torino!" continued Prandicelli, touching my forearm with his finger. "How could I forget-a Torino? *Che successo, che trionfo!* I not esaggerate-a . . . believe-a me, Maestro, I am not-a one to esaggerate-a . . . but in Torino, when the opera, she finish, the public it do not-a leave! No, signore, it-a refuse to leave the *teatro!* Schipa, he come out-a to receive the *acclamazione* twenty-five, no, thirty time-a, but the *applauso,* it not stop and the public, it-a refuse to go home and — " But before he could evoke another of Tito Schipa's triumphs, the waiter appeared with a tureen of steaming chicken broth, whose succulent aroma brought an approving twitch to the nostrils of my guest.

"You see, Signor Prandicelli," I resumed, "I would like to begin this group wtih Signor Schipa singing the *'Ella mi fu rapita'* . . ."

" *'Ella mi fu rapita'?*" he exclaimed. *"Ma bravo, bravo! Bravissimo!"* He pushed his chair slightly back from the table to give his arms more leeway. " *'Ella mi fu rapita!'* " He savored the Italian syllables with the gustatory appreciation of a connoisseur. "Tito Schipa, he will sing-a *'Ella mi fu rapita.'* You have-a good taste, Maestro. Because-a, I tell you, this aria, *'Ella mi fu rapita,'* Schipa, he cannot ever-a sing it once-a! You surprised? Ha, ha! Do not-a be surprised. Tito, he alaways sing it-a twice-a! A la Scala, must-a repeat and sing it-a twice-a, and at San Carlo, a la Fenice, alaways twice! Also in Bologna, in Pisa, in Firenze . . . as soon as he finish *'Ella mi fu rapita,'* the public, it go crazy. Is *impossibile* to sing-a once-a! And in Torino, when public, it refuse to leave the *teatro,* Schipa, he have to sing-a this aria three time-a! Believe me, Maestro, I not esaggerate. But this . . . this is-a nothing! Five year before, in Parma, I was there and saw it-a with these two eye . . ." Prandicelli pulled up his chair again, so that he could grasp my left forearm. "You do not-a know the Parmigiani? No? *Ebbene,* they are *terribile* public, *terribile!* When they not like *il tenore,* they are *rabbiosi,* like bitten by mad dog! They ready to kill-a! Si, signore! The police-a, she must-a take the *tenore* rapidissimo from-a the *teatro* and put him on the train, to save-a his life-a!

"But when they like the *tenore,* he must do what-a they say!" went on Prandicelli, energetically shaking the upraised thumb of his right hand. "So Schipa, he sing *'Ella mi fu rapita,'* and then . . ." Here he raised the index finger, "he sing it again. He know he always sing aria twice-a. Then the *choristi,* they come out on stage, but Parmigiani scream-a so, the *choristi* go back-a fast-a and" — now the middle finger joined the others — "he sing-a third-a time. But wait-a, wait-a! Now come-a the best. After he sing-a third-a time, the public, it jump and stamp-a feet, cry *'Bravo! Bis, bis!'* Schipa, he afraid he get-a tired, *faticato,* must sing-a the whole-a last act! Schipa, he point to his throat, beg public, 'Please, *per piacere, non posso piu!* I sing already three time-a, *tre volte, tre volte, basta!' Ma no,* for Parmigiani *non basta,* three time-a not enough! They are *assassini,* these Parmigiani, they make-a Schipa sing four time-a!"

He lifted both hands, with the four fingers extended on each, to emphasize the enormity of these four encores, then sank back in his chair, as though personally exhausted by Schipa's superhuman effort. There was a moment of silence as the soup plates were removed, after which we were presented with Luccioni's famous polpettone alla Napolitana.

"How wonderful," I said, after the waiter had withdrawn. "But here, as you know, the audiences are less demonstrative."

Prandicelli nodded, as he took another gulp of Chianti.

"When Schipa finishes the *'Ella mi fu rapita,'* " I went on, determined to bring the conversation back to Cleveland, "the club members will sing the chorus, *'Duca, Duca.'* They sing it in Italian, by the way, and do it very well, I assure you. After my singers get through with this number, we come to the final section of this scene, and it is here that I probably will need your help, dear Signor Prandicelli, because at this point there is an aria for the Duke, a very fine, exciting aria in D Major — *'Possente amor mi chiama'* — where the chorus joins at the end, and . . . you see, I am not sure that Signor Schipa knows this aria. I wrote him about it, but, as you know, there was no answer. Now I wonder . . . if he does not know this aria, maybe you could ask him to learn it for our concert?"

Prandicelli stopped his fork in midair and stared at me in amazement. "What-a you say?" he finally spluttered. "I should-a ask-a Schipa to learn aria from *Rigoletto*? Because, he, Schipa, he not-a know aria from *Rigoletto*." Putting down his fork, he pulled a large handkerchief out of his trouser pocket and passed it over his forehead, as though to rid himself of a bad dream. "You say, Schipa, he not know aria from *Rigoletto*!" he continued, putting away the handkerchief and pointing an accusing finger at me.

"*Gran Dio!* I, Egidio Prandicelli, I have-a to travel in this barbarian country, all-a the way to Clayvelando, Oheeo, to hear a young man — esacuse-a me, I do not remember your name-a — hear a young American maestro tell-a me, Prandicelli, that Schipa, *he not know aria from Rigoletto*! Tito Schipa sing-a *Rigoletto* in every *teatro,* in every opera'ous-a in the world-a, but here-a in Clayvelando, Oheeo, he, Schipa, he not know-a . . . *not know aria* . . . he must-a learn-a *Rigoletto*! *Dio mio, che ignoranti!*"

He lifted both hands to heaven, as though imploring divine forgiveness for such a sacrilege. "Esacuse me, young-a man, I do not remember your name-a, but it is-a for me, Egidio Prandicelli, not possibile to go to Tito Schipa and-a say to him-a, '*Per piacere,* Signor Schipa, in Clayvelando, Oheeo, they ask-a you to learn aria from *Rigoletto.* There is there young *maestro americano* who, he is not-a certain, but he not think-a you know aria from *Rigoletto,* so he ask-a me, Prandicelli, to ask-a you, Tito Schipa, to please learn aria from *Rigoletto,* so you can-a sing aria in Clayvelando!'"

The rest of the dinner, notwithstanding the excellence of the polpettone and Luccioni's best Chianti, was a dismal and chilly postlude of mercifully short duration.

All I could do now, I realized later that same evening as I made my way sorrowfully home, was hope for the best. To clear my conscience, I wrote another letter to Schipa, saying that it did not matter to us whether he sang the aria from memory or not. That way the door was diplomatically left open, and if the worst came to the worst, we could spare the great man the effort of having to learn the aria by heart.

The day before the concert, Tito Schipa arrived in Cleveland and was taken out to dinner by the senior members of the club. I told them to take their time and not to rush the meal prior to the late evening dress rehearsal. I wanted my singers to be well warmed up by the time Schipa reached Severance Hall so as to make a good impression on our famous guest. When Schipa finally appeared, he was in the best of spirits. He sang *"Ella mi fu rapita"* like an angel, then listened respectfully to the choristers as they went through their *"Duca, Duca,"* even complimenting them on the clarity of their Italian enunciation.

At the conclusion of this, I gave the upbeat for the introduction to the D Major aria. But when the moment came for him to sing, Schipa simply stood there looking at me with a puzzled smile.

"*Un momento,* Maestro," he said in his melodious voice, "what is-a this music they are playing?"

It was all I could do not to explode on the spot. "Dear Mr. Schipa," I said, trying to speak in a level tone of voice, "this is the aria about which I kept writing to you. I sent you three letters. Surely you must have received at least one of them. If you are not going to sing this aria, then how on earth are we going to end this scene? It cannot just be left hanging there in the air."

"Please, Maestro, may I see the score?" asked Schipa, who had remained completely unruffled during my rather heated outburst.

"Why here it is," I said, pointing to the words *"Possente amor mi chiama"* " . . . where it has always been, ever since Verdi composed it eighty years ago!" I was too upset to put up a pretense at good manners.

Schipa inspected the music and then shook his head sadly. "Oh, that is-a too bad," he said, "that is-a too bad!"

He handed back the score with a look of sincere regret. "You, young American Maestri, should ask-a somebody who know Italian opera, you should-a consult and ask-a. You could save much-a trouble if you ask-a. Anybody who know Italian opera could-a tell you that this aria, *she never-a done-a!* But it is not-a such a *gran disturbo.* When your singers, they finish the chorus, I sing-a *'La donna è mobile.'* The people out-a there" — he indicated the empty rows in the auditorium — "they like-a very much *'La donna è mobile.'* You will see, Maestro, it will be a great *successo!*"

And so it came to pass. Under the circumstances, it was the

only possible solution. I was horrified beyond words, of course, at the fantastic notion of having the Duke of Mantua sing of the fickleness of women after learning that Gilda (who is just about the most faithful of all Italian opera heroines) is in his palace. Tito Schipa, in a way, proved his point. Nobody noticed the preposterous nonsequitur, and both soloist and chorus scored an enormous *successo.*

There was one thing, however, that I found hard to forgive, and the sheer indignity of it rankles with me to this day. The Clevelanders in the auditorium of Severance Hall gave the performers such a thundering ovation after the *Rigoletto* group that Schipa had to repeat *'La donna è mobile'* as an encore. The look he gave me as he sang it has left a mark which the passage of the years has not erased.

The first work I chose for the new opera department I had been asked to direct at the Cleveland Institute of Music was Mozart's *Marriage of Figaro.* It has remained to this day one of my all-time favorites, and I have developed such a proprietary feeling about this particular opera that I cannot bear to see it performed by any company or group that I have not personally trained or influenced in some way. I realize that I am hopelessly prejudiced in this respect, and it has even led me, on occasion, to emit the harshest and most unfair judgments on other producers' interpretations of this wonderfully effervescent work. But because it was the first opera I both stage-directed and conducted from start to finish, *The Marriage of Figaro* has retained a unique place in my affections.

The dramatic scheme that I prepared for the singing actors, indicating what each was to do and think at every moment, was worked out with almost choreographic precision. In the process, all the basic problems I had to cope with received what I am tempted to call "definitive" solutions. In later years, when I returned to this Mozart opera, I was unable to add any fundamental improvements. My initial staging, as worked out in Cleveland, seemed to have attained a degree of appropriateness which I personally could not improve on.

Beryl Rubinstein had not been idly boasting when he had told me that his Institute of Music contained a number of gifted singers. They proved it on the evening of our performance. The opera was sung in English rather than in Italian, not only for the benefit of the audience, who otherwise would have missed most of librettist Lorenzo da Ponte's delightful humor, but more specifically for the sake of the performers.

This is a principle I have adhered to ever since. It is almost impossible, I believe, to teach young American singers to "live" their roles with maximum intensity when they are forced to sing in a foreign tongue. Gifted linguists, persons who can acquire such a knowledge of a language that they can think and joke in it, can develop a capacity for "feeling" their roles in a tongue that is not native to them. But these people tend to be rare. For most singers the strangeness of the language they are made to sing in is like an ill-fitting garment they might be forced to wear. They feel uncomfortable and it inhibits the naturalness of their gestures and expressions; in a word, they are not "at home" in it. And when one is not "at home" in a language, it is almost impossible to be, or to appear to be, spontaneous.

Since the major roles in this production of *Figaro* were all sung by students of the Cleveland Institute of Music, there could be no question of my slipping Margaret into the role of Cherubino. Her condition in any case would not have allowed it, for she was "expecting" for most of this period, and on January 19, 1937, she was finally delivered from her pains by giving joyous birth to a little baby boy with buttonlike brown eyes, whom we named Michael.

In February I began training my Cleveland Institute students in Puccini's *Gianni Schicchi*. The academic season was already fairly far advanced, and I decided that it would be better to concentrate on a relatively short, one-act *opera buffa,* which, though it is nowhere near as well known or as often performed as *Tosca, La Bohème,* and *Madame Butterfly,* is as good as anything Puccini ever wrote.

The truth of the matter is that I was already over extended in my activities and fighting desperately for time. In Philadelphia Fritz Reiner had several big projects planned, while Rodzinski was now preparing Richard Strauss's *Elektra.* The first orchestral rehearsals of this opera were an ordeal, for once again I was called upon to sing all the parts for the benefit of the orchestra's instrumentalists, who were as unfamiliar with the vocal line as their conductor. Later, while reading Halina Rodzinski's book, *Our Two Lives,* I came upon a description of how, during some summer rehearsals for the Salzburg Festival of 1935, Toscanini made Erich Leinsdorf sing most of the parts of Verdi's *Falstaff.* But I believe I am not exaggerating when I say that I am the only person alive who has had an opportunity to render *all* the parts of both *Der Rosenkavalier* and *Elektra* accompanied by a major symphony orchestra.

The final *Elektra* performances were most satisfactory, even though the stage-directing of Herbert Graf (specially brought in from New York for the occasion) was no more inspired than Wymetal's had been for Reiner's production in Philadelphia. The German soprano Gertrude Kappel sang the role of Elektra very well, but Enid Szantho's rendition could not, alas, stand comparison with Margaret Matzenauer's magnificent portrayal of Klytemnestra in the earlier Reiner production.

Although my multiple activities in Cleveland kept me extremely busy, I still had to shuttle back and forth and spend two days of every week in Philadelphia. Under Reiner's iron-fisted direction, the Curtis Institute orchestra had long ceased to be the musical rabble it had been under Emil Mlynarski, and it was now probably the finest student ensemble in the country. Reiner himself was so pleased with the progress made that he decided to stage two public events. The first was to be an evening of orchestral music featuring a number of brilliant student soloists; the second, even more of a sensation, was to be the world première of *Amelia al ballo,* the first opera written by Gian Carlo Menotti, an Italian-born student of the Curtis Institute who was at the time only twenty-five years old.

The preparations for the two events were quite far advanced when Reiner received a telegraphic invitation from London, asking him to conduct several operas at Covent Garden. For a man who was regarded by many connoisseurs as the world's finest opera conductor — his sense of rhythmic flexibility and his skill in achieving subtle phrasings being superior even to Toscanini's — this was too tempting an offer to turn down. Though the invitation involved two ocean crossings and an absence from Philadelphia of some two months, Reiner accepted, and I was entrusted with the job of conducting the concert and preparing the opera.

Along with compositions by Goldmark, Richard Strauss, and Liszt, two particularly interesting pieces had been chosen for the concert which the student orchestra was due to play in Philadelphia's Academy of Music. The first was Saint-Saëns' Violin Concerto No. 3 in B Minor; the second were the Scherzo and Nocturne movements from Mendelssohn's *A Midsummer Night's Dream.*

The institute's violin department, where Mother was teaching, was now headed by Efrem Zimbalist, who had succeeded his former Petersburg teacher, Leopold Auer, in 1950. His most brilliant pupil at this time was Oscar Shumsky, who, though he had officially graduated from the institute in 1936, had stayed on in some postgraduate capacity.

I have always been an avid reader of books, and particularly of books dealing with the past history of music and musicians. One of these, which I had read with great interest, was a small volume by Leopold Auer analyzing a number of violin concertos. Among them was precisely the Third Concerto by Saint-Saëns, which Oscar Shumsky was due to play. Auer, furthermore, had had a chance to discuss its playing with the composer, who had complained to him about the way in which the middle movement was generally performed. Saint-Saëns wanted it conducted, not in 6 but in 2 beats to the measure so that it should be grazioso and allegretto — that is, graceful and lively rather than grave and portentous.

I took the book to Shumsky and showed him the passage. "Look at this. Here we have some absolutely first-class information, straight from Saint-Saëns, who told it to the teacher of your teacher. Now shouldn't we follow the wishes of the composer?"

"Sure," said Shumsky, "let's try it." Accordingly we rehearsed the middle movement at the faster tempo. I was delighted with the result. It was more in keeping with Saint-Saëns's sprightly temperament.

Before the final rehearsal, however, Shumsky came to see me. "You can forget about that change you were proposing for the middle movement," he said. "We're going to play it slower."

"But why?" I asked, surprised by this last-minute volte-face.

"Because Mr. Zimbalist wants it that way. He says that's all poppycock, what Saint-Saëns said. Saint-Saëns wasn't a violinist and didn't know what he was talking about. It's got to be played slowly, and that's the way it's going to be."

There was no point in my arguing about it. But I couldn't help marveling at the casual way in which the composer's wishes were blandly disregarded in favor of a performer's preference, which was given automatic right of way. But even though we were now forced to play it in this manner, was Saint-Saëns necessarily wrong and Zimbalist necessarily right?

My own opinion, for what it is worth, is that in this case Zimbalist was wrong. The reason why he wanted this particular movement played at the slower tempo was because this was the speed at which he personally excelled. Just as there are singers who love to sing slowly and to sustain high tones, so there are violinists who can move a bow across the strings with extraordinary slowness. I don't believe I have ever heard a violinist who could do this more impressively than Efrem Zimbalist. The result was amazing, and for me literally breathtaking. For when Zimbalist, at a concert, began playing in this extraordinarily deliberate manner, I would often find myself beginning to gasp and would have to leave at once for fear of fainting.

The reason I preferred the faster tempo desired by Saint-Saëns was thus probably subjective and closely linked to my particular musical temperament. It is a mistake, however, to believe that the composer is always right in his tempo and other indications. When Rachmaninoff, who was one of the greatest pianists of all time, recorded his piano concertos, the results are completely convincing and can hardly be improved on. But such a combination of gifts is exceedingly rare. It is common knowledge that Brahms could not conduct his own symphonies anywhere near as well as Hans von Bülow, Artur Nikisch, or Toscanini. Many composers have been poor performers of their own compositions. In Budapest I heard Béla Bartók play some of his piano pieces in a way that was rather dull, whereas other pianists do the most exciting things with these same compositions. Schumann's symphonies are now almost never played with his clearly defective orchestration, but instead in the vastly improved versions which gifted conductors such as George Szell and others have provided. Gustav Mahler, on the other hand, was that rarest of combinations: a great composer who was also a superlatively gifted conductor. He was *total begabt,* and the markings in his scores are consequently *massgebend,* as the Germans put it — that is, standard-setting, authoritative, and definitive.

Mendelssohn's *Midsummer Night's Dream* confronted us with a problem of a different order. The Nocturne movement of this composition is famous for its beautiful French horn solo — one of the most demanding in the horn player's repertoire. Now as ill luck would have it, the student who was to play this particular solo with the Curtis orchestra came down with appendicitis and had to be rushed to the hospital one week before the concert.

We were thus faced with a major crisis. It was too late to omit this piece since the programs had already been printed. The other French horn players in the orchestra were adequate, but not one of them was skilled enough to play the exposed and exceedingly difficult solo passage.

Much troubled by this contretemps, I went to see Anton Horner, a charming Old World gentleman who, like Marcel Tabuteau and so many Curtis Institute teachers, was a veteran member of the Philadelphia Orchestra. I explained to him what had happened, and suggested that since no other student was good enough to play the solo, we should bring in a professional horn player from the Philadelphia Orchestra. We would of course be cheating, since all the instrumentalists at this concert were supposed to be students, but given the critical circumstances, this seemed to me the only solution.

"Now wait a moment," said Horner. "Maybe there is a better way . . . I have a pupil here who, I think, can manage the solo very well."

I looked at him in astonishment. "You mean to say, Mr. Horner, that you have a Curtis pupil who is good enough to play this passage? Then how come he is not in the student orchestra?" The Curtis orchestra was supposedly composed of the institute's most talented instrumentalists.

"Well," said Anton Horner, "it's a bit unusual. You see, this pupil of mine has only been studying the French horn for about three months."

"Three months!" I exclaimed. "What are you talking about, Mr. Horner? You have a pupil here who has only been taking lessons for three months, and you say he is better than the other players who've been studying with you for years?"

"Yes," he answered quietly, "it happens to be the case."

The newcomer who had learned to master the French horn in three short months was a twenty-year-old prodigy named Mason Jones. Of all orchestral instruments the French horn is with little doubt the most unpredictable, and even very experienced performers can never be sure that at some point or other their instrument won't run amuck with a "blooper" — as it is called in the trade. But during his first three months of playing, Mason Jones, for reasons that seemed to defy logical analysis, had not once perpetrated such an error. He seemed to have been born to play this instrument, which in his hands was as docile as a Shetland pony.

On the evening of the concert, Jones played the solo beautifully, impeccably, just as he has played everything else since then. The applause at the conclusion of the two Mendelssohn pieces was deafening and well deserved. But I doubt that many of the clappers gathered in the Academy of Music that evening realized that they had just heard a miracle.

When Fritz Reiner returned from London, his first concern was to see how the rehearsals were going for Gian Carlo Menotti's new opera, translated into English and retitled *Amelia Goes to the Ball.* While I dealt with the musical side of the production, Ernst Lert, who was now teaching dramatic acting at the Curtis Institute, had taken care of the staging.

Once again Lert demonstrated great aptitude. The only fault I could find with his staging had to do with his summary rejection of several very sensible ideas I suggested but which Lert rejected out of hand, simply because, I believe, he had not thought of them himself. For I should add that for all his talents, which were great, Lert was not an easy person to deal with. He had been gassed during the First World War, and this seems to have affected his disposition, for he could at times be as stubborn as a mule. He was also a specialist and, like most specialists, he had his idées fixes and his prejudices and things had to be done *his* way.

I learned many things from Ernst Lert and I owe him a great deal. But I am happy to say that I also learned a thing or two from his failings. Nobody in this world of ours is omniscient and it is ridiculous to claim that one can think of everything or imagine only the very best. Perhaps because I did not start out as an opera specialist but drifted into this field more or less accidentally I have always welcomed other people's good ideas.

Although Lert was too old and experienced to be troubled by such apprehensions, the rest of us were full of fear and trembling at the thought of how the great man (Fritz Reiner) was going to react to our preparation of Menotti's opera. I had to conduct, while Reiner, seated in the auditorium, watched in silence. To my considerable relief, he did not once try to stop us, let me conduct, the cast sing, and the orchestra play through to the very end. When I turned around at last, there was actually a smile on his face instead of the thundercloud we had more or less anticipated.

Coming forward to congratulate me, he shook my hand warmly, then said, "Come, I'll treat you to a good dinner and some fine entertainment."

I remember little of the dinner, but I have a vivid recollection of the entertainment that followed.

"Shall we take in a show?" asked Reiner, as we stepped out of the restaurant.

"Anything you say, Meister," I answered, wondering what he had in mind.

He hailed a taxi. "Is there a good burlesque show in town?" he asked the driver as we climbed in.

"Why sure," said the cab-driver. "What about the Bijou?"

I knew nothing about the Bijou, and I don't think Reiner did either. But to the Bijou we were driven.

It turned out to be a kind of "strip joint," situated in one of Philadelphia's less reputable quarters. The show, we were informed at the box office, had already started, but there were still seats available. Reiner asked for two — "way up front." The two tickets handed back were for the very first row.

As we walked down the aisle, behind the flashlight-swinging usherette, I was surprised to see some of the spectators raise their hands or programs to their faces, while some even turned away. Intrigued, I looked over my shoulder and understood why. Half of the members of the Curtis student orchestra seemed to have converged on the Bijou and they were now shame-facedly trying to hide from their boss's critical gaze.

I felt like laughing, but Reiner, continuing on down the aisle, noticed nothing. His eyes were riveted on the naked female bodies that were undulating all over the stage in the most gruesome fashion. There wasn't one of them who could have passed as a semibeauty, and the gaudy stockings and make-up they wore did nothing to improve their looks. The jokes that issued from their heavily rouged lips were painfully grotesque and corny.

After fifteen minutes of visual and aural punishment, Reiner decided he had had enough. He rose from his seat and I followed. Back up the aisle we marched, as spectators to the left and right of us hurriedly ducked or shielded their faces with their sleeves. Reiner noticed nothing once again, and I carefully refrained from telling him the awful truth. What he would have thought of *them,* I have no idea, but I have a pretty good notion of what they must have thought of us!

7

A Three-Ring Opera Season

NOT UNTIL the autumn of 1937 did I begin to realize how profoundly my life had been affected by my chance encounter with Ernst Lert. What I would have become if his piano accompanist had not been taken ill and I had not seen him in action in Philadelphia, I have no idea. But I might never have become "Mr. Opera," as I am now known to quite a few people, for those lessons with Lert, during the summer of 1936, altered the course of my career.

Until then, my life had lacked any clear direction. Like a mountain stream, I had been trying to find my way down to the plain, only to run into formidable obstacles. The first, a wall-like mass of rock, had been Josef Hofmann's veto against my piano playing. A second and no less daunting impediment was soon to loom when I discovered that I was not really made to be an outstanding symphony conductor. But now, unexpectedly, a new channel had been opened up for me by Ernst Lert's engineering genius, and it was down this waterway that my concentrated energies were soon to be plunging.

At the time I had no clear idea of what lay in store for me, save for the fact that I had agreed to set up an opera department at the Cleveland Institute of Music. Beyond this first step my future was a blank and I had no idea that I was fated to become that essentially hybrid creature: an opera "expert" and even more, an opera "pioneer." I still fancied myself as destined to become another Fritz Reiner, not realizing that my polymorphous talents, being more diffuse, might be creative in a different way and that the precision-loving mathematician who lay dormant within me was one day going to blossom into a kind of operatic Euclid and the author of the first, and so far as I know, only basic textbook yet written on operatic acting and stage directing.

When Margaret and I returned to Cleveland in the autumn of 1937, after another summer that was partly spent in Rockport, I decided to sever my lingering connection with the Curtis Institute in Philadelphia. I did so first of all because I now had more than enough to keep me busy in Cleveland, where I had an opera department to run and two large choral groups to train, quite aside from my active participation in chamber-music concerts and the piano lectures I had to prepare for the symphony orchestra's Women's Committee (about which I shall have more to say anon).

My second reason for leaving Philadelphia was the sobering realization that I was not really made to be a symphony conductor. At a time when orchestra conductors have reached such a pinnacle of importance that their faces now frequently replace those of composers on the covers of recordings, it has become a commonplace to say that a good orchestra conductor needs to have an exceptionally keen ear to do the job he does. But it is not generally realized that he must have a very special kind of ear. The closest instrumentalists — the first semicircle of string players — are not more than six feet from the conductor's podium. From them and the instruments behind them and, as it were, from all points of the compass come whispers or gusts of music, which engulf the conductor in successive waves of sound. In the midst of all this tumult, which in large orchestral compositions can reach a truly deafening volume, the good conductor must be able to cut through these cloudbursts of sound and identify any instrument that is not being played correctly.

No conductor can hope to survive for long if, unable to spot the trouble quickly, he has to stop the players and say, "Sorry, gentlemen, something went wrong. Let's do it over again." To such embarrassed requests most orchestra players react with disdain. They look at each other questioningly and mumble, "What kind of a lout is this anyway? What does he mean, 'Something went wrong'?" Indeed, if orchestra players begin to suspect that their conductor cannot pick out the "guilty" instruments immediately, they are apt to play wrong notes deliberately. A trumpeter will get off a "fixer" or a tympanist will let one of his sticks fall on the drumhead just to enjoy the conductor's flustered frustration as he cries, "Who did that? Who made that noise?"

I had known all this for years, and at least as far back as my first exposure to orchestra conducting with the students of the Franz Liszt Academy in Budapest. But not until the spring of 1937, when I had to take the Curtis orchestra through those Saint-Saëns, Mendelssohn, Goldmark, and Liszt pieces, did I fully realize that I might not have the right kind of ear to be a truly first-rate symphony conductor. If I went back into the auditorium and put forty feet or more between myself and the nearest instruments, I could hear everything quite clearly and could immediately spot errors and pick out instrumentalists who were playing incorrectly. But when I was on the conductor's podium, it was as though my hearing faculties had lost their acuteness, seriously impairing my ability to detect mistakes.

Even experienced musicians are often surprised to discover how inept composers can be when they climb onto the podium and undertake to conduct their own works. The reason is simply that they lack the special noise-resisting and discriminating kind of ear that is the sine qua non of every truly competent symphony conductor. I say "symphony conductor" advisedly, because this problem of massive, overwhelming waves of sound only presents itself in large symphonic works. For an opera conductor, who needs many other important gifts, the lack of an outstanding "symphonic ear" is not a serious liability.

For the start of our second opera season with the Cleveland Institute of Music I chose Humperdinck's *Hansel and Gretel* because of its fairy-tale charm. It was performed in Severance Hall in November 1937 by students whom I had carefully coached in acting, along the lines of Ernst Lert's teaching. The audience loved every minute of it and gave the student performers a long and well merited ovation. In the next day's issue of the Cleveland *Plain Dealer,* Herbert Elwell pulled out all the stops in a rave review, which helped to reinforce my local reputation as an "opera expert" and which, above all, was a marvelous fillip for the Institute of Music's students.

Elwell's words of praise also elicited a quite unexpected response from — of all people — Josef Hofmann, who happened to be in Ohio on a concert tour. He wrote me a kind letter, saying he had been pleased to read of the great success I had just had in Cleveland with *Hansel and Gretel.* He felt sure that this was only a beginning and that it would lead to great things later on in the field of opera. I had the impression, while reading his letter, that Hofmann was a bit conscience-stricken at having taken such a dim view of my piano playing in the past, and this may well have been the case. But when I look back on those years, I am forced to admit that Hofmann might after all have been right in steering me away from a career as a piano virtuoso and in another direction, where my special gifts could find their full and fruitful expression.

While my popularity with various Cleveland groups was growing, my relations with Artur Rodzinski had begun to sour. It had become glaringly evident from our collaboration on a number of operatic productions that in such matters he had more to learn from me than I did from him, even though he was supposed to be the boss. He, who was so bearish in social gatherings, was also jealous of my success with the members of the Women's Committee, who were much too excited about Boris Goldovsky's talents as a raconteur. It had started with *Der Rosenkavalier,* an opera with which Cleveland's music-loving ladies were not familiar. I had been asked to deliver an explanatory lecture in the small Chamber Music auditorium of Severance Hall. The lecture was such a spectacular success that in preparation for the later *Parsifal* production, I was offered the main auditorium, which was fully sold out for the occasion. Willy-nilly, I became the "darling" of Mrs. Adella Prentiss Hughes, who introduced me to her influential society friends — Mrs. Blossom, Mrs. Taplin, Mrs. Rorimer, and many others — who sang my praises in their turn — much to Rodzinski's annoyance.

Rodzinski, furthermore, was now involved in a major row with the orchestra's board of directors, who refused to give him money for hiring additional string players. To avenge himself, he decided not to produce any more operas during the forthcoming season. He even began to neglect the orchestra, spending increasingly long periods of time in New York to audition and select instrumentalists for the new NBC Symphony Orchestra, which David Sarnoff, its president, had decided to form with Arturo Toscanini as the main conductor.

Although Rodzinski's decision to abandon operatic ventures did not affect the Cleveland Orchestra's normal concert performances, it left one person particularly disgruntled. This was Richard Rychtarik, the talented artist who had designed the sets for all of the operas put on at Severance Hall. He and his attractive German wife had become good friends of Margaret and myself, and we spent many evenings together in each other's apartments.

One evening, while we were lamenting this state of affairs, Rychtarik said to me, "You know, Boris, it's really too bad when you think of all those talented young singers you are training at the institute. What are they going to do when they graduate? Now that Severance Hall is no longer in the business of producing operas, there's no place for them to go — at any rate in Cleveland."

He looked at me and I looked at him, and the next thing we knew, we were both saying more or less simultaneously, "Well, why don't we found an opera company of our own to fill the gap?"

It would be tedious to relate in detail everything that followed. As is usually the case with such ventures, we encountered some skeptical resistance, but also an encouraging amount of support. And thus was born the Civic Opera Company of Cleveland.

Since there is no point in launching an opera company unless one has some idea of what works it should perform, we had to begin by selecting a particular opera for our debut.

"As far as I'm concerned," said Rychtarik, "you can keep Mozart, Verdi, Wagner, Puccini, and the rest. There's only one opera we can start with."

"Oh," I said. "And which is that?"

"Why, *our* national opera," he replied. "I mean Smetana's *Prodaná Nevěsta,* or as you would say, *The Bartered Bride.*"

Well, I thought to myself, why not? Though Smetana's most famous opera was far less well known in America than Dvořák's *New World* Symphony, there was no reason why it should go on being neglected and ignored. The young Czechoslovakian republic, which Tomáš Masaryk had founded and which his successor, Eduard Beneš, was now guiding, was already being menaced by a rising tide of Sudeten irredentism, fanned to white heat by Nazi propaganda, and though these political considerations had no direct bearing on our operatic plans, it did not seem a bad idea to dust off one of the cultural glories of a people who had finally achieved nationhood after centuries of political and religious oppression.

Before we could get very far with our new operatic venture, I received a summons from Rodzinski. As conductor of the recently formed Philharmonic Chorus, I had been rehearsing the singers in the Chôros No. 10 by the Brazilian composer Heitor Villa-Lobos, which was to be publicly performed in January. The season's second big choral event had not yet been chosen, and Rodzinski was very anxious that it should be Bach's *St. Matthew Passion,* as shortened and arranged for concert presentation by Ossip Gabrilowitsch, the conductor of the Detroit Symphony Orchestra. Gabrilowitsch had died some months earlier, but his widow — who happened to be a daughter of Mark Twain — had firmly rebuffed Rodzinski's request that the Cleveland Orchestra be allowed to play the Passion in honor of her deceased husband, saying (or with words to that effect) that "this was Ossip's masterpiece and will die with him."

The reason why Rodzinski was so anxious to obtain the right to perform this version of the St. Matthew Passion is that Gabrilowitsch had accomplished the tour de force — for such he imagined it to be — of reducing Bach's great work, which was originally written to be performed on two consecutive days, each performance lasting more than two hours, to a single oratorio which, with an intermission, lasted less than one hundred and fifty minutes. When first played in Detroit in this streamlined version, it had caused a sensation so much so indeed that Gabrilowitsch subsequently took it to New York. Rodzinski was now determined to repeat this success in Cleveland, but his efforts had been frustrated by the obstinacy of Mrs. Gabrilowitsch.

All of this was explained to me in Rodzinski's office, after which he said: "Borischikov, you who are so clever in dealing with elderly women" — a pointed reference to my success with the members of the Women's Committee — "maybe you can persuade her. I would like you to go to Detroit and talk to her."

I asked for a few days to think the matter over. I rang up some friends in Detroit who were close to the local orchestra and through them I discovered that Ossip Gabrilowitsch's widow was currently attending some spiritist séances, apparently in the hope of entering into posthumous communication with her recently deceased spouse. This gave me an idea of which I am today rather ashamed. I went back to see Rodzinski and asked him to telephone Mrs. Gabrilowitsch and say that Boris Goldovsky urgently wished to see her about an important message which he had been asked to transmit to her. The call was put through, and Mrs. Gabrilowitsch agreed to receive me.

Several days later I drove over to Detroit on this strange mission.

I was still young enough to be flattered by the thought that I was being asked to tackle a problem which my "boss," Artur Rodzinski, had been unable to solve. When I was finally seated before her, I explained that I had come all the way from Cleveland to see her because of a curious dream I had had on two successive nights. Dr. Rodzinski and I had been discussing the possibility of putting on the St. Matthew Passion in another version, but then one night her deceased husband had appeared to me in a dream and, speaking in Russian, had told me that he wanted us to perform the St. Matthew Passion in his version. Dr. Rodzinski, with whom I had discussed this extraordinary dream — one I had had not once, but twice — felt that I should tell her about it, which was the reason for my trip.

The moment I uttered the word "dream" I could see a glimmer of interest light up in the depths of the old lady's eyes. "Young man," she said, in a quavering but excited voice, "I am glad to meet the person to whom my dear departed Ossip saw fit to entrust this important message. Of course, if it is Ossip's wish that Dr. Rodzinski and his orchestra and your singers should perform this work in Cleveland, then his will be done. But you must promise me, young man, and Dr. Rodzinski must promise me that you will respect dear Ossip's wishes and that you will play the St. Matthew Passion *exactly* as he arranged it."

I gave her an absolute guarantee that the wonderful version her late husband had prepared would be treated with the utmost respect. I swore on the Bible and assured her that Dr. Rodzinski, who was a devout Catholic, was also prepared to swear on the Bible that not a note would be changed.

Had I been able to foresee what I was letting myself and my singers in for, I would have thought twice before inventing this fancy tale about the dear departed Ossip's portentous apparition in my dreams. For it was only after I had been granted the coveted permission and had been entrusted with a copy of the precious score that I realized what a hideous job of butchery had been perpetrated on the Passion.

The complete work, as I have said, was originally composed for two successive church performances; not only that, it is scored for two orchestras, divided choruses, and seven soloists (five men and two women) — which is why it is rarely, if ever, performed in American churches. In May 1908, during a Bach Festival held in Leipzig, a particularly hardy group of Germans undertook to perform the uncut Passion on one day: it began at 3:00 P.M. and — with a two-hour break — ended at 10:00 P.M. Even with "normal" cuts, the Passion lasts three and a half hours. Gabrilowitsch had therefore decided to cut it down to concert size by omitting several choruses, recitatives, and chorales. All of this was perfectly legitimate, and indeed unavoidable. But not content with that, he had butchered half a dozen arias by simply lopping off the concluding section in each. Many of the solos and ensemble numbers in this mighty work are composed along a standard A–B–A pattern — with a first section being played in one key, followed by a second section in which new thematic material is developed in another key, with a concluding section repeating the theme in the original key. Gabrilowitsch had simply chosen to hack away the concluding A sections, with the result that many pieces were left dangling in the air at the end of the B section. I could not understand how a sensitive and educated musician could bring himself to perpetrate such an act of mutilation on a composition by Bach. It was as though in reproducing a full-face portrait by a Renaissance painter, one were to show only the left side of the face, and the nose, while omitting the right eye, cheek, ear, and the rest on the grounds that they were simply "repetitions" of what was to be seen on the left.

By now, however, the machinery was in action and it was too late to turn back. From the moment Rodzinski heard that I had managed to wrest a copy of the precious score away from Gabrilowitsch's widow, along with her consent that it be played in Cleveland, he went ahead and hired several famous singers — Margaret Matzenauer (contralto), Jeannette Vreeland (soprano), Chase Baromeo (baritone) among them — and let everyone know that the

Cleveland Orchestra was going to perform this special version of Bach's St. Matthew Passion in mid-April. He himself left in early March for New York to conduct several concerts with the NBC Symphony Orchestra, leaving the Cleveland musicians in the hands of guest conductors, while I was busy training the choristers.

On April 10, Rodzinski reappeared in Cleveland, newly aureoled with glory as a result of a nationally broadcast American première of Shostakovich's Fifth Symphony, which he had conducted in New York. He probably felt a bit guilty for having so neglected his own orchestra, and he may have been feeling the strain of overwork in New York. The deteriorating international situation may also have been affecting him, for Hitler's recent invasion of Austria had induced Rodzinski to follow Toscanini's example in renouncing his scheduled participation in the following August's Salzburg Festival. An inhibited and often unpredictable person, Rodzinski was prone to fits of moodiness all winter, for he had been greatly upset by the news of his brother's death in November. The convergence of these troubling events seems to have undermined his self-confidence and plunged him once again into a state of almost panicky depression, for the man I found waiting for me in his office was in a frankly defeatist mood.

"Borischikov," he said to me, "I'm sorry to tell you this, but frankly, I cannot conduct the St. Matthew Passion."

"Come on," I said, trying to cheer him up. "Of course you can do it."

"I haven't looked at it. I don't know anything about it," he insisted.

"Dr. Rodzinski," I said, "I will play it for you, and you will see there is nothing to it. You don't have to know it all that well."

"Oh, yes, I realize that. Of course I can conduct the solo numbers. There's no problem there. But the choruses — single chorus here, double chorus there, and the dozens of entrances that have to be given to tenors, basses, sopranos, and altos — all that's very complicated. I haven't time to learn it. I just can't do it."

"But Dr. Rodzinski," I protested, "we have to do something. We can't call the whole thing off a couple of days before the concert since it has been scheduled and particularly now that we've rehearsed the chorus and engaged famous singers."

"Listen," said Rodzinski, "I have an idea that might solve the problem. I'll conduct the solo pieces, and you will conduct the choruses."

I stared at him in stupefaction. Having his assistant conduct *Die Fledermaus* in his place was one thing, but to elevate him to the status of simultaneous co-conductor for this magnificent (even though mutilated) choral work was quite another matter. "But, Dr. Rodzinski, what are you saying? This will be a public scandal! This just cannot be done. There is just no way to explain it. People will be wondering what on earth is going on. They'll cover us with ridicule. They'll laugh both of us out of town."

My outburst seemed to crush the poor man even more. He sat there behind his desk, looking the picture of dejection.

"Well, what do you suggest?" he finally asked in a weary voice.

It was clear that Rodzinski hadn't given proper thought to the consequences of his extraordinary proposal. But I soon realized that without my active assistance this misguided enterprise would come to almost certain grief. Some sort of salvaging action had to be undertaken.

We finally hit upon a risky *faute de mieux* solution. Margaret Matzenauer sat on a chair facing the audience, while I was seated on another chair, placed back to back against hers, facing the chorus. Her bulk was so enormous that I was completely invisible to the audience. Rodzinski was thus able to conduct from his podium, where he was the focus of most eyes, while I quietly gave the choristers their cues.

*

While I was having problems with Rodzinski, who was still nominally my boss, Margaret was actively pursuing her singing career. As our son, Michael, was now a year old, she was less tied down by maternal and domestic chores and able to resume her public appearances. She accordingly entered a nationwide contest — the Metropolitan Auditions of the Air — which the Sherwin-Williams Paint Company was sponsoring.

On February 15, she went to New York for the quarter finals, at which time she sang *"Martern aller Arten"* from Mozart's *Die Entführung aus dem Serail.* Having passed this test with flying colors, she was asked to return to New York three weeks later to sing *"Ach, ich liebte"* from the same opera. She passed this test too, and it was as a finalist that she appeared again in Manhattan on March 20. Although she charmed everyone with her rendition of *"Come per me sereno"* from Bellini's *La Sonnambula,* she was told that the management of the Metropolitan Opera was looking for a first-class baritone, and she was therefore not unduly surprised to learn that the first prize had been awarded to Leonard Warren, whose glorious voice was to become one of the Met's great ornaments for more than two decades. It was nevertheless a bitter blow to Margaret, who had outsung all her feminine rivals, and when one year later, Edward Johnson, the general manager of the Met, suggested that she come to New York for a private audition, she turned the offer down. She had decided in the meantime to have another child, and in January of 1939 she gave birth to a daughter, who was given the lovely, sea-swept Russian name of Marina.

Part of the summer of 1938 was again spent at Rockport, Maine. Though we no longer stayed in Mother's bayside house, which now had to provide beds for my sister Irene's three children, we still saw quite a bit of Lubo, who continued to amuse us with her imperiously incorrect pronouncements.

On one memorable occasion, when Irene and I were casually

(but attentively) eavesdropping, we heard her issuing instructions to the local bank. She had just come home and had left a bag near one of the bank's desks. We heard her say, "Allo, this is Lea Luboshutz speaking . . . What? You do not know me? Arre you the young mahn who seets in the third row from right on the second chair?" Apparently the person at the other end of the line wasn't, for a moment later we heard her add, "You are seeting in ze wrong seat!"

When Margaret and I returned to Cleveland that autumn, we found that Artur Rodzinski was in even greater conflict with his symphony orchestra's board of directors now that its chairman, Dudley Blossom, was dead. Once again no operas were scheduled for the season. My own opera programs, on the other hand, were going very well. The student singers and instrumentalists from the Cleveland Institute of Music had scored a third resounding success with the presentation of Donizetti's *Don Pasquale,* and the new Civic Opera Company, which Richard Rychtarik and I had founded, had created a minor sensation with a sparkling rendition of *The Bartered Bride.* The Clevelanders' appetite for opera — presented in a more modest but livelier style than Rodzinski's major orchestral productions — seemed just about insatiable, and our professional singers and instrumentalists were soon hard at work rehearsing Bizet's *Carmen* and Verdi's *La Traviata.*

But this, as it turned out, was merely a beginning, for the entire region now seemed in the grip of an operaphilic contagion. I was approached by a singers' group from nearby Akron, who had heard of the success we had had with *The Bartered Bride* and wanted to put it on in their own town. They could provide most of the singers and the instrumentalists if we — which is to say Richard Rychtarik and myself — could provide the scenery, the stage-directing expertise, and, if necessary, a singer or two from the Civic Opera Company for the most exacting roles.

One of our ace performers at this time was an entertaining Irish American named Mike Ryan, who had a fine tenor voice. He had learned both tenor roles in *The Bartered Bride,* an opera which deals with two half brothers, Jeník and Vašek, who have the same father but different mothers. Vašek is a comic character, a young stutterer who is not very bright, while Jeník is a romantic wooer. Though the two roles are quite different, Mike Ryan was prepared to sing either one, depending on the needs of the Cleveland or Akron opera group.

All was going well when suddenly, in the spring of 1939, we were confronted with a crisis. The Akron group had a fairly good singer who, by working hard, had mastered the role of Jeník. But a few days before the scheduled performance, he was injured in an automobile accident. Nobody had been picked to be his understudy, while Ryan was already slated to play the comic part of Vašek, the stutterer. What were we to do? A large theater, which was not usually available for such events, had been specially hired and every seat had been sold. We couldn't cancel the performance at this late date without provoking an uproar and queering the pitch for opera in the town of Akron forever.

I finally decided that there was only one solution. It so happens that in *The Bartered Bride* the two half brothers are never on stage at the same time except at the very end. It was thus possible for Mike Ryan to play both roles. The first act posed no problem since Vašek is not present at all. He does, however, appear at the beginning of the second act, and shortly after he leaves the stage Jeník comes in. Since this involved a costume change, I reshuffled the sequence slightly, moving up the peasants' dance to give Ryan time to climb out of Vašek's clothes and into Jeník's costume.

I made a similar change in the third act. But there was still the problem of the final scene, when Vašek rushes in disguised in a bearskin and is finally recognized as being Jeník's half brother. I solved this dilemma by having a member of the Akron troupe put on the bearskin, as well as Vašek's red wig, and come out on stage with his back turned to the audience. When he removed his bear's-head hood, the assembled villagers pointed at him, laughing and crying, "Vašek!" after which his mother led him hastily away.

The opera was thus performed, on schedule, thanks to the ambidextrous talents of Mike Ryan, who sang and acted both tenor roles to perfection. Indeed, so artful was he in his dual impersonation that he completely took in a brilliant musician and opera conductor who had fled from Czechoslovakia after the Wehrmacht's mid-March invasion and who was now living in Cleveland as a refugee.

As we drove home in my white Packard, he told me how much he had enjoyed the evening, even though it sounded a bit strange to his Prague ear to hear *Prodaná nevěsta* sung in English. "But tell me one thing, for this really amazed me," he added. "How on earth did you manage to get two tenors who look so much alike?"

For the first time in almost a decade, neither Margaret nor I visited Rockport during the tense, prewar summer of 1939. Instead, we retired to the little town of Twinsburg, about an hour's drive from Cleveland, with our son, Michael, who was now two and a half years old, and little Marina, who was entering her sixth month.

In late June or early July I received a totally unexpected invitation from Emporia, Kansas. Word had apparently reached this distant Corn Belt town that in Cleveland there was a fellow named Goldovsky who liked to work with amateur opera groups, and it had fired the dean of the local college with musical ambition. Already known for its newspaper, the Emporia *Gazette*, the enterprising Kansas town wanted to stake out a second claim to national fame with an epoch-making presentation of Rossini's *The Barber of Seville*. To impersonate Figaro, the dean and faculty had accordingly engaged the famous Australian baritone John Brownlee (who had been singing this role at the Met), and now they wanted the obscure but well-spoken-of Goldovsky to come from Ohio to stage direct and conduct the final performances.

By the time I reached Emporia, in mid-August, the temperature had hit 100° Fahrenheit and showed no inclination to descend. It was all we could do to get through our rehearsals without passing out. The singers, fortunately, were fairly well rehearsed, though the tall and ample-bosomed lady (an English teacher at the college) who had been chosen for the leading female role was as unlike Rosina as it was possible to be, and there was an equal incongruity with the diminutive chemistry teacher who had been selected for the role of Don Basilio.

For two weeks we were stuck there, having to spend our restless nights in non-air-conditioned rooms and our days rehearsing in a hall which was like a baking oven. Before the fortnight was over, more than one of us showed signs of dog-day madness. To amuse ourselves, John Brownlee and I invented a private quarrel of the kind that prima donnas like to cultivate. Brownlee insisted on being permitted to take a solo curtain call, while I no less imperiously announced that "when I stage operas, individual bows are out! Only ensemble curtain calls are allowed."

We carried this ridiculous quarrel to quite extraordinary lengths, looking daggers at each other and coldly refusing to converse at the dinner to which we were invited by the worried dean, who had been told that the two "stars" from out of town were no longer on speaking terms. We even managed to rise from the table as implacably wooden-faced and hostile as it was possible for two pranksters to look.

How we survived the ordeal, I honestly don't know, for we were driven quite silly by the relentless heat. On the eve of the final performance, just to complicate matters, the orchestra's one and only double bass collapsed with some acute gastric attack, and I was forced to plug the instrumental gap by playing the double-bass part on the spinet, which had been installed in the orchestra pit for the *secco* recitatives. Since I had to conduct the orchestra with my right hand and needed my left hand for the double-bass part, I had no way of turning the pages of the score. A young man was accordingly conscripted for this particular job, which was not simple, since it meant hastily replacing the recitative music with the full orchestral score, and vice versa, as we went along. A second acolyte hovered just behind, ready to thrust a straw into my mouth and feed me an ice-cold drink each time it looked as though I was about to keel over, while a third, armed with a Turkish towel, kept wiping the sweat from my forehead and neck. I felt and must have looked a bit like an Ottoman pasha in a Turkish bath, or like Primo Carnera in his corner of the ring between two heavyweight boxing bouts.

As a final treat, we were all invited to dinner by William Allen White, the distinguished editor of the Emporia *Gazette* and "the sage of Emporia." His wife was also present, and it was she, as I recall, who turned on the radio toward the end of the evening to hear the latest news. A couple of days before, Moscow and Berlin had startled the world by announcing the conclusion of a nonaggression pact between Hitler's Third Reich and Stalin's U.S.S.R. The purpose of this diabolical agreement was to aggress a third party, and it came as a nasty shock to all of us to realize that while we had been nitwittedly sweating it out, singing, and playing jokes on each other, a hopelessly surrounded Poland was being overrun by foreign tanks.

Not long after my return to Cleveland, during this fateful autumn of 1939, a delegation of singers from the town of Canton (located some distance to the south of Akron) came to see me with the request that I help them organize an opera group, as I had done with the Akronites. I told them that regretfully it was out of the question: I was much too busy as it was, trying to direct an opera department, teach the piano, and keep two opera groups going, to take on a new assignment. They then asked if by any chance I knew of someone who could come out to Canton to get them started.

Unfortunately I knew of no one, but I said that I would try to find somebody who could do the job.

I had little time to give the matter much thought until a few weeks later when, out of the blue, I received a telephone call from a Hungarian named Julius Toldi. Like so many others, he had been forced to flee his homeland to escape the jackbooted advance of Hitler's legions, and he had found momentary refuge in Cleveland. He was a well-trained musician, he told me, he was looking for a job, he was starving, his wife was starving and so on. Having been a refugee myself, I listened with sympathy to his tale and told him to come see me.

Toldi's credentials seemed fairly good. He had studied in Vienna under Schönberg and Webern, and he had even managed to obtain a recommendation from Bruno Walter. His wife was a painter, but as they had had to leave most of her canvases behind, she would have to start again from scratch in a country where her name meant nothing. Meanwhile they were starving.

I asked Toldi what he could do as a musician.

"Anything you want me to do," he answered confidently.

"Do you play the piano?"

"Yes, though not particularly well."

"Can you train choruses?"

"Of course."

"And can you train soloists?"

"Certainly," he answered. "I'll do anything you want."

I should have known better after the Bach-Gabrilowitsch fiasco, but I felt sorry for this poor fellow, whom the Wehrmacht and the Gestapo had run out of Vienna. It occurred to me that Toldi might be just the person needed for the opera group in Canton. So without further ado I arranged for him to coach the Canton chorus and singers. It meant two trips a week and a $10 fee for each training session — enough to keep him and his painter wife from dying of hunger.

At first everything went well. The Canton group seemed

pleased with Toldi's coaching. After three months, or thereabouts, one of them telephoned to say that they had learned *The Bartered Bride* — "except that we haven't got a tenor. But you promised to give us a tenor from Cleveland."

Yes, I replied, I could give them a tenor from Cleveland. I asked a few questions about the opera to find out how far along they were with their preparations, and finally I said that I would drive out to Canton to see how everything was going.

When I reached Canton, I was agreeably surprised to discover that they really had studied and rehearsed their parts. They wanted to put on the opera in the auditorium of the Timkin High School. Rychtarik would truck his scenery out from Cleveland, while I attended to the staging. Except for the tenor whom we were to supply from our opera group, they had all the necessary singers and enough players to supply the orchestral accompaniment. Not least of all, they had managed to do all this without going bankrupt.

Every major problem seemed to have been solved, and the future look auspicious.

"By the way," I asked Toldi, "can you conduct?"

He laughed. "Who can't conduct? Anybody can conduct. That's no problem."

"Oh," chimed in his wife, "you know, Gyuli" — the diminutive of Julius, which she used to designate her husband — "Gyuli is so excited by the prospect that he stands before the mirror and beats time, like this." And she offered me a demonstration of her dear Julius in action.

His ridiculous affirmation — "Anybody can conduct" — should have given me pause. But compassion had momentarily got the better of my caution. And so, on the day scheduled for the first orchestral rehearsal, I drove to Canton and took my place in the Timkin High School auditorium next to the opera group's directors.

Raising his baton, Toldi had his instrumentalists launch into the overture of *The Bartered Bride*. But it was soon painfully evident that he had not the faintest idea of how to direct an orchestra, and still less singers on a stage. He didn't know how to give a proper downbeat, nor a second beat, nor a third. The instrumentalists, as long as they kept their eyes on the score, were able to play fairly well, but if their eyes strayed toward the conductor, their sense of tempo began to vary and became confused. The singers, who had no score to go by, were even more perplexed by Toldi's random gesticulations and were soon hopelessly out of time with the orchestra.

The directors looked at me questioningly, and I felt like crawling under my chair. Finally, to spare everyone further embarrassment, I stood up and said, "I think we'd better call it a day. Everybody's tired, so why don't we all go home and get a good night's sleep, and then everything will go fine for tomorrow's dress rehearsal."

I then withdrew to a schoolroom office for a private meeting with the directors.

"What is the meaning of this?" they asked me, looking considerably put out.

"Gentlemen," I said, "I am as surprised as you are. Mr. Toldi, I thought, had done a good job so far."

"Oh, yes," they agreed. "We have nothing against Mr. Toldi as a teacher. We like Mr. Toldi as a coach for the chorus and the leading singers. Only" — and here all nodded their heads in agreement — "he doesn't seem able to conduct."

"Well," I said, "I'll be honest with you. Because he could do those other things, I too thought that he could conduct. I should have known better. This is my fault. But I'm not going to leave you in the lurch. I'm going to cancel my engagements in Cleveland for tomorrow and the day after, and I'll stay here and conduct the dress rehearsal and the performance."

After the meeting, from which he had been deliberately excluded, I rang up Toldi and said I wanted to see him the next morning for breakfast. He came round to the hotel where I was staying, and over two cups of steaming coffee I broke the bitter truth to him. "You know, Toldi, you've done a fine job training the singers and the chorus, and you deserve full credit for it. But training singers is not the same thing as conducting an orchestra. I thought you could conduct because you told me you could and because of that letter you showed me from Bruno Walter, which made it sound as though you had studied with him. But I realize now that you have never in your life conducted a symphony, still less an opera. So you must let me conduct the dress rehearsal and the performance."

"Aha!" he exclaimed, with a steely look in his eye. "I knew it all along! I told my wife, 'You know, Goldovsky wants me to do all the dirty work, but Goldovsky wants to have all the glory.' Well, I'm sorry, Mister, this is not going to work. This is my show and I am going to conduct the dress rehearsal and I am going to conduct the performance, because my name is on the program. So don't think for a moment that you're going to get away with this."

"Toldi," I said, "you're being silly, really silly. You have a good thing going here, you have a small income, you have made a nice impression on these people, they like you for what you have taught them to do. So why spoil everything at the last moment by doing more than you know how to do well? You say I'm trying to steal this conducting job away from you, as though I didn't have a dozen more important things to do in Cleveland. I need this job like a hole in the head."

But Toldi just laughed sarcastically. *"Ja, Ja, Ja!* How wonderful it all sounds! But you're not kidding me for one second. I can see right through you. But I'm not going to let you get away with this. I'm going to do the rehearsal and I'm going to do the performance."

"Listen," I said, beginning to lose patience, "don't kid yourself about this. If you insist on making it so hard for everybody, you are not going to keep this job. You won't be reengaged for another season — that I can guarantee. Because these people are very upset about this whole business."

"Aha! Now you are threatening me! Ha-ha-ha!" he cried with an even more sarcastic laugh. "But just wait, I will show you! I will sue you!"

There was clearly no point in continuing the argument. If Toldi was stubbornly determined to be his own worst enemy, there was no way I could stop him.

Fortunately there was a baby grand piano in the pit, and so when the time came for the dress rehearsal, I approached the orchestra players and said, "I'm going to play the piano for this rehearsal."

Toldi made no objection. "Sure, you play the piano. You'll be part of the orchestra."

"Don't pay any attention to him," I told the instrumentalists. "Play along with me as I play the piano. The singers are well trained and should be able to follow."

This dress rehearsal was one of the weirdest experiences imaginable. The orchestra played and the singers sang along with the piano, while Toldi stood on the podium waving his baton ecstatically.

We went through the same incredible rigmarole for the public performance. When it was all over, I mopped my brow with relief. Singers and orchestra players were loudly applauded, while Toldi stood out in front, bowing and smiling and taking credit for everything.

But a little later he got a nasty shock, just as I had predicted. The directors of the Canton opera group informed him that his services would not be required for the next season.

Julius Toldi's rage against Boris Goldovsky — the scoundrel who had tried to steal his glory and who had later pulled the rug out from under him by taking over the group he had so brilliantly trained — now knew no bounds. He raved and foamed at the mouth, and later, dipping his pen in vinegar, he wrote a furious book about his Canton experiences, in which I (though not actually named) was portrayed as the instrument of Satan, a scheming blackguard and master plotter, a sort of Iago or Scarpia of the orchestra pit.

8

Tanglewood and Koussevitzky

IN SEPTEMBER of 1939 I had received a letter from Herbert Graf informing me that Serge Koussevitzky, the conductor of the Boston Symphony Orchestra, was opening a summer music school at Lenox, Massachusetts, in July of the following year. He had asked Graf to head the new music center's opera department, but not being an opera conductor, Graf, who knew me well from our work together in Philadelphia and Cleveland, had suggested that I be chosen as his musical assistant. The proposal had apparently met with Koussevitzky's approval, for he and George Judd, the manager of the Boston Symphony Orchestra, were prepared to pay me $500 to help Dr. Graf during the Berkshire Music Festival of 1940.

Although we were both of Russian origin, this was the first time I had ever had any dealings with Serge Koussevitzky. Mother, I knew, was an old friend of his, and Uncle Pierre had often accompanied him on the piano at a time when Koussevitzky was touring Russia as a double-bass virtuoso. Pierre had also helped him later, playing orchestral scores on the piano when Koussevitzky was so laboriously learning to become a conductor, and he had even sailed down the Volga with him on one of Koussevitzky's famous pre–First World War orchestral tours.

I had heard Uncle Pierre tell many stories about this singularly warm-hearted, temperamental, hypersensitive human being, but it wasn't until I reached the Tanglewood estate the following summer that I realized how well Koussevitzky knew my family. A couple of days after my arrival I was invited to have tea with him at his luxurious country house, situated on a nearby hill. I told him how honored I felt at having been given this opportunity to preside over the musical activities of his opera department, particularly since he knew so little about me and my abilities.

"You are mistaken," he said to me in Russian — the only language, as I was soon to discover, in which he could express himself with ease — "I know a great deal about you. But even if I knew less, I would still give you a chance. Being your father's son, you will be certain to do a good job.

"Yes," he went on, much amused by my look of astonishment, "I knew your father, Onissim Goldovsky, very well and am, as a matter of fact, deeply obligated to him." He then explained that while still a young man, but already the leading double-bass player at the Bolshoy Opera House, he had married one of its ballerinas, Nadejda Galat. The marriage had not worked out, and the two had soon separated. Later, Koussevitzky had fallen in love with Natalya Ushkova, the daughter of a wealthy tea merchant. Before marrying her, he had to obtain a divorce from his ballet dancer. But the young lady would not hear of it, and when Koussevitzky sent over a lawyer to work out some kind of settlement, "she horsewhipped that fellow all the way down the steps of her apartment house."

Koussevitzky had then appealed to my father, a well-known member of the Moscow bar and, he claimed, "famous for his gentle powers of persuasion." Father managed to placate the irascible lady. Not only was he able to leave her apartment unscathed, but he even prevailed on her to grant the desired divorce. Koussevitzky did not tell me what sort of financial settlement had been offered to the ballerina wife, but Lubo later told me that the amount provided by the bride-to-be was truly astronomical. "So you see," Koussevitzky concluded, "I know more about you than you think. And because you are your father's son, I have high hopes for you."

It did not take me long to realize that family ties and past services were not enough to keep Koussevitzky happy if one failed to live up to the high expectations he entertained about all those who worked for and under him. He wanted the Berkshire Music Center to differ from other music schools in every possible respect. There was to be no official curriculum, there were to be no examinations nor any graduating diplomas. Instead there was to be a deliberate mixing of generations, with talented young people being exposed to gifted veterans for six intensive weeks of musical inspiration. And in this informal, experimental atmosphere, Koussevitzky was convinced, great things would burgeon.

All this was explained to me personally by Koussevitzky, who began the summer course by calling in the various teachers to find out what they would like to undertake during the summer session. "Here, in Tanglewood," he said to me, "you will be able to realize your secret dreams, to experiment with ideas you could not try out elsewhere. Now tell me, have you anything of the sort in mind?"

"Some of my ideas may seem utopian," I replied, "but still, I would like to find out what would happen if we were to treat opera singers like full-fledged artists and not like unmusical and clumsy marionettes who cannot be trusted to think for themselves."

"You expect opera singers . . . to be artists who think for themselves?" — Koussevitzky's hazel eyes seemed to widen as he stared at me fixedly. "But, Good Lord," he said, as though he had just listened to some scandalous enormity, "this certainly cannot be done."

"You may be right," I said. "Perhaps it cannot be done. But would you mind if I try?"

"Oh, no," he said. "Go ahead and try. By all means, go ahead and try. I give you carte blanche."

The gifted luminaries whom Koussevitzky had assembled to inspire the carefully screened and sifted summer students (312 accepted out of about 600 applicants) included Paul Hindemith and Aaron Copland for composition, Olin Downes for musical history, G. Wallace Woodworth and Hugh Ross for choral music, and Herbert Graf and myself for opera. The conducting classes — a larger one for general instruction and a smaller one for particularly gifted youngsters (like Leonard Bernstein and Lukas Foss) — he was going to handle himself.

Whereas the other teachers had little trouble finding rooms where they could train and rehearse their students, we had to start the opera department virtually from scratch. Well-intentioned though he was, Koussevitzky — or Koussie, as everyone called him behind his back — had not the faintest idea what an opera department needed to function properly. We did not have enough rehearsal rooms, we did not have enough pianos. But our complaints were soon attended to, and before long a dozen or more Baldwin spinets were installed in the gabled manor house and the adjoining barns and garages of the Tanglewood estate. For if there was one quality that distinguished Koussevitzky, it was an unflagging devotion to projects and persons he believed in. He had long been generous in commissioning and financing the publication of works by contemporary composers, and he was not going to be stingy with his latest brain child: the Berkshire Music Center.

Our main problem, however, was the absence of a theater. All that was available was an open-air platform, covered by a large circus tent. When it rained, the marquee would gradually fill with water and begin to sag, and we would have to interrupt rehearsals to shake off the water. The tent was also too small to shelter the spectators, who had to sit, beyond its protective canopy, on chairs lined up on the grass.

For all these reasons we had to limit our ambitions to short excerpts and one-act operas. The first complete work chosen, in obvious deference to its composer, Paul Hindemith, was a musical and dramatic prank entitled *Hin und Zurück.* In this curious piece — the kind one is willing to see once but never again — the music, like the action, moves forward and then begins reversing backward, like a cinematographic reel, to its original point of departure. The result was clever, but that was about all one could say for it. I doubt that the performers — led by Richard Burgin, the concert master of the Boston Symphony Orchestra — enjoyed it any more than I, who had to play the four-hand piano part along with the composer.

Hindemith — a very opinionated gentleman from Frankfurt who had been offered a teaching post at Yale — may have sensed our lukewarmness toward his elaborate leg-pull, for he was soon complaining to Koussevitzky about the opera department, warning him that if he wasn't careful, "it will develop an insatiable appetite and devour everything else around here." Unfortunately for himself, he was so overbearing in pressing his strong feelings on every possible subject that he finally got on Koussevitzky's nerves. They had a violent argument about something, and Hindemith left Tanglewood in a huff. He was never invited back.

One of our main problems — as is true of all operatic ventures — was with scenery. For the first-act duet between Rodolfo and Mimi in Puccini's *La Bohème,* which was rehearsed in a garage, we were reduced to borrowing a stove, a table, and two chairs from the nearby home of the estate's superintendent of grounds.

Our pièce de résistance, if such it can be called, was Handel's *Acis and Galatea.* Herbert Graf selected this pastoral masque of nymphs and shepherds because it could be played out of doors against the lovely background of Tanglewood's formal garden, lake, and the wooded Berkshire hills behind.

Since there was nothing remotely resembling an orchestra pit available, the instrumentalists whom I conducted were placed behind a hedge, which hid them from the spectators. Unfortunately, from my oblique position I could not see the singers on the stage, nor could they see me. Our ability to communicate was further compounded by the wind. If it blew in one direction, I could no longer hear the singers; if it blew in the opposite direction, they could not hear the orchestra. The wind also played havoc with the music on the stands, and during rehearsals we had to station special assistants by each stand to hold down and turn the pages. Nor was this the end of our troubles. The rays of the August sun, as it descended toward the west during the hot afternoons, tended to blind the musicians and to melt the varnish on the violins. There were angry protests and we were faced with a mutiny until we could provide the players with sunglasses and parasols, held over them by hastily recruited acolytes. All in all, we were quite a sight, and I myself looked like the half-baked product of some Arabian desert, with a kefiyeh-like handkerchief draped over my head to save me from sunstroke.

On the afternoon of the final performance we were blessed with exactly the kind of weather we needed. The sun was veiled by an overcast so that we could dispense with the dark glasses and umbrellas. There was no wind. The singers could hear the orchestra and I could hear the singers. And the clouds sheltering us from the hot August sun thoughtfully refrained from drenching us with rain.

At the end of the performance, Koussevitzky joined us behind the hedge and congratulated us warmly. He had greatly enjoyed the gay cavorting and singing on the stage, and he proposed that we give a repeat performance the next afternoon. I had to say no. We had tempted fate once and got away with it. But it was really asking too much of the elements to be as cooperative a second time.

Mother, who journeyed down from Rockport while the summer school was still in session, was greatly impressed by what she saw and heard. Finally, when we were seated *à trois,* conversing as usual in Russian, she remarked to Koussevitzky, "I have been observing all this tremendous activity here and all these wonderful things. And I wonder, Sergei Alexandrovich, if you realize who you are."

"What do you mean? Who do you think I am?" asked Koussevitzky with a puzzled frown.

"I mean, Sergei Alexandrovich," said Lubo, "that you are God Almighty!"

Koussevitzky looked at her, not in the least surprised by this extravagant compliment. "Well," he nodded quietly, "I know my *responsábilities.*" He pronounced this sentence in English, but with the accent incongruously placed on the third syllable. *"Je suis responsable!"* was indeed one of his favorite expressions. It was Sergei Alexandrovich's way of saying that he was the boss, and proud of it.

During those six chaotic weeks we were repeatedly told by Koussevitzky that he expected us to "deliver 200 percent." Apparently we did, for at the end of the summer school he informed Herbert Graf and myself that he would like us back at Tanglewood next year. He had great plans for the summer school of 1941, and if all went well we would have an "opera house" to perform in when we returned.

He was as good as his word. Mrs. Curtis Bok, who had attended some of the 1940 concerts, had generously donated $10,000, and Koussevitzky had persuaded a number of other wealthy patrons to give him the money needed to build a theater concert hall capable of seating 1200 spectators.

The summer school's activities were once again opened with a formal "commencement" address, *prononced* by Koussevitzky, who, as I was beginning to discover, loved to "*prononce* a speech" on every possible occasion. He expressed gratitude to the "trusties" of the Boston Symphony Orchestra whose generosity was making it possible to bring music to the "maces" ("masses"). He was also pleased to *annonce* a special ceremony, which was to take place exactly three days hence, on Thursday, to inaugurate the new Theater Concert Hall.

Working at a "200 percent delivery" tempo, Herbert Graf and I managed to prepare a few scenes from Mozart's *Così fan tutte* so as to have something to put on stage when the Theater Concert Hall was formally inaugurated. These musical offerings were accompanied by several speeches, one of which was made by Graf, as head of the center's opera department. This noble building, he declared, was a symbol of the drawing of a new age when, instead of importing our traditions from Europe, we would begin to cultivate our own American ways of doing things.

The tone of this brief address struck me as most apropos. But when I approached Koussevitzky at the conclusion of the ceremonies, there was an angry look on his face.

"The scenes were all right," he told me in Russian, "but I will never forgive Dr. Graf for that speech."

"But why, Sergei Alexandrovich, what do you mean?"

"How dare he *prononce* a speech in my new *teatr* and say that we must import our traditions from Europe?"

"But, Sergei Alexandrovich, he did not say that at all. In fact, he said the exact opposite."

"Are you sure?" he asked, giving me a searching look.

"Absolutely positive," I answered.

"Well, then, that's different," he said. And there was no more talk of pardoning Dr. Graf for crimes the poor fellow had not committed.

If Koussevitzky's skill in communicating his thoughts in English left something to be desired, so did his ability to understand the language. I was not affected by this particular failing, for I always spoke to him in Russian, but I trembled for the many less fortunate souls who often aroused his wrath through some innocent remark which he had totally misunderstood.

On a later occasion, when a number of faculty heads had been summoned to a meeting in New York to discuss the Berkshire Music Center's next season, Koussevitzky began to unfold his grandiose plans for an annual Greek "puhgahn," which was to be a regular feature of the Tanglewood Festival. He was going to construct an "amphiteatr" on the hill opposite the lake, and there the puhgahn would take place with specially composed music and hundreds of participants, not to mention the tens of thousands of spectators who would come to watch this event. In the middle of this almost lyrical description, Koussevitzky was called away from the conference table by a long-distance telephone call. All eyes turned to me in search of an explanation. I had to confess, with some embarrassment, that puhgahn was not a Russian word, at least not one that I was familiar with. It could be Nordic, it might be Mongolian, it was even possibly some strange Hindi term he had picked up somewhere in a description of a maharajah's fantasy. But why he was using this term in connection with Tanglewood, I was at a loss to explain. Only much later did it dawn on me that what he was trying to describe was a "pageant."

One of his choice heteroglot expressions, always addressed to the string players of the student orchestra, was "You must change the bow so *personne* knows." The *personne* part of this admonition could be traced to the early 1920s, when he was living in Paris and was entertaining music lovers with the fashionable "concerts Koussevitzky." The first time I heard this phrase I was reminded of the picturesque pronouncement which the violin teacher Karl Flesch used to make to his students at the Curtis Institute of Music and which had caused us endless merriment: "The nearer the bridge the bow it plays, the more she jumps by himself."

Koussevitzky's "You must change the bow so *personne* knows" phrase was illustrated by an appropriate movement of the right arm and wrist, and so eloquently was this gesture performed that after a few rehearsals even the least gifted student violinists and cellists of the Berkshire Music Center would begin to produce the velvety string sound which was the hallmark of every orchestra Koussie conducted.

Occasionally he sensed that the players he was instructing had difficulty understanding him. Once, while he was rehearsing the student orchestra, I heard him pleading with the cellists, from whom he wished to elicit a soft, yet intensely singing tone. "*Weicher, weicher, Kinder,*" he implored, "but without losing 'substahnce.' " The students tried various approaches in an earnest but vain endeavor to figure out what was required of them. Finally, after ten minutes of frustration, Koussie stopped, fixed the first-stand players with an intense gaze, and said with slow, deliberate emphasis, "More . . . less!" That did it!

Having begun the summer course with several extracts from Mozart's *Così fan tutte,* Herbert Graf and I decided to finish it with a full-length performance of the opera. When the time came for the dress rehearsal, Koussevitzky made a dramatic appearance, striding majestically down the aisle in his famous black cape and taking a seat in the middle of the auditorium. In accordance with the ideas that Richard Wagner had first put into practice at Bayreuth, the orchestra pit in our new Theater Concert Hall had been so constructed that neither the conductor nor the instrumentalists could be seen by the audience. So I was not unduly surprised, in the middle of the overture, to see Koussevitzky leaning over the balustrade and observing us intently.

A short scene followed the overture, and then, while the scenery was being changed, I hopped out of the pit and made my way back to the middle of the auditorium, where Koussevitzky was now seated. He was obviously upset. His forehead was clouded and the blue vein over his left eyebrow was pulsating ominously — a sure sign that he was angry.

"How was the ensemble? How was the balance?" I asked a bit nervously.

"Both the ensemble and the balance are good," he replied in a sepulchral tone.

"Please, Sergei Alexandrovich," I pleaded with him, "tell me what is wrong. Something is obviously wrong. But this is only the dress rehearsal. Maybe there is still time to correct it."

He let a long moment go by before answering. "Yes," he finally said, "something is wrong, something is disgracefully wrong. And it is all your fault!" he went on, with sudden vehemence. "How can you? How could you? That baseball bat! That telephone pole! Break it into a thousand pieces, throw it away, get rid of it at once!"

I heard the blistering words in a kind of dream, while my dazed brain sought to understand what he was referring to. Suddenly I knew: it was my baton, the nice, harmless stick with the thin cork handle which I had learned to use under Fritz Reiner, but which was very different from the pencil-thin wand which Koussevitzky dangled between the middle and ring fingers of his right hand. Sergei Alexandrovich was hurt, hurt at the thought that one of *his* faculty members, conducting in *his* theater, for one of *his* Tanglewood rehearsals, someone who had had ample chance to study *his* conducting technique and who could easily have procured himself *his* kind of stick, had nevertheless chosen to use a different, foreign, disgraceful utensil. After returning to the orchestra pit, I broke Reiner's "telephone pole" into two ignominious stumps. I have never used a baton since that day.

At the end of my first summer at Tanglewood, Koussevitzky had asked me if there was anything unusual I would like to try my hand at for the following year, and I had told him that in Cleveland I had been doing research into the problems of musical tempo — one of the areas in which, I might add, Koussevitzky was rather weak as a conductor. I said that I would like to give some lectures on the subject since I had developed some interesting ideas. Sergei Alexandrovich gave me carte blanche to go ahead.

Among those who came to listen to these lectures was G. Wallace Woodworth, chairman of the music faculty at Harvard, who had returned to Tanglewood in 1941 to teach choral conducting. Woodward was so interested in what I had to say that he invited me to come to Harvard in the autumn to give two tempo lectures to his university students. I accepted his kind invitation, little suspecting what it was going to lead to.

In Cleveland my musical activities had undergone a kind of horizontal spread. It had started with Beryl Rubinstein, who had suggested that in addition to the opera department, I also give advanced piano lessons at the Cleveland Institute of Music. Not long afterward I was asked to take over the piano department at Western Reserve University. This proved a boon, for it brought me into contact with a brilliant musical theorist named Melville Smith. Smith, who was a singularly alert person with an omnivorous curiosity, drew my attention to a book, written by Arnold Schultz, entitled *The Riddle of the Pianist's Finger.* This book was a revelation, for it offered me something I had never come across before: an anatomical analysis of piano technique.

It is impossible to do justice to a technical work of this kind in a few words. So, at the risk of committing an injustice, let me say that there were two important things I learned from Schultz's book. The first was the vital distinction — which nobody had pointed out to me before — between the flexor muscles of the hand, which push the fingers down, and the extensor muscles, which lift the fingers up. Conventionally, piano-playing technique, when reduced to its essentials, can be defined as a way of using these muscles successively at a very rapid pace. But — and here was the revolutionary notion propounded by Schultz — this alternating movement is wasteful and inefficient, rather like trying to drive a car by constantly moving one's right foot back and forth from the accelerator to the brake. Since each piano key is fitted with a spring, it rides up naturally when the pressure on it is relaxed, which means that by letting one's finger ride up with it, one can learn to play the piano by ignoring the extensors and using only the flexor muscles of the hand.

The second thing I learned from this book concerned the use of the middle joints of the fingers, which are of paramount importance in evaluating the various speeds with which piano keys are pushed downward. The real breakthrough in the development of my piano technique, however, only came when I hit on the idea of applying Schultz's anatomical analysis to the activities of the finger's nail joint. All of the piano teachers I have known have insisted that their students keep their forefingers rigid. The reason for this can probably be traced to the fact that most children have very loose fingertips and teachers develop a subconscious fear that unless these dangling fingertips are kept rigid, they may be in danger of breaking off. Inspired by Schultz's scientific approach to these problems, I developed an ability to use the nail joint actively and to such good effect that I found that I could handle almost any piano piece with complete technical assurance without having to put in hours of preparatory drillwork limbering up the muscles of my hands.

Melville Smith, who had first introduced me to Schultz's theories, had meanwhile left Cleveland, having been appointed director of the Longy School of Music in Cambridge, Massachusetts. So between my two tempo lectures at Harvard, I decided to call on the old friend I had known at Western Reserve.

While he was taking me on a guided tour of his establishment, of which he was justly proud, I asked him about his piano department.

"It's none too good," he admitted to me ruefully, "not at all what it should be. We really ought to have somebody to organize and improve it. Somebody like yourself. But unfortunately we cannot afford you."

A little later that same day, I called on Wallace Goodrich, director of the New England Conservatory of Music. He had seen me at work at the Berkshire Music Center and was apparently impressed, for he went out of his way to show me around the conservatory.

"Tell me about your opera department, Mr. Goodrich," I said, as we walked around.

Goodrich was a rather pompous gentleman, but he frankly admitted that the conservatory's opera department was not too good. After which he added, as a kind of afterthought, "You know, we really could do with someone like yourself to improve it. But of course we cannot afford you."

I was struck by the similarity of sentiment, and even of phrasing, and it gave me an idea.

"Mr. Goodrich," I said, "I heard the same sentence earlier today in Cambridge from Melville Smith of the Longy School of Music. Why don't you two get together? If you can't afford me singly, maybe you can do it by joining forces?"

The truth of the matter was that I was no longer happy in Cleveland, notwithstanding the kindness I had met with from so many of its citizens. My relations with Artur Rodzinski had turned completely sour, and the last straw, as far as Margaret and I were concerned, was a reception at his house, at which, under the influence of some Moral Rearmament teaching he had recently absorbed, he craved our forgiveness and asked us to submit the names of all the persons we felt he might at one time or another have offended. ("What should we do — send him the Cleveland telephone directory?" one of our friends asked, after witnessing this spectacle of self-abasement.)

A couple of weeks after my visit to Cambridge and Boston I received a joint letter from Melville Smith and Wallace Goodrich. They wrote to say that they had talked the matter over between them and they had come to the conclusion that by pooling their resources they could afford an expensive fellow like myself. I lost no time accepting their joint offers. And so it was decided that next June, at the conclusion of the current academic year, Margaret and I would say goodbye to Cleveland and move to Boston.

In January of 1942 Koussevitzky lost Natalya Konstantinovna, the devoted wife and patroness of the arts who had financed his orchestral beginnings in Moscow and Berlin and enabled him, after the Revolution, to found a publishing company in Paris for the editing of scores by contemporary composers. Her first name had been joined to his to form the composite "Seranak" — the name given to the splendid country house they had bought near Lenox, in the Berkshires, not far from the Tanglewood estate. True to his generous form, the widower honored Natalya's death by setting up a Koussevitzky Music Foundation, designed to sponsor works by new composers. The first beneficiaries were Samuel Barber, Benjamin Britten, and Nicolai Berezowsky.

Natalya Konstantinovna's death inevitably brought back to mind a story my Uncle Pierre liked to tell about his first visit to Koussevitzky in Boston, during a concert trip he was making in the United States with the violinist Paul Kochanski. Many of Koussevitzky's eccentricities could be traced back to a childlike need for reassurance, affection, and admiration. So Uncle Pierre was not unduly surprised when, over a cup of tea, his friend Sergei Alexandrovich began plying him with questions: "Tell me, Petya, you who know everybody in New York, you who circulate among musicians there, do they talk a lot about me and my organization?"

The question, of course, was asked in Russian. It was an odd term to use, but whether he was speaking in his native Russian or in his fragmentary and often confusing English, Koussevitzky invariably referred to the Boston Symphony Orchestra as "my organization."

Pierre, who knew exactly how to reply to this kind of question, undertook to reassure him: "Sergei Alexandrovich, let me tell you what everybody is saying in New York. All the musicians there are saying that Sergei Alexandrovich Koussevitzky is the only honest musician left in the world."

"Ah, no, no, Petya," said Koussevitzky, raising his hand in a gesture of protest. "No, no, Petya. *C'est exagéré!* You must not *exagérer.* I do not like *exagération,*" he continued, as usual peppering his Russian speech with French words. "It is not true. I am not the only honest musician in the world. I will name you several other honest musicians. No, Petya, no . . . Just a moment, I will name you some others. For instance, there is . . . uh . . . uh . . . uh . . . there is . . . for instance . . . uh . . ." His eyes wandered around the room, as he kept repeating, "honest musicians? . . . honest musicians?" But somehow they were unable to focus on the name of a single one.

Finally, unwilling to give up, Koussevitzky called to his wife, "Natashok! Natashok! Tell me, *dushka,* tell me, who are the other honest musicians?"

When Herbert Graf and I returned to Tanglewood in July of 1942, we were in for a surprise. One of my duties, as the person responsible for the musical side of the opera department, was to audition singers applying for admission to the Berkshire Music Center, selecting the best ones for our summer program. Almost all of them had already been examined, and those accepted had been given their assignments. But among the few who still needed to be auditioned on the first Monday of the summer-school term was a young truckdriver from Philadelphia who had been admitted to the Berkshire Music Center on instructions from Sergei Alexandrovich himself.

Alfredo Cocozza — or Mario Lanza, as he now called himself (having adopted his mother's maiden name) — had managed to attract Koussevitzky's attention in Philadelphia during one of the Boston Symphony Orchestra's periodic visits to that city. After finding where Koussevitzky was staying, he had persuaded the desk clerk to give him a room next to Sergei Alexandrovich's suite, and once installed he had given full throat to bel canto tunes and snatches of operatic arias. Intrigued by the extraordinary sound he heard issuing from his neighbor's room, Koussevitzky had introduced himself and invited Cocozza-Lanza to come to Tanglewood.

When the time came, on that first Monday, to test Lanza's tenor voice, Sergei Alexandrovich came in person to listen to his protégé. Lanza was paired off with a young Mexican soprano named Irma Gonzalez, and the two were asked to sing part of the duet from the third act of *La Bohème* — this being something that Lanza had learned by heart (probably by listening to phonograph recordings). The tenor sound that issued from that simple truckdriver's throat was gorgeous, unforgettable, out of this world. I could hardly believe my ears. Koussevitzky, seated next to me, was so excited that the tears began rolling down his cheeks, as they had a way of doing in moments of intense emotion.

"Caruso *redivivus!* Caruso *redivivus!*" he whispered to me ecstatically, as he wiped his cheeks. He was overjoyed at the thought that his "discovery" was genuine, a priceless addition to the world of music, and that his first, favorable impression in Philadelphia was not mistaken.

"Listen," Koussevitzky said to me after the audition, "five weeks from now we are going to do Beethoven's Ninth Symphony, and I want this boy to sing the tenor part in it."

"Very well, Sergei Alexandrovich," I assured him, "I will prepare him personally."

I gave instructions to have Lanza report to me the next morning for special coaching. But once we were together in the rehearsal room I realized that I was faced with an uphill job. Lanza, to begin with, could not read a line of music. Even worse, he had never had any solfège instruction and his ear was totally untrained. I would play one note on the piano and he would sing another. I would move up the scale, and, instead of following me, his voice would move down.

After several coaching sessions, I was ready to throw in the sponge. We were getting nowhere in a great hurry. At the lunch table I confessed my predicament to Ifor Jones, one of the choral directors at Tanglewood, who was also leader of the Bach Choir in Bethlehem, Pennsylvania: "Koussie wants Lanza to sing the tenor part in the Ninth Symphony, and he asked me to prepare it. But how can I coach somebody who can't read a note of music and whose ear is totally untrained?"

"You can't," was Ifor Jones's answer. "I know Lanza. I wanted to engage him for my festival performances. No good. It can't be done. You can't teach him anything."

We finally decided to go together to break the news to Koussevitzky. To avoid a scene, I decided to broach the subject as diplomatically as possible: "Dr. Koussevitzky, I just don't know how to teach this boy. He's got a beautiful tenor voice — there's no denying it — but he's musically untrained. Neither Dr. Jones nor I know how to go about teaching him the fundamentals. So why don't you select someone else who will prepare him for you?"

Koussevitzky was no fool. He realized immediately that if the two of us could not teach Lanza to sing the tenor part, then nobody could. The idea was allowed to die a quiet death.

Finally, after putting our heads together with Herbert Graf, we decided that Lanza might after all be taught to sing Fenton in Otto Nicolai's *The Merry Wives of Windsor*. Even though we shortened this small role as much as possible, it still required a lot of work. Somehow we managed to pound the words and music into Lanza's head, and he even scored a great hit with the audience when he sang the serenade in the second act. But most of the teachers and students of the opera department developed a hearty dislike for this fat, uncouth individual, who behaved like a vulgar lecher, pawing the girls and luring them into empty practice rooms.

His voice, of course, was phenomenal, and later on in Hollywood, his musical promoters were able to splice together bits of arias and other pieces to make him sound like a great opera star. But it was a bogus star, which glittered for some years like a supernova before going out forever. Today his name is not even recorded in most operatic textbooks or encyclopedias, and this is as it should be, for someone who cannot perform a role on stage has no right to be considered an opera singer.

Years later, when he was at the pinnacle of his fame, he came back to visit Tanglewood during another summer session. When the news was brought to me that "Mario Lanza is here, don't you want to see him?" I answered, "No. I don't want to have anything to do with him. He is not the kind of singer or person I even want to shake hands with."

*

Among the surprises that lay in store for me when Margaret and I moved to Boston in the autumn of 1942 was the presence in Cambridge of Nadia Boulanger. Scores of famous musicians had passed through her composition school at Fontainebleau, France, and now that she had sought refuge from the Nazis in America, Melville Smith had had the bright idea of inviting her to teach at the Longy School of Music.

I had once heard her speak in public before leaving Cleveland. To attend a talk given by this slender, alert, extremely vital lady, who was already a legend to musicians, was a real event, and I can still recall the sense of anticipation with which I waited for her to appear on the platform. The lecture that followed was dazzling, like a display of fireworks. She began with some general remarks about music and composers, dwelt for a moment on Rameau, then jumped to Brahms, moving on from him to Stravinsky (her favorite among the moderns). I listened with bated breath, thinking to myself: "Here is a real master! She is going to connect Rameau, Brahms, and Stravinsky in some marvelously new and illuminating way." Having done quite a bit of lecturing myself, I was by now familiar with the technique of building up interest and suspense. But to my surprise she mentioned another composer, devoted a few words to him, and then veered off in a totally different direction. The linking thread I had been eagerly expecting was never supplied, and the listeners were left with a series of disconnected strands of thought rather than with a closely woven and meaningful whole.

I was left wondering how a supremely gifted woman who had taught composition to so many successful musicians could be so lacking in a basic sense of organization, and precisely of the kind that composition requires. There is a mystery here I have never been able to fathom. For it is a fact, and not a mere prejudice, that whereas there have been great women writers and poets, there has never been a great woman composer — even though music is an art in which women have long been encouraged to excel.

Be that as it may, Nadia Boulanger was as gifted a musician as it was ever my good fortune to meet. Once again I owed this privilege to Melville Smith, who, shortly after I had started teaching at the Longy School, arranged a recital so that I could show off my keyboard talents as the new head of the piano department. I played all sorts of things, and after the recital Nadia Boulanger came up and was particularly warm in complimenting me on the way I had played Debussy. This praise, from such a legendary figure and a Frenchwoman to boot, did a great deal to reassure me in my new job, for I now felt myself "protected," as it were, by a truly superior authority.

This was the beginning of an informal association, based on the fact that both of us were pianists. I soon discovered the first of her great gifts. As a sight-reader, she was a match for Dohnányi. She could read the manuscript of a modern orchestral score she had never before seen and reproduce it on the piano with miraculous facility. No new style seemed too unfamiliar or complex to throw her off her incredibly sure stride.

I made the second discovery a little later, when she asked me to join her in a fund-raising concert in honor of her sister, the composer Lily Boulanger, who had died in 1918. She chose some four-hand pieces by Schubert, as well as a Stravinsky sonata for two pianos. It became apparent to me during our very first rehearsal that this woman had the most precise sense of time divisions I had ever encountered in a human being. I had long prided myself on my excellence in this field, but Nadia Boulanger was quite clearly my peer, for she was sensitive to fractions of time of which I was hardly aware. To keep up with her I had to remain on the qui vive and exercise a maximum alertness. It was both a thrilling and a challenging experience.

The third of her distinctions was an encyclopedic knowledge of music. She seemed to be at home with every style and to know all that was worth knowing about each and every one. She paraded this knowledge in the most stimulating way, giving one the impression that she knew everything. And the marvel of it was that it wasn't just an air, it was a fact. She did indeed know everything that was worth knowing, and she could impart it with a charm which kept it from being overpowering. No wonder so many musicians were delighted to study under her! She generated so much warmth and enthusiasm that one was prepared to forget and forgive everything — even the somewhat disconnected nature of her observations when she was on the lecture platform.

My relations with Serge Koussevitzky had by this time grown so cordial that I was granted the special privilege of calling him Dyadya Seryozha (Uncle Serge) whenever I was invited to his home on Buckminster Road in the Boston suburb of Brookline or when I went backstage after a concert at Symphony Hall to congratulate him on his latest performance. These pilgrimages to the green room, each marked by ceremonial Russian kisses on both cheeks and a gush of complimentary words about the glorious musical event just experienced, were part of the ritual one had to observe if one wished to remain in the good graces of Sergei Alexandrovich, for they were not events to be taken lightly. He was always careful to note just who was present, and he listened with an attentive ear to one's rapturous remarks. One had to say just the right thing for fear of offending this most sensitive of human beings — as my sister, Irene, once discovered to her cost at Tanglewood. After making the ritual visit at the end of a Thursday night concert, she returned two days later to hear him conduct the same program. Feeling particularly moved and, thinking to please him, she declared that what she had just heard was "the most beautiful concert I ever had the privilege of attending." To which Dyadya Seryozha replied in all seriousness: "And what was wrong with last Thursday's concert?"

At Tanglewood, Koussevitzky had been much impressed by my piano playing as well as by the little explanatory talks I would give when introducing some opera scene. In essence, these were outgrowths of the piano lectures I had given with such success to the members of the Women's Committee in Cleveland. Another person whom they impressed was Aaron Richmond, a most affable gentleman and one-time pianist who was now the undisputed managerial tsar for the entire region of New England. Since I was so adept at illustrating opera themes on the piano, why, he suggested, couldn't I do the same for the symphonic works that were played each week by the Boston Symphony Orchestra?

Thus were born the Symphony Luncheons, as they came to be known, which were very chic affairs, attended by some three hundred of the choicest and most blue-blooded Bostonians. The music-loving ladies and the well-groomed gentlemen (most of them retired bankers or businessmen) who could find time to attend would assemble in the Oval Room of the Copley Plaza at eleven-thirty, then proceed to eat lunch until one — at which point I would sit down at the piano and explain how and why Brahms, Schumann, Prokofieff, Stravinsky, or whoever it might be, had chosen to develop this or that theme in a particular manner in one of the works we were to hear that afternoon. The piano lecture was over around two o'clock, and we would all leave the hotel and flock over to nearby Symphony Hall on Huntington Avenue.

These Symphony Luncheons soon became so popular that I found myself being called upon to give lecture recitals even when the orchestra was away on tour. In March of 1943, for example, I decided to illustrate the development of piano literature through the ages by playing short pieces by Scarlatti, Bach, Mozart, Beethoven, Chopin, Liszt, Debussy, Scriabin, Bartók, and Balakireff. In the next day's issue of the *Boston Herald,* Rudolf Elie remarked that "as always, Mr. Goldovsky prefaced the performance of each composition with a few remarks as to its character, its treatment of the instrument, and its place in the scheme of things. As always, too, his ebullient asides and his ready wit enlivened the affair considerably. In short, his approach to the subject, although seemingly light (and certainly shocking to the Onward and Upward with the Arts school of thought), proves on closer analysis to be as sound as it is entertaining."

I have quoted these lines because they well describe the informal yet educational ambiance which used to reign at these Symphony Luncheons. On a later occasion, when the Boston Symphony Orchestra was out of town, I persuaded Margaret to join me for an all Brahms recital. I invented a program called "Invitation to the Waltz" at which I showed how that dance had developed from its origins in the late eighteenth century down to the present, and I did much the same, though on a smaller scale, with a program entitled "An Afternoon with Chopin" in which I began by playing his very first composition and ended up playing his very last to illustrate his evolution as a composer.

I also persuaded Mother to travel up from Philadelphia with her precious Stradivari violin, known as "The Nightingale," in order to prove to the distinguished dowagers from Beacon Hill and Commonwealth Avenue that women too can be superior instrumentalists. This mother-and-son recital stirred up a lot of interest in the local press, and at the end of our joint recital Lubo was approached by an eager young reporter, who began plying her with questions. Frank Sinatra had just made a dazzling breakthrough as America's latest crooning sensation, so inevitably the question was popped at her: "What do you think of Frank Sinatra?"

Lubo had never heard of Frank Sinatra. But thinking that the young interviewer was referring to one of her favorite violin and piano pieces — by César Franck — she replied, "Oh, I like the Franck sonata very much."

When the Boston Symphony's programs consisted of standard works, these piano lectures of mine required little preparation. But when new, unknown compositions were to be played, as was often the case with Koussevitzky, I was granted the rare privilege of being allowed to attend his rehearsals in Symphony Hall. I was always impressed by the workmanlike diligence with which he studied and rehearsed these new compositions, managing to communicate his own extraordinary enthusiasm to his instrumentalists, who thus gave young composers a chance to hear their works played under exceptionally favorable circumstances. Some of these composers were invited to participate in my Symphony Luncheons, and on such occasions I would vary the usual piano-playing routine by interviewing them for the benefit of the Oval Room luncheoners.

One of these guest composers was my old friend Samuel Barber, whom I had got to know when we were fellow students at the Curtis Institute. Some time after Pearl Harbor, Barber had been drafted into the army, made a corporal, and assigned the brain-numbing task of collating the pages of U.S. Army songbooks and band parts. He might have eked out his military career in total obscurity but for Dmitri Shostakovich in distant Russia, who celebrated the heroic defense of Leningrad against the besieging Germans by dedicating his latest symphony — the Seventh — to the great imperial city. Galvanized by this distant musical challenge, some enterprising U.S. Air Force colonel decided that what a Rooskie could do for Leningrad, one of Uncle Sam's warrior-musicians could do even better. Barber, already blessed with the auspicious name of Sam, was accordingly singled out, told to abandon his collating activities, promoted to the rank of sergeant, and ordered to compose a heroic symphony extolling the glories and achievements of the U.S. Air Force.

The colonel in charge of this particular project decided to take no chances. To make sure that the composition was truly "realistic" in its inspiration, he had Barber taken aloft in different bombers and fighter planes, some of which went into dizzying gyrations just to give the sergeant-composer a "real-life feel" of what it was like to be a pilot. He was made to listen to different engine whines and to the chattering of Morse code and other communications devices in the hope that these sonorous experiences would help him develop the right kind of descriptive music for his "Air Force Symphony." Unfortunately for all concerned, Barber's modern style of composition was not of the programmatic type, but this embarrassing fact was quietly kicked under the rug. He had been promoted to the rank of sergeant, and this was his chance to prove that he had really earned that extra stripe.

Sam first tried to convince the commanding officer that the symphony's opening theme was inspired by the sweep of an airplane's wings, but the officer found this interpretation a bit too glib. Barber then decided to weave a plane's radio signal into the basic pattern of the symphony's slow movement. The colonel was charmed by the suggestion, and since there was no point in doing things halfway, he ordered the Bell Telephone Laboratories to build a special instrument which could be tuned to any desired pitch and intensity.

Sam told me all this while we sat in the balcony of Symphony Hall listening to Koussevitzky rehearse the first movement of his symphony. "But I am deathly afraid that Koussevitzky will refuse to use the new instrument, and if he throws it out, it will be no joking matter for me. Unless that signal plays on that gadget, my military career is going to take a very sinister turn."

"But what makes you think that Koussie is going to dislike this machine?"

"Well, you know how it is," said Sam. "Stokowski is crazy about these new-fangled gadgets, and since one conductor's electronics are another conductor's poison, I have reason to fear the worst."

Having finished the first movement, Koussevitzky launched into the second. After a few introductory measures we heard the *peep-pe-pe-peep* of the radio signal. Koussevitzky stopped, frowned, started to say something, then glanced at the clock and announced that it was time for an intermission.

We immediately repaired to his dressing room, where Uncle

Serge was being helped into a dry shirt by his faithful valet, Victor.

"You know," I said, wishing to broach the subject gently, "this new instrument has a very interesting sound. It is sort of . . . in-human. No, that's not the right word. Maybe — fleshless."

"No, no, not 'inhuman,' not 'fleshless.' I know what you mean," said Koussevitzky. He was inordinately fond of words, and one could usually quicken his interest by searching for the *mot juste*. "Not 'inhuman' — no, no, you mean . . . *abstrahct*. Of course, that is what is wrong with it! The sound should be more *abstrahct*. Listen, Barber," he added, getting quite excited, "we must make it more *abstrahct*."

Sam was delighted. He didn't care how abstract the gadget was made to sound provided it remained in the orchestra in the full solidity of its Bell Telephone metal box.

"Barber, why did you mark it mezzo-forte?" Koussevitzky asked. "Go down quickly and tell the man to play it pianissimo. Find out how to adjust it to pianissimo. Make it *abstrahct*, as *abstrahct* as possible!" That was his way. He loved nothing better than to tell young composers how to annotate and improve their music.

We hurried to the stage to examine the signal machine's abstract possibilities. It was calibrated from 0 to 100. At 80 it was quite loud, at 25 or 30 barely audible. Barber finally set it at 40. If played any softer, the air force colonel who was going to attend the performance might have difficulty hearing it clearly.

The rehearsal resumed. Koussevitzky began the second movement again, listened to the signal motif, and then stopped the orchestra to ask the percussion player: "You marked it pianissimo, yes?"

"Yes, sir," replied the player. "It's right on forty."

"Not forte," said Koussevitsky. "It was forte before, but now I want it pianissimo."

"Yes, sir," repeated the signal player. "Mr. Barber has changed it to forty, just as you asked."

"But don't you understand?" said Koussevitzky, beginning to lose his calm. "I do not want it played forte!"

"But Mr. Barber came down during the intermission and said you wanted it set at forty."

"Who is running this *orchestre?*" asked Koussevitzky, his face getting redder by the second. "Mr. Barber or me? And I am telling you I do not want it played forte!"

By this time I was running down the steps to the stage. I reached it in time to be able to whisper furiously into the percussion player's ear, "Set it at thirty-five and keep still, for heaven's sake!"

We had almost lost a member of the Boston Symphony while trying to save the Bell Laboratories machine and Barber's army career.

There was, I might add, an amusing postlude to this incident when Sam came to the Symphony Luncheon at the Copley Plaza on the following Friday to be interviewed about his new symphony. Among the guests was the wife of a four-star general. Pleased to see that Barber was in military uniform, she asked to meet him. I escorted Sam over to her table and introduced him: "Madam, it gives me great pleasure to present to you Samuel Barber."

"Sergeant," she addressed him in a condescending tone, "we are delighted that we are going to hear this music of yours. But tell me, sergeant, had you studied music earlier or did you pick it up in the army?"

Sergeant Samuel Barber managed to hold his sharp tongue, but it was all I could do to keep from guffawing.

Although these Symphony Luncheons were beginning to turn me into a local celebrity, I was quite unknown in New York City when, in the spring of 1944, the Metropolitan Opera Company made one of its annual visits to Boston. To liven things up during the Saturday afternoon broadcasts, the producers of the intermission period were now going in for opera quizzes, and it was their practice when on tour to add a "local boy" to the panel as a kind of courtesy gesture. So a letter was sent to Wallace Goodrich, asking if he could recommend anybody in Boston who knew enough to take part in the opera quiz during the Met's stay in Boston. Goodrich himself had done some opera conducting, even though he no longer headed the New England Conservatory of Music, but he volunteered my name.

Shortly afterward I received a letter from the Souvaine Agency in New York asking me if I would be willing to participate in the intermission quiz program, which was to take place during the Saturday afternoon perfromance in Boston. The fee, if I was willing, was $50, and I was also invited to join the other quiz experts for lunch before the performance at the Ritz-Carlton Hotel on Arlington Street.

When I turned up at the Ritz dining room at the appointed hour, I was ushered over to a table where a number of important-looking gentlemen were engaged in an animated conversation with a most attractive blond lady.

"Ah, Mr. Goldovsky," said one of the gentlemen, rising to greet me. "Allow me to introduce you to my wife, Mrs. Geraldine Souvaine." She extended an exquisitely manicured hand and gave me a condescending smile. I was next introduced to Olin Downes, the well-known *New York Times* music critic who was to act as quizmaster, to a tall, portly gentleman named Sigmund Spaeth, and to two other opera experts who were taking part in the quiz.

After I had given my order to the waiter, I sat there feeling out of place. The others continued chatting about this and that, enjoying their carefully cultivated "in" jokes, which were quite beyond my depth. Knowing my place, I kept my mouth shut. I was the local yokel, and, this being the case, the best thing to do was to be as quiet as a church mouse.

After luncheon, we were driven to the opera house and ushered into a specially reserved box. Toward the end of the first act, we were led to the room where the broadcast quiz was to be held. Here I was invited to take a seat next to the other opera experts, who didn't imagine that there would be much competition.

Picking up a card from a small stack in front of him, Olin Downes read off the first question before turning the card over to look at the answer written on the back. He had hardly finished the question when Sigmund Spaeth's arm shot up.

"Yes, Mr. Spaeth?" said Olin Downes, and back came the answer.

I don't recall the first questions and answers on this particular Saturday afternoon, but I do remember my first intervention very well. The question was: "Who was the opera composer whose father was a trumpeter?"

Once again Sigmund Spaeth's hand was in the air before any of us could open our mouths. Olin Downes gave him the nod, and back came the answer: "Robert Schumann."

"Mr. Spaeth," I said, "I am afraid you are mistaken. It was Rossini's father who was a trumpeter. Schumann's father was a bookseller."

This must have been one of my red-letter days, for Spaeth, in his eagerness to get in his answer first, made several other blunders, which I was able to correct. I even answered a couple of questions which had everyone else stumped.

Suddenly I was somebody. I was no longer the tongue-tied hick whose presence had been tolerated at the luncheon table.

Several weeks later I received a letter from Henry Souvaine, who ran the advertising outfit that handled the Met intermission, asking me how often I could come to New York to take part in the Saturday afternoon opera quizzes during the Met's next season. I was soon a regular participant. My knowledge was apparently impressive, though personally I could see nothing particularly extraordinary in being able to answer questions which I had been asking my various opera students for the past twelve years.

At the end of my first season on the quiz panel, I received a telephone call from the Souvaine Agency. Henry Souvaine wanted me to come down to New York to talk over a new project. "This is a brand new idea and I have a hunch it could be terrific. I want you to take charge of the first intermission of each Saturday broadcast. You will act as a master of ceremonies, discuss the opera of the day with various guests, and illustrate the music on the piano. Think it over, and then we'll decide on the price we should ask Texaco for such a project." This unexpected offer set my head reeling. Having listened fairly regularly to the Saturday broadcasts, I was aware of the importance attached to these first intermissions. During my Cleveland days, I had heard talks from the Met given by ex-president Hoover, Carl Sandburg, Walt Disney, and the Nobel Prize winner Robert Millikan. Later, these first intermissions become known as Opera Victory Rallies and featured an amazing array of world-famous personalities including Mayor Fiorello La Guardia, Eleanor Roosevelt, Jan Masaryk, and Archibald MacLeish. To replace these luminaries on a regular basis was a dizzying prospect.

It seems that the idea of devoting the first intermissions to a musical and dramatic analysis of the opera of the day, came from Henry Souvaine's wife, Geraldine. Some ten years earlier she had heard a program given at the Italian Club of Columbia University, where the eminent conductor Tullio Serafin, assisted by Rosa Ponselle and Ezio Pinza, talked about Mozart's *Don Giovanni*. Having, at some gathering or other, heard me play the piano, Geraldine Souvaine became convinced that I could handle a presentation of a similar type.

All this I did not learn until much later. In the meantime, I had to decide what fee I should ask for a job which, I knew, would give me an extraordinary amount of national exposure.

Before taking the "Night Owl," which was to put me in New

York in the early hours of the morning, I rang up Uncle Pierre and said I had to see him about an important matter. In Manhattan I took a cab to the apartment house where he and Aunt Genia lived. Their welcome, as usual, was wonderfully warm.

"So you're going to make a radio career?" said Uncle Pierre, after I had told him of Henry Souvaine's idea. "How perfectly wonderful! Wonderful! But tell me, how much are you going to charge them?"

I named a figure, and he looked appalled.

"You're crazy!" he said. "Completely crazy! Out of your mind! Why you should ask for at least twice that much!"

"So you want me to lose this job, you want me to ruin this opportunity?"

"Well, if that's the way you feel about it, do as you wish," said Uncle Pierre. "Don't let me interfere. Only I'm telling you that you're out of your mind. You should be asking double that amount."

That afternoon I went to call on Henry Souvaine. It was always a pleasure to meet with him, for he was a live wire, forever brimming over with exciting new ideas and projects. As the minutes went by both of us got more and more excited by this idea of a one-man intermission program, during which I would do what I had done for the Women's Committee in Cleveland and, in a slightly different form, at the Symphony Luncheons in Boston: talk about the opera being performed at the Met, illustrating it musically on the piano.

"So you like the idea?" he finally said. "That's great, great! It's going to be a knockout, I tell you. Now what do you think? How much should we charge Texaco?"

I took a deep breath and quoted the figure Uncle Pierre had recommended. There was a long moment of silence. Now that I had thrown caution to the winds, what the hell, I might as well go the whole hog. "Plus," I added, "round-trip transportation from Boston."

"Well," said Henry Souvaine, finally breaking his silence, "you know, that's what I always tell my sponsors: 'If you want first-class talent, you have to pay first-class money!' "

This phrase too has remained engraved on my memory. Until then, I had had my doubts. But now I knew for sure that I was really first-class talent.

⁓(9)⁓

Two Mozart Triumphs

IN 1944, in the very middle of the war, Margaret and I acquired a gabled house on Clinton Road, in Brookline, only a couple of blocks from Serge Koussevitzky's home. Behind this three-story house is a small sloping garden which we often show to visitors, saying proudly, "Where you see those poplars, there once stood a gallows, the same gallows that Verdi introduced into the second act of *Un Ballo in Maschera.* And under those gallows, strange herbs used to grow, and it was right here, in what is now our garden, that Amelia, the wife of the Governor's friend Renato, came to pick the mandrake root that was to help her forget her guilty love for the Governor."

"You don't say?" our visitors usually exclaim with obvious disbelief, until, going to the shelves of the music library, which fill the house from top to bottom, I pull out the score of Verdi's opera and point to the scenic indication: "A lonely field, on the outskirts of Boston, at the foot of a steep hill," and then show them the soothsayer Ulrica's description: "to the west of the city, where the pale moon strikes the barren field."

The truth, of course, is that Verdi's opera was based on a libretto written in 1832 by Eugène Scribe for Daniel Auber. It deals with the eighteenth-century Swedish king Gustavus III, who was shot to death during a masquerade ball held at the Royal

Opera House in Stockholm. Verdi, using an Italian version of Scribe's libretto, composed his opera in the fall of 1857, and as ill luck would have it, the rehearsals got under way in January of 1858 — the very month in which an Italian revolutionary named Felice Orsini tried to assassinate Napoleon III with an "infernal machine," which killed ten people and wounded 150 others, though the Emperor himself escaped unscathed. Under the circumstances the Neapolitan censor refused to clear Verdi's work in its original form. The composer was told that the story might be interpreted as an "encouragement to regicide," and to get around this veto, Verdi was forced to shift the scene of action from the Royal Court in Stockholm to the remote and more plebeian Governor's mansion in seventeenth-century Boston. Which is why, in the opera's second act, Amelia finds herself several miles to the west of Boston — which means in Brookline — looking for a magic herb under the gallows, which, by a process of logical deduction, Margaret and I figured must once have stood at the bottom of our little garden.

For this and other reasons too, *Un Ballo in Maschera* has long been one of my favorite Verdi operas. It was thus with considerable anticipation that, in December 1945, I traveled down to New York on one of my Metropolitan broadcast trips to watch Bruno Walter conduct it.

If there is one word that really fits Bruno Walter, it is "charm." He was the personification of Viennese graciousness; it permeated and embellished all of his musical performances, overlaying them with a kind of venerable, impalpable patina. It was thus a shock for me to see the curtain of the Metropolitan Opera rise at the start of the second act on a moonlit stage adorned by several tall poles, which looked more like limbless trees than gallows. I was even more surprised to see the Yugoslav soprano Zinka Milanov, who was singing the role of Amelia, make not the slightest attempt to stoop under the gallows and look for the magic herb which Ulrica had instructed her to pick. I heard her sing these tremulous lines with her eyes glued to Bruno Walter's stoop-shouldered form, as though he were the cause of her sudden fright:

> *Mezzanotte! Ah! che veggio?*
> *Una testa di sotterra si leva . . .*
> *e sospira!*
> *Ha negli occhi il baleno dell'ira*
> *e m'affisa e m'affisa*
> *e terribile sta!*
>
> (Midnight! Ah, what do I see?
> A head rises from the ground
> And it sighs!
> It has the flash of wrath in its eyes,
> And it stares at me, and stares at me,
> And it is terrifying!)

Verdi's music could not be more explicit. Distant church bells, accompanied by a shuddering tremolo in the cellos and basses, indicate that it is midnight. Then, as Amelia comes upon the skull, lying under the gallows, and sees its empty eye sockets staring at her, the entire orchestra erupts into a poignantly descriptive tumult — with shudders, gasps, and descending chromatics in the strings, eerie pipings in the flutes, and somber tremolos in the kettledrums. But on the Metropolitan Opera stage there was no skull to be seen, so the horror so vividly described in Verdi's music and the lines Zinka Milanov sang referred to some nonpresent, invisible entity. In short, the action on the stage had nothing whatsoever to do with the music, with the result that it reduced all three of opera's vital elements — the sung words, the dramatic action, and the orchestral music — to total meaninglessness.

One may well ask how Bruno Walter, a skilled, sensitive, sophisticated artist, could preside over this disgraceful spectacle. The answer is that matters pertaining to dramatic action were not part of his responsibilities. It was his job to direct and supervise all musical nuances on stage and in the pit, and to keep singers and orchestra together; it was not part of his duties to see to it that the singers acted sensibly. That was the stage director's function.

Instinctively, I had always deplored this lamentable dichotomy, this often flagrant contradiction between what the words and the music were trying to express and what the singers were actually doing on stage. Ernst Lert too had deplored it, and ever since the summer of 1936, when he had given me those eye-opening lessons, I had decided that if there was one contribution I could make to the field of opera it was to try to bridge the yawning chasm which so often separates the conductor's from the stage director's realm.

In Cleveland this had been no problem. I had been forced to supervise the dramatic side of my productions because Beryl Rubinstein could not afford to hire a professional stage director. I was thus in every sense the boss and could personally see to it that music, voices, gestures, and action all fitted harmoniously and intelligently together. But during those first summers at Tanglewood when I was Herbert Graf's musical assistant I could not develop much enthusiasm for his system of dramatic instruction in which the singers were asked to "express" themselves in a rather vague, undefined manner.

Koussevitzky, whose theatrical ideas had been strongly influenced by his Moscow friend Konstantin Stanislavsky, soon became disenchanted with Graf's work. "He talks big," Koussevitzky told me at one point, "but the results are mediocre." And so, at the end of the second Tanglewood summer, I was summoned to Sergei Alexandrovich's office and informed that Dr. Graf would not be reengaged for the summer of 1942 and that I was to take over. I had to tell Koussevitzky that this was out of the question. His face flushed red and the telltale vein began throbbing on his forehead, for he could not bear to have anyone dispute and disobey his decisions.

"What do you mean you are not going to accept this job?" he exclaimed. "How dare you? And why not?"

"Dr. Koussevitzky, I am very sorry," I said. "But I was brought here on the recommendation of Dr. Graf, and I am not going to take his place. Because it will look before all the world as though I had intrigued against him."

Koussie's anger died down as swiftly as it had risen. Grudgingly he swallowed my refusal, and Graf was not fired.

In the winter of 1945–1946 we began making plans for the following summer, when the Berkshire Music Center was due to reopen after a wartime lapse of three years. Aided by the generous stipend he had received from the Koussevitzky Foundation, the English composer Benjamin Britten had dedicated his opera, *Peter Grimes,* to the memory of Natalya Koussevitzky. Its London première in 1945 had moved critics to hail it as a masterpiece, and Koussevitzky, who had long taken an almost paternal interest in the young composer — one of his many gifted *Kinder* — was determined to have its first American performance occur at Tanglewood.

The preparations were already far advanced when he was informed that Dr. Herbert Graf would be unable to take part in the summer session, because he had been asked to go to Hollywood to help produce a film involving opera. Koussevitzky hit the roof. He demanded absolute loyalty of all those who had the privilege of working under him, and this for him was an act of betrayal.

There was a stormy scene with Graf's manager, who claimed that his client had not broken his word since no contract had been signed. Shortly afterward I was summoned to Sergei Alexandrovich's house on Buckminster Road and informed that Graf, who had run out on him in the most despicable manner, would never work for him again. "You see what happened? Graf himself quit. Now will you be head of the department?"

"Ah," I said, "that's different. If Graf walked out on you, I can take his place. But not if you fired him."

So I was appointed head of the opera department of the Berkshire Music Center, a post I was to hold for the next sixteen years.

The main trouble with Herbert Graf — one which persists with stage directors to this day — is that he had never worked with singers who had mastered the fundamentals of stage behavior. Thorough dramatic training is something that opera singers should acquire when still relatively young, for by the time they move to stardom it is already too late. They become set in their ways and develop postures and attitudes which cannot be easily changed.

Three or four years after Koussevitzky's run-in with Herbert Graf, I was asked by the Columbia Broadcasting System to direct the first big television opera ever presented to an American audience. The opera chosen was Bizet's *Carmen,* specially trimmed to ninety minutes to make it acceptable to a nationwide TV public. I was given first-rate singers to work with — including the famous mezzo-soprano Gladys Swarthout as Carmen and the baritone Robert Merrill for the role of Escamillo.

Though she was a bit beyond her prime, Gladys Swarthout was still very beautiful and had exactly the right kind of expressive face for the role of the fiery gypsy. I guided her step by step, seeing to it that her every move and gesture would be perfectly coordinated with the music. She grew increasingly excited as we went along, for she had never been exposed to this kind of drill before. But because it was all so new to her, she had a lot of trouble assimilating the new ideas and coordinating them with the music. I had a particularly difficult task in the smugglers' cave scene of the third act, when I was teaching her how to turn up the fortune-telling cards (announcing her impending death) in precise time with the long, premonitory notes played by the trombone, clarinet, and oboe. We had to practice the scene over and over until she could do it correctly. But it cost her such an effort that she finally broke down and wept: "My God, if only I had known you when I was a young girl!"

As a rule, I have been fortunate in being able to work with singers whom I have personally trained. Graf, on the other hand, suffered from the terrible impediment most stage directors encounter when they find themselves dealing with operatic stars, or what the French call *monstres sacrés*. Many of these singers are endowed with magnificent voices but are too busy and "self-important" to bother with unfamiliar dramatic ideas, and because they have to be handled with kid gloves, they end up doing exactly what they please. I had seen it happen with Fritz Reiner, who did not suffer fools gladly, but who nevertheless had to swallow Emanuel List's poor musicianship simply because there was no one else around to replace him.

Some years ago, after I had founded my own touring opera company, we put on a particularly successful performance of Mozart's *Don Giovanni* in Shreveport, Louisiana. People came from near and far to see it. Quite a few were thrilled and returned home with glowing accounts of the production. Among them were several board members of a well-known provincial theater. They went to see its director, saying: "We've just seen Goldovsky's *Don Giovanni,* and it's wonderful. Now listen, you're planning to put on this opera here next season, aren't you? So why don't you ask Goldovsky to come here and stage it?"

"Say, that's not a bad idea," said the director. "He's a good man. Sure, I'll call him."

I was at home in Brookline when the long-distance call came through. "Boris," said the director, "I understand you have a fine *Don Giovanni* production. Why don't you come out and stage it here for us next fall?"

"Well," I said, "but when exactly?"

I was given a date in November. I checked my calendar and saw that I had two weeks free in that month.

"This is wonderful," I said. "I think I can do it. Now tell me — who is going to be in the cast?"

The director reeled off an extraordinary list of names, including some of the best-known singers in the world. They would sing in Italian, so there would be no problem with a translation.

Wow! I thought to myself. This was quite a challenge. It would offer me a rare chance to transmit my ideas to a group of really brilliant professionals who were intimately familiar with the music of this opera.

There was only one hitch, the director told me. "We don't have much time available for rehearsals. How many hours do you think you'd need to put it all together?"

"Oh, that should not be too much of a problem," I answered. "I've done it recently and I know every inch and every whisker of *Don Giovanni*. I can tell you exactly: not counting the dress rehearsal, I can manage it in twenty-eight hours."

"Okay, Boris. I think this is going to work out. I'll ring you back tomorrow."

The director phoned me the next day and announced in an excited voice, "I have good news for you. I've put it all together and, believe it or not, I can give you thirty-five hours of rehearsal time."

"Say, that's great!"

"Now, do you have a pencil handy?"

"Sure," I said, "but why?"

"Because you must write down how it is all going to be allocated."

"Okay," I said, "I'm listening."

"Well, to begin with, you can have nineteen hours with the Commendatore."

That brought me up with a start. The Commendatore comes in for exactly five minutes near the beginning of *Don Giovanni* and doesn't sing again until the final two scenes, when he appears as a virtually motionless statue. What I was to do with the seventeen or eighteen spare hours that would be left over after I had spent an hour on the Commendatore, I had no idea. Since the other singers would not be available during that time, according to the director's breakdown, I could have two hours or so with Masetto and maybe an hour with Zerlina. Don Giovanni, himself, however, was terribly tied up with other engagements, so I couldn't see him until the very end. And since the bass who was to play the part of Leporello was also unavailable, I couldn't have him and the Don together until the day of the dress rehearsal.

"Listen, my dear friend," I said, after I had noted it all down, "you don't need a stage director. As a matter of fact, I advise you not to hire anyone for this job. These singers know their business. They've performed in this opera dozens of times. What you really need is a janitor."

"A janitor! Now, Boris, what is this? You're joking?"

"No, I'm not joking. I mean just that. You need someone to show the singers which doors they should use to come on and off the stage. They know this opera backwards and forwards, and the only thing they aren't familiar with is the scenery you're going to use. Show it to them. But otherwise, don't annoy them by imposing upon them unfamiliar ideas. Just leave them to their own devices. Believe me, they'll be a lot happier that way."

One of the troubles with opera productions, as I had learned early on in the game, is that there is no one really in charge. The conductor is allowed to lead the orchestra, but that is about all he is permitted to do. He may request certain singers, but he won't necessarily get them, and he may end up with substitutes about whom he knows less than nothing. He does not choose the scenic designer or the costumer, as these belong to the realm of the stage director, with whom the conductor may or may not get along. The stage director, as often as not, lacks the musical expertise to do justice to the composer's intentions, and so, to build up his own prestige and to demonstrate his originality, he resorts to gimmicks.

A good deal of what passes today for "ingenious stage directing" is, in fact, nothing more than gimmickry run riot. I once saw a performance of Béla Bartók's *Bluebeard's Castle* in which the composer's "jewelry music" — with the glitter of gold and gems vividly suggested by the use of harps, celesta, muted trumpets, French horns, and a solo violin — was not illustrated on the stage by a display of the husband-murderer's prized possessions, since treasure chambers and that sort of thing are terribly old hat. Instead, the evil man's wealth was represented by towering edifices and skyscrapers, whose looming bulk on the thoroughly scenic sets contradicted Bartók's music.

Not long ago, in Chicago, I witnessed a dress rehearsal of *The Tales of Hoffmann* in which a full-sized locomotive was placed on the stage and two obtrusive elevators were evident at either side. Many such gimmicks come and go as passing fads. At one time, it was a passion for platforms and steps, cluttering the boards and impeding normal stage movement. At another time it was a predilection for mirrors. I remember a performance of Mozart's *Idomeneo* in Vienna, where the ceiling was composed of reflectors, slanted in such a way that everything that happened on the floor of the stage was repeated in reverse on the ceiling. And since very little was happening in either place, the combination was quite amazing.

The Italians are apt to become upset if the operas they go to see don't contain some kind of dramatic "event" or "happening." So the stage directors clutch at any kind of trickery to jazz up their productions. In Palermo I witnessed a performance of Rossini's hilarious (and far too little known) *Le Comte Ory,* in which a beggar was brought in on crutches during the peasants' scene in the first act and made to fall down so that he could be lifted up again, though this sensational "event" was in no way related to either the story or the music. In Milan's La Scala, I was astonished to behold a high, fairy-tale-like tower, which the stage designer had constructed above Juliet's bed in Bellini's *I Capuletti ed i Montecchi.* Shortly before the duet which Romeo and Juliet were to sing, Romeo appeared at the top of the tower, and while the snare drum in the orchestra rattled away, he clambered down the overhanging tower and scooted to the ground like a squirrel. Once on the stage floor, he never looked at Juliet, preferring to move over to one side of the stage while she remained on her own side. A more absurd "love duet" it would have been impossible to conceive, but the spectators were satisfied; they had been treated to a bit of athletic drama.

In Rome, however, I saw something even more spectacular. In the final scene of this same opera, Romeo, or more exactly somebody dressed to look like him, came sliding, like a circus gymnast, hand over hand, down a rope strung from a crossbeamed ceiling. Once on the ground he darted behind a column so that the real Romeo could come out and sing, "Oh, there she lies amid the flowers and the roses and the grass," etc. Of flowers, roses, and grass there was not so much as a blade or a bud to be seen, since Juliet lay on the cold concrete. But here too the spectators were happy, because they had witnessed a kind of *salto mortale*.

One of the latest absurdities consists of illuminating the actors from below by means of floodlights placed under the stage floor, which is fashioned out of aluminum mesh — a technique of lighting which reverses the usual shadow lines in the faces of the actors. Some stage directors like to jazz up their productions with pornographic touches. In a fairly recent production of *La Bohème,* Marcello is shown in the opening scene painting a nude. In a freezing attic on Christmas Eve the model stands with her back to the audience so that the spectators can enjoy the sight of her rosy buttocks, while the two Bohemians on stage shiver in their winter clothing.

I could extend the list, almost ad infinitum. One of my former students, who was engaged to sing the role of Musetta in the Covent Garden production of *La Bohème,* was made to run up a flight of steps to the second floor of the Café Momus, where there was a billiard table. She was directed to turn her back to the audience and, while the harp was plucking the three introductory notes, to hit three separate billiard balls in time with the music and then quickly whirl around to start her waltz song. This is how young singers who are making their debuts are often treated by stage directors who are only interested in flaunting their extraordinary ingenuity. Is it surprising that so many of them make a poor impression on such occasions?

As for the mass invasion of contemptible buffoonery which recently invaded Bayreuth, the less said about it the better. But Wagner, who had the clearest possible idea of what one should or should not do on a stage, must be squirming in his grave.

From the very start of my operatic activities in Cleveland I had been fascinated by the way in which music and drama influence each other. The conclusion I soon reached was that if something in the published scores did not seem to make sense, it was most probably the accidental result of some unusual and unfavorable conditions existing at the time the opera was written rather than a careless "lapse" on the part of the composer.

Not long after the grotesque *Ballo in Maschera* scene I had witnessed in New York, I happened to have a long conversation with Fausto Cleva, one of the most brilliant opera conductors of that time. During the Metropolitan's coming season he was going to conduct Gounod's *Faust.* I told him how puzzled I had long been as to why the *"Dies Irae"* hymn in the church scene was always sung in French rather than in Latin. He had never thought about it, but he agreed that it was distinctly odd and not at all in accordance with Roman Catholic usage. Another thing that had puzzled me, I went on, was why this "Requiem" was not sung at the funeral of Marguerite's brother, Valentin, rather than for nobody in particular, as was the case in all the performances of the opera I had ever seen.

"But that would not be possible," objected Cleva. "Valentin is still alive — he is killed only in the episode that follows the church scene."

"That's just it," I said. "Wouldn't it be more sensible to reverse the order of these events and end the third act with the 'Requiem' scene?"

"Bravo!" exclaimed Cleva in a sudden burst of enthusiasm. "These are excellent ideas. And you know what — I'm going to have these changes made when I conduct *Faust* next season."

I was consequently much surprised, several months later, when I went to see his production. Everything was being done in the conventional, time-honored manner. The *"Dies Irae"* was still sung in French and Valentin still died in the following scene.

"What happened?" I asked Cleva after the performance. "Didn't you want to make those changes?"

"I did indeed," he replied. "I pleaded with the management to let me do so, but to no avail. I was told not to rock the boat. Extra rehearsals would have been required to teach the Latin words to the choristers, and, so it was explained to me, Valentin's death, with the entire cast on stage, provided a more effective ending for the third act."

Bruno Walter too must have discovered, early on in his career, that in trying to change traditional habits or in finding fault with dramatic actions, one only makes oneself unpopular with singers, stage directors, and the management. So he — along with other conductors — simply closed his eyes and minded his business. But my eyes had been opened — by Ernst Lert — and I refused to close them. Being both conductor and stage director, I was not afraid to rock the boat. In the case of *Faust* I became convinced that the substitution of French for Latin in the *"Dies Irae"* and the absence of the slain Valentin in the church scene were both due to the fact that the Catholic church authorities in midnineteenth-century France frowned on stage representations of religious rituals. Such strictures do not exist in the United States, and it is thus possible, and in my opinion most desirable, to change the traditional procedures.

The close scrutiny to which I subjected opera scores led me eventually to some interesting "finds." In the third act of *Carmen,* for example, I noticed that the toreador Escamillo mentions two fights with Don José though there is only one fighting sequence in the score. The mystery was cleared up when I finally obtained a microfilm of Bizet's original manuscript from the Bibliothèque Nationale in Paris and discovered that some forty pages of that priceless score had been cut out in the printed edition. The restoration of this amputated music added a most exciting second encounter between the bullfighter and Don José.

Already in Philadelphia, when I was helping Margaret to prepare the role of Cherubino for Reiner's production of *The Marriage of Figaro,* I had been struck by the fact that the page boy participates in almost none of the opera's many ensemble scenes. In fact, he has only one tiny duettino in the second act, and here his total singing time is less than thirty seconds. I eventually found an explanation for Mozart's peculiar treatment of this important role in the memoirs of Michael O'Kelly, the voluble Irishman who doubled in the roles of Don Basilio and Don Curzio under the composer's own direction. O'Kelly describes in detail the difficulties Mozart encountered in 1786 in casting the première of *Le Nozze di Figaro.* The Italian company in Vienna had only three female singers, while the opera required five. The girl who was eventually entrusted with the role of Cherubino was Sardi Bussani, the stage manager's wife. Though she possessed a sweet singing voice, she was basically an actress, who had had no previous training in music. She could thus be taught the simple melodies of the solo sections, but — as is not unusual with beginners — she was incapable of handling the middle lines in passages where another singer carried the upper voice. Here too was the explanation for another anomaly: why, during the wedding ceremony of the third act, Mozart entrusted the charming "glorification" duet to two girls who have no intrinsic connection with the plot. Since nowadays no Cherubino suffers from Sardi Bussani's shortcomings, it is infinitely more appropriate to have this duettino sung by Barbarina and Cherubino. It justifies the guffawing, which is so charmingly illustrated by the orchestra, not to mention other musical and dramatic advantages which result from this simple and logical reorganization of the score.

As an educator of young singers I then felt (and still feel today) that a detailed analysis and careful acting out of short sections of standard operas is the best method for learning the fundamentals of stage technique. My dedication to this "workshop" style of study led me, during the winter of 1945–1946, to the most serious disagreement I ever had with Koussevitzky. For the reopening of the Berkshire Music Center he wanted something more spectacular and ambitious than the relatively well known *Acis and Galatea* (Handel), *Così fan tutte* (Mozart), and *The Merry Wives of Windsor* (Nicolai), with which we had launched the opera department at Tanglewood in the early 1940s. Benjamin Britten's *Peter Grimes,* which had been commissioned by the Koussevitzky Music Foundation, was obviously the perfect choice. I had, however, lost all desire to conduct any of Graf's opera productions after seeing several examples of his shoddy workmanship at the Met in New York. I therefore suggested to Sergei Alexandrovich that the opera department be reorganized. Graf would remain in charge and be responsible for the major productions, while I would work independently with a different group of singers in a workshop program based on scenes from standard operas. Somewhat reluctantly Koussevitzky agreed to let Graf choose the singers for the *Peter Grimes* production, while I recruited others for my workshop. He also accepted my suggestion that Britten's opera be conducted by Leonard Bernstein, a brilliantly gifted symphonic conductor and the favorite of Koussie's many *Kinder.*

By the middle of May I had selected all of my workshop students and assigned them the roles they were to have memorized by the beginning of July. But two weeks before the summer school was due to open, Koussevitzky informed me of Herbert Graf's sudden "desertion." He expected me to take over as head of the opera department. "You will immediately embark on the task of organizing and staging the performance of *Peter Grimes,*" he told me in tones that brooked no contradiction.

"Please don't ask me to do this, Sergei Alexandrovich," I said. "To begin with, I have not even seen the score of the new opera — "

"Don't be ridiculous," he interrupted, "you will have plenty of time to familiarize yourself with the opera, and by the time the singers learn the music, you will — "

"No, I will not," I insisted. "I have chosen twenty singers who have all received assignments. Were I to prepare a complicated modern work, I would have to spend so much time and effort that I would neglect those young singers who are counting on me to instruct them. So I have to say no. But there must be some other way of solving the *Peter Grimes* problem."

Koussevitzky was furious, and he would almost certainly have fired me on the spot had he not needed my help to get him out of an awkward predicament. He eventually agreed to my suggestion that Eric Crozier, who had directed the London première, be brought over to take Graf's place, and that, for the preparatory training of the singers, we should engage Fritz Cohen, whose opera department at the Juilliard School of Music in New York was highly praised by many experts.

And so it came to pass. Leonard Bernstein proved more than equal to the task. Unfortunately, in his youthful zeal, he insisted that everyone should sing and play with full intensity during all of the rehearsals. This worked well with the instrumentalists, but it had a devastating effect on the two tenors who had to alternate in the exacting leading roles. William Horne and Joseph Laderoute had so forced their voices during the weeks of preparation that in the two actual performances they could hardly croak their topmost tones. The opera nevertheless was widely acclaimed, and Koussevitzky was so overjoyed by the new work's success that he declared to everyone that *Peter Grimes* was the greatest opera since Bizet's *Carmen*.

Ever since our successful production of Mozart's *Così fan tutte* at the end of our second Tanglewood season, my conscience had been troubled by the same problem that had cropped up in Cleveland. I felt I had no right to train exceptionally gifted people to become outstanding artists unless I could provide them with a professional outlet for their talents. There seemed to be only one solution: to form an opera company in Boston. In April of 1946 I accordingly wrote twenty letters to well-to-do Boston friends, asking each to donate $250. If, at the end of the first season, they were not pleased with the results, I promised that I would not trouble them a second time.

Today it seems almost inconceivable that thirty-three years ago one could seriously envisage the prospect of producing four operas in one season on the strength of a $5000 advance, and that one could do it, furthermore, with the most expensive seats being priced at $3.60. Yet this is how the New England Opera Theater was launched. Here, as in Cleveland, I decided to start with *The Marriage of Figaro*. It was such a shoestring operation that we could not afford to hire Jordan Hall except for the dress rehearsal and the two performances scheduled in November. Most of the preparation had to be undertaken in the living room and dining room of our Brookline home. To cut down on the cost of a hotel accommodation, we lodged the costume designer, Leo Van Witsen, whom we had brought in from New York City, on the third floor of our house, under the gabled roof, where our children, Michael and Marina (aged respectively nine and seven), had their rooms. They now had to sleep and move around in a jungle of costumes that were hung from every peg and clothes rack available.

But our greatest headache was the scenery. The sets were built and painted in what had once been the basement garage, but which now began to look like a combination workshop and warehouse. Margaret, while stirring the soup or preparing something for lunch in the kitchen, would be almost nauseated by the smell of burning glue rising from below. Yet the garage kept filling up relentlessly, until it was so crammed with sets that we had to push hard to open the door and get inside.

The week preceding the first performance was absolute bedlam, as the members of the chorus trooped in to be instructed by the make-up man. Margaret, in addition to her duties as a mother and a Susanna-to-be, had to busy herself preparing sandwiches for the cast. But the performance that followed fully justified our frantic efforts, generously encouraged by Serge Koussevitzky, whose friendly sendoff was printed on the program's first page: "May I take this opportunity to stress my belief in the success of Boris Goldovsky's long-visioned idea — the realization of a New England Opera Theater. This idea should meet with the wholehearted support of all musical Boston. For it would help to initiate a new era in operatic art and bring about the development of a new, real American opera." Jordan Hall was packed, and, what was even more encouraging, it was packed by enthusiasts who behaved at the end with most un-Bostonian abandon, shouting themselves hoarse and clapping till their hands were sore. Among them was Rudolf Elie, the Boston *Herald*'s "Roving reporter," who dropped in for five minutes but stayed on, riveted to his seat by the sprightly action on the stage. At the end, as he later described it, he found himself "hollering bravo . . . like a madman," along with the rest of the audience, "who practically cheered the gold leaf off the proscenium arch."

A few days later, he managed to ambush me in a drugstore near the New England Conservatory of Music, where he found me seated on a stool chewing a piece of sponge cake between swigs of coffee. He seemed much amused by the red feather I had stuck into the band of my shapeless cloth hat and by the tartan muffler which I had carelessly wrapped around the collar of my overcoat. He began asking me questions about our *Figaro* production. I told him that I had decided to perform it with twenty-six instruments in the orchestra pit, exactly as Mozart had done for its Prague première at the Nostitz Theatre in the autumn of 1786. I had, furthermore, been greatly helped by a new analysis of Mozart's original manuscript made by the German scholar Rudolf Gerber by variations in the oldest known copies of the score which had been discovered by Professor Edward Dent and Siegfried Anheisser in the small German town of Donaueschingen. On the basis of these findings I altered the vocal lines for Susanna and the Countess in the trio of the second act and I lengthened the ensuing duettino between Cherubino and Susanna. For similar reasons I had Barbarina and Cherubino sing the "glorification" duet in the third act's wedding scene.

But that wasn't all, I continued. I had even managed to correct a glaring error committed by both Mozart and Da Ponte in the sextet of the third act: "Just imagine, this opera has been performed thousands of times in the last one hundred and sixty years, and yet no one has ever noticed the fact that in the sextet scene Susanna has no real reason for bringing in the money to pay off Marcellina. Mozart overlooked it and so did Da Ponte."

"How on earth did you notice this?" asked Elie, with a look of intense surprise.

"I didn't notice it," I answered, "any more than other conductors or stage directors before me. It was discovered by the two singers who sang the role of Susanna in our two performances — my wife, Margaret, and Nancy Trickey. And all because of an unusual method of study I dreamed up during our rehearsals. I asked each of our singers to figure out what he or she — that is, the character being impersonated — was doing when not actually on stage. They had to fill out the employment of their time off stage, and in particular, they had to be able to tell me exactly why they returned to the stage. The singers were quite fascinated by this probing inquiry — almost as though they were being asked to sustain an alibi — and none of them had any difficulty telling me why they returned to the stage, except for Margaret and Nancy Trickey. Both of them shamefacedly confessed that they couldn't figure out how Susanna knew the money was needed.

" 'When I leave the stage after my duet with the Count,' said Margaret, 'I am absolutely certain of his good will. So much so that when I run into Figaro, I whisper to him that he won't need a lawyer since his case against Marcellina has already been won.'

" 'Yes,' chimed in Nancy Trickey, 'and convinced as I am that the Count will rule in Figaro's favor, I wouldn't dream of giving any money to that old biddy.'

"At first I thought there was something in the libretto they had overlooked, but after carefully examining the text I realized that their reasoning was sound. So I went back to Beaumarchais' play *Le Mariage de Figaro,* which was the basis for Da Ponte's text, and here I found a very different situation. Susanna's uncle, the gardener Antonio, is present at the judgment scene and, after hearing the Count's unfavorable verdict, he leaves the stage with the words, 'I'm off to tell my niece all about it.' So it's quite natural for Susanna to rush in a few minutes later with a purse in her hand, exclaiming, 'My Lord, stop everything! I have come to pay this lady with the dowry Madame has given me.' "

"But why," asked Elie, "didn't Da Ponte use Antonio just as Beaumarchais did?"

"He couldn't. You see, in the Viennese première of *Figaro,* the roles of Dr. Bartolo and Antonio were sung by the same performer, and since Bartolo's presence in the sextet is essential, Antonio had to be sacrificed."

"And how did you manage to correct this omission?" asked Elie.

"It was fairly simple," I explained. "I had Susanna come in earlier with the others, and after hearing the Count's adverse decision, she runs off stage, realizing that truly heroic measures are now needed to save her tottering marriage prospects."

I went on to develop certain of my pet ideas: "No musical assistants on stage, no prompters, no stage managers, no cuing from the conductor or anyone else. I wouldn't dream of insulting my performers by implying that they need that sort of help."

Elie asked me about our financial situation. I told him frankly that though we had performed twice to packed houses, we had ended up $1000 in debt. "But that we can stand," I added. "A small deficit with a full house is one thing. But a deficit with a half-full house is another. That I will not risk, nor ask anyone else to risk."

A full account of this impromptu interview was published in

two successive numbers of the *Boston Herald.* Forthright as ever, Rudolf Elie even referred rather critically to the "rank ollapodridas" which had been coming to the Boston Opera House for the last thirty years "under various highly suspect auspices." It was almost embarrassing to have such an ardent champion ready to take up the cudgels for us at the drop of a few casual remarks.

He helped us again later by writing a moving appeal on our behalf, in which he lamented the cluttered state of our Brookline home. He quoted Margaret as declaring "with her black eyes flashing . . . 'Either those things go out of the house, or I do.' " The article ended with a plea: "We have to save the Goldovsky marriage. So please, people who have a barn, write in!"

Three barn owners responded to this eloquent appeal, and we heaved a thankful sigh of relief. We accepted two of the offers — one from somebody who owned an empty barn in Brookline, another from some wealthy people who lived out in the country near Harvard, Massachusetts. Three full furniture vans were needed to truck the stuff away.

Shortly before Christmas of the previous year, when I was in New York for a Saturday afternoon quiz program, I happened to be wandering around backstage in the Metropolitan's old opera house on 39th Street when I ran into Cesare Sodero, whom I had vaguely known ever since the time in Philadelphia when I had acted as his backstage assistant for *Rigoletto.* I was a bit embarrassed by this accidental encounter, for I had not much cared for the way in which he had just conducted the first two acts of *La Traviata.* So in order to say something, I asked him if he had ever conducted the section immediately following the baritone aria — *"Di Provenza il mar"* — toward the end of the second act, which is usually omitted when this opera is performed. Sodero stared at me, surprised, and said, "Of course not," adding a moment later, "I have no idea what's there. I have never looked at that part of the score."

His answer left me speechless. That an opera conductor should choose to delete a section of an opera is a perfectly defensible procedure, provided that he knows exactly why he is doing it. Many operas have to be cut in this way when the action on the stage begins to drag and the spectators begin to yawn. I once tried to restore this particular section of *La Traviata* in my own production and I discovered that it really didn't work and the traditional cut was justified. But at least I had put tradition to the test. I hadn't accepted it blindly, without even bothering to examine what Verdi had originally composed, as had Cesare Sodero.

I have always deplored this uninquisitive attitude on the part of conductors, who should after all be interested in problems of operatic composition. (We can learn almost as much from a composer's weaknesses as from his strengths.) But this is not to say that I approve of the opposite tendency, which has begun to manifest itself in recent years, and which consists of scrupulously preserving every line and every note. The amount of music that an average spectator can absorb in any given afternoon or evening is limited. This is a basic truth about this complex art form which even the most rabid opera fan must accept. Those who choose to disregard this inbuilt limitation do as great a disservice to themselves as to the work they think they are honoring. No amount of cultural snobbishness can alter the fact that audiences prefer operas that are lively and tuneful to those that are full of dissonances and harsh sounds. Mozart, who felt that ugliness has no place in music, had a far keener appreciation of what an average audience can take than, let us say, an ultramodern composer who forces his captive audience to sit through several hours of excruciating cacophony and tumult. An audience can absorb a piece of atonal music when it is sandwiched into a symphony program between solid chunks of popular favorites. But two or three hours of unrelieved dissonances, even when accompanied by lively action on a stage, are just too much for most human ears. This is why, with the sole exception of Alban Berg's *Wozzeck,* in which familiar march music, dance tunes, and lullaby themes are deliberately introduced to relieve the nerve-racking tension, no opera written in the atonal style has ever achieved enduring success.

In the winter of 1946–1947 I was much concerned with these problems of what an opera audience can or cannot take in connection with the work that I wanted to present at the following summer's Berkshire Festival. In the course of my research into Mozart, whose finest operas in my opinion are second to none, I made an astounding discovery. In the year 1780, when he was only twenty-four, the young Wolfgang Amadeus was commissioned by Karl Theodor, Elector of Bavaria, to write a serious opera. The result was a monumental work entitled *Idomeneo,* which was first performed at the Ducal Court in Munich in January 1781. The somewhat ponderous Bavarians gave it a moderate acclaim, but later efforts to have it performed in the imperial city of Vienna did not materialize. The lighthearted, and often light-witted, Viennese — many of whom preferred the Italian Salieri to *il tedesco* ("the German") Mozart — were such a frivolous lot that even Mozart's comic operas tended to be too musically sophisticated for their shallow tastes. But whereas *Le Nozze di Figaro, Don Giovanni, Così fan tutte,* and *Die Zauberflöte* were later played and replayed in every major opera house in Europe, *Idomeneo* was allowed to gather dust. Not until March 1934, a full century and a half after its composition, was it able to cross the Channel, when some hardy Scots undertook to perform it in Glasgow. Four years later some daring Londoners had a crack at it, but no one had ever ventured to put it on in the United States.

There was a puzzle here I decided to unravel, for I had read that *Idomeneo,* along with *Don Giovanni,* was Mozart's favorite. It did not take me long to understand why he valued it so highly. *Idomeneo,* being an *opera seria,* is devoid of light comic touches. It was meant to be a mighty tragic drama in the classic Greek tradition, and this all along was Mozart's supreme ambition. He wanted to shine as a creator of serious works rather than as a purveyor of *opera buffa* or *dramma giocoso.* I can put it in slightly different terms by saying that had he lived one hundred years later, he would have preferred to write in the manner of Verdi and Wagner rather than in the style of Johann Strauss or Offenbach. Of course, Mozart could transform even comic opera into serious art, and in *Don Giovanni,* which is one of the most sublime musical and theatrical creations of all time, he raised the *dramma giocoso* to unprecedented heights by blending tragic and supernatural elements to achieve a truly Shakespearean mixture of the pathetic, the fantastic, and the droll.

What astounded me, as I delved into the score, was the stupefying mastery which a young composer of twenty-four could display in this, for him, unfamiliar genre of serious opera. Elettra's first aria left me spellbound. In order to portray her all-consuming jealousy and psychological disarray, Mozart injected triple-time phrases into the 4/4 meter of the orchestral accompaniment. The result is an earthquakelike upheaval, in which the universe tilts and ends up out of joint. So too the storm which later breaks out as Idamante and Elettra are about to embark for Argos. It is a musical miracle — with sudden, startling changes of keys which no eighteenth-century composer had even begun to imagine might exist, and orchestral innovations — including the use of muted trumpets — I had never encountered in any of Mozart's other works. No less breathtaking was the chorus of lamentation in the last act, the accompaniment to which Beethoven imitated in his *Moonlight* Sonata.

This said, the opera displayed glaring weaknesses. It went on endlessly, losing focus as it proceeded and finally degenerating into hopeless, even if beautiful, confusion. I was not the first person to have pored over these defects. A number of eminent musicians had sought to revise *Idomeneo,* including Richard Strauss, who had fashioned a version of his own. Yet none of these attempts to rescue the work from the faults of its labyrinthine construction had saved it from practical oblivion. The question was: Could I succeed where others had failed?

The first act offered no problems. The action takes place on the island of Crete. King Idomeneo is about to return home from the Trojan wars after many years of absence. Ilia, daughter of the recently vanquished King Priam of Troy, is already in Crete with other Trojan captives. She is in love with Idomeneo's son, Idamante, but she struggles against her emotions out of loyalty to her native city. Electra, Agamemnon's daughter, is also in Crete, having been banished from her own land of Argos. She too is in love with Idamante. He, however, prefers Ilia and declares his love for her, much to the anger of the jealous Elettra. So much for the general situation. The action gets under way with Arbace, the Cretan nobleman, arriving with the sad news that Idomeneo and his men have been shipwrecked. The scene changes to the seacoast. Threatened with destruction by the violence of the storm, Idomeneo makes a vow to Poseidon, promising to sacrifice the first human being he encounters once he has reached the shore if the irate God of the Seas will but call off his howling winds. The winds abate and Idomeneo disembarks on the rocky shore. Anxiously he waits for the appearance of the first Cretan, whom he will have to seize and sacrifice. Idamante enters and, not recognizing his father (whom he imagines has perished in the storm), offers him shelter. Eventually they recognize each other — at which point the unhappy king hurries away in terror, not daring to tell his son of his rash vow.

Up to this point in the story everything was clear. But with the start of the second act the action comes to a standstill. For a long time nothing of real importance happens. Idomeneo has meetings and discussions with Ilia and Elettra, both women sing lovely arias, but the story is not one whit advanced. Finally Idomeneo resolves to break his solemn vow to Poseidon and to send his son away from Crete. The best way of effecting this is to order him to accompany Elettra back to her native Argos. Elettra is delighted, since she will be alone with her loved one, while Idamante is downcast, since he is being separated from Ilia. The conclusion of the second act, when it finally comes after endless digressions, is sublime. Idamante agrees to accompany Elettra to Argos, but just as the happy-unhappy pair are about to embark, another terrible storm breaks loose. Idomeneo, realizing that Poseidon is outraged by his attempt to deceive him, offers to sacrifice himself in order to save his son. In vain. The winds rise to gale force and the terrified islanders flee the harbor and take refuge from the elements elsewhere.

The start of the third act merely aggravated the meanderings of the second. Here Princess Ilia, blissfully unaware of the disasters that have befallen Crete, spends her time in pleasant meditations. No longer able to contain her love for Idamante, she confides her rapture to the zephyrs and the flowers.

It was only too obvious that the story line had been hopelessly blurred. Like the other musicologists who had carefully studied the score, I placed the blame for this squarely on the shoulders of the librettist, a Salzburg chaplain named Giambattista Varesco. Wishing to imitate the illustrious poet Pietro Mestastasio, he had adhered to the rigid eighteenth-century conventions governing the composition of serious opera. Each of the principal protagonists in the opera had to have three arias apiece, and even the secondary characters were granted at least one aria. These arias, furthermore, were joined by endless *secco* recitatives. The result was an immensely long work, which even the glories of Mozart's music had been unable to save from neglect and oblivion.

Only much later did I discover that Varesco was not wholly to blame. All he had been asked to do, in reality, was to fashion an Italian version of a French text which Antoine Danchet had provided, some seventy years earlier, for the *Idoménée* of the French composer André Campra. In Danchet's libretto, however, King Idomeneo is not only confronted with the need to sacrifice his son, he has also fallen desperately in love with Ilia. This additional element of amorous rivalry — between father and son — made the situation much more tense and dramatic. But Varesco — to judge by the correspondence between Mozart and his father — was specifically instructed to omit this additional romantic entanglement from his libretto, doubtless because a stage portrayal of an amorous rivalry between a reigning monarch and his heir would have been embarrassing to Karl Theodor, the Prince Elector of Bavaria who had commissioned this opera.

Although I knew nothing at the time of the libretto's historical antecedents, my theatrical instincts told me that something drastic was needed. Well intentioned though they were, my predecessors had all failed to make *Idomeneo* palatable because they had approached Mozart's work as musicians and had sought to save as much as they could of the opera's wonderful arias and melodic passages. If I was to succeed, I would have to adopt an entirely different approach, recalling Jean Racine's judicious advice (in the preface to his *Mithridate,* a tragedy which, curiously enough, also deals with an amorous rivalry between a king and his two sons): "Do not put anything on the stage which is not absolutely necessary, for the most beautiful scenes risk becoming a bore the moment they begin to interrupt the action instead of leading it towards the end."

In keeping with Racine's advice, I ruthlessly decided to excise everything not directly connected with the basic plot. I did away with the prime minister and merged his role with that of the high priest, thereby eliminating two arias which (in Varesco's libretto) are sung about nothing in particular. I cut out the second-act arias given to Ilia and Elettra, and moved Ilia's third-act aria, her love duet with Idamante, and the quartet of the four principals into the second act. Miraculously everything fell into place, and by a happy accident the different keys of my streamlined version were so closely related that the reshuffled sections fitted together in a most harmonious sequence.

While engaged on this elaborate cutting and restitching job, I heard that an English version of the opera existed. I accordingly wrote to London to obtain a copy. Unfortunately, it arrived too late for us to be able to use it at our first Tanglewood production.

Having always worked on the principle that opera, to be theatrically valid, must be sung in a language that is second nature to the performers, I asked my able assistant, Sarah Caldwell, to help me prepare an English translation, and it was in this version that *Idomeneo* was later given in Boston.

We were rehearsing the opera at Tanglewood, in July of 1947, when it suddenly dawned on me that *Idomeneo* was anything but an old-fashioned story bequeathed to us by the bards of ancient Greece; it was a cautionary tale that had immense relevance to the present. And so, before the curtain rose on August 4 I came out and delivered a short speech, as I had been doing with all of our operatic productions. This opera, I explained, was really an allegory about what was happening in the world today. By exploding the atomic bomb, the United States had unleashed the awesome forces of nature. But the world was going to have to pay a price to keep these forces tamed and from wreaking universal havoc and destruction. This price was the sacrifice of national sovereignty, a sacrifice comparable to the one that Idomeneo had promised to make by killing his son. But unfortunately, like Idomeneo, the nations of the world had taken to cheating. They, or at any rate their rulers, were not prepared to surrender their respective sovereignties for the establishment of a world order capable of harnessing and controlling the gigantic forces which the splitting of the atom had released. So one day they would be punished for their devious ways; they would then have to abdicate their powers and, like King Idomeneo, place authority in the hands of young, uncorrupted people, capable of governing their subjects under the reign of international law.

My introductory words made a considerable impression and helped put the audience in a receptive mood for this unfamilar Mozart work. Once again my painter friend Richard Rychtarik designed some splendid stage sets; Leo Van Witsen created fine classical Greek robes and military gear; and I was most ably seconded at rehearsals by two outstanding musicians, Jan Meyerowitz and Felix Wolfes. Joseph Laderoute, who had already shone in *Peter Grimes,* was a magnificently tortured Idomeneo, Nancy Trickey was a moving Princess Ilia, and Paula Leuchner a tempestuous Elettra. Since the operatic use of *castrati* went out with the French Revolution — which from the strictly vocal point of view is to be regretted, since many of them were the most accomplished singers the world has ever known — the adolescent role of Idamante had to be entrusted to a mezzo-soprano. In this case there were two of them: Ann Bollinger for the première, Dorothy Dawson for the second performance.

The applause at the conclusion of both performances was quite simply stupendous. Koussevitzky was radiant, beaming from ear to ear while tears of pleasure trickled down his venerable cheeks. The première of a major Mozart work that had never before been heard in the United States — this was just the kind of great creative event he had always wanted his Berkshire Music School to produce.

The critics were equally enthusiastic. The music editor of *Time* devoted an entire column to it. Noel Straus in the *New York Times* could not contain his admiration: "For its astounding choral writing alone, *Idomeneo* would be worthy of frequent hearings. No two choruses are alike, and they cover the widest range of emotion, from the joy and serenity of the enchantingly graceful *'Placido è il mar'* to the anguish of the *'Pietà'* of the shipwrecked sailors.

"Never was Mozart to write a finer operatic ensemble than the great quartet in this opera, or more remarkable accompanied recitatives, while Idomeneo's 'prayer,' with its striking pizzicato accompaniment, has a quality all its own among the composer's creations . . . The orchestration of this work is a treasure-mine of novel and fascinating combinations and effects. In no other opera of Mozart is the instrumental scoring so rich in color and daring."

Our friend Rudolf Elie, of course, pulled out all the stops in covering the event for the *Boston Herald.* "I will leave it to others to discuss the finer points of the musical vocabulary. But here, in what seemed to me the finest student performance I ever heard in my life, was a thesaurus of everything that ever happened in music up to Mozart, and the clue to everything that has happened since. Beethoven? He's there, in the opening of the third act (in a scene of incomparable tragedy). Verdi? He's there, in a foreshadow of his last and greatest works. Brahms, Schumann? They're all there, even the moderns, for Mozart's daring is beyond belief. Dissonances which in his own day must have been far more shocking than any conceived today for far more callous ears; musical devices only now coming into use. And all underlining perhaps the most perfect marriage of words and music ever conceived. The love scene of the second act (I would be willing to perjure myself forever on it) is the most marvellous love scene in all music." And so on.

We encountered the same response four months later when we performed the same opera in Boston's Jordan Hall. Harrison Keller, who had succeeded Quincy Porter as director of the New England Conservatory of Music, wrote me a most appreciative letter, saying what enormous pleasure it had given him to see *Idomeneo* performed in Boston: "I am convinced by yesterday's performance that I have never before heard Mozart at his 'greatest' great. Somehow his orchestra takes fire and with such startling changes of color and pace that I have seldom, if ever, found in his symphonies. Opera surely was his great love, and I hope (and who knows) perhaps he heard it."

Mrs. H. V. Greenough, a resident of Brookline like myself was even more generous. "My dear Mr. Goldovsky," she wrote, "it gives me great pleasure to send you this $200. After seeing 'Idomeneo' on Sunday, I am surprised that mink coats, diamond tiaras, engagement rings, and bill folds were not showered on the stage!"

10

Farewell to Uncle Serge

THE YEAR 1947 was not a particularly happy one for Serge Koussevitzky. In the late spring a former music critic named Moses Smith came out with a biography devoted to him. Smith, as is often the case with critics, was a frustrated musician, and by the time I got to know him, he was so crippled by arthritis that he had to move around in a wheelchair. He had turned into an embittered man, and some of his personal unhappiness had worked its way into this biography.

Before writing his book, Smith had gone around interviewing as many of Koussevitzky's friends, acquaintances, and members of the Boston Symphony as possible. One of the persons he had talked to, or rather, who had talked to him at great length — for he was an extraordinarily voluble individual — was Nicolas Slonimsky, a pint-sized live wire who was a walking encyclopedia of both musical and philological information. Slonimsky had made a name for himself as a pianist in pre-Revolutionary Russia, and, like Uncle Pierre, he had spent many hours helping Koussevitzky while the latter, who until then had only been known as a double-bass player, studied assiduously to become an orchestra conductor.

It is difficult for a person who has helped a contemporary develop a special skill to view him with undiluted awe and respect. This was particularly true of Slonimsky, a peppery individual who knew so much that he tended to be impatient with people who knew less — which is to say, with just about everybody. Having had a chance to work with Koussevitzky at the outset of his conducting career, he knew perfectly well how wobbly those beginnings were. For Sergei Alexandrovich was not a born conductor — like, let us say, his *Wunderkinder,* Lukas Foss and Leonard Bernstein. He came to conducting relatively late in life, and from the very start he displayed weaknesses that he was never able to overcome completely. His beat, to begin with, was unclear. His ear was not as sharp as that of some other conductors, and his understanding of certain musical styles was limited. His most serious weakness, however, was an inability to decide at exactly which tempo a piece should be played until he had actually started conducting it. He realized this himself and spent a good part of his life covering up this particular deficiency.

Koussevitzky's great strength, of course, was in his very special feeling for the sound of string instruments. In his youth he had been a virtuoso on the double bass, a very difficult instrument to play without making rather unpleasant scratching noises. Koussevitzky had solved this particular problem, and he demanded the same smooth bowing from all of his string players, torturing them into producing the most velvety and even singing tone. There was a Concerto for Strings by Corelli in which his initial downbeat was so slow and vague that none of the players knew precisely when to start. The result was quite astonishing. The opening chord came into being without any ictus, the slight attacking "uh" noise which normally precedes it. It emerged from the silence out of nothing, like a rainbow or an apparition hovering in the air.

But this vague downbeat, which occasionally worked wonders with the strings, had a pernicious effect on wind players, who need a very clear signal from the conductor and who cannot make their entrances in a tentative manner. At rehearsals it was always painful to watch Koussie trying to get two oboes or three trombones to produce a simultaneous attack. He would have the players repeat the same passage over and over; he would scold them, saying they were incompetent musicians, until finally, by watching each other and devising their own independent system of communication, the players would achieve the desired unanimity — at which point Koussie would say, "You see, it is very simple."

No one could deny that Moses Smith's book was carefully researched. It was even full of praise for Koussevitzky's achievements. But it also contained a number of unflattering comments. Thus, in describing the conductor's early years in Boston, he wrote that there "were times in those days when Koussevitzky was close to tears with frustration, induced by a confused awareness that he was not prepared for his task. The most dramatic achievement in his career lay in . . . learning after fifty what a student of conducting often learns before twenty." Smith pointed out several specific failings in his conductorial equipment, noting, for example, that "bad orchestral balance is one of Koussevitzky's recurring sins." Elsewhere he observed that he "seems never to have mastered the essential (and elementary) meaning of *ritardando,* which he seems to construe as a different tempo instead of a gradual slowing down." Though these failings did not by any means overshadow the equally specific virtues, they combined to form — or so at least the author claimed — a psychological study of how a man with glaring weaknesses had risen to greatness in the musical world through sheer force of will, immense exertion, and, not least of all, a highly profitable marriage with a wealthy heiress.

Uncle Serge, as it happened, was vacationing in Florida when the book was published. But one of his secretaries who had read it and made notes on the more critical passages called him on the telephone long-distance and repeated some of the uncomplimentary statements made about him. In a situation like this, Ernö Dohnányi would have laughed and said, "Excellent! I shall add it to my anthology of stuff written about me by musical ignoramuses." But Koussevitzky was not built of the same robust material, and the news that an uncomplimentary book about him had just appeared made him tremble with rage.

Interrupting his vacation, he took the first train back to Boston. Along with other trusted friends, I was summoned to his Brookline home, where he was waited upon by his faithful valet, Victor, fed by a Russian cook named Dasha, and assisted in all of his business activities by his dead wife's niece, Olga Naumova, who had served as his amanuensis for eighteen years. A council of war was held to decide what should be done about this abomination that had just hit the bookstands. We all pleaded with Sergei Alexandrovich to let the matter rest. But no, he was determined to bring legal action against the scoundrel who had dared to splatter his good name with mud. It wasn't only an insult to him, it was an insult to the great organization, to the great orchestra he had been conducting now for close to a quarter of a century. It was an insult to the city of Boston. It was an attack on the arts, an assault on the artistic integrity and worth of musicians all over the United States.

Deaf to our pleas and remonstrances, Uncle Serge went ahead and filed a court injunction requesting that the offending book be banned and all copies forcibly removed from the bookstores. He seemed to think that because he had been personally maligned, every musician in America would flock to his side, deluging the publisher with furious letters, organizing protest meetings and public demonstrations. But nothing of the sort happened. There were no rallies, no public demonstrations, and the examining magistrate who had to deal with the injunction finally threw out the case on the grounds that in the United States prominent public figures cannot protect their privacy from the scrutiny of critics unless the statements made about them can be proved to be demonstrably false and malicious. Considerable publicity was aroused by the hubhub, and the result, as we had vainly tried to impress on Sergei Alexandrovich, was a boon to the publisher, who sold thousands of copies of Moses Smith's book.

*

It is easy to criticize the comportment of others when they behave like innocents in matters of this kind. So it is only proper that I should mention another case of unfortunate publicity where I was the principal offender.

Several years after this uproar over Moses Smith, at a time when I was preparing the first national tour of my Opera Theater, our public relations expert set up an interview for me with Jay Harrison, who was then the music critic of the *New York Herald Tribune*. He was a pleasant fellow who knew quite a lot about opera and who had often participated in the broadcasts of the Metropolitan Opera's Saturday afternoon quiz programs.

Harrison was curious to learn how my ideas about producing opera differed from those of other conductors and stage directors. I explained to him that the trouble with opera, in the United States and elsewhere, was that the emphasis was placed almost entirely on musical nuances, while the dramatic values were neglected or ignored. I cited as an example the average conductor's insistence that the singers keep their eyes glued on him, whereas in my productions they were trained *never* to look at the conductor.

"But why do conductors insist that singers watch them?" asked Harrison.

"I will tell you why," I answered. "The trouble is that singers are not trusted by most conductors. These gentlemen are totally preoccupied with musical matters and are intent on controlling all details of tempo and phrasing not only in rehearsals but also during the actual performances. I believe, however, that singers need not be treated like puppets whose strings must be pulled by the puppet master, but that they can be trained to be completely self-reliant musicians. Furthermore, music is by no means the only element of importance in opera. And, unfortunately, singers who are forced to focus all their attention on the conductor are quite unable to act convincingly. In a way," I added, "one might say that many opera conductors are the greatest enemies of the musical theater because they destroy its dramatic values."

A day or two later, the *New York Herald Tribune* published a long article by Harrison in which my ideas were expounded at some length. The headline was startling: CONDUCTORS ARE THE GREATEST ENEMIES OF OPERA! SAYS GOLDOVSKY

As ill luck would have it, Fritz Reiner was at that moment guest-conducting at the Metropolitan Opera in New York. The day the article appeared I got a long-distance telephone call from Mrs. August Belmont, who headed the Metropolitan Opera Guild and who had given me a lot of precious support both in New York and in Boston. "Boris," she said, "what is the matter with you? Have you lost your mind? I just had a telephone call from Fritz Reiner, and he's very bitter. He said, 'How can Goldovsky say a terrible thing like that? I taught him, and he knows how carefully I train singers, how much attention I pay to everything, and yet he says that I am an enemy of opera.''

I told Mrs. Belmont that Reiner was completely mistaken. I hadn't meant it personally, for I had learned a great deal from Reiner and considered him the finest opera conductor in the business. But not all conductors were like Reiner, and the truth of the matter was that it was their inattention to dramatic values that was doing so much damage to opera as a valid form of art.

"All right," she said. "I understand. But you absolutely must write to Reiner, you must see him, you must explain all this to him, because he's terribly upset and hurt."

I sat down and wrote a long letter to Fritz Reiner, explaining my remarks to Harrison and saying that they were not in any way directed at him, since I had the highest regard for his work as an opera conductor. My letter, however, had no effect, and for months thereafter Reiner refused to speak to me and would not even shake my hand whenever we chanced to meet.

Because Russian — a beautifully correct, grammatical Russian which he spoke with an elegant Moscow accent — was the only language he was really at home in, Koussevitzky remained almost umbilically attached to the culture of the motherland he had left in 1921. He was, of course, completely cosmopolitan in his musical tastes, and he was ready to play the works of any modern composer regardless of his origin, yet he was always particularly interested in the compositions of contemporary Russians — like Stravinsky and Prokofieff, whose scores he had published in the early 1920s in Paris under the imprint of his Editions Koussevitzky.

One of these contemporary Russians was Alexander Tikhonovich Grechaninov, in whose dacha, near Moscow, I had taken lessons in theory and harmony during the summer of 1921. Like Koussevitzky, Stravinsky, Balanchine, Vladimir Nabokov, and so many other Russian refugees from Bolshevism, Grechaninov had finally found a haven in the New World, and he was now living in New York.

Alexander Tikhonovich was much too conservative in his style of composition to suit Koussevitzky's somewhat avant-garde tastes. And so when, in 1943, Grechaninov sent him the score of one of his recent compositions, little attention was paid to it at first. This was not unusual, for unsolicited manuscripts and scores of all kinds were constantly being brought by the mailman to Symphony Hall, and I would often see them piled up on a table in a corner of the green room, waiting (sometimes for months) for the Master to inspect them. There was, however, one thing about this particular composition of Grechaninov's which intrigued Uncle Serge: its title — *Ecumenical Mass*. He asked one of his friends what the word "ecumenical" meant and got very excited when he was told that it meant "belonging to all religions."

Like my father, my mother, and Uncle Pierre, Koussevitzky, though Jewish-born, had been brought up in a distinctly liberal and unfanatical tradition. He was so lukewarm to orthodox Judaism that to please his second wife, Natalya, he had agreed to be converted to the Russian Orthodox faith. But deep down within him Sergei Alexandrovich had remained an agnostic, or more exactly, a nonpartisan believer. He had no use for narrow-minded bigotry, preferring to believe that there was something good in every creed. He felt that if only people of different faiths could learn to be more charitable about the religious beliefs of others, a major source of international tension and conflict would be removed.

The title of Grechaninov's opus thus struck a responsive chord, and Koussevitzky decided to perform the *Ecumenical Mass* at one of his regular Boston Symphony concerts. A choir master was engaged to train the choristers, and in due course the composer himself appeared in Boston to be present at the rehearsals. By this time the old gentleman, who had been born one year after the battle of Gettysburg and who was now entering his eightieth year, was almost completely blind. Since he spoke almost nothing but Russian, he needed to be led around by an English-speaking "seeing-eye dog" — a job for which I was picked out when Koussevitzky learned that I had once studied under the old man in Russia.

Alexander Tikhonovich was touched by this unexpected welcome on the part of one of his former pupils, but he was considerably less pleased by the changes Koussevitzky wished to make in his *Ecumenical Mass.* Musically speaking, this was not a work of great originality. Parts of it sounded more like a lighthearted Ukrainian operetta than the twentieth-century religious music it was supposed to be, and in one place there was even a sprightly melody played by a clarinet, which reminded one of a folksy dance tune.

Koussevitzky was most upset by this passage. Stopping the orchestra, he turned toward the auditorium, where we were seated side by side, and said in Russian: "Alexander Tikhonovich, would you please come up here for a moment? I would like to talk to you."

I accompanied Grechaninov to the podium, where Koussevitzky undertook to explain to him why this clarinet passage should be eliminated. The scene that ensued was truly comical. Normally, composers whose works Koussevitzky had agreed to perform stood in fear and trembling before him, saying, "Yes, sir . . . of course, sir . . . if that's the way you want it, sir, by all means let's do it that way!" and so on. But Grechaninov was not going to kowtow to a younger man whom he had known back in Moscow when Koussevitzky was no more than a dilettante whom no one took seriously. And so, when Koussevitzky said to him, "This melody is impossible! It will have to go!" Alexander Tikhonovich answered him in a loud, high-pitched, almost singsong voice, "But I like it!" And that was that!

We had no such problems in the summer of 1948 when I decided to produce Grechaninov's comic opera *The Marriage* (based on an amusing play by Gogol). The only hitch occurred immediately after the overture. Just as Sonia Stolin, who was playing the role of the prospective bride, Agafia, was about to burst into song, someone flushed a backstage toilet, and one of the pipes in the theater's plumbing system emitted a soft but penetrating whining tone. The startled girl, believing that an instrument in the orchestra was giving her the pitch, obediently began singing her unaccompanied solo passage almost a major third higher than written.

On August 14, 1947, shortly after our two triumphal performances of *Idomeneo* at Tanglewood, Sergei Alexandrovich Koussevitzky and Olga Alexandrovna Naumova, his faithful secretary of eighteen years' standing, were secretly married in a private ceremony held in his country estate (Seranak) near Lenox. Koussevitsky at this time was much preoccupied by the future of his "organization." He was seventy-three years old and feeling the strain of having to rehearse and conduct one hundred concerts every year. It was too heavy a load for a person of his age to carry, so he proposed to delegate a good half of this crushing burden to an assistant conductor, who would eventually succeed him as musical director of the Boston Symphony Orchestra. The person he wanted for this prestigious post was his favorite Tanglewood *Kind,*

Leonard Bernstein — or Lenushka, as Uncle Serge preferred to call him.

The "trusties" of the Boston Symphony, however, did not take kindly to his proposal that Leonard Bernstein, a local Jewish boy from Brookline, be named assistant director, on the understanding that he would eventually succeed Koussevitzky as resident conductor of the Boston Symphony. Deciding to play his ace, Sergei Alexandrovich then tended his resignation. To his intense mortification it was accepted in the spring of 1948 by the board of overseers, who announced that Dr. Koussevitzky would be retiring the following year and that his place would be taken, in October 1949, by Charles Munch, the conductor of the Orchestre de Paris. Although this formally ended Koussevitzky's ties with the Boston Symphony, it left the problem of the Berkshire Music Center unresolved, for whereas he had inherited an already well established orchestra when he had first come to Boston, Koussie regarded the Tanglewood school, which he had done so much to promote, as his particular "baby," and he was not going to let the "trusties" force him to relinquish it as well.

In the autumn of 1949, after another successful Berkshire Festival, I was invited to spend several days with Uncle Serge and Olga Alexandrovna at Seranak. Such invitations were extremely rare, and I was of course most honored to be granted this exceptional mark of favor.

I found Sergei Alexandrovich much preoccupied by the future of *his* Berkshire Music Center, which he rightly felt had proved itself to be an extraordinarily innovative and beneficial institution. "As you know," he explained to me, "when we started out, we were the only ones doing this sort of thing. So we got the most brilliant students to come here — youngsters like Lenushka, Lukas Foss, Eleazar de Carvalho — and we had no rivals. But now other organizations are competing with us. Just think, the Juilliard School of Music is now *paying* youngsters to study there in the summer. They are bribing them by giving them fellowships as well as scholarships, even though the students would much prefer to come here." For with Sergei Alexandrovich it was, of course, axiomatic that any musical enterprise he was directing was ipso facto more desirable than any other. "They are buying these young students away from us, they are seducing them in the most improper fashion. Now I ask you, what can we do about it?"

"Dyadya Seryozha," I said, "I think we are going to have to fight fire with fire. I mean, if the others offer them scholarships and subsistence grants, maybe we should too. Of course I cannot really advise you about this since I know nothing about the overall financial situation. But if you can tell me how much profit the festival has been making from the summer concerts, then maybe I can help you develop a special scholarship program. But," I added hastily, knowing how touchy Koussevitzky was about outsiders trying to pry into his affairs, "it's probably none of my business."

"Oh," he said, "I would tell you gladly, but I can't."

"And why can't you?"

"Because they won't tell me."

"Who won't tell you?" I asked.

"They, the *trusties,*" he answered, meaning of course the trustees of the Boston Symphony Orchestra, who had been underwriting the cost of the Berkshire Music Center since 1942.

I stared at Uncle Serge in amazement, unwilling to believe my ears.

"Yes, that is the way it is," he went on, making a gesture of helplessness. "Every year I ask for a detailed financial report. But do you think I get one? No. These people, you know, Judd and the *trusties,* they are in cahoots. They won't tell me, and there is no way for me to find out."

"But that's incredible!" I said. "It's inconceivable, Dyadya Seryozha. How dare they do such a thing?"

I was flabbergasted at the idea that someone might have the nerve not to inform the Creator as to what was happening in His own backyard. At the same time, I knew many of these trustees personally, and in particular the general manager of the Boston Symphony Orchestra, George Judd, who would gladly have given his lifeblood to please his musical director. Unfortunately, Koussie and Judd had never been able to communicate effectively. Koussevitzky only partially understood Judd's English, while Judd understood not a word of Koussevitzky's Russian. The result was a perpetual mismeeting of minds — with the tragic result that over the years George Judd had become Koussie's special bête noire and the source of all sorts of imaginary plots and machinations.

"You see, Olechka," he said to his wife, Olga, who had joined us around the fireplace, "Boris too is amazed that we cannot get any financial statements."

"Yes," she chimed in, in her quietly submissive way, "they send us these volumes every year, but there is not a word in them about finances." She went over to a shelf where about a dozen neatly bound volumes were stacked in a row. She pulled out one of them and handed it to me. "Have a look. You'll see."

I opened the volume and found the table of contents. Chapter one, chapter two, chapter three — the entire history of the Boston Symphony Orchestra's activities for that particular summer had been systematically chronicled and analyzed in these various chapters. Finally I came to chapter ten. Opposite it was the mention: "Financial statement." I flicked through to the indicated page, and there it all was: a tabulated list of the festival's and Berkshire Music Center's complete expenses over the six summer weeks, almost down to the cost of the toilet paper provided for the washrooms.

I sat there, speechless with amazement as my eyes ran down the long list of incredibly detailed figures. My situation was most uncomfortable. I had inadvertently landed myself in a most dangerous fix. For several minutes I had listened to Sergei Alexandrovich getting increasingly steamed up against the iniquity of these "trusties" and of that dirty dog Judd, who were deliberately keeping him in the dark and who were obviously hiding the fact that they had been making pots of money, which is why the rogues were keeping these dark financial secrets to themselves, and I too had worked myself up to a high pitch of indignation, saying, "How disgraceful! Why the nerve of them! And to think that the Boston Symphony is supposed to be a nonprofit organization!" And now here were all the particulars laid out before my eyes without the slightest effort at dissimulation, and to make it even more embarrassing, there was Olga Alexandrovna watching me from her armchair like a lynx. She, who for eighteen years had been Koussevitzky's private secretary and in charge of all his business affairs, was no more capable of reading a table of contents in English than he was.

It was obvious from my silence that I had stumbled upon something that had riveted my attention.

"What have you found? Is there anything there?" asked Uncle Serge anxiously.

"Well," I said, trying to sound nonchalant, "there are some figures here, but who can make heads or tails of all this?"

"Yes," nodded Koussevitzky, "that's the trouble. Who can make it all out? I can't. Olga here can't. But Boris, maybe you can."

"Well, perhaps," I said, deciding to play a close hand. "But Dyadya Seryozha, it won't be easy, it will take time."

"Oh, don't worry about that," he reassured me. "Take all the time you need. In fact, I tell you what — why don't you take all these volumes back home with you, and once you have been through them, write me a report on what you have found."

And so it was agreed. When I left Seranak the next day, the dozen tomes were piled in the back seat of my car, and I took them to Brookline with me. Needless to say, I never wrote a line of that report, and after Uncle Serge's death, I returned those meticulously compiled volumes to the "wicked" trustees of the Boston Symphony Orchestra.

*

Although Koussevitzky managed to retain his hold on the Berkshire Music Center, his running battle with the purse-wardens of the Boston Symphony Orchestra remained unresolved — particularly during the summer of 1950, when Charles Munch tactfully withdrew to France for the holidays, while an outsider, Victor de Sabata (who had made a name for himself at La Scala in Milan), was brought in to conduct two concerts.

Fortunately for us, the opera department was not directly affected by this squabbling, even though the trustees of the Boston Symphony Orchestra had begun to question the wisdom of spending so much money on an opera school which did not benefit the Boston concert seasons in any tangible way.

The conjunction of these various factors merely heightened Koussevitzky's personal interest in our department. Though he had never made a specialty of conducting opera, Koussevitzky had been a close friend and admirer of Stanislavsky's in his youth and he was very fond of theatrical productions. But for this love of the stage I doubt that he would have let our opera department at Tanglewood expand and thrive as it did, becoming in the process a kind of operatic laboratory of a unique and unprecedented kind. Sergei Alexandrovich was immensely proud of our continuing successes — Rossini's *The Turk in Italy* in 1948 (an opera that had not been performed in the United States for over a century), Benjamin Britten's *Albert Herring* in 1949, and Mozart's *La Finta Giardiniera,* which was staged in 1950 by Sarah Caldwell while I was in the hospital recovering from an operation — successes which awoke in him a desire to conduct the next summer's opera himself. The choice fell on Tchaikovsky's *The Queen of Spades,* based on Pushkin's famous short story "Pikovaya Dama."

One of Koussevitzky's distinguishing characteristics was a fussiness about his personal attire which, I feel sure, was much appreciated by the Boston Brahmins. He was extremely fastidious about his mode of attire, and whether dressed in his trim winter coat with the expensive silk scarf around his neck, in his famous flowing cape à la Franklin Roosevelt, or in a midsummer blazer, impeccably creased white trousers, and two-tone shoes, Sergei Alexandrovich was invariably a model of sartorial elegance. And so, when we began planning our production of *The Queen of Spades,* he insisted on discussing every detail of the costumes with the costume designer Leo Van Witsen.

Well do I remember those long, laborious sessions in his Brookline home. To make absolutely certain that they understood each other perfectly, I repeated Koussevitzky's statements in *sotto voce* asides to Leo Van Witsen, and I translated Van Witsen's answers into Russian for the benefit of Uncle Serge. He seemed surprised by this laborious procedure and even questioned me about it. I explained that I was doing this in order to clarify my own thinking, which was why I was also taking notes.

Notwithstanding these precautions, we almost came to grief after we had successfully settled on the dresses to be worn by Lisa and the old countess. There was now the question of Herman's cape, which was to be worn for the outdoor scenes. "What color would you like the cape to be?" asked Van Witsen. I translated the question into Russian, simultaneously noting it on my pad.

"The cape should be dark green," answered Koussevitzky. I repeated his English words in Russian, as I had been doing, whereupon he turned on me with flashing eyes: "Why are you writing down 'dark green'?" he stormed at me in Russian. "You heard me say 'dark gray' quite clearly!"

As usual he had been thinking half in English, half in French, and what he had actually said, and what my ear had failed to catch, was "dark *gris.*"

Sergei Alexandrovich, unfortunately, was never able to conduct *The Queen of Spades.* But like the trips abroad which he indulged in during the last years of his life, the preparations for this opera kept him busy and contented. Liberated at last from the onerous responsibility of having to direct a major symphony orchestra, he discovered a freedom to move around and to do what he pleased that he had not known in years. He received invitations to conduct other orchestras in Europe and Israel, and he began to savor the joys of being a guest conductor.

I was made personally aware of this new *Wanderlust* one day when, shortly before his return from one of these tours abroad, I received a telegram from Uncle Serge: "EXPECT YOU FOR DINNER ON FRIDAY TO DISCUSS IMPORTANT PLANS." I was all agog with curiosity when I turned up at his house, but not until after dinner, when he led me into the drawing room so that we could talk undisturbed, did I discover what was on his mind.

"I am sending you to Israel," he announced without further ado. "You will have to stay there for a year or two, for I want you to organize all the local forces, singers and choruses in particular. They have a fine orchestra in Israel, but we will need hundreds of vocalists, oratorio singers, operatic artists, and choristers. For I am preparing an international festival. It will be the most grandiose festival ever conceived. I will have music composed especially for the occasion by several of the greatest living composers. It will be a tremendous ecumenical event."

I was bewildered but impressed. "When will all of this take place?" I asked.

He seemed surprised at my question. "Why, in the fall of nineteen fifty-two. You know, of course, what great musical anniversary will be celebrated in nineteen fifty-two?"

Since we were now in the spring of 1950 I had not given much thought to the autumn of 1952, but having participated in dozens of quiz programs during the Saturday intermission broadcasts of the Met I was used to questions of this nature and I had the dates of the great composers clearly catalogued in my mind. "Give me a few seconds," I said, "and I will figure out what anniversary you are referring to."

"Go ahead," he said. He lit a cigarette and sat watching me intently as I began running back in fifty-year leaps to catch a great name that had been born or had died in 1902, 1852, 1802, and so on. When I reached 1402, I stopped, greatly puzzled. There was no one. For safety's sake, I went back another hundred years and then retraced my steps. I could not connect a single great composer to any of those dates — for Muzio Clementi, who was born in 1752, and Giuseppe Sarti, who died in 1802, were far too obscure to have inspired the kind of monster festival Uncle Serge was envisaging.

Finally I had to admit defeat: "I am sorry, Dyadya Seryozha, I give up. I cannot think of anyone. My mind is not functioning well. It must be that wonderful wine we had for dinner."

"You cannot think of anyone?" Uncle Serge said sadly. The tears came to his eyes, as they always did when he was profoundly moved. "Don't you know?" he said, taking out his handkerchief. "Don't you know that in nineteen fifty-two we will be commemorating the three-thousandth anniversary of the death of King David?"

Being busy with his handkerchief, Uncle Serge did not notice the look of startled disbelief on my face. But I soon realized that this colossal festival he was planning was essentially a transposition to a foreign land of the grandiose scheme he had once envisaged for staging a Greek *puhgahn* (pageant) at Tanglewood. Fortunately, it was scheduled far enough ahead not to interfere with our plans for the Berkshire Festival of 1951, when he was to conduct *The Queen of Spades.*

In the winter of 1950–1951 Koussevitzky's health took a turn for the worse. I had to make a special trip to Arizona, where he had acquired a house for the cold winter months, to discuss the problems of Tchaikovsky's opera. Uncle Serge told me that he was having trouble with his doctors. They were all ignorant quacks, trying to persuade him that he was a sick man, affected by some strange blood disease which caused the body to manufacture too many red corpuscles. Even the famous heart specialist who had examined him was dismissed as something of a charlatan. "How silly these people are! All they know is what their statistics tell them. But that does not apply to me."

The "charlatans" unfortunately were right, and not long after Sergei Alexandrovich's return to Boston, his health began deteriorating steadily. His third wife, Olga, who had never shared his "ecumenical" enthusiasms, decided that the time had come to bring Sergei Alexandrovich back to the "true faith" — which is to say, to Russian Orthodoxy. It was an absurd decision, given his Jewish origins, but he was by now too weak to resist. When I went to call at his Buckminster Road home, I found a Russian priest, with a long beard and a black cassock, in almost permanent attendance on the sinner who had agreed to return to the fold.

In May Uncle Serge had to be hospitalized at the New England Medical Center, but when it became clear that nothing could save him, Leonard Bernstein was hastily summoned from Mexico. He arrived at his bedside just in time to see Sergei Alexandrovich draw his last breath on June 4.

It was Uncle Serge's wish to be buried at Lenox, not far from his Saranak estate and next to his beloved Natalya Konstantinovna. But in the meantime there was the question of the funeral service. Since there was no Russian Orthodox church in Boston, Koussevitzky's widow arranged with Father Hale to have the funeral held at the Church of the Advent, not far from the Charles River at the foot of Beacon Hill. A compromise was worked out so that part of the liturgy should be conducted according to the Russian Orthodox rites, the rest following the High Church Episcopalian (or "Anglo-Catholic") ceremonial.

I was chosen to be one of the honorary pallbearers, while Mother traveled up specially from Philadelphia. It was a dreadfully hot June day when we left our Brookline home, and on our way into Boston a truck which suddenly turned right damaged the left side of my car. I got out to exchange insults with the truckdriver, but even so we managed to reach the church in time.

This harrowing incident was a mild foretaste of what was to follow. The Church of the Advent was crammed. All the members of the Boston Symphony, most if not all of its "trusties," the board members of my opera company, and hundreds of ladies who had been Koussevitzky admirers and the mainstay of our Symphony Luncheons were all there, packed into an airless church, which was soon thick with clouds of incense. The heat was unbearable, and as we were forced to stand for long periods during the Orthodox Russian part of the ritual, I was afraid that more than one of those faithful old ladies would pass out before the two services were over.

But as though these tribulations were not enough, we were also forced to listen to some atrocious, off-key singing on the part of seven or eight Russian Orthodox practitioners who had been hastily imported from Worcester, where there was a Russian church. It pained me to think that Serge Koussevitzky, who, for a quarter of a century, had ruled like a king over Boston's musical activities, should be honored at this parting ceremony with such dreadful caterwauling.

It was particularly shocking for a man who had turned the Boston Symphony Orchestra into one of the world's finest musical ensembles because of an almost mystical cult and enthusiasm for music which he had been able to communicate to all who worked with him. I shall never forget his reaction, during a faculty meeting held at the end of the first summer season at Tanglewood, when I had rashly remarked that "many things next year will be easier because we will be familiar with the regular routine of what we're doing."

"No," exploded Koussevitzky, reddening with anger, "here there will never be routine!" The idea that at *his* School one of *his* faculty members could speak of doing things in a "routine" fashion was sheer heresy. It was something he would never tolerate.

I was tremendously impressed by this almost visceral reaction. A great orchestra, like any aggregate of individuals, needs a lot of drillwork to become a great ensemble, and drillwork in the nature of things is deadening, dispiriting. This is particularly true of the strings — the *tutti* players, as they are known in the trade — who must operate collectively by "doubling" and who are never granted their moment or two of individual glory, as happens with the woodwinds and the brasses. No wonder they are so often disenchanted, these humble rank-and-filers, these "little" or "forgotten" men and women without which no orchestra can function. Koussevitzky overcame this demoralization by forcing his players to surpass themselves in virtually every performance. For he expected total dedication from all who worked under his direction.

To see him on stage was to realize that a ritual was taking place. He was not a mere musician like the rest of us, he was a high priest and the concert hall was his cathedral. And who can ever forget his entrance? "Entrance" is too prosaic a word; it was an introit, the revelation of a presence. But the moment he began making music the pose disappeared and the greatness triumphed, for he felt and made all those with him feel that music is sacred. Not only the performance but every single rehearsal was a matter of cosmic importance. He convinced each participant that this particular piece of music-making, no matter how ordinary or "routine" it might seem, was far and away the most momentous event taking place at that instant in the entire universe. He was officiating at a cult, and those playing with him were his high priests.

As I look back on that incredibly hot June day in 1951, I realize that I owe Sergei Alexandrovich Koussevitzky a great deal. At the anniversary dinner given to celebrate his twenty-five years with the Boston Symphony I was asked to make a speech. If I had to make it again today, I don't think I would change a word. There are three levels of greatness available to musicians, I said. A musician can become a virtuoso — which was the case with Koussevitzky when he played the double bass. A musician can also achieve greatness by developing an orchestra into one of the world's finest musical ensembles — which Koussevitzky did with the Boston Symphony. But there is also a third level of greatness, which can only be reached by a musician when he has a vision of the future and wishes to be the architect thereof. Such a musician was Serge Koussevitzky, and on this level his crowning achievement was the Berkshire Music Center, which shaped and influenced the musical future of the United States.

All orchestra conductors are colossal egocentrics. In a sense they have to be in order to impose a particular approach or "style" which each is persuaded is not only the best but the only possible way a particular composition should be played. Sergei Alexandrovich, Lord knows, was no exception. But of all the great conductors I have known, Koussevitzky was the only one who really cared about the future, who was really interested in young composers and performers. In promoting their works and their careers, he was sharing in their future glory, but the fact is that he really loved them — they were in a genuine sense his children.

At Tanglewood he made a point of attending our opera rehearsals because he was truly interested in what we were doing. We all felt that in his fastidious, watchful way he loved us, and this inspired us to heights we could not have reached without him. The theater building, whose construction he persuaded Mrs. Curtis Bok and other generous patrons to finance, was an eloquent example of this tender solicitude. Designed by Eliel Saarinen and his son Eero, it was a miracle of intelligent architecture. Walls and roof were suspended from a steel-ribbed frame which looked like a suspension bridge, with the result that there was not a single supporting beam to interfere with the spectators' view of the stage. The tentlike side walls, ending a foot or two above the ground, made possible a natural ventilation, which was as much appreciated by instrumentalists and singers as by their audiences. The dressing rooms, the backstage machinery for flying the sets, the curved plaster cyclorama ideally suited for the projection of sky, cloud, and other visual effects were all beyond reproach. But above and beyond all this was Serge Koussevitzky, who watched over us like a guardian angel and who never refused us any reasonable sum of money for the purchase of needed equipment.

Such was the strength of his enthusiasm and support that it outlived his death by more than a decade. Throughout that time Tanglewood was the foremost laboratory for operatic experimentation in the United States, and perhaps even in the world. The list of American premières of twentieth-century works includes Benjamin Britten's *Peter Grimes* and *Albert Herring*; Luigi Mennini's *The Rope* (also commissioned by the Koussevitzky Foundation); Bucci's *A Tale for Deaf Ears*; Lukas Foss's *Griffelkin*; Ibert's *Le Roi d'Yvetot*; three operas by Jan Meyerowitz — *Simoon, The Bad Boys in School, Port Town*; Joseph Horovitz's *Gentlemen's Island*; and Bernstein's *Trouble in Tahiti*. Here also took place the first American productions of three Mozart operas — *Idomeneo, La Clemenza di Tito,* and *Zaide* — and of Paisiello's *King Theodore in Venice*. And this is not to mention the production of operas that in those days were virtually unknown to most American music lovers — Gluck's *Iphigenia in Tauris* and *The Drunkard Reformed*; Rossini's *The Turk in Italy* and *Count Ory*; Grétry's *Richard the Lion-hearted*; Pergolesi's *Livietta and Tracollo*; Milhaud's *Ariane*; Chabrier's *The Incomplete Education*; Puccini's *La Rondine*; Ravel's *The Spanish Hour*; Ibert's *Angélique*; Holst's *Savitri*; Tchaikovsky's *The Queen of Spades*; Richard Strauss's *Ariadne auf Naxos*; Vaughan Williams' *Riders to the Sea*; Stravinsky's *Mavra*; and Robert Middleton's *Life Goes to a Party*.

The carte blanche we were given during those many summers at Tanglewood changed the nature of opera in the United States. For the methods we developed there have since permeated the length and breadth of the country and will eventually, I am convinced, change the attitude toward opera throughout the world.

We even succeeded in changing Koussevitzky's opinion regarding opera singers by demonstrating beyond all doubt that they can be made into first-rate musicians and self-reliant singing actors. My hope of freeing opera singers from the stigma of musical and theatrical incompetence became a reality more exciting than any I had dreamed of. The list of gifted singers who were drawn to Tanglewood and whom I had the honor of instructing reads like a Hall of Fame for contemporary American opera: Adele Addison, Eunice Alberts, Betty Allen, Mildred Allen, Jacqueline Bazinet, Ara Berberian, Annabelle Bernard, Helen Boatwright, McHenry Boatwright, Debria Brown, Lee Cass, Richard Cassily, Gene Cox, Phyllis Curtin, Gene Deis, Justino Diaz, Mattiwilda Dobbs, Rosalind Elias, Saramae Endich, Edith Evans, Ellen Faull, Paul Franke, Robert Gay, Frank Guarrera, Marshall Heinbaugh, Ronald Holgate, Edmund Hurshell, Donna Jeffrey, Junetta Jones, Jean Kraft, Heidi Krall, Joseph Laderoute, David Lloyd, John Macurdy, John McCollum, Robert McFerrin, Spiro Malas, Robert Mesrobian, Mildred Miller, Sherrill Milnes, Robert Minser, Mariquita Moll, Frank Monachino, Mac Morgan, Joan Moynagh, Robert Nagy, Marni Nixon, Julian Patrick, Thomas Paul, James Pease, David Poleri, Mary Ellen Pracht, Leontine Price, Tommy Rall, Robert Rounseville, Arthur Schoep, George Shirley, Leonard Treash, Nancy Trickey, Luigi Vellucci, Shirley Verrett, James Wainner, Claire Watson, Nancy Williams, Raymond Wolansky, Beverly Wolff, and Ed Zambara are only the better known of the hundreds of talented students who helped to make Tanglewood the creative crucible it became. Quite a few went on to become world-famous opera stars. Others — Jacqueline Bazinet, David Lloyd, Robert Mesrobian, Robert Minser, Frank Monachino, James Pease, Arthur Schoep, Leonard Treash, Ed Zambara — eventually turned to stage directing and joined the ranks of those — like Anthony Addison, Edward Alley, Harold Blumenfeld, Ted Blumfield, Sarah Caldwell, Peggy Donovan, Robert Evans, Howard Jarrett, James Lucas, Nathaniel Merrill, Karlos Moser, Thomas Philips, Fred Popper, George Posell, Ross Reimueller, Mauritz Sillem, and Justine Votipka, who were specifically trained to be operatic coaches, conductors, and producers. All, in one way or another, have carried the gospel of Tanglewood to every corner of the United States and to many opera centers in Europe.

Directly or indirectly, all of us owe a debt of thanks to Serge Koussevitzky, without whose generosity, energy, and vision, none of us would have become quite what we are. And if there is one respect, above all others, in which I can say I am a Koussevitzky disciple, it is in the joy I have found in educating people — young singers, young musicians, and, not least of all, opera audiences. Nothing in my life has given me greater satisfaction, and I am proud to have been able to reach millions through my opera broadcasts.

With Koussevitzky I came to appreciate something I had already learned from Ernö Dohnányi. This is the realization that music is one's friend. It may sound like an odd thing to say, but many performers are basically afraid of music. So too are many conductors. Stage directors, of course, tend to be absolutely petrified of music. But I tell my students, "There is nothing to be afraid of. Music is your friend. If something goes wrong, well, all right, we'll fix it."

This has been my religion, just as it was Uncle Serge's. Like him, I have never felt the need for an additional creed, since I had already found it in music. We are lucky, those of us who feel this way, for wherever we may be, on the podium or at the keyboard, we are very close to heaven.

Index

MY ROAD TO OPERA

The Recollections of Boris Goldovsky

as told to Curtis Cate

Boris Goldovsky has had one of the most colorful careers of any modern man of music. Born in 1908 in Moscow, the son of a well-known concert violinist, Goldovsky began his life in music as a child performer on the piano. When he and his mother fled Russia after the revolution, he was introduced to the wider arena of European music, studying in Berlin under Artur Schnabel and in Budapest under Ernst Dohnányi. The reminiscences of these and other European musical centers in the 1920s and '30s are spiced with wit and shrewd observation of the great and near great.

Goldovsky's fifty-year career in American music began at the Curtis Institute in Philadelphia where, under Josef Hofmann and Fritz Reiner, he taught, conducted and, finally, became involved in what was to become one of his great successes —the staging of opera. His dramatic innovations and consummate skill in production were enough to attract the attention of Artur Rodzinski, who invited him to Cleveland to become Rodzinski's assistant for opera production. In 1942, Goldovsky moved to Boston as director of the New England Conservatory's opera department, then as founder of the New England